W9-ARL-259

Clinton Pierce

SAMS
Teach Yourself

Perl

in 24 Hours

SECOND EDITION

SAMS

201 West 103rd St., Indianapolis, Indiana, 46290 USA

Sams Teach Yourself Perl in 24 Hours, Second Edition

Copyright © 2002 by Sams Publishing

All rights reserved. No part of this book shall be reproduced, stored in a retrieval system, or transmitted by any means, electronic, mechanical, photocopying, recording, or otherwise, without written permission from the publisher. No patent liability is assumed with respect to the use of the information contained herein. Although every precaution has been taken in the preparation of this book, the publisher and author assume no responsibility for errors or omissions. Neither is any liability assumed for damages resulting from the use of the information contained herein.

International Standard Book Number: 0-672-32276-5

Library of Congress Catalog Card Number: 99-64533

Printed in the United States of America

First Printing: October 2001

04   03   02   01   4   3   2   1

Trademarks

All terms mentioned in this book that are known to be trademarks or service marks have been appropriately capitalized. Sams Publishing cannot attest to the accuracy of this information. Use of a term in this book should not be regarded as affecting the validity of any trademark or service mark. ActiveState, ActivePerl, and PerlScript are trademarks of ActiveState Tool Corp.

Warning and Disclaimer

Every effort has been made to make this book as complete and as accurate as possible, but no warranty or fitness is implied. The information provided is on an "as is" basis. The author and the publisher shall have neither liability nor responsibility to any person or entity with respect to any loss or damages arising from the information contained in this book or from the use of the CD or programs accompanying it.

ACQUISITIONS EDITOR
Scott D. Meyers

DEVELOPMENT EDITOR
Scott D. Meyers

MANAGING EDITOR
Charlotte Clapp

COPY EDITORS
Jerome Colburn and Dave Mason, Publication Services, Inc.

INDEXER
Chris Wilcox

PROOFREADERS
Publication Services, Inc.

TECHNICAL EDITOR
Rafe Colburn

TEAM COORDINATOR
Amy Patton

MEDIA DEVELOPER
Dan Scherf

INTERIOR DESIGN
Gary Adair

COVER DESIGN
Aren Howell

PRODUCTION
Publication Services, Inc.

Contents at a Glance

Appendixes 417

Contents

About the Author

CLINTON PIERCE is a software engineer, freelance programmer, and instructor. He has been answering questions about Perl on USENET for many years and has been writing courseware and teaching Perl to his co-workers and anyone else who will listen for about as long. He is a Web Architect for Decision Consultants who, when not designing middleware software to integrate legacy systems to the Web, teaching Unix and Perl to consultants at Decision Consultants, writing books and articles, or writing programs at home Just For The Fun Of It, harbors secret dreams of being abducted by wood nymphs and living in the deep forest without technology. You can visit his Web site at `http://www.geeksalad.org` for updates and corrections, or just to say hello.

Dedication

To Heidi and Calvin, for not killing me this summer and supporting me during this
adventure. Without your support, I'd have lost even more of my marbles.

Acknowledgments

"If I have seen further, it is by standing on the shoulders of Giants" —Isaac Newton.

Any book on Perl should first recognize the Giant who gave us Perl in the first place. Thanks, Larry.

I not only stood on the shoulders of Giants, but also was led by hoards of others. To make sure this book came out as error-free as possible, I invited perfect strangers to watch, criticize, and correct me when necessary. This has been a humbling experience. In no particular order, the people who annoyed me the most and who deserve the most thanks are Abigail, Greg Bacon, Sean Burke, Ken Fox, Kevin Meltzer, Tom Phoenix, and Randal Schwartz. Also, thanks to Michael Schwern, Tom Grydeland, Matt Bielanski, Mark Jason-Dominus, Jeff Pinyan, Gary Ross, Andrew Chen, and John Bell for finding bugs and offering suggestions. Thank you Dave Rolsky, Jonathan Swartz, and Ilmari Karonen for the HTML::Mason help.

Some small credit should also go to #perl for letting me sound my ideas off them and for giving me their honest—and sometimes brutal—opinions.

Somewhat responsible for this book are Bill Crawford and Donna Hinkle for getting me into this whole training mess in the first place. Thanks, I think.

Of course, I'd like to thank the people at Sams Publishing behind the scenes that I didn't get to talk to but who are just as important. I'd never have put together anything like this.

Tell Us What You Think!

As the reader of this book, *you* are our most important critic and commentator. We value your opinion and want to know what we're doing right, what we could do better, what areas you'd like to see us publish in, and any other words of wisdom you're willing to pass our way.

You can e-mail or write me directly to let me know what you did or didn't like about this book—as well as what we can do to make our books stronger.

Please note that I cannot help you with technical problems related to the topic of this book, and that due to the high volume of mail I receive, I might not be able to reply to every message.

When you write, please be sure to include this book's title and author as well as your name and phone or fax number. I will carefully review your comments and share them with the author and editors who worked on the book.

E-mail: webdev@samspublishing.com

Mail: Mark Taber
           Associate Publisher
           Sams Publishing
           201 West 103rd Street
           Indianapolis, IN 46290 USA

Introduction

"Any sufficiently advanced technology is virtually indistinguishable from magic." — Arthur C. Clarke

Remember this and hold it deep in your mind: *There's nothing magical about programming a computer.*

Like anything that seems magical, there's always a trick to it—and programming is no different. All you need are some analytical thinking skills, the desire to learn, and some time to learn Perl. The best way to learn how to program a computer—or any task really—is to have a goal. Your goal could be to spice up your Web pages, to convert a program you already have to Perl, or to satisfy idle curiosity—it doesn't really matter.

Now, given that you've established a goal and have some thinking skills, what does this book have for you?

This book will teach you the basics of the Perl programming language. You'll learn just enough Perl to do something useful. You will not be overwhelmed with details that, although interesting, will only get in your way and that you'll probably never use again. Each new concept in this book is demonstrated with lots of working code examples. Go ahead—flip through the book and see.

But why Perl? Almost every company that does programming of some kind uses Perl. Perl is found in finance, manufacturing, genetics, the military, and every other application known to humankind. And, of course, Perl is used on the Internet and the World Wide Web. Perl isn't going away any time soon, which is why learning it is an investment in your time that will pay off for years to come.

It's also possible to create really stunning Perl programs with just a small bit of code. Using a little bit of Perl to glue together other applications, languages, and technologies, you'll be creating useful Perl programs in no time.

How to Use This Book

This book is divided into 24 segments that each take roughly an hour to complete. You can work through the lessons in the space of a day (if you don't plan to eat or sleep), or you can take your time and work through the hour lessons at your own pace.

At the end of each hour, you'll be able to accomplish a new set of tasks. The lessons contain clear explanations of the language features and how they work. In addition, each hour provides you with the opportunity for hands-on training, simply by following the steps described.

Conventions Used in This Book

Sams Teach Yourself Perl in 24 Hours uses a number of conventions that are consistent throughout this book:

- Each hour begins with an overview of what you will learn.
- Step-by-step instructions are preceded by a To Do icon.
- Every hour ends with a summary and a series of commonly asked questions and answers; hopefully, you'll find the answers to your questions among them.

In addition, these elements appear throughout the book:

Notes provide you with comments and asides about the topic at hand.

Tips offer shortcuts and hints on getting the task done.

Cautions explain roadblocks you might encounter when you work with Perl and tell you how to avoid them.

New terms are emphasized by being placed in italics for your easy reference.

PART I
Fundamentals

Hour

HOUR 1

Getting Started with Perl

Perl is a general-purpose programming language. It can be used for anything that any other programming language can be used for. It has been used in every industry imaginable for almost any task you can think of. It's used on the stock market; in manufacturing, design, customer support, quality control, systems programming, payroll, and inventory; and, of course, on the Web.

Perl is used in so many places because Perl is what's known as a *glue language*. A glue language is used to bind things together. You probably wouldn't want to write a word processor in Perl—although you could—because good word processors are already available. Writing a database, a spreadsheet, an operating system, or a full-featured Web server in Perl would be silly—but again, possible.

But what Perl is good at is tying these elements together. Perl can take your database, convert it into a spreadsheet-ready file, and, during the processing, fix the data if you want. Perl can also take your word processing documents and convert them to HTML for display on the Web.

As a side effect of being a language designed to glue elements together, Perl is very adaptable. It runs under, at last count, about two dozen operating systems—and probably more. Perl's programming style is very flexible, so you can do the same things in many ways. Your Perl programs may look nothing like mine, but if they both work, that's okay. Perl can be a strict language when it needs to be, and it can be forgiving to new programmers if you want. It's all up to you.

Let me just clear up a few points. The name of the programming language is *Perl*. The name of the program that runs your programs, the interpreter, is *perl*. The distinction usually isn't very important to you—except when you're trying to start your programs; then it's always *perl*. Sometimes—but not here—you will see Perl written as *PERL*, probably because one explanation of Perl's name is as an acronym for *Practical Extraction and Report Language*. Nobody ever really called it PERL; it's too pretentious. It's just Perl to its friends.

Many of Perl's features were "borrowed" from other languages. This borrowing gave rise, early on, to Perl's other acronym-expansion: *Pathologically Eclectic Rubbish Lister*.

In this hour we'll cover

- Installing Perl
- Accessing Perl's internal documentation
- Writing your first Perl script

Installing Perl

To play with Perl, you first have to install it. Perl's installation is designed to be easy and error free. In fact, as part of the installation steps, Perl should do a self-test to make sure that it's okay. The installation procedures vary widely depending on what operating system you have. So, to get things moving, pick which operating system you have from the sections here, and follow along.

Stop! Wait! Maybe You Already Have Perl

Before you go through all the trouble to install Perl on your system, you should check to see whether you already have it. Some Unix vendors ship Perl with the operating system. Windows NT comes with Perl as part of the Windows NT Resource Kit (but that version is a bit old). To see whether you have Perl properly installed on your operating system, you need to get to a command prompt.

1

Under Unix, simply log in to the system. If you have a graphical environment, you need to open a terminal window. After you've logged in or opened your window, you may see a prompt like this:

$

It might be a % or it might look like bash%, but either way, it is called the *shell prompt* or *command prompt*. For the first few hours, you'll need to be at this prompt to interact with Perl.

To see whether Perl is properly installed on your system, type the following (but not the $ prompt):

$ **perl -v**

Either the system responds with an error message such as command not found, or Perl responds and prints its version number. If Perl prints its version number, then it's installed. You probably do not have to reinstall it.

> The version number reported should be at *least* 5—perhaps 5.004, 5.005, 5.6, and so on—but no lower. If Perl responds with a version of 4.x, then you must install a new copy. Perl version 4 is old, buggy, and no longer maintained; few of the examples in this book will work with Perl version 4. At the time of this writing, 5.6.1 is considered the current version of Perl.

If you have a Windows machine, to see whether Perl is properly installed, you need to get to an MS-DOS prompt, similar to Figure 1.1.

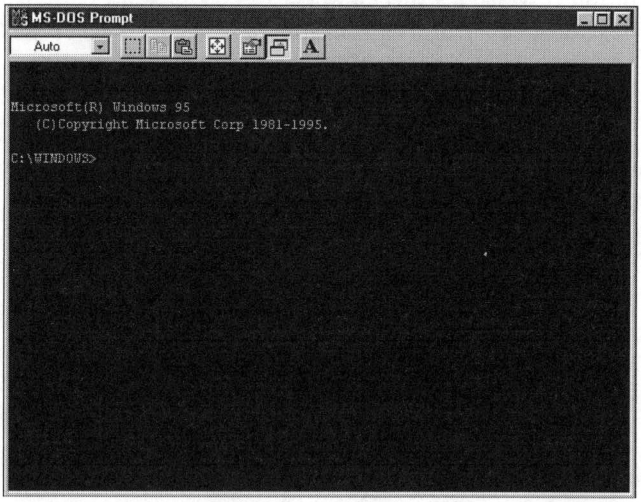

FIGURE 1.1

You can check your version of Perl at this DOS prompt.

```
MS-DOS Prompt
Auto

Microsoft(R) Windows 95
    (C)Copyright Microsoft Corp 1981-1995.

C:\WINDOWS>
```

At that prompt, type the following (but don't repeat the prompt):

```
C:\> perl -v
```

If Perl is properly installed, it answers with its version number. As noted in the previous caution, it should be at least version 5. If MS-DOS replies with `Bad command or file name`, you need to install Perl properly.

On the Macintosh, you can check to see whether Perl is installed by running File Find (Command-f) for 'MacPerl' as shown in Figure 1.2. If the application is found, open it and look at the "About MacPerl" option under the Apple menu. You should have at least Version 5.2.0 Patchlevel 5.004; otherwise, you should install a new version of MacPerl.

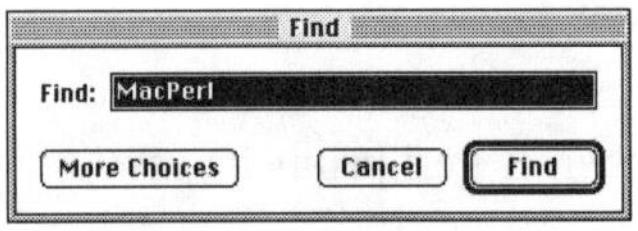

FIGURE 1.2

Looking for Perl on the Macintosh.

Installing Perl on Windows 95/98/NT

To install Perl under Windows, keep in mind that, as with many things in life, you can take the Easy Way or the Hard Way. If you're proficient with a C compiler and the tools needed in a development environment—makefiles, shells, and so on—you can take the Hard Way and build your own Perl from scratch. The source to the `perl` interpreter is free for you to look at, modify, and change to suit your needs; see Hour 16, "The Perl Community," for details. Building Perl from scratch under Windows is not easy and probably more hassle than it's worth for most people.

Installing Perl the Easy Way really is easy. ActiveState Tool Corp. provides a self-installing Perl distribution, and installation works as it does for any other Windows application, as shown in Figure 1.3. This Perl is distributed under the ActiveState Community License, which you should read. The URL is `http://www.ActiveState.com`.

FIGURE 1.3

Installing Perl under Windows with ActiveState.

1

This is exactly the same Perl you would get if you had built it yourself. ActiveState has simply done the hard parts for you and wrapped it up with an installation program. ActiveState also offers commercial support for Perl, if you require it, and offers add-on products such as debuggers and other development tools and libraries.

> A copy of ActiveState's Perl distribution is on the CD-ROM included with this book. You can install directly from this CD or go to ActiveState's Web site to get the latest version of Perl.

Installing Perl on Unix

To install Perl on Unix, you need a couple of things. First, you need a copy of the Perl source bundle. You can always download the latest bundle from the Downloads area of `http://www.perl.com`. You can find multiple versions there, but the one you want is always labeled "Stable" or "Production." You also need an ANSI C compiler. Don't worry if you don't know what that means. Perl's configuration program checks for one, and if the compiler is not there, you can install a prebuilt version, as described at the end of the section.

> If your Unix has a system for installing prebuilt packages, you may be able to install a prebuilt version of Perl. Linux, Solaris, AIX, and other Unixes have prebuilt bundled versions of Perl that can be installed easily. Consult your documentation on where to obtain these packages.

After you have the Perl source bundle—which comes in a file named something like stable.tar.gz—then you need to unpack and install it. To do so, enter these commands:

```
$ gunzip stable.tar.gz
$ tar xf stable.tar
```

These commands take a while to run. If you don't have the gunzip decompression program, you can obtain a copy from `http://www.gnu.org`. The program bundle is called gzip. When you're all done with unpacking, type the following command at a prompt:

```
$ sh Configure
```

The `configure` program starts and asks you a *lot* of questions. If you don't know the answers to most of them, that's fine; just press Enter. The default answer is usually the best one. Perl can be built without problems on almost any Unix system imaginable. When that's all done, type this command:

```
$ make
```

Building Perl takes quite a while. Get some coffee. If you have a slow system, get lunch. When the build is complete, type two more commands:

```
$ make test
# make install
```

The `make test` command ensures that Perl is 100 percent okay and ready to run. To run `make install`, you might need to be logged in as root—that's why the prompt is #, root's prompt, in the example—because it wants to install Perl into system directories.

When `make install` is correct, you can test Perl's installation by typing the following at the prompt again:

```
$ perl -v
```

If this command works, congratulations!

> A copy of the source files for building Perl under Unix is on the CD-ROM included with this book. You can copy the installation bundle directly from here, or you can go to `http://www.perl.com` for the latest version of Perl.

Installing Perl on Macintosh

> The latest release of the Macintosh Perl—called MacPerl—is available from the CPAN ports directory. To get the release, you need to go to
> `http://www.perl.com/CPAN/ports/mac`
> and download the installation file from there. You should download the most recent version of MacPerl appl.bin from that directory. Install it by using StuffIt Expander to extract the MacPerl installation program from the downloaded file, and then running the installation program.

When you're finished, you will want to set up a helper for the Perl documentation reader, Shuck, which was installed with MacPerl. MacOS 8 users can do this in the Internet Control Panel by selecting File Mapping from the Advanced menu and adding a file extension mapping for `.pod` to the Shuck application. This will give you easier access to the documentation. You might also want to set up mappings for `.ph`, `.pl`, `.plx`, `.pm`, `.cgi`, and `.xs` (all extensions used by Perl) to the MacPerl application. Be sure to set the file type to 'TEXT'.

MacOS 7 users will have to use the InternetConfig utility to perform similiar mappings. In the InternetConfig, select Helpers, and add a new helper application `shuck` for `.pod`. Also add helpers for the other extensions mentioned previously to the MacPerl application.

> A copy of MacPerl's installation bundle is on the CD-ROM included with this book. You can install directly from the CD-ROM, or you can go to `http://www.perl.com/CPAN/ports/mac` and get the latest version there.

Documentation

This point is important, so please pay close attention: With *every* Perl installation, you receive a *full* copy of the current documentation for the Perl language and the interpreter.

That's right. The entire set of documentation available for Perl comes with the installation bundle. You get it for free. The 5.6 distribution includes more than 1,700 pages of documentation. This documentation includes reference material, tutorials, FAQs, history, and even notes on Perl's internals.

You can access this documentation using a variety of methods. On Windows and Unix, a utility called `perldoc` is installed with Perl. You can use the `perldoc` program to search the documentation and provide formatted output for the manuals. To run `perldoc`, you need to be at a command prompt. The following example uses a Unix prompt, but a DOS command prompt is fine:

```
$ perldoc perl

PERL(1)          13/Oct/98 (perl 5.005, patch 02)          PERL(1)

    NAME
        perl - Practical Extraction and Report Language

    SYNOPSIS
        perl [ -sTuU ]        [ -hv ] [ -V[:configvar] ]
             [ -cw ] [ -d[:debugger] ] [ -D[number/list] ]
             [ -pna ] [ -Fpattern ] [ -l[octal] ] [ -0[octal] ]
             [ -Idir ] [ -m[-]module ] [ -M[-]'module...' ]
             [ -P ]        [ -S ]        [ -x[dir] ]
             [ -i[extension] ]        [ -e 'command' ] [ --
             ] [ programfile ] [ argument ]...

        For ease of access, the Perl manual has been split up into a
        number of sections:
    :
```

The manual sections are divided into pieces with names like perlfunc (Perl Functions), perlop (Perl Operators), and perlfaq (Perl FAQ). To access the perlfunc manual page, you enter the command `perldoc perlfunc`. The names of all the manual sections are listed in the perldoc Perl manual page.

To search the manual for a function name, you can run the `perldoc` utility with a `-tf` switch. The following example finds the manual page for Perl's `print` function:

```
$ perldoc -tf print
```

The FAQs are Frequently Asked Questions about Perl. They are questions that people learning Perl ask over and over again. To save people time and trouble, the questions have been collected into files called FAQs. To search a FAQ for a keyword, you should use the `-q` switch along with a word that might appear in the FAQ's title. For example, if you want to know about Perl support, you could use the following query:

```
$ perldoc -q support
```

In this case, the entry for the FAQ questions `"Who supports Perl? Who develops it? Why is it free?"` is displayed.

Some Special Documentation Cases

When Perl is installed on a Unix system, the installer is given the option to install manual pages in traditional "man" format. If the installer chooses yes, the standard Perl documentation is converted into man format and stored in an appropriate place. To access the Perl documentation, you can use either the `perldoc` program or the `man` program as you normally would with UNIX:

```
$ man perl
```

When ActiveState's Perl distribution is installed on a Microsoft Windows system, the manual pages are converted to HTML format and can be accessed with a Web browser. If you want to read the manuals, point your frame-capable Web browser to the local directory `C:\Perl\html` if you used the standard installation directory; if you didn't, use your selected directory instead.

For the Macintosh, MacPerl comes with a utility called `Shuck` that is located in the MacPerl folder. You can use it to read and search the Perl documentation as shown in Figure 1.4.

What If You Can't Find the Documentation?

If you can't find the documentation, only two things can be wrong. The first is you're not looking in the right places. Perhaps the `perldoc` utility is installed in a directory that's not in your shell's search path. Or perhaps your search path is overly restrictive. Hunt around for the `perldoc` utility, and add that directory to your shell's `PATH` environment variable.

The second reason is the documentation was removed, either by accident or malice. Perl's installation includes documentation. You can't install Perl without it. If the documentation

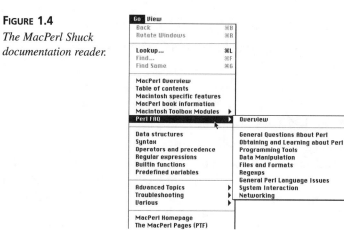

FIGURE 1.4

The MacPerl Shuck documentation reader.

isn't there, then a good argument can be made that Perl wasn't properly installed or that it has since been corrupted. Perhaps you—or the system administrator—should consider reinstalling Perl. The documentation is an integral part of the Perl development environment, and without it some pieces of Perl will not function.

If all else fails, and you can't get a local copy of the documentation, you can fall back to the Web. On Perl's primary distribution site (http://www.perl.com), you can access the standard set of documentation. Having the actual documentation that came with your version of Perl would be better—it's tailor-made to your particular version and installation—but this online documentation will do in a pinch.

Your First Program

To write your Perl programs, you need a utility called a *text editor*. A text editor is a program that allows you to enter plain text, without any formatting, into a file. Microsoft Windows Notepad and the MS-DOS EDIT.EXE program are both examples of text editors. For Unix, vi, emacs, and pico are all text editors. At least one of them will be available on your system. Under the Mac, the MacPerl application contains a rudimentary text editor; to open a new program, select New under the File menu.

You should *not* use a word processor to type in your Perl programs. Word processors—such as Microsoft Word, WordPad, WordPerfect, and so on—embed formatting codes by default when they save documents, even if the documents contain no boldface, italic, font changes, or other special formatting. These formatting codes will confuse Perl, and your programs will not work correctly. If you need to use a word processor, be sure to save your programs as plain text.

Typing Your First Program

Open your text editor, and type the following Perl program exactly as shown:

```
#!/usr/bin/perl

print "Hello, World!\n";
```

The `#!` line should be the first line in the file.

After you type this program into your text editor, save it in a file named `hello`. You don't need an extension on the filename, but Perl permits you to put one there. Some Windows and Macintosh utilities use extensions to tell what kind of file this is. If you need or want to use an extension, `.pl` or `.plx` is common; for example, you can use `hello.pl`.

One of the most common problems here besets users of Microsoft Notepad. When you save the file, Notepad always appends a `.txt` extension to the file, whether or not you asked it to. If you want a `.pl` extension, you have to specify the filename in quotes, like this: `"hello.pl"`, as shown in the following figure. This forces Notepad to save the file without the `.txt` extension.

Running the Program

To run the program, for now, you need to get to a command prompt. In Unix, open a terminal window or log in. On a Microsoft Windows machine, open an MS-DOS prompt. You should also change into the directory where you stored the hello program by using your shell's `cd` command.

When you're at the prompt, type the following. (A DOS prompt is shown here; Unix has a slightly different prompt.)

`C:\PROGRAMS>` **perl hello**

If all goes well, Perl should respond with the following message:

`Hello, World!`

If typing this command worked, congratulations! Remember how you ran this program, because this is how you will start your programs for the rest of the book. (You can use some other ways, which will be covered shortly.)

If it did not work, check for the following:

- If you receive the error message `Bad command or file name` or `perl: command not found`, then the Perl program is not in your execution path. You need to figure out where the Perl program is installed and add that directory to the `PATH` variable in your shell.

- If you receive the error message `Can't open perl script hello: A file or directory does not exist`, then you're probably not in the same directory as the file named `hello` that you saved earlier, or you saved the file under a different name. To change into the proper directory under Unix or Windows, use the `cd` command. For example, if you saved the file on your desktop in Windows 98, the command would be:

  `c:\> c:\Windows\Desktop>` **perl hello**

  Remember, if you used an extension on the filename (such as .pl or .plx), you need to specify that extension when you run the program.

- If you receive an error such as `syntax error`, then Perl starts normally but cannot figure out what is in the file named `hello`. You've either mistyped the file's contents, or you've used a word processor that applied formatting to the saved file. The `cat` command (Unix) or the `type` command (DOS) can be used to verify what is in the file. If you mistyped, check everything; the quotation marks and punctuation are important.

If you're using MacPerl, simply select `Run "hello"` from the Script menu to run your first Perl program. If you're not using MacPerl's built-in editor to write your program, use the Open command from the File menu to open your program in MacPerl, and then select Run.

It Worked! So What Happened?

When you typed the command `perl hello`, a program named `perl` was started on your computer. This program is called the *Perl interpreter*. The Perl interpreter is the heart and soul of Perl. Its job is to take the file it has been given (`hello`, in this case), find the program inside it, and run it.

By "run it," I mean "first check the statements, functions, operators, math, and every-thing else that makes up the Perl program to make sure the syntax is correct, and then execute the statements one at a time."

When the Perl interpreter is all done reading your program from disk, it begins to run the program and continues running that program until it's all done. When it's finished with your program, the Perl interpreter exits and returns control to your operating system.

Now let's look at how the `hello` program is "run."

Perl Play-by-Play

The first line of the `hello` program is

```
#!/usr/bin/perl
```

To Perl, anything following a `#` on a line is considered a comment line. A comment is something that Perl otherwise ignores. The `#!` on the first line of a program is different in some cases. The pathname that follows—`/usr/bin/perl`—is the path to the Perl inter-preter. If a Unix file begins with `#!` followed by the path of an interpreter, then Unix knows that this is a program (rather than a shell script) and how to interpret it. See the "Q&A" section at the end of the hour for an explanation of how to run programs.

Some Web servers that can execute Perl programs—Apache, for example—also pay attention to the `#!` line and can call the programs without having to use an explicit `perl` command.

For now, just consider `#!` a comment line.

The next line of the program is

```
print "Hello, World!\n";
```

A whole lot is going on here. This line constitutes a Perl statement; it marks off for Perl one thing to do.

First, this line contains a function called `print`. The `print` function takes whatever fol-lows it and displays it—to your screen by default. What the `print` function is supposed to print lasts all the way up to the semicolon (`;`).

The semicolon in Perl is a *statement separator*. You should put a semicolon between state-ments in your Perl program to show where one statement ends and the next one begins.

In this case, the `print` function displays the phrase `Hello, World!`. The `\n` at the end of the line tells Perl to insert a new blank line after it prints the phrase. The quotation marks around the phrase and the `\n` tell Perl that this is a literal string, and not another function. Strings are discussed at great length next hour.

Something You Should Know

Perl is called a *free-form* programming language. This means that Perl statements aren't very picky about how they're written. You can insert spaces, tabs, and even carriage returns—called *whitespace*—nearly anywhere in a Perl statement, and it really doesn't matter.

The only places that you really can't insert whitespace willy-nilly are places you'd expect restrictions to be. For example, you can't insert spaces in the middle of a function name; `pr int` is not a valid function. Nor can you insert them in numbers, as in `25 61`. Also, whitespace inside literal strings like `"Hello, World!"` shows up as, well, whitespace. Almost everywhere else it's valid. You could write the sample Perl program like this:

```
#!/usr/bin/perl

print
    "Hello, World!\n"
    ;
```

It would have functioned identically to the original. This free-form nature gives you a lot of range in "style" in your Perl programs. Feel free to express yourself with form. Just remember, someday other users may have to look at your programs. Be kind to them.

The style used in the examples in this book is fairly conservative. Sometimes statements are broken across several lines for clarity or to save space, because Perl statements can get quite long. The Perl documentation even has a suggested style guide, if you want to browse it for suggestions. You should search for the document named perlstyle.

> Style in Perl programs can be taken to extremes. Valid Perl programs can be written as poetry, even haiku. Some memorable Perl programs actually look like pictures but do something useful. Every year *The Perl Journal* (`http://www.tpj.com`) runs a contest that's all about writing obscure-looking Perl programs: the Obfuscated Perl Contest. You should not take style lessons from the entries.

Summary

In this hour, you learned a little about what Perl is and how it works. As you go through this book, you'll pick up more details here and there. You also learned how to install Perl on your system and verify that it's working properly and that all the documentation is in place. Finally, you typed in—and, I hope, ran—your first Perl program. Afterward, you dissected that program and learned a little bit about how Perl works.

Q&A

Q **These things that Perl runs, are they called Perl *scripts* or Perl *programs*?**

A The name really doesn't matter. Traditionally, *programs* are compiled into machine code and stored that way, and the machine code can be run many times. On the other hand, *scripts* are fed to an external program that translates them into actions every time they're run. Larry Wall, creator of Perl, has said that a "script is what you give an actor, a program is what you give an audience." Take that any way you'd like. For the remainder of this book, I'll call them *Perl programs,* and if you learn well, you can then be known as a *Perl programmer.*

Q **Do I have to type the listings from this book? Some of them are pretty long.**

A All the program listings and examples from this book, as well as any data files needed by the programs, are on the accompanying CD-ROM.

Q **I found my program under Windows using the Explorer and double-clicked on it. A DOS window opened, printed something, and then immediately closed. What's wrong?**

A Nothing! The Perl interpreter is associated with the `.pl` extension as a DOS-mode program. When you clicked on it, a DOS window was opened and the interpreter ran your program and then immediately exited. (It was a short program.) If you actually need to see your Perl program run, then open a window and run it manually.

Q **In the "Running the Program" section, you hinted at an easier way to run Perl programs under Unix. How?**

A First, you must make sure that the `#!` line of the program is correct, and that the pathname there really points to a perl interpreter; `/usr/bin/perl` is the usual place for it, or `/usr/local/bin/perl` on some machines. Next, you must make the program executable by using the `chmod` command. For the `hello` program, the UNIX shell command would be `chmod 755 hello`. After that's done, you can run the Perl program by typing `hello` or `./hello`. Hint: Don't ever name your program "test" under Unix. The Unix shells have a command called `test`, and you'll be very frustrated when the wrong one runs. See your shell's documentation for other names you should avoid.

Also, if you use the listings on the CD-ROM, you will need to change the `#!` line to match the location of `perl` on your system, or you will have to run your programs from the command prompt by typing **perl *programname*.**

Workshop

Quiz

1. *Perl* is the name of the language; *perl* is the name of

   a. The language also

   b. The interpreter

   c. A DOS command

2. Where can you always find a copy of the Perl documentation?

   a. `http://www.microsoft.com`

   b. `http://www.perl.com`

   c. `http://www.perl.net`

3. In which manual page can you find a description of Perl's syntax?

   a. perlsyn

   b. perlop

   c. perlfaq

Answers

1. b. Although, after it's installed, `perl` is a valid command in a DOS shell. So c is acceptable also.

2. b. And installed on your system as well.

3. a. Unless you actually run `perldoc perl`, there's no way you could have known for sure, now is there?

Activities

- Browse through the FAQ. Even if you don't understand everything in there, you should get a feel for what kind of information is in the FAQ.

   If you prefer reading it on a browser, surf to `http://www.perl.com` and read it there, but do peruse it.

HOUR 2

Perl's Building Blocks: Numbers and Strings

Every programming language—and every human language—has a similar beginning: You have to have something to talk about. In Perl, numbers and strings are the basic unit of conversation, and these are called *scalars*.

Every hour in this book deals in some way with scalars—increasing, decreasing, querying, testing, collecting, clearing, separating, folding, sorting, saving, loading, printing, and deleting them. Scalars are Perl's singular nouns; they can represent a word, a record, a document, a line of text, or a character.

Some scalars in Perl can represent information that does not change over the life of the program. Some programming languages call these values *constants* or *literals*. Literal data is used for things that simply do not change, such as the value of π, the rate of acceleration of a body falling to Earth, and the name of the 15th President of the United States. If these values are needed by a Perl program, they would, at some point in the program, be represented by a scalar literal.

The other kinds of scalars in Perl are those that change, called *scalar variables*. Variables hold data while you manipulate it. You can change the contents of variables, because they merely act as handles for the data they represent. Variables are given names—convenient and easy-to-remember names, ideally—that enable you to refer to the data you are manipulating.

This hour also introduces Perl's operators. They are one kind of verb in the Perl language. Operators take Perl's nouns and do the actual manipulations you need to write programs that perform useful tasks.

In this hour, you'll learn about

- Literal numbers and strings
- Scalar variables
- Operators

Literals

Perl has two different types of scalar constants called *literals:* numeric literals and string literals.

Numbers

Numeric literals are numbers, and Perl accepts several different ways of writing numbers. All the examples shown in Table 2.1 are valid numeric literals in Perl.

TABLE 2.1   Samples of Numeric Literals

Number	Type of Literal
6	An integer
12.5	A floating-point number
15.	Another floating-point number
.7320508	Yet another floating-point number
1e10	Scientific notation
6.67E-33	Scientific notation (e or E is acceptable)
4_294_296	A large number with underscores instead of commas

Numbers are expressed as you think they would be. Integers are just groups of consecutive digits. Floating-point decimal numbers contain a decimal point in the correct position, even if there are no digits to the right of it. A floating-point number can be expressed in scientific notation as an exponent preceded by the letter e (or E) and a decimal number called the mantissa. The value of the scientific-notation literal is 10 raised to the power indicated by the exponent, multiplied by the mantissa; for example, 6.5536E4 = 65,536.0. (Strictly speaking, a mantissa is the decimal part of a logarithm, where it serves the same purpose as it does here.)

You cannot put commas into a numeric literal to improve readability, but you can use underscores where commas would normally appear. Perl removes the underscores when using the value.

> Do not use a leading zero in front of a number, such as 010. To Perl, a leading zero means that the literal represents an octal number—base 8. Perl also allows you to use literal hexadecimal numbers—base 16— and binary numbers—base 2. More information on these is in the online documentation in the perldata section.

Strings

String literals in Perl are sequences of characters, such as Hello, World. They can contain as much data as you want; strings have no real limit on their size except the amount of virtual memory in your computer. Strings can also contain any kind of data—simple ASCII text, ASCII with the high bits on, even binary data. Strings can even be empty.

In Perl you must enclose string literals, with very few exceptions, in quotation marks. This process is called *quoting* the string. The two primary ways of quoting strings are to use single quotation marks (' ') or double quotation marks (" "). The following are some sample string literals:

```
"foo!"
'Fourscore and seven years ago'
"One fish,\nTwo fish,\nRed fish,\nBlue fish\n"
""
"Frankly, my dear, I don't give a hoot.\n"
```

What if you need to put another quotation mark inside your string literal? For example, the following string literal would make no sense to Perl:

```
"Then I said to him, "Go ahead, make my day""
```

Here, the quotation mark in front of the word Go marks the end of the string literal started by the first quotation mark, leaving the phrase Go ahead, make my day outside the string literal—in which case it would have to be valid Perl code, which it isn't. To prevent this situation, you must use a *backslash* (\) in front of the quotation marks that are inside the string. A backslash inside of a string literal tells Perl that the character that follows should not be treated as Perl would normally treat it—in this case, it should be handled as a character in the string literal rather than as the marker for the end of the

string literal. Put a backslash character in front of each quotation mark that you want
Perl to treat simply as a character, as shown here:

```
"Then I said to him, \"Go ahead, make my day.\""
```

The backslashes let Perl know that the quotation mark that follows is not the match for
the first quotation mark that started the string literal. This rule applies to single quotation
marks as well as double quotation marks, as you can see here:

```
'The doctors\'s stethoscope was cold.'
```

The primary difference between double-quoting and single-quoting a string is that single-
quoted strings are quite literal; every character in a single-quoted string (except the
sequence \') means exactly what is there. In a double-quoted string, on the other hand,
Perl checks to see whether variable names or *escape sequences* are present and translates
them if they are. Escape sequences are special strings that allow you to embed characters
in strings when just typing the characters would cause problems. Table 2.2 shows a short
list of Perl's escape sequences.

TABLE 2.2   Sample String Escape Sequences

Sequence	Represents
\n	Newline
\r	Carriage return
\t	Tab
\b	Backspace
\u	Change next character to uppercase
\l	Change next character to lowercase
\\	A literal backslash character
\'	A literal ' inside of a string surrounded by single quotation marks (' ').
\"	A literal " inside of a string surrounded by double quotation marks.

You can find the full list of escape sequences in the online manual. As I indicated in Hour 1, "Introduction to the Perl Language," you can find the
entire Perl language documentation by using the perldoc utility included
with the Perl distribution. The escape sequences are listed in the "perlop"
manual page under the heading "Quote and Quote-like Operators."

Having many quotation marks embedded in a string can make typing the string error-prone and difficult, because each embedded quote mark has to be escaped, as shown here:

```
"I said, \"Go then,\", and he said \"I'm gone.\"."
```

Perl provides another quoting mechanism: the qq and q operators. To use qq, you can surround the string literal with qq( ) instead of quotation marks:

```
qq(I said, "Go then," and he said "I'm gone")
```

qq replaces the double quotation marks; this mechanism behaves exactly like double quotes in almost all respects.

You can use the q operator to surround text instead of using single quotation marks:

```
q(Tom's kite wedged in Sue's tree)
```

The qq and q operators can use any nonalphabetic, nonnumeric character to mark the beginning and ending of a string. Those markers are called *delimiters*. In the preceding examples, I used parentheses, but any other nonalphabetic or nonnumeric character could have been used:

```
q/Tom's kite wedged in Sue's tree/
```

```
q,Tom's kite wedged in Sue's tree,
```

The character you want to use as a delimiter must appear immediately after the qq or q operator.

If you use any of the character pairs (), <>, {}, or [] as delimiters, they will nest properly. That is, if you use them in matched pairs inside the qq or q operators, you do not need to use a backslash escape sequence:

```
q(Joe (Tom's dad) fell out of a (rather large) tree.);
```

However, doing this doesn't make your Perl programs very readable. Usually it's easier just to pick delimiters that don't appear in your string:

```
q[Joe (Tom's dad) fell out of a (rather large) tree.];
```

Scalar Variables

To store scalar data in Perl, you must use a scalar variable. In Perl, you indicate a scalar variable with a dollar sign followed by the name of the variable. The following are some examples:

```
$a
$total
$Date
$serial_number
$cat450
```

The dollar sign—called a *type identifier*—indicates to Perl that the variable contains scalar data. Other variable types (hashes and arrays) use a different identifier or no identifier at all (filehandles). Variable names in Perl—whether for hashes, arrays, filehandles, or scalars—must conform to the following rules:

- Variable names can contain alphabetic (a to z, A to Z) characters, numbers, or an underscore character (_) after the type identifier. The first character of a variable name can't be a number, though.

- Variable names are case sensitive. This means that upper- and lowercase are significant in variable names. Thus, each of the following represents a different scalar variable:

```
$value
$VALUE
$Value
$valuE
```

Perl reserves to itself single-character variable names that do not start with an alphabetic character or underscore. Variables such as $_, $", $/, $2, and $$ are *special variables* and should not be used as normal variables in your Perl programs. The purpose of these special variables will be covered later.

Scalar variables in Perl—in contrast to some other languages—do not have to be declared or initialized in any way before you can use them. To create a scalar variable, just use it. Perl uses a default value when an uninitialized variable is used. If it's used as a number (such as in a math operation), Perl will use the value 0 (zero); if it's used like a string (almost everywhere else), Perl will use the value " ", the empty string.

Using a variable before it has been initialized with a value is considered a bad programming practice. Perl can be made to warn you when this situation happens. If your program has -w on the #! line at the beginning, or if you invoke Perl with the -w switch on the command line, then if you try to use the value of a variable that you haven't previously set, Perl responds with this error message when your program runs and you try to use the value: Use of uninitialized value.

The Special Variable $_

Perl has a special variable, $_, whose value is used as a "default" by many operators and functions. For example, if you simply state print by itself—without specifying a scalar variable or string literal to print—Perl will print the current value of $_:

```
$_="Dark Side of the Moon";
print;    # Prints the value of $_, "Dark Side..."
```

Using $_ like this can understandably cause some confusion. It's not really apparent what `print` is actually printing, especially if the assignment to $_ occurs higher up in the program.

Some operators and functions are actually easier to use with the $_variable, notably the pattern-matching operators discussed in Hour 6, "Pattern Matching." In this book, however, I'll keep the use of $_to a minimum so that the lessons are easier to follow.

Expressions and Operators

Now that you've learned what scalar data is and know how to use scalar variables, you can start doing something useful with Perl. Perl programs are just collections of expressions and statements executed in order from the top of your Perl program to the bottom (unless you specify otherwise with flow-control statements, covered in Hour 3, "Controlling the Program's Flow"). Listing 2.1 shows a valid Perl program.

LISTING 2.1   A Simple Perl Program

```
1:   #!/usr/bin/perl -w
2:
3:   $radius=50;
4:
5:   $area=3.14159*($radius ** 2);
6:   print $area;
```

Line 1: This line is the path to the Perl interpreter, as explained in Hour 1. The `-w` switch tells Perl to inform you of any warnings encountered.

Line 3: This line is an *assignment*. The numeric scalar data value 50 is stored in the scalar variable $radius.

Line 5: This line is another assignment. On the right side of the assignment operator is an expression. This expression contains the scalar variable $radius, operators (* and **, explained later), and a numeric scalar (2). The expression's value is computed and assigned to $area.

Line 6: This line prints the result of the calculation stored in $area.

An expression in Perl is simply something that has a value. For example, 2 is a valid expression. So are 54*$r, "Java", sin($pi*8), and $t=6. The values of expressions are computed when your program is run. The program evaluates the functions, operators, and scalar constants in the expression and reduces it to a value. You can use these expressions with assignments, as part of other expressions, or as part of other Perl statements.

Basic Operators

As you saw in Listing 2.1, to assign scalar data to a scalar variable, you use the assignment operator, =. The assignment operator takes the value on the right side and puts it in the variable on the left:

```
$title="Gone With the Wind";
$pi=3.14159;
```

The operand on the left side of the assignment operator must be something that a value can be assigned to—namely, a variable. The operand on the right side can be any kind of expression. The entire assignment itself is an expression; its value is that of the right-hand expression. This means that, in the following snippet, $a, $b, and $c are all set to 42:

```
$a=$b=$c=42;
```

Here, $c is first set to 42. $b is set to the value of the expression $c=42 (which is 42). $a is then set to the value of the expression $b=42.

The variable being assigned to can even appear on the right side of the assignment operator, as shown here:

```
$a=89*$a;
$count=$count+1;
```

The right side of the assignment operator is evaluated using the old value of $a or $count, and then the result is assigned to the left side as the new value. The second example has a special name in Perl; it's called an *increment*. You'll read more about incrementing values later.

Numeric Operators

Perl has many operators to manipulate numeric expressions. Some of these operators are familiar to you already; some you will be meeting for the first time. The first kind of operator you should already know—the arithmetic operators. Table 2.3 shows a list of these operators.

TABLE 2.3 Arithmetic Operators

Example	Operator Name	Expression Value
5 + $t	Addition	Sum of 5 and $t
$y - $x	Subtraction	Difference between $y and $x
$e * $pi	Multiplication	Product of $e and $pi
$f / 6	Division	Quotient of $f divided by 6
24 % 5	Modulus	Remainder of 24 divided by 5 (4)
4 ** 2	Exponentiation	4 raised to the 2nd power

Arithmetic operators are evaluated in the order you would think: exponentiation first; multiplication, division, and modulus next; and then addition and subtraction. If you're unsure of which order elements will be evaluated in an expression, you can always use parentheses to guarantee the evaluation order. Nested parentheses are always evaluated from the inside out:

```
5*6+9;        # Evaluates to 39
5*(6+9);      # Evaluates to 75
5+(6*(4-3));  # Evaluates to 11
```

String Operators

Numeric values aren't the only values in Perl that can be affected by operators; strings can be manipulated as well. The first string operator is the concatenation operator, represented by a period (.). The concatenation operator takes the string on the left and the string on the right and returns a string that is both strings put together:

```
$a="Hello, World!";
$b=" Nice to meet you";
$c=$a . $b;
```

$a and $b are given simple string values in this example. On the last line, $a and $b are concatenated to become Hello, World! Nice to meet you and stored in $c. $a and $b are not modified by the concatenation operator.

There is another way to put strings together. Earlier, you learned that inside a double-quoted string Perl looks for variables. If Perl finds a variable inside a double-quoted string, it is *interpolated*. This means that the type identifier and variable name inside the double-quoted string are replaced by the variable's actual value:

```
$name="John";
print "I went to the store with $name.";
```

In this example, Perl looks inside the double-quoted string, sees $name, and substitutes the string John. This process is called *variable interpolation*. To prevent something that looks like a variable in a string from being interpolated, you either can use single quotation marks—which do not perform interpolation of any kind—or put a backslash in front of the variable identifier:

```
$name="Ringo";
print 'I used the variable $name';     # Will not print "Ringo", prints $name
print "I used the variable \$name";    # Neither will this.
```

The last two print statements in the preceding example print I used the variable $name; the value of the variable $name is not interpolated. So, to perform concatenation without using the concatenation operator, you can simply use double-quoted strings, as follows:

```
$fruit1="apples";
$fruit2="and oranges";
$bowl="$fruit1 $fruit2";
```

If a variable name is followed immediately by letters or numbers, Perl will not be able to tell clearly where the variable name ends and the rest of the string begins. In that case, you can use curly braces {} around the variable name. This syntax allows Perl to find the variable name where it might be ambiguous:

```
$date="Thurs";
print "I went to the fair on ${date}day";
```

Without the braces, Perl would think you wanted to interpolate a variable named $dateday in the double-quoted string, not to interpolate $date and follow it with the string day. The braces make it clear what you meant to be interpolated. For historical reasons, apostrophes following variable names have the same issue:

```
$name="Bob";
Print "This is $name's house"; # does not print Bob.
```

This can also be fixed with a judicious use of curly braces:

```
$name = "Bob";
print "This is ${name}'s house"; # Does print Bob
```

The other string operator presented here is the repetition operator, x. The x operator takes two values—a string to repeat and the number of times to repeat that string—as you can see here:

```
$line="-" x 70;
```

In the preceding example, the - character is repeated 70 times by the x operator. The result is stored in $line.

More Operators

Perl has so many operators that there isn't enough space in this book to document them all fully. (You can read about them all in the "perlop" manual page.) But for the remainder of this hour, you'll read about the most commonly used operators and functions in Perl.

One-Operand (Unary) Operators

Until now, all the operators you've read about take two *operands*—that is, two expressions, from whose values the operators make a new value in some way. For example, division (6/3) requires a dividend (6) and a divisor (3), multiplication (5*2) requires a multiplicand (5) and a multiplier (2), and so on. Another kind of operator, called a *unary operator,* takes only one operand. You're probably familiar with one example of these already—the unary minus (-). The unary minus returns the value of its operand with the sign reversed: negative if the operand is positive, positive if the operand is a negative number:

```
6;      # Six
-6;     # Negative six.
-(-5);  # Positive five, not negative five.
```

Many of Perl's unary operators are actually *named operators;* that is, instead of a symbol—like the - for unary minus—they use a word. The parentheses around the operand with named unary operators are optional but are shown in Table 2.4 for clarity. Named unary operators in Perl look and act like functions (discussed in Hour 8), and their operands are called *arguments*—the term used for the expressions that Perl functions act on.

Some named unary operators are listed briefly in Table 2.4.

TABLE 2.4 Some Named Unary Operators

Operator	Sample Usage	Result
int	int(5.6234)	Returns the integer portion of its argument (5).
length	length("nose")	Returns the length of its string argument (4).
lc	lc("ME TOO")	Returns its argument shifted to lowercase letters ("me too").
uc	uc("hal 9000")	Returns the reverse of lc ("HAL 9000").
cos	cos(50)	Returns the cosine of 50 in radians (.964966).
rand	rand(5)	Returns a random number from 0 to less than its argument. If the argument is omitted, a number between 0 and 1 is returned.

You can find the full list of named operators in the online manual. As discussed in Hour 1, you can find the entire Perl language documentation by using the `perldoc` utility included with the Perl distribution. All of the operators are listed in the "perlop" manual and in the "perlfunc" manual. (Operators that are symbols, such as *, are listed in perlop, whereas named unary operators are listed in perlfunc.) More operators will be presented in later lessons as they are needed.

Increment and Decrement

In the "Numeric Operators" section, you read about a special type of assignment called an increment, which looks like the following:

```
$counter=$counter+1;
```

An increment is typically used to count things, such as the number of records read, or to generate sequence numbers, such as numbering the items in a list. It's such a common idiom in Perl that you can use a special operator called an *autoincrement operator* (++). The autoincrement operator adds 1 to its operand:

```
$counter++;
```

When this code is executed, `$counter` is increased by 1.

Perl also offers a shortcut for decreasing a variable's value called, not surprisingly, the *autodecrement operator* (--). You use the autodecrement exactly the same way you use the autoincrement:

```
$countdown=10;
$countdown--;        # decrease to 9
```

Let me add a final note on the autoincrement operator: When the operator is applied to a text string, and the text string starts with an alphabetic character and is followed by alphabetic characters or numbers, this operator becomes magical. The last (rightmost) character of the string is increased. If it's an alphabetic character, it becomes the next letter in sequence; if it's numeric, the number increases by 1. You can carry across alphabetic and numeric columns as follows:

```
$a="999";
$a++;
print $a;            # prints 1000, as you'd expect
$a="c9";
$a++;
print $a;            # prints d0.  9+1=10, carry 1 to the c.
$a="zzz";
$a++;
print $a;            # prints "aaaa".
```

The autodecrement operator does not decrement strings like this.

Angle Operator (<>)

The angle operator (<>), sometimes called a diamond operator, is primarily used for reading and writing files; it will be covered fully in Hour 5, "File I/O." However, a brief introduction now will make the exercises more interesting, and when you begin Hour 5, the operator will look somewhat familiar to you.

Until then, you can use the angle operator in its simplest form: <STDIN>. This form indicates to Perl that a line of input should be read from the standard input device—usually the keyboard. The <STDIN> expression returns the line read from the keyboard:

```
print "What size is your shoe? ";
$size=<STDIN>;
print "Your shoe size is $size. Thank you!\n";
```

The preceding code, when executed (assuming you type 9.5 as your shoe size), would print this on the screen:

```
What size is your shoe?  9.5
Your shoe size is 9.5
. Thank you!
```

The `<STDIN>` expression reads from the keyboard until the user presses the Enter key. The entire line of input is returned and is placed in `$size`. The line of text returned by `<STDIN>` also includes the newline character that the user typed by pressing Enter. That's why the period and "Thank you!" appear on a new line in the preceding display— the newline was part of the value of `$size`. Often, as here, you don't want the newline character at the end of the string—just the text. To remove it, you can use the `chomp` function as follows:

```
print "What size is your shoe?";
$size=<STDIN>;
chomp $size;
print "Your shoe size is $size. Thank you!\n";
```

`chomp` removes any trailing newline character at the end of its argument. It returns the number of characters removed, which is usually 1 but is 0 if nothing needs to be removed.

More Assignment Operators

Earlier, you learned that to assign a value to a scalar variable you use the assignment operator (=). Perl actually has an entire set of operators for doing assignments. Every Perl arithmetic operator and quite a few others can be combined to do an assignment and an operation all at the same time. The general rule for building an assignment with an operator is as follows:

variable operator=expression

This form of the assignment produces the same result as the following:

variable=variable operator expression

Using combined assignments generally doesn't make your programs any more readable but can make them more concise. Following this rule, the statement

```
$a=$a+3;
```

can be reduced to

```
$a+=3;
```

The following are some more examples of assignments:

```
$line.=", at the end";        # ", at the end" is appended to $line
$y*=$x                        # same as $y=$y*$x
$r%=67;                       # Divide by 67, put remainder in $r
```

A Few Words on Strings and Numbers

For the most part, Perl allows you to use numbers and strings interchangeably; the representation it uses depends on what Perl is looking for in that situation.

- If something looks like a number, Perl can use it as a number when it needs a number:

```
$a=42;          # A number
print $a+18;    # displays 60.
$b="50";
print $b-10;    # Displays 40.
```

- If something looks like a number, when Perl needs a string, it uses the string representation of the number:

```
$a=42/3;
$a=$a . "Hello";   # Using a number like a string.
print $a           # displays "14Hello"
```

- If something doesn't look like a number, but you've used it where a number was expected, Perl simply uses the value 0 in its place:

```
$a="Hello, World!";
print $a+6;     # displays the number 6
```

If you have warnings enabled, Perl emits a warning if you do this, however.

All these uses are in keeping with Perl's philosophy of Least Surprise. Even when given nonsense—as in the last example here—Perl tries to do something sensible with it. If you have warnings enabled in your Perl program—by putting a -w on the #! line or invoking the Perl interpreter with the -w option—Perl warns you that you're doing something nonsensical by giving you the following message: Argument X isn't numeric.

Exercise: Interest Calculator

For this exercise, you're going to perform a compound interest calculation. This program will calculate the interest on a savings account, given some information about interest rates, deposits, and time. The formula you're going to use is as shown here:

$$\text{accrued} = \text{payment} \left(\frac{(1 + \text{monthly interest})^{\text{number of deposits} - 1}}{\text{monthly interest}} \right)$$

Using your text editor, type the program from Listing 2.2 and save it as Interest. Do not type in the line numbers. Make the program executable according to the instructions you learned in Hour 1.

When you're done, try running the program by typing the following at a command line:

```
perl Interest
```

Listing 2.3 shows a sample of the Interest program's output.

LISTING 2.2 The Interest Program

```
1:   #!/usr/bin/perl -w
2:
3:   print "Monthly deposit amount? ";
4:   $pmt=<STDIN>;
5:   chomp $pmt;
6:
7:   print "Annual Interest rate?  (ex. 7% is .07) ";
8:   $interest=<STDIN>;
9:   chomp $interest;
10:
11:  print "Number of months to deposit? ";
12:  $mons=<STDIN>;
13:  chomp $mons;
14:
15:  # Formula requires a monthly interest
16:  $interest/=12;
17:
18:  $total=$pmt * ( ( ( 1 + $interest) ** $mons ) -1 )/ $interest;
19:
20:  print "After $mons months, at $interest monthly you\n";
21:  print "will have $total.\n";
```

Line 1: This line contains the path to the interpreter (you can change it so that it's appropriate to your system) and the -w switch. Always have warnings enabled!

Line 3: The user is prompted for an amount.

Line 4: $pmt is read from the standard input device (the keyboard).

Line 5: The newline character is removed from the end of $pmt.

Lines 7–9: $interest is read in from the keyboard, and the newline is removed.

Lines 11–13: $mons is read in from the keyboard, and the newline is removed.

Line 16: $interest is divided by 12 and stored back in $interest.

Line 18: The interest calculation is performed, and the result is stored in $total.

Lines 20–21: The results are printed.

LISTING 2.3 Output from the Interest Program

```
1:   Monthly deposit amount? 180
2:   Annual Interest rate?  (ex. 6% is .06) .06
3:   Number of months to deposit? 120
4:   After 120 months, at 0.005 monthly you
5:   will have 29498.2824251624.
```

Summary

In this hour, you learned that Perl's most basic type of data is a scalar. Scalars can consist of almost any kind of data. Scalar values can be represented by string or numeric literals. Numeric literals can be have many different formats representing integers and floating-point numbers. String literals are sequences of characters surrounded by either double or single quotation marks. Scalar values are stored in scalar variables, which have a dollar sign $ in front of their names. Perl provides operators for performing string manipulation and basic arithmetic.

Q&A

Q The output of the Interest program looks sloppy. How do I control how many digits are displayed?

A The easiest way to control the number of decimal digits is to use the `printf` function, which is covered in Hour 9, "More Functions and Operators."

Q Does Perl have a function for rounding?

A The `printf` function usually does what you want for rounding when displaying numbers. If you really need the `round` function, check out the POSIX module, which has this function and many more.

Q How large (or small) of a number will Perl let me manipulate?

A The answer depends on your operating system. A typical Intel Unix system's double-precision floating-point numbers can have more than 300 places in the exponent. This means you can manipulate numbers with 300 zeros to the right (or left) of the decimal point. Typically, however, large numbers have only 14 digits of precision.

Workshop

Quiz

1. Variables are interpolated inside `qq` quotes.

   a. True

   b. False

2. What value is stored in `$c` after running the following code?

   ```
   $a=6;
   $a++;
   $b=$a;
   $b--;
   $c=$b;
   ```

a. 6

b. 7

c. 8

3. Concatenation can be performed only with the concatenation operator (.).

a. True

b. False

2

Answers

1. a. True. qq behaves in every way like a pair of double quotation marks. This means it can interpolate variables.

2. a. $a is set to 6. $a is then incremented to 7, and assigned to $b. $b is decremented to 6, and assigned to $c.

3. b. False. A motto in the Perl community is "There Is More Than One Way To Do It" (TIMTOWTDI). Concatenation can be performed by including two (or more) scalars in a double-quoted string, as follows:

```
qq($a$b$c);
```

Activities

- Write a short program that prompts the user for a Fahrenheit temperature and prints the temperature in Celsius. Converting Fahrenheit temperature to Celsius can be accomplished by taking the Fahrenheit temperature and subtracting 32, and then multiplying by 5/9. For example, 75 degrees Fahrenheit is 23.8 degrees Celsius.

- Modify the Interest program in Listing 2.3 to print the amount with no more than two decimal places. You can do so without printf with clever use of the int operator, multiplication, and division.

HOUR 3

Controlling the Program's Flow

In Hour 2, "Perl's Building Blocks: Numbers and Strings," you learned about statements, operators, and expressions. All the examples in that hour had one thing in common: All the statements were executed in order from top to bottom and were executed only once.

One of the reasons that you use computers is that computers are very good at performing repetitive tasks—over and over again—without getting tired or bored and without developing carpal tunnel syndrome. So far, you haven't had any way of telling Perl to "do this task *X* times" or to "repeat this task until it's done." In this hour, you will learn about Perl's control structures. Using them, you can group statements into something called a *statement block* and run the group of statements repeatedly until they've done what you want.

The other chore that computers excel at is making decisions quickly. It would be tiresome—not to mention silly—if a computer had to ask you every time it made a decision. The very act of retrieving and reading your email causes your computer to make millions of decisions that you really don't want to deal with: how to assemble network traffic, which colors to make each pixel on your screen, how your incoming mail should be pulled apart and displayed, what should be done when your mouse cursor moves even a tiny bit, and countless others. All these decisions are made up of other decisions, and some of them are made thousands of times per second. In this hour, you will learn about *conditional statements*. Using these statements, you can write blocks of code that will be executed or not, depending on decisions made in your Perl program.

In this chapter we'll cover the basics of

- Block statements
- Operators
- Looping
- Labels
- Exiting Perl after a program execution

Blocks

The fundamental way to group statements in Perl is the *block*. To group statements in a block, just surround the statements with a matched set of curly braces, as shown here:

```
{
    statement_a;
    statement_b;
    statement_c;
}
```

Within the block, statements execute from the top down, as they have until now. You can have other, smaller blocks of statements nested within a block, as you can see here:

```
{
    statement_a;
    {
            statement_x;
            statement_y;
    }
}
```

The format of the block, like the rest of Perl, is free-form. The statements and curly braces can be on one line or on several lines, as shown here, and with any kind of alignment you want, as long as you always have a matched set of curly braces:

```
{ statement;  { another_statement; }
     { last_statement;              } }
```

Although you can arrange blocks any way you would like, programs can be hard to read if they're just thrown together. Good indenting, although not necessary, makes for human-readable Perl. It can help you keep track of your program's logic.

Blocks that occur by themselves within a program are called *bare blocks* or *naked blocks*. Most of the time, however, you will encounter blocks attached to other Perl statements.

The `if` Statement

To control whether statements are executed based on a condition in a Perl program, you usually use an `if` statement. The syntax of an `if` statement is as follows:

```
if (expression) block
```

The statement works like this: If the *expression* evaluates to true, the *block* of code is run. If the *expression* is false, the *block* of code is not run. Remember that the block includes the braces. Consider this example:

```
if ( $r == 5 ) {
   print 'The value of $r is equal to 5.';
}
```

The expression being tested is `$r == 5`. The `==` symbol is an equality operator. If the two operands on either side—`$r` and `5`—are numerically equal to one another, the expression is considered to be true, and the `print` statement is executed. If `$r` is not equal to `5`, the `print` statement is not executed.

The `if` statement can also run one set of statements if a condition is true and another set of statements if it's not. That structure is called an `if-else` statement. The syntax looks like this:

```
if (expression)      #If expression is true...
   block1            # ...this block of code is run.
else
   block2            # Otherwise this block is run.
```

The first block, *block1*, is run only if the *expression* is true; if the *expression* is not true, *block2*, following the `else`, is run. Now consider this example:

```
$r=<STDIN>;
chomp $r;
if ($r == 10) {
   print '$r is 10';
} else {
   print '$r is something other than 10...';
   $r=10;
   print '$r has been set to 10';
}
```

In the preceding example, notice that to assign a value to $r, I used the
assignment operator, =. To *test* the value of $r, I used the numeric equality
test operator, ==. Do not confuse them in your programs, because debugging can be very difficult. Remember that = assigns a value and == tests for
equality. If you use the -w option to turn warnings on, Perl can sometimes
warn you if you have made this error.

Yet another way of structuring an if statement is to check multiple expressions and run
code depending on which expressions are true:

```
if (expression1)     # If expression1 is true ...
   block1                # ...run this block of code.
elsif (expression2)  # Otherwise, if expression2 is true...
   block2                # ...Run this block of code.
else
   block3                # If neither expression was true, run this.
```

You can read the preceding block like this: If the expression labeled *expression1* is true,
then the block *block1* is run. Otherwise, control falls to the elsif and *expression2* is
tested; if it's true, then *block2* is run. If neither *expression1* nor *expression2* is true, then
block3 is run. The following is an example of real Perl code that demonstrates this syntax:

```
$r=10;
if ($r==10) {
   print '$r is 10!';
} elsif ($r == 20) {
   print '$r is 20!';
} else {
   print '$r is neither 10 nor 20';
}
```

The Other Relational Operators

So far, you've been comparing numeric quantities in your if statements with the equality
operator, ==. Perl actually has quite a few operators for comparing numeric values, most
of which are listed in Table 3.1.

TABLE 3.1 Numeric Relational Operators

Operator	Example	Explanation
==	$x == $y	True if $x equals $y
>	$x > $y	True if $x is greater than $y
<	$x < $y	True if $x is less than $y

continues

TABLE 3.1 Continued

>=	$x >= $y	True if $x is greater than or equal to $y
<=	$x <= $y	True if $x is less than or equal to $y
!=	$x != $y	True if $x is not equal to $y

To use these operators, you can simply put them in anywhere that your program needs to test relations between numeric values. An example of the use of these operators in an `if` statement is shown in Listing 3.1, which you can type in and run (do not type the line numbers—"1:" and so forth).

LISTING 3.1 A Small Number Guessing Game

```
 1:   #!/usr/bin/perl -w
 2:
 3:   $im_thinking_of=int(rand 10);
 4:   print "Pick a number:";
 5:   $guess=<STDIN>;
 6:   chomp $guess;    # Don't forget to remove the newline!
 7:
 8:   if ($guess>$im_thinking_of) {
 9:    print "You guessed too high!\n";
10:   } elsif ($guess < $im_thinking_of) {
11:          print "You guessed too low!\n";
12:   } else {
13:          print "You got it right!\n";
14:   }
```

The various parts of the program work as follows:

Line 1: This line is the standard first line of a Perl program; it indicates the interpreter you want to run and the -w switch to enable warnings. See Hour 1, "Introduction to the Perl Language"; your first line may need to look slightly different.

Line 3: The (rand 10) function picks a number between 0 and 10, and the int() function truncates it so that only integers 0 to 9 are assigned to $im_thinking_of.

Lines 4–6: This line asks the user for the guess, assigns it to $guess, and removes the trailing newline character.

Lines 8–9: If $guess is greater than the number in $im_thinking_of, then these lines print an appropriate message.

3

Lines 10–11: Otherwise, if $guess is less than the number in $im_thinking_of, these lines print that message.

Lines 12–13: The only choice left is that the user guessed the number.

The operators in Table 3.1 are used only for testing numeric values. Using them to test non-alphabetic data results in behavior that you probably don't want. Consider this example:

```
$first="Simon";
$last="simple";
if ($first == $last) {      # == is not what you want!
   print "The words are the same!\n";
}
```

The two values $first and $last actually test *equal* to each other. The reason was explained in Hour 2, " Perl's Building Blocks: Numbers and Strings": If nonnumeric strings are used when Perl is expecting numeric values, the strings evaluate to zero. So the preceding if expression looks something like this to Perl: if (0 == 0). This expression evaluates to true, and that's probably not what you wanted.

 If warnings are turned on, trying to test two alphabetic values (simple and Simon in the preceding snippet) with == will generate a warning message when the program runs to alert you to this problem.

If you want to test nonnumeric values, you can use another set of Perl operators, which are listed in Table 3.2.

These operators decide "greater than" and "less than" by examining each character left to right and comparing them in ASCII order. This means that strings sort in ascending order: most punctuation first, then numbers, uppercase, and finally lowercase. For example, 1506 compares less than Happy, which compares less than happy.

TABLE 3.2 Alphanumeric Relational Operators

Operator	Example	Explanation
eq	$s eq $t	True if $s is equal to $t
gt	$s gt $t	True if $s is greater than $t
lt	$s lt $t	True if $s is less than $t
ge	$s ge $t	True if $s is greater than or equal to $t
le	$s le $t	True if $s is less than or equal to $t
ne	$s ne $t	True if $s is not equal to $t

What Truth Means to Perl

Up to this point, you've been reading about "if this expression is true..." or "...evaluates to true...," but you haven't seen any formal definition of what Perl thinks "true" is. Perl has a few short rules about what is true and what is not true, and the rules actually make sense when you think about them for a bit. The rules are as follows:

- The number 0 is false.
- The empty string (`""`) and the string `"0"` are false.
- The undefined value `undef` is false.
- Everything else is true.

Make sense? The only other point to remember is that when you're testing an expression to see whether it's true or false, the expression is simplified—functions are called, operators are applied, math expressions are reduced, and so on—and then converted to a scalar value for evaluation to determine whether it is true or false.

Think about these rules, and then take a look at Table 3.3. Try to guess whether the expression is true or false before you look at the answer.

TABLE 3.3 True or False Examples

Expression	True or False?
`0`	False. The number 0 is false.
`10`	True. It is a nonzero number and therefore true.
`9>8`	True. Relational operators return true or false, as you would expect.
`-5+5`	False. This expression is evaluated and reduced to 0, and 0 is false.
`0.00`	False. This number is another representation of 0, as are 0x0, 00, 0b0, and 0e00.
`""`	False. This expression is explicitly mentioned in the rules as false.
`" "`	True. There's a space between the quotes, which means they're not entirely empty.
`"0.00"`	True. Surprise! It's already a string, but not `"0"` or `""`. Therefore, it is true.
`"00"`	True also, for the same reason as `"0.00"`
`"0.00" + 0`	False. In this expression, 0.00+0 is evaluated, the result is 0, and that's false.

Until now, you've seen only expressions with relational operators as the conditions in `if` statements. Actually, you can use *any* expression that will evaluate to true or false the way you would want:

```
# The scalar variable $a is evaluated for true/false
if ($a) {  ...  }

# Checks the length of $b.  If nonzero, the test is true.
if (length($b)) { ....  }
```

Recall from Hour 2, "Perl's Building Blocks: Numbers and Strings," that the assignment operator = returns a value—the value that was assigned. That value, of course, is also true or false:

```
$a = 1;
$b = 2;
print qq(The statement "$a = $b" is );
if ($a = $b) { # value is 2, therefore true
   print "true";
} else {
   print "false";
}
```

This code prints `The statement "1 = 2" is true`. Now you see why using = when you meant == is such a pitfall.

The value `undef` is a special value in Perl. Variables that have not yet been set have the value of `undef`, and some functions return `undef` on failure. It's not 0, and it's not a regular scalar value. It's kind of special. In a test for truth, `undef` always evaluates to false. If you try to use the `undef` value in a math expression, it's treated as though it were 0.

Using variables that haven't been set yet is usually a sign of a programming error. If you're running your Perl programs with warnings enabled, the value `undef` in an expression or as an argument to some functions causes Perl to generate the warning `Use of uninitialized value`.

Logical Operators

When you're writing programs, you sometimes need to code something like the following: Do this if `$x` is true and if `$y` is true, but not if `$z` is true. You can code this example into a series of `if` statements, but it's not pretty:

```
if ($x) {
   if ($y) {
        if ($z) {
                # do nothing
        } else {
                print "All conditions met.\n";
        }
   }
}
```

Perl has a whole class of operators for connecting together true and false statements like this, called *logical operators*. The logical operators are shown in Table 3.4.

TABLE 3.4   Logical Operators

Operator	Alternative Name	Example	Analysis
&&	and	$s && $t	True only if $s and $t are true
		$q and $p	True only if $q and $p are true
||	or	$a || $b	True if $a is true or $b is true
		$c or $d	True if $c is true or $d is true
!	not	! $m	True if $m is not true
		not $m	True if $m is not true

Using the operators in Table 3.4, you could rewrite the previous snippet much more concisely as follows:

```
if ($x and $y and not $z ) {
    print "All conditions met.\n";
}
```

Expressions connected with logical operators are evaluated from left to right, until a value of true or false can be determined for the entire expression. Examine the following code:

```
1:   $a=0;
2:   $b=1;
3:   $c=2;
4:   $d="";
5:   if ($a and $b) {  print '$a and $b are true'; }
6:   if ($d or $b) { print 'either $d or $b is true'; }
7:   if ($d or not $b or $c)
8:     { print '$d is true, or $b is false or $c is true'; }
```

Lines 1–4: These lines give the variables default values.

Line 5: $a is evaluated first. It is false, so the `and` expression cannot possibly be true. $b is never evaluated; it doesn't have to be, because the truth of the expression is known after evaluating $a. The `print` is not executed.

Line 6: $d is evaluated first. It is false. Even if $d is false, the expression might still be true—because it contains a logical `or`—so $b is examined next. $b turns out to be true; therefore, the expression is true, and the `print` happens.

Line 7: $d is evaluated first. It is false. But although $d is false, the expression might still be true—as seen in line 4—because it contains a logical or. Next, the truth of $b—1, so true—is negated, so this expression becomes false. The truth of the or statement cannot be determined yet, so $c is evaluated. $c turns out to be true, so the whole expression is true, and the print happens.

This behavior—stopping the evaluation of a logical expression as soon as the truth can be determined—is called *short-circuiting*. This feature is used by Perl programmers to construct simple flow-control statements out of logical operators and to avoid the if statement entirely:

```
$message="A and B are both true."
($a and $b) or $message="A and B are not both true.";
```

In the preceding example, if either $a or $b is false, the right side of the or must be evaluated, and the message is changed. If both $a and $b are true, the or must be true, and it's not necessary to evaluate the right side. The truth value of the entire expression isn't used at all; this example uses the short-circuit side effects of the and and or operators to manipulate $message.

> The || operator and or aren't completely alike. They differ in that || has higher precedence than or. This means that in an expression, || tends to be evaluated sooner than or. This is similar to multiplication having higher precedence than addition in normal mathematical expressions. The same caution applies to &&/and, and !/not. If you're unsure, use parentheses to guarantee the order in which the expression will be evaluated.

An interesting property of Perl's logical operators is that they don't simply return true or false. They actually return the last value evaluated. For example, the expression 5 && 7 doesn't just return true—it returns 7. This allows constructs like this:

```
# Set $new to old value if $old is true,
# otherwise use the string "default".
$new=$old || "default";
```

which is a little more concise than the code

```
$new=$old;
if (! $old) {  # was $old empty (or false)?
  $new="default";
}
```

This trick can make your code less readable. Understanding how it works can be helpful, though, if you are going to be looking at much Perl code written by others.

Looping

As you read in the Introduction, sometimes just making decisions and running code conditionally are not enough. Often you need to run pieces of code over and over again. The exercise presented in Listing 3.1 wasn't much fun, because you could take only one guess (well, that and because it's a pointless game). If you want to be able to take multiple guesses, you need to be able to repeat sections of code conditionally, and that's what looping is all about.

Looping with `while`

The simplest kind of loop is a `while` loop. A `while` loop repeats a block of code as long as an expression is true. The syntax for a `while` loop looks like this:

```
while (expression) block
```

When Perl encounters the `while` statement, it evaluates the *expression*. If the *expression* is true, the *block* of code is run. Then, when the end of the block is reached, the *expression* is re-evaluated. If it's still true, the *block* is repeated, as in the following snippet:

```
1:   $counter=0;
2:   while ($counter < 10 ) {
3:    print "Still counting...$counter\n";
4:    $counter++;
5:   }
```

Line 1: `$counter` is initialized to zero.

Line 2: The expression `$counter < 10` is evaluated. If it's true, the code in the block is run.

Line 4: The value of `$counter` is incremented by 1.

Line 5: The `}` marks the end of the block started on line 2 with a `{`. At this point, Perl returns to the top of the `while` loop and re-evaluates the conditional expression.

Looping with `for`

The `for` statement is the most complicated and versatile of Perl's looping constructs. The syntax looks like this:

```
for ( initialization; test; increment ) block
```

The three sections of the `for` statement—*initialization*, *test*, and *increment*—are separated by semicolons. When Perl encounters a `for` loop, the following sequence takes place:

1. The *initialization* expression is evaluated.

2. The *test* expression is evaluated; if it's true, the *block* of code is run.

3. After the *block* is executed, the *increment* is performed, and the *test* is evaluated again. If the *test* is still true, the *block* is run again. This process continues until the *test* expression is false.

The following is an example of a `for` loop:

```
for( $a=0; $a<10; $a=$a+2 ) {
   print "a is now $a\n";
}
```

In this snippet, `$a` is set to 0, and the test `$a<10` is performed and found to be true. The body of the loop prints a message. The increment is then run—`$a=$a+2`—which increases the value of `$a` by 2. The test is performed again, and the loop repeats. This particular loop repeats until the value of `$a` is 10, when the test will be false and the program will continue running after the `for` loop.

You don't have to use the increment in the `for` statement for counting; it simply iterates until the test is false. In fact, you should be aware that each of the three parts of the `for` statement is *optional,* although the two semicolons are required. The following `for` statement is missing some pieces but is still perfectly valid:

```
$i=10;                    # initialization
for( ; $i>-1; ) {
   print "$i..";
   $i--;                  # actually, a decrement.
}
print "Blast off!\n";
```

Omitting the test portion means that you have to have some other way to exit the loop, or it will loop forever.

Other Flow Control Tools

Controlling the way your program executes with loops and condition statements is fine, but other flow control statements are needed to make readable programs. For example, Perl has statements to exit a `while` loop early, to skip certain portions of a `for` loop, to exit an `if` statement before the end of a block, or even to exit your program without falling off the end. Using some of the constructs explained in this section can make your Perl programs more concise and easier to read.

Odd Arrangements

The `if` statements have one more possible syntax. If you have only one expression inside the `if` block, the expression can actually precede the `if` statements. So, instead of writing

```
if (test_expression ) {
   expression ;
}
```

you can write

```
expression if (test_expression );
```

The following are a couple of examples of this variation of the syntax:

```
$correct=1 if ($guess == $question);
print "No pi for you!"  if ( $ratio != 3.14159);
```

You usually use this syntax in Perl code for clarity; sometimes reading the code is easier if you see the action before the condition. The expression preceding the `if` must be a single expression. The `if` statement must also be followed by a semicolon.

Fine-Grained Control

In addition to blocks, `for`, `while`, `if`, and other flow-control statements that control blocks of code, you can use Perl statements to control the flow *within* the blocks.

The simplest statement that gives you this control is `last`. The `last` statement causes the innermost currently running loop block to be exited. Consider this example:

```
while($i<15) {
   last if ($i==5);
   $i++;
}
```

The `last` statement causes the `while` loop to exit when the value of `$i` is 5, instead of normally when the `while` test is false. When you have multiple nested loop statements, `last` exits the loop currently running.

The set of nested loops in Listing 3.2 finds all the whole numbers less than 100 whose products are 140—2 and 70, 4 and 35, and so on—rather inefficiently. The point to note here is the `last` statement. When a product is found, the result is printed, and the inner loop (the loop iterating over `$j`) is exited. The outer loop continues executing (by incrementing `$i`) and reruns the inner loop.

LISTING 3.2 Example of the **last** Statement

```
1:   for($i=0; $i<100; $i++) {
2:    for($j=0; $j<100; $j++) {
3:          if ($i * $j == 140) {
4:                print "The product of $i and $j is 140\n";
5:                last;
6:          }
7:    }
8:   }
```

The `next` statement causes control to be passed back to the top of the loop and the next iteration of the loop to begin, if the loop isn't finished:

```
for($i=0; $i<100; $i++) {
   next if (not $i % 2);
   print "An odd number=$i\n";
}
```

This loop prints all the even numbers from 0 to 98. The `next` statement causes the loop to go through its next iteration if `$i` is not even; the `$i % 2` expression is the remainder of `$i` divided by 2. In this case, the `print` statement is skipped. (A much more efficient way to write this loop would be simply to increase `$i` by 2, but that wouldn't demonstrate `next`, would it)?

The redo statement is similar to next, except that the condition isn't re-evaluated. Perl resumes execution back at the beginning of the block and doesn't check whether or not the termination condition has been met yet.

Labels

Perl allows blocks and some loop statements (`for`, `while`) to be *labeled*. That is, you can place an identifier in front of the block or statement:

```
MYBLOCK: {
}
```

The preceding block is labeled as MYBLOCK. Label names follow the same conventions as variable names, with one small exception: Label names do not have an identifying character—%, $, @—as variables do. It's important to make sure that label names do not clash with Perl's built-in keywords. As a matter of style, it's best if label names are all uppercase. You should not have any conflicts with any current or future Perl keywords that way. The `for` and `while` statements can all have labels as well.

```
OUTER: while($expr ) {
   INNER: while($expr) {
         statement;
   }
}
```

The `last`, `redo`, and `next` statements can each take a label as an argument. You therefore can exit a specific block. The code in Listing 3.2 found two factors of 140 by using a nested pair of `for` loops. Suppose you wanted to exit the loops as soon as a factor is found. Without labels, you would need a complex arrangement of flag variables (variables whose only purpose is to store a true or false value for program flow control) and `if` statements between the two loops, because you cannot exit the outer loop from within the inner loop. Labels solve this problem:

```
OUTER: for($i=0; $i<100; $i++) {
   for($j=0; $j<100; $j++) {
         if ($i * $j == 140) {
               print "The product of $i and $j is 140\n";
               last OUTER;
         }
   }
}
```

Now the last statement can specify *which* loop it wants to exit—in this case, the OUTER loop. This snippet prints only the first pair of factors of 140 that it finds.

Leaving Perl

The `exit` statement is the ultimate flow-control tool. When Perl encounters an `exit` statement, the program stops executing, and an *exit status* is returned by Perl to the operating system. This exit status is usually used to indicate successful completion of the program. You'll learn more about exit statuses in Hour 11, "System Interaction." For now, an exit status of zero means everything went okay. The following is an example of `exit`:

```
if ($user_response eq 'quit') {
   print "Good Bye!\n";
   exit 0;          # Exit with a status of 0.
}
```

The `exit` statement has some side effects that are important to your operating system. When an `exit` is performed, any open files are closed, file locks are released, memory allocated by Perl is released to the system, and the Perl interpreter performs a clean shutdown.

Exercise: Finding Primes

What computer language primer would be complete without this little gem? In this exercise, you will examine a small program to find and print prime numbers. Prime numbers are divisible only by 1 and themselves; for example, 2 is prime, 3 is prime, 4 is not (because it is divisible by 1, 4, and 2), and so on. The list of primes is infinite, and they take a lot of computer power to find.

Using your text editor, type the program from Listing 3.3 and save it as `Primes`. Do not type in the line numbers. Make the program executable according to the instructions you learned in Hour 1.

When you're done, try running the program by typing the following at a command line:

```
perl -w Primes
```

LISTING 3.3   The Complete Source for Primes

```
1:   #!/usr/bin/perl -w
2:
3:   $maxprimes=20;          # Stop when you've found this many
4:   $value=1;
5:   $count=0;
6:   while($count < $maxprimes) {
7:               $value++;
8:               $composite=0;
9:   OUTER: for ($i=2; $i<$value; $i++) {
10:              for($j=$i; $j<$value; $j++) {
11:                      if (($j*$i)==$value) {
12:                              $composite=1;
13:                              last OUTER;
14:                      }
15:              }
16:        }
17:        if (! $composite) {
18:              $count++;
19:              print "$value is prime\n";
20:        }
21:   }
```

Line 1: This line contains the path to the interpreter (you can change it so that it's appropriate to your system) and the -w switch. Always have warnings enabled!

Line 3: `$maxprimes` is the maximum number of primes you want to find.

Line 4: `$value` is the value you're going to test for primeness.

Line 5: `$count` is the number of primes so far.

Line 6: The `while` loop continues as long as the program hasn't found enough primes.

Line 7: `$value` is incremented, so the first number to be checked for prime quality is 2.

Line 8: `$composite` is a flag used in the `for` loops to indicate that the number found is *composite,* not prime.

Lines 9–10: The `for` loops iterate through all the possible factors of `$value`. If `$value` were 4, the loops would produce 2 and 2, 2 and 3, 3 and 2, 3 and 3.

Lines 11–14: The values of `$i` and `$j` are multiplied together; if the product is `$value`, then `$value` is composite. The flag `$composite` is set, and both `for` loops are exited.

Lines 17–20: After the `for` loops, the `$composite` flag is checked. If it's false, the number is prime. These lines then print a message and increment the counter.

> The algorithm used here to find primes isn't particularly speedy or efficient—but it makes for a good demonstration of looping. A better method can be found in a good book on numerical algorithms.

Summary

In this hour, you learned about Perl's many flow control constructs. Some constructs, such as `if` and the logical operators, are used to control whether portions of the program run, depending on true or false values. Other constructs, such as `while`, `until`, and `for`, are used for looping over pieces of code as many times as necessary. You also learned what Perl's particular idea of truth is, which is used by virtually all test conditions in Perl.

Q&A

Q **I'm familiar with another programming language, C, which has a `switch` (or `case`) statement. Where is Perl's `switch` statement?**

A Perl doesn't have one! Perl provides such a variety of tests that figuring out the best syntax for a `switch` statement is nightmarish. The simplest way to emulate a `switch` statement is as follows:

```
if ($variable_to_test == $value1) {
    statement1;
} elsif ($variable_to_test == $value2) {
    statement2;
} else {
    default_statement;
}
```

The online syntax manual page—which you can view by typing `perldoc perlsyn` at a command prompt—contains many clever examples of how to emulate a `switch` statement in Perl, some with very `switch`-like syntax.

Q **How many `for` (`while`, `if`) blocks can I nest inside each other?**

A As many as you like, within memory restrictions of your system. Usually, however, if you have deeply nested loops, it is a sign that you should approach the problem differently.

Q **Help! Perl is giving me the message `Unmatched right bracket` (or `Missing right bracket`). The line number reported is the end of the file!**

A Somewhere in your program, you've used an open brace (`{`) without a close brace (`}`), or vice versa. Perl can sometimes guess where the typo is in your program, but sometimes not. Because control structures can nest arbitrarily deeply, Perl doesn't know you've made a mistake until it unexpectedly reaches the End of File without finding the balancing brace. A good program editor (such as vi, Emacs, or UltraEdit) has features to help you find mismatched braces. Use one.

Workshop

Quiz

1. The `while` statement loops as long as a condition is true. What statement loops as long as a condition is false?

   a. `if (not ) {}`

   b. `while (! condition) {}`

2. Is the following expression true or false?

```
(0 and 5) || ( ("0" or 0 or "") and (6 and "Hello")) or 1
```

a. True

b. False

3. What is the value of `$i` after this loop is run?

```
for($i=0; $i<=10; $i++) {      }
```

a. 10

b. 9

c. 11

Answers

1. b. The `while (! condition ) {}` syntax loops until the condition is false.

2. a. The expression can be reduced in these steps:

   > (false) || ((false) and (true)) or true

   > false || false or true

   > true

3. c. The test is `$i<=10`, so when the test is finally false, `$i` must be 11. If you got this one wrong, don't worry. It's such a common mistake that it even has a special name among programmers: a *fence post* error or an *off-by-one* error.

Activities

- Modify Listing 3.1 to keep playing the game until a successful guess is made.

- Listing 3.3, as it is written, is actually quite inefficient at finding primes. For example, it analyzes all the even numbers above 2—which cannot possibly be prime. Make additions to the algorithm to make the Primes program more efficient.

HOUR 4

Stacking Building Blocks: Lists and Arrays

Scalars are Perl's singular nouns. They can represent any one thing—a word, a record, a document, a line of text, or a character. Often, though, you need to talk about collections of things—many words, a few records, two documents, fifty lines of text, or a dozen characters.

When you need to talk about many things in Perl, you use *list data*. You can represent list data in three different ways: by using lists, arrays, and hashes.

Lists are the simplest representation of list data. A list is simply a group of scalars. Sometimes they're written with a set of parentheses encasing the scalars, which are separated by commas. For example, `(2, 5, $a, "Bob")` is a list that contains two numbers, a scalar variable `$a`, and the string `"Bob"`. Each scalar in a list is called a *list element*. In keeping with the philosophy of Least Surprise (see Hour 2, "Perl's Building Blocks: Numbers and Strings"), Perl's lists can contain as many scalar elements as you like. Because scalars can also be arbitrarily large, a list can hold quite a lot of data.

To store list data so that you can refer to it throughout your program, you need an array variable. Array variables are represented in Perl with an "at" sign (@) as the type identifier followed by a valid variable name (as discussed in Hour 2, "Perl's Building Blocks: Numbers and Strings"). For example, @foo is a valid array variable in Perl. You can have the same name for an array variable as a scalar variable; for example, $names and @names refer to different things—$names to a scalar variable, and @names to an array. The two variables have nothing to do with each other.

Individual items in an array are called *array elements*. Individual array elements are referred to by their position within the array, called an *index*. That is, we can refer to the third array element of the array @foo, the fifth array element of the array @names, and so on.

The other list type, a *hash,* is similar to an array. Hashes will be discussed further in Hour 7, "Hashes."

In this hour you will learn

- How to fill and empty arrays
- How to examine arrays element by element
- How to sort and print arrays
- How to split scalars into arrays and join arrays back into scalars

Putting Things into Lists and Arrays

Putting things into a literal list is easy. As you just saw, the syntax for a literal list is a set of parentheses enclosing scalar values. The following is an example:

```
(5, 'apple', $x, 3.14159)
```

This example creates a four-element list containing the numbers 5, the string `'apple'`, whatever happens to be in the scalar variable $x, and pi.

If the list contains only simple strings, and putting single quotation marks around each string gets to be too much for you, Perl provides a shortcut—the qw operator. An example of qw follows:

```
qw( apples oranges 45.6 $x )
```

This example creates a four-element list. Each element of the list is separated from the others by whitespace (spaces, tabs, or newlines). If you have list elements that have embedded whitespace, you cannot use the qw operator. This code works just as though you had written the following:

```
('apples', 'oranges', '45.6', '$x')
```

Notice that the $x is encased in single quotation marks. The qw operator does not do variable interpolation on elements that look like variables; they are treated as though you wanted them that way literally. So '$x' is not converted to whatever the value of the scalar variable $x is; it's left alone as a string containing a dollar sign and the letter x.

Perl also has a useful operator that works in literal lists; it's called the *range operator*. The range operator is designated by a pair of periods (..). The following is an example of this operator:

```
(1..10)
```

The range operator takes the left operand (the 1) and the right operand (the 10) and constructs a list consisting of all the numbers between 1 and 10, inclusive. If you need several ranges in a list, you can simply use multiple operators:

```
(1..10, 20..30);
```

The preceding example creates a list of 21 elements: 1 through 10 and 20 through 30. Giving the range operator a right operand less than the left, such as (10..1), produces an empty list.

The range operator works on strings as well as numbers. The range (a..z) generates a list of all 26 lowercase letters. The range (aa..zz) generates a much larger list of 676 letter pairs starting with aa, ab, ac, ad and ending with zx, zy, zz.

Arrays

Literal lists are usually used to initialize some other structure: an array or a hash. To create an array in Perl, you can simply put something into it. With Perl, unlike other languages, you don't have to tell it ahead of time that you're creating an array or how large the array is going to be. To create a new array and populate it with a list of items, you could do the following:

```
@boys=qw( Greg Peter Bobby );
```

This example, called an *array assignment,* uses the array assignment operator—the equals sign, just as in a scalar assignment. After that code runs, the array @boys contains three elements: Greg, Peter, and Bobby. Notice also that the code uses the qw operator; using this operator saves you from having to type six quotation marks and two commas.

Array assignments can also involve other arrays or even empty lists, as shown in the following examples:

```
@copy=@original;
@clean=();
```

Here, all the elements of @original are copied into a new array called @copy. If @copy already had elements before the assignment, they are now lost. After the second statement is executed, @clean is empty. Assigning an empty list (or an empty array) to an array variable removes all the elements from the array.

If a literal list contains other lists, arrays, or hashes, these lists are all flattened into one large list. Observe this snippet of code:

```
@boys=qw( Greg Peter Bobby );
@girls=qw( Marcia Jan Cindy );
@kids=(@girls, @boys);
@family=(@kids, ('Mike', 'Carol'), 'Alice');
```

The list (@girls, @boys) is flattened by Perl to a simple list containing first all the girls' names and then all the boys' names before the values are assigned to @kids. On the next line, the array @kids is flattened, and the list ('Mike', 'Carol') is flattened into one long list; then that list is assigned to @family. The original structures of @boys, @girls, @kids, and the list ('Mike', 'Carol') are not preserved in @family—only the individual elements from Greg through Alice. In other words, the preceding snippet for building @family is equivalent to this assignment:

```
@family=qw(Marcia Jan Cindy Greg Peter Bobby Mike Carol Alice );
```

The left side of an array assignment can be a list if it contains only variable names. The array assignment initializes the variables on that list. Consider this example:

```
($a, $b, $c)=qw(apples oranges bananas);
```

Here, $a is initialized to 'apples', $b to 'oranges', and $c to 'bananas'.

If the list on the left contains an array, that array receives *all* the remaining values from the right side, no matter where it is in the list. The reason is that an array can contain an indefinite number of elements. Observe here:

```
($a, @fruit,$c) = qw (peaches mangoes grapes cherries);
```

In this example, $a is set to 'peaches'. The remaining fruits in the list on the right are assigned to @fruit on the left. No elements are left for $c to receive a value (because the array on the left side of an assignment absorbs all the remaining values from the right), so $c is set to undef.

It's also important to note that if the left side contains more variables than it has elements, the leftover variables receive the value undef. If the right side has more variables than the list on the left has elements, the extra elements on the right are simply ignored. The following figure shows another example to help understand that concept.

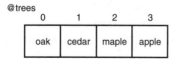

In the first line, $t, $u, and $v all receive a value from the right side. The extra right-side element ('quail') is simply not used for this expression. In the second line, $a, $b, and $c all receive a value from the right. $d, however, has nothing to get from the right ($c takes the last value, 'gopher'), so $d is set to undef.

Getting Elements Out of an Array

So far in this hour, you've been slinging around whole arrays and lists and putting information into arrays. How can you get that information back out?

One way to get the contents of the entire array is to put the array variable in double quotation marks:

```
print "@array";
```

An array in double quotes is interpolated, and its elements are returned separated by spaces. This example prints the elements of @array with a space separating each element.

Many times, though, you need to get to individual elements of arrays. You may need to search for an element, change the value of an element, or to add or remove individual elements in an array.

Individual elements in an array are accessed by a numeric index. The index for array elements starts at the number 0 and increases by 1 for each additional element. Each element of the array has an index value, as shown in the following figure.

@trees

0	1	2	3
oak	cedar	maple	apple

The number of elements in an array is limited only by your system's memory. To access an element, you use the syntax

`$array[index]`

where `array` is the array name and `index` is the index of the element you want (also called a *subscript*). The array doesn't have to exist before you refer to individual elements; if it does not already exist, it just automagically springs into existence. Some examples of accessing array elements follow:

```
@trees=qw(oak cedar maple apple);
print $trees[0];          # Prints "oak"
print $trees[3];          # Prints "apple".
$trees[4]='pine';
```

Notice that to talk about an individual element of `@trees`, the code uses a `$`. "I thought the `$` marker was usually reserved for scalars; what's going on?" you might ask. The answer is that the `$` in `$trees[3]` does refer to a scalar: one scalar value within `@trees`. (Scalars are also indicated by a dollar sign because they're singular as well. You should notice a pattern here.)

At the beginning of this hour, you discovered that scalars and arrays can have the same variable names and remain unrelated. Perl can tell the difference between `$trees`, a scalar variable that has nothing to do with the `@trees` array, and `$trees[0]`, the first element in the `@trees` array, because of the square brackets in `$trees[0]`. Perl knows that you're taking about the first element of `@trees` and not talking about `$trees` at all.

You can also talk about a subgroup within an array, called a *slice*. To take a slice of an array, you use both the `@` type identifier—to indicate that you're talking about a group of things—and square brackets—to indicate you're talking about individual elements of an array, as shown here:

```
@trees=qw(oak cedar maple apple cherry pine peach fir);
@trees[3,4,6];              # Just the fruit trees
@conifers=@trees[5,7];   # Just the conifers
```

Finding the End of an Array

Sometimes you need to find the end of the array—for example, to see how many trees are in the `@trees` array or to cut some trees out of the `@trees` array. Perl provides a couple of mechanisms for finding the end. The first is a special variable in the form

$#*arrayname*. It returns the number of the last valid index of the array. Check out this example:

```
@trees=qw(oak cedar maple apple cherry pine peach fir);
print $#trees;
```

This example contains eight elements, but you must remember that arrays are numbered starting at 0. So the preceding example prints the number 7. Modifying the value of $#trees changes the length of the array. Making it smaller truncates the array at whatever index you specify, and making it larger gives the array more elements. The newly added elements all have their values set to undef.

The other method of finding the size of an array is to use the array variable in a place where a scalar is expected:

```
$size=@array;
```

This puts the number of elements in @array into $size. This takes advantage of a Perl concept called *context,* explained in the next section.

You can also specify negative indexes for arrays. Negative index numbers start counting from the end of the array and work backward. For example, $array[-1] is the last element of @array, $array[-2] is the next to the last element, and so on.

4

Learning More about Context

What is *context?* Context means the things that surround an item of interest to help define what that item means. For example, seeing a man in surgical scrubs can have different meanings depending on where he is: In a hospital, the fact that the man is wearing scrubs might mean that he's a doctor; at a Halloween party, he could be just another party guest in costume.

Human language uses context to help determine the meaning of words. For example, the word *level* can have several different meanings depending on how it's used and what context it's in:

- The carpenter used a level to hang the door straight.
- The moderator spoke in a level tone.
- The water in the pool was at waist level.

It's the same word each time, but the meaning has changed. It becomes a noun, an adjective, and a different kind of noun depending on how it's used in a sentence.

Perl is also sensitive to context. Functions and operators in Perl can behave differently depending on what context they're used in. The two most important contexts in Perl are *list context* and *scalar context*.

As you've seen, you can use one operator—the equals sign—to perform assignment with both arrays and scalars. The type of expression (list or scalar) on the left side of the assignment operator determines what context the things on the right side are evaluated in, as shown in the following lines of code:

```
$a=$b;        # Scalar on the left: this is scalar context.
@foo=@bar;    # Array on the left: this is list context.
($a)=@foo;    # List on the left: this is also list context.
$b=@bar;      # Scalar on the left: this is scalar context.
```

The last line is interesting, because it puts an array into scalar context. As was stated in the previous section, evaluating an array in a scalar context returns the number of elements in the array.

More about the Size and End of an Array

Observe $a and $b in the following few lines of code; they do almost the same thing:

```
@foo=qw( water cola juice lemonade );
$a=@foo;
$b=$#foo;
print "$a\n";
print "$b\n";
```

At the end of this code, $a contains the number 4, and $b contains the number 3. Why the difference? $a is @foo evaluated in a scalar context, and it contains the *number of elements.* $b, on the other hand, is set to the *index of the last element,* and indexes start counting at 0.

Because arrays in a scalar context return the number of elements in the array, testing whether an array contains elements becomes this simple:

```
@mydata=qw( oats peas beans barley );
if (@mydata) {
   print "The array has elements!\n";
}
```

Here, the array @mydata is evaluated as a scalar, and it returns the number of elements— in this case, 4. The number 4 evaluates to true in an if statement, and the body of the if block is run.

> Actually, @mydata here is used in a special kind of scalar context called a *Boolean* context, but it behaves the same way. Boolean context occurs when Perl expects a true or false value, such as in an `if` statement's test expression. One other context, called *void* context, will be explained in Hour 9, "More Functions and Operators."

Context with Operators and Functions

Many of Perl's operators and functions force their arguments to be either scalar context or list context. Sometimes the operators or functions behave differently depending on what context they're in. Some functions you've already encountered have these properties; however, this fact hasn't been important until now, because they have only had scalars to work on.

The `print` function expects a list as an argument. It doesn't particularly matter what context the list is evaluated in, though. So printing an array with `print` like this causes the array to be evaluated in a list context, yielding the elements of @foo:

```
print @foo;
```

You can use a special pseudofunction called `scalar` to force something into a scalar context:

```
print scalar(@foo);
```

This example prints the number of elements in @foo. The `scalar` function forces @foo to be evaluated in a scalar context, so @foo returns the number of elements in @foo. Then the `print` function simply prints the number returned.

The `chomp` function you learned about in Hour 2, "Perl's Building Blocks: Numbers and Strings," takes either an array or a scalar as an argument. If `chomp` is presented with a scalar, it removes the record separator from the end of the scalar. If it is presented with an array, it removes the record separator from the end of each scalar in the array.

Also in Hour 2 you learned how to read a line of input from the keyboard by using `<STDIN>`. The angle brackets (`<>`) are really an operator in Perl, and they behave differently depending on context. In a scalar context, this operator reads one line of input from the terminal. In a list context, however, it reads *all* the input from the terminal—until the End of File is read—and places the data in the list. Examine the following:

```
$a=<STDIN>;    # Scalar context, reads one line into $a.
@whole=<STDIN>; # List context, reads all input into the array @whole.
($a)=<STDIN>; # List context, reads all input into the assignable list.
```

4

In the third example, what does $a receive? Remember from earlier in this hour that if the left side in a list assignment doesn't have enough variables to hold all the right-side elements, the extra right-side elements are dropped. So here all input from the terminal is read, but $a receives only the first line.

> What's an *End of File*? When Perl reads all input from a terminal, you need
> to signal when you're done feeding Perl data. You usually do so typing an
> end-of-file (EOF) character. That character differs depending on your operat-
> ing system. Under Unix, that character is usually a Ctrl+D at the beginning
> of a line. On MS-DOS or Windows systems, that character is Ctrl+Z two times
> anywhere in the input.

Also in Hour 2 you learned about the repetition operator x. The repetition operator has a special behavior in list context. If the left operand is in parenthesis, and the operator itself is used in a list context, it returns a list of the left operand repeated. The following example builds an array of 100 stars:

```
@stars= ("*") x 100;
```

The left operand of x—"*"—is in parentheses, and assigning it to an array puts it in a list context. This syntax is useful for initializing an array's elements to a particular value.

Another operator that you've been using—and probably didn't know it was an operator—is the comma (,). Until now, you've been using the comma to separate elements of literal lists, like this:

```
@pets=('cat', 'dog', 'fish', 'canary', 'iguana');
```

The preceding snippet has the list being evaluated in a list context, as normal. In a scalar context, on the other hand, the comma is an operator that evaluates each element from left to right and returns the value of the rightmost element:

```
$last_pet=('cat', 'dog', 'fish', 'canary', 'iguana');   # Not what you think!
```

In this snippet, the pets named on the right side of the assignment operator aren't really a list, despite the parentheses around them. The right side of the expression is evaluated in a scalar context because of the scalar $last_pet on the left of the equals sign, so the group of string literals is evaluated as a scalar. The result is that $last_pet is set equal to 'iguana'.

Another example of a function that acts in two completely different ways depending on which context it's in is the localtime function. In a scalar context, the localtime func-tion returns a nicely formatted string with the current time. For example, print `scalar(localtime);` would print something like: `Thu Sep 16 23:00:06 1999`. In a list context, `localtime` returns an list of elements that describe the current time:

`($sec, $min, $hour, $mday, $mon, $year_off, $wday, $yday, $isdst)=localtime;`

What these values represent is shown in Table 4.1.

TABLE 4.1 Return Values from `localtime`, in List Context

Field	Value
$sec	Seconds, 0–59
$min	Minutes, 0–59
$hour	Hour, 0–23
$mday	Day of the month, 1–28, 29, 30, or 31
$mon	Month of the year, 0–11 (be careful here!)
$year_off	Number of years since 1900 (add 1900 to this number for the correct 4-digit year)
$wday	Day of the week, 0–6
$yday	Day of the year, 0–364 or 365
$isdst	True if Daylight Savings Time is in effect

Do *not* attempt to get a four-digit year by concatenating '19' in front of the year returned by `localtime`. The year returned is an offset from 1900—in 1999, year is '99'; in 2001 it is '101'. Adding 1900 to this value will work correctly well beyond year 2000. Perl has no Y2K bugs, but simply concatenating '19' (or '20') with the year will cause a Y2K problem in your programs.

How do you know what context a function or operator forces on its arguments and how it's going to function depending on whether it's in a scalar context or a list context? Quite simply, you don't, and there's really no good way to guess. The online documentation lists each function and operator and explains these factors for each one if you're unsure. For the remainder of this book, if a function or operand forces a context on its arguments, or behaves differently depending on what context it's evaluated in, I will indicate all these points when the function is first presented. It doesn't happen often, but when it does, I'll be sure to tell you.

Manipulating Arrays

Now that you've learned the basic rules for building arrays, it's time to learn some tools to help you manipulate those arrays to perform useful tasks.

Stepping Through an Array

In Hour 3, "Controlling the Program's Flow," you learned about making loops with `while`, `for`, and other constructs. Many tasks you'll want to perform involve examining each element of an array. This process is called *iterating* over the array. One way you could do so is to use a `for` loop, as follows:

```
@flavors=qw( chocolate vanilla strawberry mint sherbet );
for($index=0; $index<@flavors; $index++) {
    print "My favorite flavor is $flavors[$index] and..."
}
print "many others.\n";
```

The first line initializes the array with ice cream flavors, using the `qw` operator for clarity. (If I had included a two-word flavor such as Rocky Road, I would have needed a regular, single-quoted list.) The second line does most of the work. `$index` is initialized to 0 and incremented by 1 until `@flavors` is reached. Because it is being compared to the scalar `$index`, `@flavors` is evaluated in a scalar context, so it evaluates to 5—the number of elements in `@flavors`.

The preceding example seems like an awful lot of work for just iterating over an array. Usually in Perl, if something seems like an awful lot of work, you can find an easier way to do it. This is no exception. Perl has another loop statement that wasn't mentioned in Hour 3, called `foreach`. The `foreach` statement sets an index variable, called an *iterator*, equal to each element of a list in turn. Consider this example:

```
foreach $cone (@flavors) {
    print "I'd like a cone of $cone\n";
}
```

Here, the variable `$cone` is set to each value in `@flavors`. As `$cone` is set to each value in `@flavors`, the body of the loop is executed, printing the message for each value in `@flavors`.

In a `foreach` loop, the iterator isn't just a variable that is assigned the value of each element in the list; it actually refers to that list element itself. If you modify the iterator, the corresponding element in the list will remain modified after the loop is done. Check out this example:

```
foreach $flavor (@flavors) {
    print "I'd like a bowl of $flavor ice cream, please.\n";
```

```
    $flavor = "$flavor (I've had some)";
  }
print "The available flavors are\n";
foreach $flavor (@flavors) {
  print "$flavor\n";
}
```

In the first loop, the second line prints "I'd like a bowl of chocolate ice cream, please." continuing with vanilla, strawberry, and so on. The third line, however, modifies $flavor, and therefore the corresponding element of @flavors, by appending (I've had some) on the end. After the first loop finishes, the second loop lists the flavors, showing for each one the fact that I've had some.

> In Perl, the foreach and for loop statements are actually synonyms; they can be used interchangeably. For clarity, throughout this book, you'll find that I use the foreach() loop statement to iterate over arrays and the for() loop statement for the kind of for loops presented in Hour 3, which did not involve arrays. Keep in mind that they are interchangeable.

Converting Between Arrays and Scalars

Perl doesn't have one general rule about converting between scalars and arrays. Rather, Perl provides many functions and operators for converting between the two types.

One method to convert a scalar into an array is the split function. The split function takes a pattern and a scalar, uses the pattern to split the scalar apart, and returns a list of the pieces. The first argument is the pattern (here surrounded by slashes), and the second argument is the scalar to split apart:

```
@words=split(/ /, "The quick brown fox");
```

After you run this code, @words contains each of the words The, quick, brown, and fox—without the spaces. If you don't specify a second argument, the variable $_ is split. If you don't specify a pattern or a string, whitespace is used to split apart the variable $_. One special pattern, // (the null pattern), splits apart the scalar into individual characters, as shown here:

```
while(<STDIN>) {
  ($firstchar)=split(//, $_);
  print "The first character was $firstchar\n";
}
```

The first line reads from the terminal one line at a time, setting $_ equal to that line. The second line splits $_ apart using the null pattern. The split function returns a list of each character from the line in $_. That list is assigned to the list on the left side, and the first element of the list is assigned to $firstchar; the rest are discarded.

> The patterns used by split are actually *regular expressions*. Regular expressions are a complex pattern-matching language introduced in Hour 6, "Pattern Matching." For now, the examples will use simple patterns such as spaces, colons, commas, and such. After you've learned about regular expressions, I will give examples that use more complex patterns to pull apart scalars with split.

This method of splitting a scalar into a list of scalar variables is common in Perl. When you're splitting apart a scalar in which each piece is a distinct element—such as fields in a record—it's easier to figure out which piece is what when you name each piece as it's split. Observe the following:

```
@Music=('White Album,Beatles',
        'Graceland,Paul Simon',
        'A Boy Named Sue,Goo Goo Dolls');
foreach $record (@Music) {
    ($record_name, $artist)=split(',', $record);
}
```

When you split directly into a list with named scalars, you can clearly see which fields represent what. The first field is a record name, and the second field is the artist. Had the code split into an array, the distinction between fields might not have been as clear.

To create scalars out of arrays—the reverse of split—you can use the Perl join function. join takes a string and a list, joins the elements of the list together using the string as a separator, and then returns the resulting string. Consider this example:

```
$numbers=join(',', (1..10));
```

This example assigns the string 1,2,3,4,5,6,7,8,9,10 to $numbers.

In Perl the output (return value) of one function can be used as an input value (argument) in another function. You can use split and join to pull a string apart and put it back together all at the same time, as seen here:

```
$message="Elvis was here";
print "The string \"$message\" consists of:",
            join('-', split(//, $message));
```

In this example, the $message is split into a list by split. That list is used by the join function and put back together with dashes. The result is the following message:

```
The string "Elvis was here" consists of: E-l-v-i-s- -w-a-s- -h-e-r-e
```

Reordering Your Array

When you're building arrays, often you might want them to come out in a different order than you built them. For example, if your Perl program reads a list of customers in from a file, printing that customer list in alphabetical order would be reasonable. For sorting data, Perl provides the `sort` function. The `sort` function takes as its argument a list and sorts it in (roughly speaking) alphabetical order; the function then returns a new list in sorted order. The original array remains untouched, as you can see in this example:

```
@Chiefs=qw(Clinton Bush Reagan Carter Ford Nixon);
print join(' ', sort @Chiefs), "\n";

print join(' ', @Chiefs), "\n";
```

This example prints the sorted list of presidents (`Bush Carter Clinton Ford Nixon Reagan`) and then prints the list again in its original order.

Be forewarned that the default sort order is ASCII order. This means that all words that start with uppercase characters sort before words that begin in lowercase letters. Numbers do not sort in ASCII order the way you would expect. They don't sort by value. For example, 11 sorts higher than 100. In cases like this, you need to sort by something other than the default order.

The `sort` function allows you to sort in whatever order you want by using a block of code (or a subroutine name, discussed in Hour 8, "Functions") as the second argument. Inside the block (or subroutine), two variables, `$a` and `$b`, are set to two elements of the list. The block's task is to return –1, 0, or 1 depending on whether the `$a` is less than `$b`, equal to `$b`, or greater than `$b`, respectively. The following is an example of the hard way to do a numeric sort, assuming that `@numbers` is full of numeric values:

```
@sorted=sort { return(1) if ($a>$b);
               return(0) if ($a==$b);
               return(-1) if ($a<$b); } @numbers;
```

The preceding example certainly sorts `@numbers` numerically. But the code looks far too complicated for such a common task. As you might suspect for anything this cumbersome, Perl has a shortcut: the "spaceship" operator, `<=>`. The spaceship operator gets its name because it somewhat resembles a flying saucer, seen from the side. It returns –1 if its left operand is less than the right, 0 if the two operands are equal, and 1 if the left operand is greater than the right:

```
@sorted=sort { $a<=>$b; } @numbers;
```

This code is much cleaner, easier to look at, and more straightforward. You should use the spaceship operator only to compare numeric values.

4

To compare alphabetic strings, use the `cmp` operator, which works exactly the same way. You can put together more complex sorting arrangements by simply making a more sophisticated sort routine. Section 4 of the Perl Frequently Asked Questions (FAQ) has some more sophisticated examples of this if you need them.

The final function for this hour is an easy function, `reverse`. The `reverse` function, when given a scalar value in a scalar context, reverses the string's characters and returns the reversed string. The call `reverse("Perl")` in a scalar context, for example, returns `lreP`. When given a list in a list context, `reverse` returns the elements of the list in reverse order, as in this example:

```
@lines=qw(I do not like green eggs and ham);
print join(' ', reverse @lines);
```

This snippet prints `ham and eggs green like not do I`. To continue this playfulness and really show off the function-stacking capability, you can add more nonsense to the mixture:

```
print join(' ', reverse sort @lines);
```

The `sort` is run first, producing the Yoda-esque list
(`I,and,do,eggs,green,ham,like,not`). That list is reversed and passed to `join` for joining together with a space. The result is `not like ham green eggs do and I`. I couldn't agree more.

Exercise: Playing a Little Game

This hour has really been full of Catch-22's: familiar operators behaving differently depending on context, a handful of new operators and functions, and quite a few new rules to remember about syntax. To keep you from developing any hang-ups, I've added this exercise, which puts your knowledge of arrays and lists to good use—a game.

Using your text editor, type the program from Listing 4.1 and save it as `Hangman`. As always, don't type the line numbers or their following colons ("1:", etc.) Be sure to make the program executable according to the instructions you learned in Hour 1, "Introduction to the Perl Language."

When you're done, try running the program by typing the following at a command line:

Hangman

or, if your system does not allow making the program executable,

perl -w Hangman

LISTING 4.1   Complete Listing of the Hangman Program

```perl
1:   #!/usr/bin/perl -w
2:
3:   @words=qw( internet answers printer program );
4:   @guesses=();
5:   $wrong=0;
6:
7:   $choice=$words[rand @words];
8:   $hangman="0-|--<";
9:
10:  @letters=split(//, $choice);
11:  @hangman=split(//, $hangman);
12:  @blankword=(0) x scalar(@letters);
13:  OUTER:
14:          while ($wrong<@hangman) {
15:                  foreach $i (0..$#letters) {
16:                          if ($blankword[$i]) {
17:                                  print $blankword[$i];
18:                          } else {
19:                                  print "-";
20:                          }
21:                  }
22:                  print "\n";
23:                  if ($wrong) {
24:                          print @hangman[0..$wrong-1]
25:                  }
26:                  print "\n Your Guess: ";
27:                  $guess=<STDIN>;  chomp $guess;
28:                  foreach(@guesses) {
29:                          next OUTER if ($_ eq $guess);
30:                  }
31:                  $guesses[@guesses]=$guess;
32:                  $right=0;
33:                  for ($i=0; $i<@letters; $i++) {
34:                          if ($letters[$i] eq $guess) {
35:                                  $blankword[$i]=$guess;
36:                                  $right=1;
37:                          }
38:                  }
39:                  $wrong++ if (not $right);
40:                  if (join('', @blankword) eq $choice) {
41:                          print "You got it right!\n";
42:                          exit;
43:                  }
44:  }
45:  print "$hangman\nSorry, the word was $choice.\n";
```

Line 1: This line contains the path to the interpreter (you can change it so that it's appropriate to your system) and the -w switch. Always have warnings enabled!

Line 3: The array @words is initialized with the list of possible words that the game can use.

Lines 4–5: Some variables are initialized. @guesses is used to hold a list of all past guesses the player has made. $wrong holds the number of wrong guesses so far.

Line 7: A word is chosen at random from the array @words and assigned to $choice. The rand() function expects a scalar argument, and because @words is being treated as a scalar, it returns the number of elements (in this case, 4). The rand function returns a number between 0 and 3—but not including 0 or 4. As it turns out, when you use a decimal number as an array index, the decimal portion is dropped.

Line 8: The hangman is defined. He's not pretty, but he gets the point across.

Line 10: The mystery word in $choice is split into individual letters in @letters.

Line 11: The hangman scalar is split into pieces in @hangman. The head is $hangman[0], the neck is $hangman[1], and so on.

Line 12: The array @blankword is used to mark which letters the player has guessed successfully. (0) x scalar(@letters) creates a list that is as long as the number of elements in @letters, which is stored in @blankword. As letters are guessed, these 0s are changed to letters in line 35—this will mark the positions of the correctly guessed letters.

Lines 13–14: The loop containing most of the program is set up. It has a label—OUTER—so that inside the loop you can have some fine-grained control over it. It continues looping until the number of wrong guesses is the same as the length of the hangman.

Lines 15–21: This foreach loop iterates over the array @blankword for each letter in the puzzle. If @blankword doesn't contain a letter in that particular element, a dash is printed; otherwise, the letter is printed.

Lines 23–25: $wrong contains the number of wrong guesses. If that number is at least one, line 24 uses a slice to print the hangman array from position 0 up to the number of wrong guesses (less 1).

Lines 26–27: These lines get the guess from the player. chomp() removes the trailing newline.

Lines 28–30: These lines search @guesses to see whether the player has already guessed that letter. If he or she has, you restart the loop at line 13. The player isn't penalized for duplicate wrong guesses.

Line 31: The letter guessed by the player is recorded in @guesses. Using @guesses in a scalar context causes the number of elements to be substituted in the brackets [], so each time this statement is run, the index one beyond the last index is set to $guess.

Lines 32–38: The meat of the program! The array @letters, which contains the puzzle, is searched. If the guess is found in the puzzle, the corresponding element of @blankword is set to the letter. The array @blankword contains either a correctly guessed letter or undef at any particular element. A flag called $right is set to 1 to indicate that at least one letter was successfully found.

Line 39: $wrong is incremented, unless the player correctly guessed a letter.

Lines 40–43: The elements of the array @blankword are joined together to form a string and compared to the original puzzle. If they match, the player has guessed all the letters.

Line 45: The player was unable to guess the puzzle, and the interpreter has dropped out of the loop started at line 13. This line prints a conciliatory message and exits the game.

This game exercises most of the concepts from this hour—literal lists, arrays, split, join, context, and foreach loops. You can implement this small game of Hangman in an almost unlimited number of ways, but I hope that you've caught on to some of the possibilities that arrays provide.

Listing 4.2 shows a sample of the Hangman program's output.

LISTING 4.2   Sample Output from Hangman

```
-------

Your Guess: t
----t-

Your Guess: s
----t-
0
Your Guess: e
----te-
0
Your Guess:
```

Summary

Arrays and lists are Perl's collective variables. You can use them to hold an almost unlimited number of scalars, and you can either manipulate them as a whole or manipulate their individual elements. Perl provides easy mechanisms for copying arrays, sorting arrays, combining arrays, and converting data back and forth between scalars and arrays. Also, many of Perl's operators and functions are sensitive to the context that they appear in, and they behave differently depending on whether they are in a scalar or list context.

Q&A

Q Can you suggest a quick way to find a particular string in an array element?

A Iterating over the array and checking each element are the usual ways to do so. If you frequently find yourself searching an array to see whether an element is in the array, you probably didn't want to store the data in an array in the first place. A much more efficient structure for random-element access is a hash, which is covered in Hour 7.

Q How can I eliminate duplicate elements from an array?

How can I count the number of unique elements in an array?

How can I see whether two arrays contain the same or different elements?

A The answer to all these questions is the same: Use a hash. Hashes allow you to do some rather interesting manipulations on arrays quickly and efficiently. All these questions are answered in Hour 7.

Workshop

Quiz

1. What's an efficient way to swap the values contained in two scalar variables `$a` and `$b`?

   a. `$a=$b;`

   b. `($a,$b)=($b, $a);`

   c. `$c=$a; $a=$b; $b=$c;`

2. What does the statement `$a=scalar(@array);` assign to the variable `$a`?

   a. The number of elements in `@array`

   b. The index of the last element of `@array`

   c. That syntax is not valid

3. What does the statement `$a=@array;` assign to the variable `$a`?

   a. The number of elements in `@array`

   b. The index of the last element of `@array`

   c. That syntax is not valid

Answers

1. b. The first choice clearly will not work; the value contained in `$a` is destroyed. Choice c answers the question but requires a third variable to hold the data during the swap. Choice b swaps the data correctly, using no extra variables, and is fairly clear code.

2. a. Using an array in a scalar context returns the number of elements in the array. `$#array` would have returned the last index of the array. The use of `scalar()` in this example is unnecessary; having a scalar on the left side of the assignment operator is enough to put `@array` in a scalar context.

3. a. Trick question, it's actually the same as #2, except that the context is implied by the assignment instead of being explicitly given with the scalar operator.

Activities

- Modify the Hangman game to print the hangman in an upright position.

4

HOUR 5

Working with Files

Until now, your Perl programs have been self-contained. They have been unable to communicate with the outside world other than to provide messages to the user and receive input from the keyboard. All of that is about to change.

Perl is an outstanding language for reading from and writing to files on disk or elsewhere. Perl's scalars can stretch to hold the longest possible record in a file, and Perl's arrays can stretch to hold the entire contents of files—as long as enough memory is available, of course. When the data is contained within Perl's scalars and arrays, you can perform endless manipulations on that data and write new files.

Perl tries very hard not to get in your way while reading or writing files. In some places, Perl's built-in statements are even optimized for performing common types of file input/output (I/O) operations.

In this hour, you will learn how Perl can give you access to all the data available to you in files.

In this hour you will learn

- How to open and close files
- How to write data to files
- How to read data from files
- How to write Perl defensively so that your programs are robust

Opening Files

To read or write files in Perl, you need to open a *filehandle*. Filehandles in Perl are yet another kind of variable. They act as convenient references (handles, if you will) between your program and the operating system about a particular file. They contain information about how the file was opened and how far along you are in reading (or writing) the file; they also contain user-definable attributes about how the file is to be read or written.

From previous hours you're already familiar with one filehandle: STDIN. This filehandle is given to you automatically by Perl when your program starts, and it's usually connected to the keyboard device (you'll learn more details about STDIN later). The format for filehandle names is the the same as that for variable names outlined in Hour 2, "Perl's Building Blocks: Numbers and Strings," except that no type identifier appears in front of the name ($, @). For this reason, it's recommended that filehandle names be in uppercase so that they do not clash with Perl's current or future reserved words: foreach, else, if, and so on.

You can also use a string scalar or anything that returns a string—such as a function—as a filehandle name. This type is called an *indirect filehandle*. Describing their use is a bit confusing for a primer in Perl. For more information on indirect filehandles, see the online documentation on the open function in the perlfunc manual page.

Any time you need to access a file on your disk, you need to create a new filehandle and prepare it by opening the filehandle. You open filehandles, not surprisingly, with the open function. The syntax of the open function is as follows:

```
open(filehandle, pathname)
```

The open function takes a filehandle as its first argument and a pathname as the second argument. The pathname indicates which file you want to open, so if you don't specify a full pathname—such as c:/windows/system/—open will try to open the file in the current directory. If the open function succeeds, it returns a nonzero value. If the open function fails, it returns undef (false):

```
if (open(MYFILE, "mydatafile")) {
    # Run this if the open succeeds
} else {
    print "Cannot open mydatafile!\n";
    exit 1;
}
```

In the preceding snippet, if open succeeds, it evaluates to a true value, and the if block is run with the open filehandle called MYFILE which is now open for input. Otherwise, the file cannot be opened, and the else portion of the code is run, indicating an error. In many Perl programs, this "open or fail" syntax is written using the die function. The die function stops execution of your Perl program and prints an error message:

Died at *scriptname* line *xxx*

Here, *scriptname* is the name of the Perl program, and *xxx* is the line number where the die was encountered. The die and open functions are frequently seen together in this form:

```
open(MYTEXT, "novel.txt") || die;
```

This line is read as "open or die," which sums up how you will usually want your program to handle the situation when a file can't be opened. As described in Hour 3, "Controlling the Program's Flow," if the open does not succeed—if it returns false—then the logical OR (||) needs to evaluate the right-hand argument (the die). If the open succeeds—if it returns true—then the die is never evaluated. This idiom is also written with the other symbol for logical OR, or.

When you are done with a file, it is good programming practice to close the filehandle. Closing notifies the operating system that the filehandle is available for reuse and that any unwritten data for the filehandle can now be written to disk. Also, your operating system may allow you to open only a fixed number of filehandles; after that limit is exceeded, you cannot open more filehandles until you close some. To close filehandles, you use the close function as follows:

```
close(MYTEXT);
```

If a filehandle name is reused—that is, if another file is opened with the same filehandle name—the original filehandle is first closed and then reopened.

Pathnames

Until now, you've opened only files with simple names like novel.txt that did not include a path. When you try to open a filename that doesn't specify a directory name,

5

Perl assumes the file is in the current directory. To open a file that's in another directory, you must use a *pathname*. The pathname describes the path that Perl must take to find the file on your system.

You specify the pathname in the manner in which your operating system expects it, as shown in the following examples:

```
open(MYFILE, "DISK5:[USER.PIERCE.NOVEL]") || die;    # VMS
open(MYFILE, "Drive:folder:file") || die;     # Macintosh
open(MYFILE, "/usr/pierce/novel") || die;     # Unix.
```

Under Windows and MS-DOS systems, pathnames contain backslashes as separators— for example, \Windows\users\pierce\novel.txt. The only catch is that when you use backslash-separated pathnames in a double-quoted string in Perl, the backslash character sequence gets translated to a special character. Consider this example:

```
open(MYFILE, "\Windows\users\pierce\novel.txt") || die;    # WRONG
```

This example will probably fail, because \n in a double-quoted string is a newline character—not the letter *n*—and all the other backslashes will get quietly removed by Perl. As you might guess from Hour 2, "Perl's Building Blocks: Numbers and Strings," one correct way to open the file is by escaping each backslash with another backslash, as follows:

```
open(MYFILE, "C:\\Windows\\users\\pierce\\novel.txt") || die;  # Right, but messy.
```

You can get rid of the double slashes by using the qq function as well. However, you can also use forward slash (/) in Perl, even under Windows and MS-DOS, to separate the elements of the path. Perl interprets them just fine, as you can see here:

```
open(MYFILE, "C:/Windows/users/pierce/novel.txt") || die;    # Much nicer
```

The pathnames you specify can be absolute pathnames—for example, /home/foo in UNIX or c:/windows/win.ini in Windows—or they can be relative pathnames— ../junkfile in UNIX or ..\bobdir\bobsfile.txt in Windows. The open function can also accept pathnames that are Universal Naming Convention (UNC) pathnames under Microsoft Windows. UNC pathnames are formatted like this:

*machinename**sharename*

Perl accepts UNC pathnames with either backslashes or forward slashes and opens files on remote systems if your operating system's networking and file sharing are otherwise set up correctly, as you can see here:

```
open(REMOTE, "//fileserver/common/foofile") || die;
```

On the Macintosh, pathnames are specified by volume, folder, and then file, separated by colons, as shown in Table 5.1.

TABLE 5.1 MacPerl Pathname Specifiers

Macintosh Path	Meaning
System:Utils:config	System drive, folder Utils, file named config
MyStuff:friends	From this folder down to folder MyStuff, file named friends
ShoppingList	This drive, this folder, file named ShoppingList

A Good Defense

Writing programs on a computer inevitably leads to a sense of optimism. Programmers might find themselves saying "This time it *will* work" or "Now I've found all the bugs." This notion of pride in your own work is good to a point; innovation comes from a sense that it is possible to accomplish the impossible. However, this self-confidence can be taken too far and turn into a sense of infallibility, which the ancient Greeks called *hubris* and that can lead to tragedy—now as then. A little hubris every so often can be a good thing; however, excessive hubris always received its punishment, called *nemesis,* from the gods. That can happen to your programs as well.

This observation has been around since computers were first programmed. In his classic work, *The Mythical Man-Month* (Reading, MA: Addison Wesley, 1975, p. 14), Fredrick P. Brooks says: "All programmers are optimists. Perhaps this modern sorcery [programming] especially attracts those who believe in happy endings and fairy godmothers. [. . . but . . .] Because our ideas are faulty, we have bugs; hence our optimism is unjustified."

Until now, all the snippets and exercises you've seen have dealt with internal data (factoring numbers, sorting data, and so on) or with simple user input. When you're dealing with files, your programs talk to an external source over which they have no control. This will also be true in situations you'll encounter in later hours, when you're communicating with data sources not located on your computer, such as networks. Here is where nemesis can strike. Keep in mind that if anything can go wrong, it will, so you should write your programs accordingly. Writing your programs this way is called *defensive programming,* and if you program defensively, you'll be a lot happier in the long run.

Whenever a program interacts with the outside world, such as opening a filehandle, *always* make sure the operation has been successful before continuing. I've personally debugged a hundred or more programs in which the programmer requested the operating system to do something, didn't check the results, and caused a bug. Even when your program is just an "example" or a "quickie," check to make sure that what you expect to happen really happens.

dieing Gracefully

The `die` function is used in Perl to stop the interpreter in case of an error and print a meaningful error message. As you've seen earlier, simply calling `die` prints a message like the following:

```
Died at scriptname line xxx
```

The `die` function can also take a list of arguments, and those arguments are printed instead of the default message. If the message is not followed by a newline character, the message has `at scriptname line xxx` appended to the end:

```
die "Cannot open";      # prints "Cannot open at scriptname line xxx"
die "Cannot open\n";    # prints "Cannot open"
```

A special variable in Perl, `$!`, is always set to the error message of the last requested operation of the system (such as disk input or output). Used in a numeric context, `$!` returns an error number, which is probably not useful to anyone. In a string context, `$!` returns an appropriate error message from your operating system:

```
open(MYFILE, "myfile") || die "Cannot open myfile: $!\n";
```

If the code in the preceding snippet fails because the file does not exist, the message prints something similar to `Cannot open myfile: a file or directory in the path does not exist`. This error message is good. In your programs, a good error message should indicate what went wrong, why it went wrong, and what you were trying to do. If something ever goes wrong with your program, a good diagnostic can help in finding the problem.

> Do not use the value of `$!` to check whether a system function failed or succeeded. `$!` has meaning only after a system operation (like file input or output) and is set only if that operation fails. At other times, the value of `$!` can be almost anything—and is wholly meaningless.

Sometimes, though, you don't want the program to die—just issue a warning. To create this warning, Perl has the `warn` function. `warn` works exactly like `die`, as you can see here, except that the program keeps running:

```
if (! open(MYFILE, "output")) {
    warn "cannot read output: $!";
} else {
    :    # Reading output...
}
```

Reading

You can read from Perl's filehandles in a couple of different ways. The most common method is to use the *file input operator,* also called the *angle operator* (<>). To read a filehandle, simply put the filehandle name inside the angle operator and assign the value to a variable:

```
open(MYFILE, "myfile") || die "Can't open myfile: $!";
$line=<MYFILE>;          # Reading the filehandle
```

The angle operator in a scalar context reads one line of input from the file. When called after the entire file has been read, the angle operator returns the value undef.

> A "line of input" is usually considered to be a text stream until the first end-of-line sequence is found. In Unix, that end-of-line sequence is a newline character (ASCII 10); in DOS and Windows, it's the sequence of carriage return and newline characters (ASCII 13,10). This default end-of-line value can be manipulated by Perl to achieve some interesting results. This topic will be covered in Hour 12, "Using Perl's Command-Line Tools."

To read and print the entire file, you can use the following if MYFILE is an open filehandle:

```
while(defined($a=<MYFILE>)) {
    print $a;
}
```

As it turns out, a shortcut for reading the filehandle is to use a while loop. If the angle operators are the *only* elements inside the conditional expression of a while loop, Perl automatically assigns the input line to the special variable $_ (described in Hour 2, "Perl's Building Blocks: Numbers and Strings") and repeats the loop until the input is exhausted:

```
while(<MYFILE>) {
    print $_;
}
```

The while takes care of assigning the input line to $_ and making sure the data in the file hasn't been exhausted (called *end of file*). This magic behavior happens only with a while loop and only if the angle operators are the only characters in the conditional expression.

> Remember that every line of data read in with a filehandle in Perl contains the end-of-line characters in addition to the text from the line. If you want just the text, use chomp on the input line to get rid of the end-of-line characters.

5

In a list context, the angle operators read in the entire file and assign it to the list. Each line of the file is assigned to each element of the list or array, as shown here:

```
open(MYFILE, "novel.txt") || die "$!";
@contents=<MYFILE>;
close(MYFILE);
```

In the preceding snippet, the remaining data in the filehandle MYFILE is read and assigned to @contents. The first line of the file novel.txt is assigned to the first element in @contents: $contents[0]. The second line is assigned to $contents[1], and so on.

In most cases, reading an entire file into an array (if it isn't too large) is an easy way for you to deal with the file's data. You can go back and forth through the array, manipulate the array elements, and deal with the array's contents with all the array and scalar operators without worrying because you're actually working with just a copy of the file in the array. Listing 5.1 shows some of the manipulations possible on in-memory files.

LISTING 5.1   Reversing a File

```
1:   #!/usr/bin/perl -w
2:
3:   open(MYFILE, "testfile") || die "opening testfile: $!";
4:   @stuff=<MYFILE>;
5:   close(MYFILE);
6:   # Actually, any manipulation can be done now.
7:   foreach(reverse(@stuff)) {
8:           print scalar(reverse($_));
9:   }
```

If the file testfile contains the text

I am the very model of

a modern major-general.

the program in Listing 5.1 would produce the output

```
.lareneg-rojam nredom a
fo ledom yrev eht ma I
```

Line 1: This line contains the path to the interpreter (change it so that it's appropriate to your system) and the -w switch. Always have warnings enabled!

Line 3: The file testfile is opened with the filehandle FH. If the file doesn't open properly, the die function is run with an error message.

Line 4: The entire contents of testfile are read into the array @stuff.

Line 7: The array @stuff is reversed—the first line becomes the last line, and so on—and the resulting list is traversed by the foreach statement. Each line of the reversed list is assigned to $_ and the body of the foreach loop is executed.

Line 8: Each line (now in $_) is itself reversed—from left-to-right to right-to-left—and printed. The scalar function is needed because print expects a list; also, reverse used in a list context reverses a list, so nothing would happen to $_. The scalar function forces reverse into a scalar context, and it reverses $_ character by character.

Probably, only small files should be reading in their entirety into array variables for manipulation. Reading a very large file into memory, although allowed, might cause Perl to use all the available memory on your system.

If you ever exceed Perl's memory by reading too large a file into memory, or do anything else to exceed your system's memory, Perl displays the following error message:

```
Out of memory!
```

and your program terminates. If this happens when you are reading an entire file into memory at once, you should probably consider processing the file one line at a time.

Writing

To write data to a file, you must first have a filehandle open for writing. Up till now, all open statements you have seen have opened the filehandle for reading only. The syntax for opening a file for writing is almost identical to that for reading:

```
open(filehandle, ">pathname")
open(filehandle, ">>pathname")
```

The first syntax line should look familiar, except for the > in front of the pathname. The > signifies to Perl that the file specified at pathname should be overwritten with new data, that any existing data should be discarded, and that filehandle is open for writing. In the second example, >> tells Perl to open the file for writing but, if the file already exists, not to discard the contents but to append the new data to the end of it. Check out these examples:

```
# Overwrite existing data, if any
open(NEWFH, ">output.txt") || die "Opening output.txt: $!";
# Simply append to whatever data may be there.
open(APPFH,   >>logfile.txt") || die "Opening output.txt: $!";
```

5

Until now, it's been almost impossible for your Perl programs to *harm* anything. Now that you know how to write to files, you must be very careful to write only to files that you mean to change. On systems in which the operating system files are vulnerable (Windows 95/98, Mac), you can damage your operating system by carelessly writing to files. Be very aware of what files you are writing to. Recovering the data in files accidentally opened with > is nearly impossible. Cleaning out data in files opened accidentally with >> also is difficult, so be careful.

When you're done with a filehandle opened for writing, closing the filehandle is especially important. Your operating system doesn't commit data to disk as you write it; it buffers the data up and writes it occasionally. The `close` function notifies the operating system that you are done writing and that the data should be moved to permanent storage on disk:

```
close(NEWFH);
close(APPFH);
```

If your program terminates with `exit`, or simply "falls off" the end, any written but not-yet-flushed information in filehandles is committed (written out to the file) as if you had closed the filehandles yourself.

After you've opened the filehandle for writing, actually putting data in the file is easy, and you're already familiar with the `print` function. Until now, you've been using `print` to simply display data to the screen. The `print` function is actually used for writing to any filehandle. The syntax for printing to filehandles is as follows:

```
print filehandle LIST
```

`filehandle` is the filehandle you want the data to be written to, and `LIST` is the list of things you want written.

In the `print` syntax, notice that no comma appears between the filehandle name and the list; this point is important. Inside the list, commas are used to separate items, as you've done until now. The lack of a comma between the filehandle and list signifies to Perl that the token following `print` is a filehandle and not the first element in the list. If you include this comma and have Perl's warnings turned on, Perl warns you with the following message: `No comma allowed after filehandle`.

Now consider the following:

```
open(LOGF, ">>logfile") || die "$!";
if (! print LOGF "This entry was written at", scalar(localtime), "\n" ) {
    warn "Unable to write to the log file: $!";
}
close(LOGF);
```

In this snippet, the file named `logfile` is opened for appending. The `print` statement writes a message to the `LOGF` filehandle. The return value from `print` is checked, and if false (meaning that the log entry could not be printed), a warning is issued. The filehandle is then closed.

You can have multiple filehandles open for reading and writing at the same time, as this snippet demonstrates:

```
open(SOURCE, "sourcefile") || die "$!";
open(DEST, ">destination") || die "$!";
@contents=<SOURCE>;                   # Slurp in the source file.
print DEST @contents;                 # Write it out to the destination
close(DEST);
close(SOURCE);
```

This snippet implements a simple file copy. As a matter of fact, you can do the read and the write at the same time and shorten the routine, just a little:

```
print DEST <SOURCE>;
```

Because `print` expects a list as an argument, `<SOURCE>` is evaluated in a list context. When the angle operator is evaluated in a list context, the entire file is read in and then printed to the filehandle `DEST`.

Free Files, Testing Files, and Binary Data

Files and file systems don't contain just the data that you put into files. On the one hand, filehandles sometimes represent more than a simple file. They may stand for such things as the keyboard, the monitor screen, network sockets, or mass storage devices such as tape drives.

Also, in addition to the data stored in the files, a file system contains what's called *metadata*—that is, data about the data in its files. Perl can be used to get metadata out of the file system; for example, to determine how big your file is, when it was last changed, who changed it, and information about what's in the file. With some operating systems, the file metadata can even determine whether the file is treated as a text file or a binary file.

Free Filehandles

Perl began life as a Unix utility, and sometimes pieces of its heritage show through—even on non-Unix platforms. When your Perl program is started, it receives three filehandles that are "free"—that is, they are opened automatically without you having to do any programming work to open them. They are STDOUT (standard output), STDIN (standard input), and STDERR (standard error). By default, they are connected to your terminal.

5

As you type, Perl can read your input from the STDIN filehandle:

```
$guess=<STDIN>;
```

When you want to display output, you use print. The reason why your output has appeared on the screen is that, by default, print uses the STDOUT filehandle:

```
print "Hello, World!\n";                    # is the same as...
print STDOUT "Hello, World!\n";
```

In Hour 12, you'll learn how to change print's default filehandle.

STDERR is usually set to your terminal, like STDOUT, but it is used for displaying error messages. In Unix, error messages and normal output can be sent to different display devices, and writing error messages to the STDERR filehandle is traditional. The die and warn functions both write their messages to STDERR. If your operating system does not have a separate error-reporting filehandle—for example, Windows or MS-DOS—your STDERR output will go to the STDOUT device.

> Redirecting error and output messages in Unix is well beyond the scope of this book, and the technique varies depending on what shell you use. Any good book on using Unix should cover this topic thoroughly.

Text Files and Binary Files

Some operating systems—such as VMS, Atari ST, and notably Windows and MS-DOS—make the distinction between binary files (raw) and text files. This distinction causes problems because Perl can't really tell the difference—and you wouldn't want it to.

Text files are simply records that end in end-of-line characters, called *record separators*. Binary files, on the other hand, are collections of bits that need to be treated literally, such as images, executable programs, and data files.

When you're writing a text file, Perl translates the \n character sequence into the record separator that your operating system uses. In Unix, \n becomes an ASCII 10 (LF); on a Macintosh, ASCII 13 (CR); and on DOS and Windows systems, it becomes the sequence ASCII 13 and ASCII 10 (CRLF). When you're writing text, this behavior is appropriate.

When you're writing binary data—GIF files, EXE files, MS Word documents, and so on—translation isn't what you want. Any time you really need to write binary data, and don't want Perl or the operating system to translate it for you, you must use the binmode function to mark the filehandle as binary. Use `binmode` after the filehandle is opened but before you do any input or output from it:

```
open(FH, ">camel.gif") || die "$!";
binmode(FH);              # The filehandle is now binary.
# Start of a valid GIF file...
print FH "GIF87a\056\001\045\015\000";
close(FH);
```

You have to use `binmode` on the filehandle only once, unless you close it and reopen it. Using `binmode` on systems that do not distinguish between binary files and text files (Unix, Macintosh) causes no harm.

File Test Operators

Before you open a file, sometimes it's nice to know whether the file exists, whether the file is really a directory, or whether opening the file will give a `permission denied` error. If you could examine the file's metadata, you could get answers to these questions. For these situations, Perl provides the *file test operators*. The file test operators all have the following syntax:

```
-X filehandle
-X pathname
```

Here, x is the particular test you want performed, and `filehandle` is the filehandle you want tested. You can also test a `pathname` without having an open filehandle. Table 5.2 lists some of the operators.

TABLE 5.2 Short List of File Test Operators

Operator	Example	Result
-r	-r 'file'	Returns true if 'file' is readable
-w	-w $a	Returns true if the filename contained in $a is writeable
-e	-e 'myfile'	Returns true if 'myfile' exists
-z	-z 'data'	Returns true if 'data' exists but is empty
-s	-s 'data'	Returns size of 'data' in bytes if it exists
-f	-f 'novel.txt'	Returns true if 'novel.txt' is a regular file rather than a directory
-d	-d '/tmp'	Returns true if '/tmp' is a directory
-T	-T 'unknown'	Returns true if 'unknown' appears to be a text file
-B	-B 'unknown'	Returns true if 'unknown' appears to be a binary file
-M	-M 'foo'	Returns the age (in days) since the file 'foo' was modified since this program began

5

You can view the full list of file test operators in the online documentation. Type **perl-doc perlfunc** at a command prompt, and look in the section "Alphabetical List of Perl Functions."

The following snippet uses file test operators to verify that files don't already exist before they are overwritten and to determine the age of the file since it was last modified:

```
print "Save data to what file?";
$filename=<STDIN>;
chomp $filename;
if (-s $filename ) {
    warn "$file contents will be overwritten!\n";
    warn "$file was last updated ",
    -M $filename, "days ago.\n";
}
```

Summary

This hour you learned about opening and closing filehandles in Perl: You open files by using the open functions and close them by using close. When filehandles are open, they can be read with <> or read and written with print. Also, you learned about some of the oddities of how your operating system handles files and how to deal with them by using binmode.

Along the way, I hope that you also learned something about defensive programming.

Q&A

Q My open statement keeps failing, and I'm not sure why. What's wrong?

A First, check the syntax of the open statement. Make sure you're opening the right filename. Print the name before the open if you need to be sure. If you intend to write to the file, make sure you put a > in front of the filename; you need to. Most importantly, did you check the exit status of open by using open() || die "$!"; syntax? The die message might be very important in helping you find your mistake.

Q I'm writing to the file, but nothing seems to go into it. Where's my output going?

A Are you sure that the filehandle opened properly? If you used the wrong filename, your data could be going to the wrong file. A common mistake is to open a file for writing by using backslashes in the pathname and enclosing the pathname in double quotation marks, as shown here:

```
open(FH, :">c:\temp\notes.txt") || die "$!";    #WRONG!
```

This line creates a file called c:(tab)emp(newline)otes.txt—probably not what you had in mind. Also, make sure that your `open` function succeeded. If you write to a filehandle that hasn't been properly opened, Perl discards the output silently unless you have Perl's warnings enabled.

Q When I try to open a file, the `open` fails and Perl reports `permission denied`. Why?

A Perl follows your operating system's rules about file security. If you don't have permission to access the file, the directory, or the drive that the file resides on, neither will your Perl program.

Q How can I read a single character at a time?

A From a file, the Perl function `getc` can do single-character input. Reading a single character from the keyboard is much more difficult, because character-at-a-time input is highly dependent on your operating system. After you've learned about modules in Hour 15, "Finding Permanence," and have read up on the Perl FAQ in Hour 16, "The Perl Community," check section 5 of the Perl FAQ. The FAQ contains a very lengthy explanation of how to read single characters for various platforms, with lots of code examples. Most of the code there is beyond the scope of this book.

Q How do I keep other programs from writing to the same file at the same time?

A What you're interested in is called *file locking*. File locking is covered in Hour 15. Be forewarned; it's not particularly easy or foolproof.

Workshop

Quiz

1. To open a file named `data` for writing, you should use which of the following:

    a. `open(FH, "data", write);`

    b. `open(FH, "data");` and simply print to `FH`

    c. `open(FH, ">data") || die "Cannot open data: $!";`

2. `(-M $file > 1 and -s $file)` is true if

    a. `$file` has been modified more than one day ago and has data.

    b. That expression cannot be true.

    c. `$file` is writeable and has no data.

Answers

1. c. Choice a is false because this is not how open opens a file for writing; b is false because it opens the filehandle only for reading. Choice c is true because it does what is asked—and uses good form by checking for errors.

2. a. -M returns the number of days old a file is (>1 is more than 1 day), and -s returns true if the file has data in it.

Activities

- Modify the Hangman program from Hour 4, "Stacking Building Blocks: Lists and Arrays," to take the list of possible words from a data file.

Hour 6

Pattern Matching

In the preceding hour, you learned about reading data from files. With that information, combined with your knowledge of scalars, arrays, and operators, you're prepared to manipulate that data to do what you want—almost. The data in the file may not have an easy-to-use format that can be broken up with a simple `split` on spaces. You may have lines that contain data you're not interested in and want to edit out.

What you need is the ability to recognize patterns in the input stream, to pick and choose data based on those patterns, and possibly to edit the data to a more usable form. One of Perl's tools for performing these tasks is regular expressions. Throughout this text, the words *regular expression* and *pattern* will be used almost interchangeably.

Regular expressions are almost a language unto themselves. Regular expressions are a formal method of describing patterns to match. In this hour, you'll learn just a little bit of this pattern-matching language.

The online documentation has a much deeper (but more terse) description of the full regular expression language used by Perl. You can look at the `perlre` documentation included with Perl. The topic is so deep that an entire book has been published on regular expressions. This book, highly recommended by the Perl community, is called *Mastering Regular Expressions* by Jeffrey E. F. Friedl (Sebastopol: O'Reilly, 1997). It is about regular expressions in general, but close attention is paid to Perl.

Regular expressions are used in other programming languages as well, including TCL, JavaScript, and Python. Many of the Unix operating system utilities also use regular expressions. Perl happens to have a very rich set of expressions—very similar to those used in other systems, but more powerful—and learning them will help you not just in Perl, but in other languages as well.

In this hour you'll learn

- How to construct simple regular expressions
- How to use regular expressions to match patterns
- How to edit strings using regular expressions

Simple Patterns

In Perl, patterns are enclosed inside a pattern match operator, which is sometimes represented as `m//`. A simple pattern might appear as follows:

```
m/Simon/
```

The preceding pattern matches the letters *S-i-m-o-n* in sequence. But where is it looking for *Simon?* Previously, you learned that the Perl variable `$_` is frequently used when Perl needs a default value. Pattern matches occur against `$_` unless you tell Perl otherwise (which you'll learn about later). So the preceding pattern looks for *S-i-m-o-n* in the scalar variable `$_`.

If the pattern specified by `m//` is found anywhere in the variable `$_`, the match operator returns true. Thus, the normal place to see pattern matches is in a conditional expression, as shown here:

```
if (m/Piglet/) {
    : # the pattern "Piglet" is in $_
}
```

Inside the pattern, every character matches itself unless it is a *metacharacter*. Most of the "normal" characters match themselves: *A* to *Z*, *a* to *z*, and digits. Metacharacters are characters that change the behavior of the pattern match. The list of metacharacters is as follows:

```
^ $ ( ) \ | @ [ { ? . + *
```

You'll shortly read about what the metacharacters do. If your pattern contains a metacharacter that you want to match for its literal value, simply precede the metacharacter with a backslash, as shown here:

```
m/I won \$10 at the fair/;      # The $ is treated as a literal dollar-sign.
```

Earlier, you read that the pattern match operator is *usually* represented by m//. In reality, you can replace the slashes with any other character you want, such as the commas in the following example:

```
if (m,Waldo,) { print "Found Waldo.\n"; }
```

The slash or other character that marks the beginning and end of the pattern is called the *delimiter*. Often you replace the delimiter when the pattern contains slashes (/) and the end of the pattern could be confused with the slashes inside the pattern. If you stick with slashes to delimit that pattern, the enclosed slashes need to have backslashes in front of them, as shown here:

```
if (m/\/usr\/local\/bin\/hangman/) { print "Found the hangman game!" }
```

By changing the delimiter, you could write the preceding example more legibly as follows:

```
if (m:/usr/local/bin/hangman:) { print "Found the hangman game!" }
```

If the delimiters around the pattern are slashes, you also can write the pattern match without the m. This way, you also can write m/Cheetos/ as /Cheetos/. Normally, unless you need to use delimiters other than slashes (//), you write pattern matches with just slashes and no m.

Variables can also be used in a regular expression. If a scalar variable is seen in a regular expression, Perl first evaluates the scalar and interpolates it, just as in a double-quoted string (recall Hour 2, "Perl's Building Blocks: Numbers and Strings"); then it examines the regular expression. This capability allows you to build regular expressions dynamically. The regular expression in the following if statement is based on user input:

```
$pat=<STDIN>;  chomp $pat;
$_="The phrase that pays";
if (/$pat/) {    #Look for the user's pattern
    print "\"$_\" contains the pattern $pat\n";
}
```

6

Regular expressions in the manual pages and in other documentation are sometimes called *REs* or *regexps*. For clarity, I'll continue to refer to them as regular expressions throughout this book.

Rules of the Game

As you begin to write regular expressions in Perl, you should know that a few rules are involved in the way Perl interprets them. There are not many rules, though, and most of them make sense after you think about them. They are as follows:

1. Normally, pattern matches start at the left of the target string and work their way to the right.

2. Pattern matches return true (in whatever context) if and only if the entire pattern can be used to match the target string.

3. The first possible match (the leftmost) in the target string is matched first. Regular expressions don't leave behind one good match to go looking for another further along. However. . .

4. The largest possible first match is taken. Your regular expressions might find a match immediately and then try to stretch that match as far as possible. Regular expressions are *greedy,* meaning they try to match as much as possible.

The Metacharacters

In all the examples that follow, the portions of text matched by patterns are represented with underlines. Remember that the entire target string is said to match even if just a portion of it matches the regular expression. The underline marks are to help demonstrate exactly what part of the target they match.

It's important to read through the following sections; however, don't worry if the information doesn't immediately make sense; it will shortly. The application of these metacharacters will be demonstrated in a bit.

A Simple Metacharacter

The first of the metacharacters is the dot (`.`). Inside a regular expression, the dot matches any single character except a newline character. For example, in the pattern `/p.t/`, the `.` matches any single character. This pattern would match <u>pot</u>, <u>pat</u>, <u>pit</u>, car<u>pet</u>, <u>pyt</u>hon, and pu<u>p t</u>ent. The `.` requires that one character be there between the *p* and the *t*, but no more.

Thus, the pattern would not match *apt* (no character at all between *p* and *t*) or *expect* (too many characters between *p* and *t*).

The Unprintables

Earlier you read that, to include a metacharacter inside a regular expression, you have to precede the character with a backslash, as shown here, to make it lose its meta-ness:

```
/\^\$/;    # A literal caret and dollar sign
```

When preceded by a backslash, normal characters *become* metacharacters. As you saw in Hour 2, some characters take on special meaning in (double-quoted) string literals when they are preceded by a backslash; almost all those same characters represent the same values in regular expressions, as shown in Table 6.1.

TABLE 6.1   Special Characters

Character	Matches
\n	A newline character
\r	A carriage return
\t	A tab
\f	A formfeed

Quantifiers

Until now, all the characters in patterns, whether text characters or metacharacters, have had a one-to-one relationship with characters in the target string they were trying to match. For example, in /Simon/, s matches an *S*, i matches an *i*, m matches an *m*, and so on. A *quantifier* is a kind of metacharacter that tells the regular expression how many consecutive occurrences of something to match. A quantifier can be placed after any single character or a group of characters (you'll learn more details on that topic momentarily).

The simplest quantifier is the + metacharacter. The + causes the preceding character to match at least once, or as many times as it can and still have a matching expression. Thus, /do+g/ would:

Match These	But Not These	Why Not
hound<u>dog</u>	badge	The required *o* is missing.
hot<u>dog</u>	doofus	The *g* is missing.
<u>doog</u>ie howser	Doogie	*D* is not the same as *d*.
<u>dooooooog</u>doog	pagoda	The *d*, *o*, and *g* do not appear in order.

6

The * metacharacter is similar to the + metacharacter, but it causes the preceding character to be matched zero or more times. In other words, the /t*/ pattern means to match as many *t*'s as possible, but if none exist, that's okay. Thus, /car*t/ would:

Match These	But Not These	Why Not
<u>car</u>ted	carrot	The *o* intrudes into the pattern, but the *ed* follows the pattern.
<u>ca</u>t	carl	The *t* in the pattern isn't optional, but the *r* is.
<u>carr</u>t	caart	The *a* in the pattern can't be repeated, but the *r* can.

One step down from the * metacharacter is ?. The ? metacharacter causes the preceding character to be matched either zero times or once (but no more). So the pattern /c?ola/ causes a *c* to be matched if it's available; otherwise, that's okay. Then it is followed by *o*, *l*, and *a*; essentially, this pattern matches any string with *ola* in it, and if *ola* is preceded by a *c*, that string is matched as well.

The difference between the ? and * metacharacters is that /c?ola/ would match *cola* and *ola*, but not *ccola*. The extra *c* requires *two* matches. The pattern /c*ola/ would match *cola*, *ola*, and *ccola* because the *c* can be repeated as many times as necessary, not just zero or one time.

If matching zero, one, or many occurrences of a pattern isn't specific enough for you, Perl allows you to match exactly as many occurrences as you need by using braces, {}. The quantifier with braces has the following format:

`pat{n,m}`

Here, *n* is the minimum number of matches, *m* is the maximum number of matches, and `pat` is the character or group of characters you're trying to quantify. You can omit either *n* or *m*, but not both. Consider the following examples:

`/x{5,10}/`	x occurs at least 5 times, but no more than 10.
`/x{9,}/`	x occurs at least 9 times, possibly more.
`/x{0,4}/`	x occurs up to 4 times, possibly not at all.
`/x{8}/`	x must occur exactly 8 times.

A common idiom in regular expressions is .*. You can use it to match *anything*—usually anything between two other things that you're interested in. For example, /first.*last/

attempts to match the word *first,* followed by anything, and then the word *last.* Observe how /first.*last/ matches the following strings:

<u>first then last</u>

The good players get picked <u>first, the bad last.</u>

The <u>first shall be last, and the last</u> shall be first.

Look at the match in the third line carefully. The match starts on the word *first* as expected. The match then matches the word *last,* but it doesn't consider itself done. It continues searching until it finds the second (and final) occurrence of the word *last.* Here, the * follows the fourth rule listed in the section "Rules of the Game": It matches the largest possible string, while still completing the match. Often, matching the largest string is not what you want, so Perl offers another solution called *minimal matching,* which is documented further in the perlre manual page.

Character Classes

Another common practice in regular expressions is to ask for a match of "any of these characters." If you're trying to match numbers, it would be nice to be able to write a pattern that matches "any digit 0–9"; if you're searching a list of names and want to match *Van Beethoven* and *van Beethoven,* a pattern that matches "either v or V" would be helpful.

Perl's regular expressions have such a tool; it's called a *character class.* To write a character class, you enclose the characters it contains in square brackets, []. Characters in a character class are treated as a single character during the match. Inside a character class, you can specify ranges of characters (where ranges make sense) by putting a dash between the upper and lower bounds. The following are some examples:

Character Class	Explanation
[abcde]	Match any of *a, b, c, d,* or *e*
[a-e]	Same as above; match any of *a, b, c, d,* or *e*
[Gg]	Match an uppercase *G* or lowercase *g*
[0-9]	Match a digit
[0-9]+	Match one or more digits in sequence
[A-Za-z]{5}	Match any group of five alphabetic characters
[*!@#$%&()]	Match any of these punctuation marks

The last example is interesting, because the characters in that class are usually metacharacters. Inside a character class, most metacharacters lose their "meta-ness"; in

6

other words, they behave like any other ordinary character. Thus, the * really represents a literal *.

If a caret (^) occurs as the first character of a character class, the character class is negated. That is, the character class matches any single character that is *not* in the class, as in this example:

```
/[^A-Z]/;        # Matches non-uppercase-alphabetic characters.
```

Because], ^, and - are special in a character class, some rules apply about trying to match those characters literally in a character class. To match a literal ^ in a character class, you must make sure it does not occur first in the class. To match a literal], you either need to put it first in the class or put a backslash in front of it (for example, `/[abc\]]/`). To put a literal hyphen (-) in a character class, you can simply put it first in the class or put a backslash in front of it.

Perl contains shortcuts for certain commonly used character classes. They are represented by a backslash and a nonmetacharacter, as shown in Table 6.2.

TABLE 6.2 Special Character Classes

Pattern	Matches
\w	A word character; same as [a-zA-Z0-9_]
\W	A nonword character (the inverse of \w)
\d	A digit; same as [0-9]
\D	A nondigit
\s	A whitespace character; same as [\t\f\r\n]
\S	A nonwhitespace character

The following are some examples:

```
/\d{5}/;         # Matches 5 digits
/\s\w+\s/;       # Matches a group of word characters surrounded by white space
```

Be careful, though. The last example here doesn't necessarily match a word; it can also match an underscore surrounded by spaces. Also, not all words are matched by the last pattern; they need to have whitespace around them, and words such as "don't" wouldn't be matched because of the apostrophe. You'll learn better patterns for word matching later in this hour.

Grouping and Alternation

Sometimes in a regular expression, you might want to know whether any of a set of patterns is found. For example, does this string contain *dogs* or *cats?* The regular-expression solution to this problem is called *alternation*. Alternation happens in a regular expression when possible matches are separated with a | character, as in this example:

```
if (/dogs|cats/) {
    print "\$_ contains a pet\n";
}
```

Alternation can be fun, but it also can be tedious when you want to match lots of similar things. For example, if you want to match the words *frog, bog, log, flog,* or *clog,* you could try the expression /frog|bog|log|flog|clog/ except that it's horribly repetitive. What you really want is to alternate on just the first part of the string, like this:

```
/fr|b|l|fl|clog/;      # Doesn't QUITE work.
```

The preceding example doesn't quite work, because Perl has no way of knowing that the alternations are one thing you want to match and og is another.

To solve this problem, you can use Perl's regular expressions to group parts of the pattern with parentheses, (), as shown here:

```
/(fr|b|l|fl|cl)og/;
```

You can nest parentheses to have groups within groups. For example, you could write the preceding expression as /(fr|b|(f|c)?l)og/ as well.

In a list context, the match operator returns a list of the portions of the expression matched that were in parentheses. Each parenthesized value is a return value to the list, or 1 if the pattern contains no parentheses. Check out this example:

```
$_="apple is red";
($fruit, $color)=/(.*)\sis\s(.*)/;
```

In this snippet, the pattern matches anything (as a group), then whitespace, the word *is,* more whitespace, and then anything (also as a group). The two grouped expressions are returned to the list on the left side and assigned to $fruit and $color.

Anchors

The last two metacharacters (I bet you thought they'd never end) are the anchors. You use anchors to tell the regular expression engine exactly where you want to look for the pattern—at the beginning of a string or at the end.

The first of these anchors is the caret (^). The caret at the beginning of a regular expression causes the expression to match only at the beginning of a line. For example, /^video/ matches the word *video* only if it occurs at the beginning of a line.

Its counterpart is the dollar sign ($). The dollar sign at the end of a regular expression causes the pattern to match only at the end of the line. For example, `/earth$/` matches *earth*, but only at the end of a line.

Patterns	What They Do
`/^Help/`	Matches only lines that begin with *Help*.
`/^Frankly.*darn$/`	Matches lines that begin with *Frankly* and end in *darn*. Everything in between is matched as well.
`/^hysteria$/`	Matches lines that contain only the word *hysteria*.
`/^$/`	Matches the beginning of a line, followed immediately by the end of the line. That is, it matches only blank lines.
`/^/`	Matches lines with a beginning (all lines). `/$/` does the same thing.

Substitution

Just finding patterns in strings and lines of input isn't enough; sometimes you need to modify the data as well. One way—but certainly not the only way—is to use the substitution operator `s///`. The syntax is as follows:

```
s/searchpattern/replacement/;
```

The substitution operator searches `$_` by default for `searchpattern` and replaces the entire matched regular expression with `replacement`. The operator returns the number of matches or substitutions performed, or 0 if no matches were made. The following is an example:

```
$_="Our house is in the middle of our street".
s/middle/end/;          # Is now: Our house is in the end of our street
s/in/at/;               # Is now: Our house is at the end of our street.
if (s/apartment/condo/) {
    #  This code isn't reached, see note.
}
```

Here, the substitutions happen as you would expect. The word *middle* is changed to *end,* and *in* is changed to *at*. The `if` statement, however, fails, because the word *apartment* does not appear in `$_` and therefore can't be substituted.

The substitution operator can also use delimiters other than slashes (/), just as the match operator can. Simply put whatever delimiter you want immediately after the s, as shown here:

```
s#street#avenue#;
```

Exercise: Cleaning Up Input Data

The "blind" substitutions in the preceding example—where substitutions are made, but the exit status isn't checked—are common when you're trying to *cook data*. Cooking data is taking data from a user or a file that is not formatted exactly the way you would like and reformatting it. Listing 6.1 shows a routine to convert your weight on the earth to your weight on the moon, which demonstrates data manipulation.

Using your text editor, type the program in Listing 6.2 and save it as Moon. Of course, don't type the line numbers. Be sure to make the program executable according to the instructions you learned in Hour 1, "Introduction to the Perl Language."

When you're done, try running the program by typing the following at a command line:

Moon

or, if you cannot make the program executable,

perl -w Moon

Some sample output is shown in Listing 6.1.

LISTING 6.1 Sample Output from Moon

```
$  perl Moon
Your weight:  150 lbs
Your weight on the moon: 25.00005 lbs
$ perl Moon
Your weight: 90 kg
Your weight on the moon: 90.9090 lbs
```

6

LISTING 6.2 Your Moon Weight

```
1:    #!/usr/bin/perl -w
2:
3:    print "Your weight:";
4:    $_=<STDIN>;
5:    chomp;
6:    s/^\s+//;   # Remove leading spaces, if any.
7:    if (m/(lbs?|kgs?|kilograms?|pounds?)/i) {
```

continues

LISTING 6.2 Continued

```
8:              if (s/\s*(kgs?|kilograms?).*//) {
9:                  $_*=2.2;
10:            } else {
11:                s/\s*(lbs?|pounds?).*//;
12:            }
13:    }
14:    print "Your weight on the moon: ", $_*.16667, " lbs\n";
```

Line 1: This line contains the path to the interpreter (you can change it so that it's appropriate to your system) and the -w switch. Always have warnings enabled!

Lines 3–5: These lines prompt the user for his weight, assign the input to $_, and chomp off the newline character. Remember that chomp changes $_ if no other variable is specified.

Line 6: The pattern /^\s+/ matches whitespace at the beginning of the line. No replacement string is listed, so the portion of $_ matching the pattern is simply removed.

Line 7: If a unit of measurement is found in the user's input, this if block removes the unit and converts it, if applicable.

Lines 8–9: The pattern /\s*(kgs?|kilograms?)/i matches whitespace and then either *kg* or *kilogram* (each with an optional *s* on the end). This means that if the input contains kg or kg (with no space), it is removed. If the pattern is found and removed, what is left over in $_ is multiplied by 2.2—in other words, converted to pounds.

Line 11: Otherwise, *lbs* or *pounds* is removed from $_ (along with optional leading whitespace).

Line 14: The weight in $_—converted to pounds already—is multiplied by 1/6 and printed.

Pattern Matching Odds and Ends

Now that you can match patterns against $_ and you know the basics of substitution, you're ready for more functionality. To be really effective with regular expressions, you need to match against variables other than $_, be able to do sophisticated substitutions, and work with Perl's functions that are geared toward—but not exclusive to—regular expressions.

Working with Other Variables

In Listing 6.2, the weight gathered from the user is stored in $_ and manipulated with substitution operators and matching operators. This listing does have a problem, however: $_ isn't exactly the best variable name to store "weight" in. It's not very intuitive for starters, and $_ might get altered when you least expect it.

> In general, storing anything in $_ for long is playing with fire; eventually, you will get burned. Many of Perl's operators use $_ as a default argument, and some of them modify $_ as well. $_ is Perl's general-purpose variable, and trying to keep a value in $_ for very long (especially after what you learn in Hour 8, "Functions") will cause bugs eventually.

Using a variable called $weight would have been better in Listing 6.2. To use the match operator and substitution operator against variables other than $_, you must *bind* them to the variable. You do so by using the *binding operator*, =~, as shown here:

```
$weight="185 lbs";
$weight=~s/ lbs//;        # Do substitution against $weight
```

The =~ operator doesn't make assignments; it merely takes the operator on the right and causes it to act on the variable to the left. The entire expression has the same value as it would if $_ were used, as you can see in this example:

```
$poem="One fish, two fish, red fish";
$n=$poem=~m/fish/;        # $n is true, if $poem has fish
```

Modifiers and Multiple Matching

Until now, all the regular expressions you've seen have been *case sensitive*. That is, upper- and lowercase characters are distinct in a pattern match. To match words and not care about whether they're in upper- or lowercase would require something like this:

```
/[Mm][Aa][Cc][Bb][Ee][Tt][Hh]/;
```

This example doesn't just look silly; it's error prone, because it would be really easy to mistype an upper-/lowercase pair. The substitution operator (s///) and the match operator (m//) can match regular expressions regardless of case if followed with the letter i:

```
/macbeth/i;
```

6

The preceding example matches *Macbeth* in uppercase, lowercase, or mixed case (*MaCbEtH*).

Another modifier for matches and substitutions is the global-match modifier, g. The regular expression (or substitution) is done not just once, but repeatedly through the entire string, each match (or substitution) taking place starting immediately after the first one.

The g modifier (and other modifiers) can be combined by simply specifying all of them after the match or substitution operator. For example, gi matches all occurrences of the pattern in the string, whether uppercase or lowercase.

In a list context, the global-match modifier causes the match to return a list of all the portions of the regular expression that are in parentheses:

```
$_="One fish, two frog, red fred, blue foul";
@F=m/\W(f\w\w\w)/g;
```

The pattern matches a nonword character, then the letter *f*, followed by four word characters. The *f* and the four word characters form a group, marked by parentheses. After the expression is evaluated, the array variable @F will contain four elements: *fish, frog, fred,* and *foul*.

In a scalar context, the g modifier causes the match to iterate through the string, returning true for each match and false when no more matches are made. Now consider the following:

```
$letters=0;
$phrase="What's my line?";
while($phrase=~/\w/g) {
    $letters++;
}
```

The preceding snippet uses the match operator (//) with a g modifier in a scalar context (which is provided by the condition of while). The pattern matches a word character. The while loop continues (and $letters gets incremented) until the match returns false. When the snippet is all done, $letters will be 11.

> You'll find much more efficient ways of counting characters presented in Hour 9, "More Functions and Operators."

Backreferences

When you use parentheses in regular expressions, Perl remembers the portion of the target string matched by each parenthesized expression. These matched portions are saved in special variables named $1 (for the first set of parentheses), $2 (for the second), $3, $4, and so on, as follows:

The pattern shown matches well-formed U.S./Canadian telephone numbers—for example, 800-555-1212—and remembers each portion in $1, $2, and $3. The values are assigned for each set of parentheses found, from left to right. If there are nested and overlapping parentheses, the captures are numbered from left to right for each opening parenthesis. These variables can be used after the following expression:

```
if (/(\d{3})-(\d{3})-(\d{4})/) {
    print "The area code is $1";
}
```

Or they can be used as part of the replacement text in a substitution, as follows:

```
s/(\d{3})-(\d{3})-(\d{4})/Area code $1 Phone $2-$3/;
```

Be careful, however; the variables $1, $2, and $3 are reset every time a pattern match is successfully performed (regardless of whether it uses parentheses), and the variables are *set if and only if the pattern match succeeds completely.* Based on this information, consider the following example:

```
m/(\d{3})-(\d{3})-(\d{4})/;
print "The area code is $1";  # Bad idea.  Assumes the match succeeded.
```

In this snippet, $1 was used without making sure the pattern match worked. This will probably cause trouble if the match ever fails.

A New Function: grep

A common operation in Perl is to search arrays for patterns—for example, if you've read a file into an array and need to know which lines contain a particular word. Perl has one function in particular that you can use in this situation; it's called grep. The syntax for grep is as follows:

```
grep expression, list
grep block list
```

The grep function iterates through each element in list and then executes the expression or block. Within the expression or block, $_ is set to each element of the list being evaluated. If the expression returns true, the element is returned by grep. Consider this example:

```
@dogs=qw(greyhound bloodhound terrier mutt chihuahua);
@hounds=grep /hound/, @dogs;
```

In the preceding example, each element of @dogs is assigned, in turn, to $_. The expression /hound/ is then tested against $_. Each of the elements that returns true—that is, each name that contains *hound*—goes into a list that is returned by grep and stored in @hounds.

You need to remember two points here. First is that $_ within the expression refers to the actual value in the list, not a copy of it. Modifying $_ changes the original element in the list:

```
@hounds=grep s/hound/hounds/, @dogs;
```

After running this example, @hounds contains *greyhounds* and *bloodhounds,* with an *s* on the end. The original array @dogs is also modified—by way of changing $_—and it now contains *greyhounds, bloodhounds, terrier, mutt,* and *chihuahua.*

The other point to remember—which Perl programmers forget sometimes—is that grep isn't *necessarily* used with a pattern match or substitution operator; it can be used with any operator or function. The following example collects just the names of dogs longer than eight characters:

```
@longdogs=grep length($_)>8, @dogs;
```

 The grep function gets its name from a Unix command by the same name that is used for searching for patterns in files. The Unix grep command is so useful in Unix (and hence, Perl) that in the culture it has become a verb: "to grep." "To grep through a book" means to flip through the pages looking for a pattern.

A related function, map, has an identical syntax to grep, except that the return value from the expression (or block) is returned from map—not the value of $_. You use the map function to produce a second array based on the first. The following is an example:

```
@words= map { split ' ', $_ } @input;
```

In this example, each element of the array @input (passed to the block as $_) is split apart on spaces, producing a list of words; this list is added to the list that the map function returns. After every consecutive line of @input has been split apart, the accumulated words are stored in @words.

Summary

In this hour, you learned what regular expressions are, how they're constructed, and how they're used in Perl. Regular expressions are made up of normal characters and metacharacters. The normal characters all stand for themselves (usually), and the metacharacters alter the meanings of the normal characters (or each other). These regular expressions can be used to test for the presence of patterns or to substitute one pattern for another.

Q&A

Q **The pattern /\w(\w)+\w/ doesn't seem to match all the words on the line, just the ones in the middle. Why?**

A You're looking for word characters surrounded by nonword characters. The first word of the line—assuming it starts at the beginning of the line—doesn't have a nonword character in front of it. It doesn't have a character in front of it at all.

Q **What's the difference between m// and //? I don't get it.**

A There's almost no difference at all. The only difference is that if you decide to specify a pattern delimiter other than /, you can do so only if you precede the pattern with an m—for example, m!pattern!.

Q **I'm trying to verify that the user typed a number, but /\d*/ doesn't seem to work. It always returns true!**

A It returns true because a pattern using only the * quantifier always succeeds. It might match zero occurrences of \d, or it might match 2 or 100 or 1,000. Using /\d+/ ensures that you have at least one digit.

Workshop

If you've started to figure out the pattern to regular expressions, try this quiz to see what you've learned.

Quiz

1. If you have lines formatted "x=y", what expression would swap the left and right sides of the expression?

    a. `s/(.+)=(.+)/$2=$1/;`

    b. `s/(*)=(*)/$2=$1/;`

    c. `s/(.*)=(.*)/$2$1/;`

2. After this code, what's the value in $2?

```
$foo="Star Wars: The Phantom Menace";
$foo=~/star\s((Wars): The Phantom Menace)/;
```

    a. $2 is not set after the pattern match because the match fails.

    b. *Wars*

    c. *Wars: The Phantom Menace*

3. What does the pattern `m/^[-+]?[0-9]+(\.[0-9]*)?$/` match?

    a. Dates in the format 04-03-1969

    b. Well-formed numbers such as 45, 15.3, -0.61

    c. Addition-looking patterns: 4+12 or 89+2

Answers

1. a. Choice c doesn't include the = symbol in the replacement string and it wasn't captured in $1 or $2 because the = occurred outside of the parentheses. Choice b is invalid; a character must appear in front of the *'s. Choice a does the job nicely.

2. a. The match fails because star is not capitalized, and the match doesn't have the case-insensitive modifier i. For this reason, you should always test whether the match succeeds before using the values $1, $2, and so on. (If the pattern match had used the i modifier or star had been capitalized, choice b would have been the correct response.)

3. b. The pattern reads, at the beginning of the line match, an optional + or -, followed by one or more digits, followed (optionally) by a decimal and possibly more digits at the end of the line. The pattern matches simple, well-formed numbers.

Activities

- See whether you can produce a pattern to match a standard time format. All the following should be acceptable: 12:00am, 5:00pm, 8:30AM. These should probably not be accepted: 3:00, 2:60am, 99:00am, 3:0pm.

- Write a short program that does the following:

    1. Opens a file

    2. Reads all the lines into an array

    3. Extracts all the words from each line

    4. Finds all words that have at least four consecutive consonants, or nonvowels (such as the words "thou*ghts*" or "yar*dstick*")

HOUR 7

Hashes

The hash is the third basic data type in Perl. The first data type you learned about was the scalar, which is a simple data type designed to hold one thing (*any* one thing—of any size—but still *one* thing). Next came the array, which is a collection of scalars. An array can hold as many scalars as you like, but searching for the scalar value you need in an array usually involves sequential access of the array until you find the scalar you need.

Hashes are another kind of collective data type. Like arrays, hashes contain a number of scalars. The difference between arrays and hashes is that hashes access their scalar data by name, not by using a numeric subscript as arrays do. Hash elements have two parts: a *key* and a *value*. The key identifies each element of the hash, and the value is the data associated with that key. This relationship is called a *key-value pair*.

Many applications lend themselves to this type of data structure naturally. For example, if you wanted to store information on licensed drivers in a state, you might use the drivers' license numbers as logical keys to store the license information; these numbers are unique (per driver). The data associated with each number would be the driver's information (license type, address, age, and so on). Each driver's license would represent an element in the hash, with the number and information as the key-value pair. Other data structures that have a hash nature are inventory part numbers, hospital patient records, telephone billing records, disk file systems, music CD-ROM collections, Rolodex information, Library of Congress numbers and ISBNs (International Standard Book Numbers), and countless others.

A hash in Perl can contain as many elements as you like, or at least as many as the available memory on your system will allow. Hashes are resized as elements are added and deleted from the hash. Access to individual elements in the hash is extremely fast and does not degrade significantly as the hash gets larger. As a result, Perl is comfortable (and quick) with your hash whether it has 10 elements or 100,000 elements. The keys to the hash can be as long as you want (they're just scalars), and the data portions of the hash can also be as large as you want.

Historically, hashes were called *associative arrays* in Perl and other languages. This term is a long-winded way of indicating that keys were associated with a value. Because Perl programmers aren't much for long-windedness, associative arrays are now simply called hashes.

Hash variables are indicated in Perl by the percent sign (%). They do not share names with arrays and scalars. You can have, for example, a hash named %a, an array named @a, and a scalar named $a. Each of these names refers to one variable unrelated to the others.

In this hour you will learn how to

- Create a hash
- Insert and remove elements from a hash
- Use hashes to manipulate arrays

Filling Your Hash

Individual hash elements are created by assigning values to them, much as with array elements. For example, you can create individual hash elements, as in the following:

```
$Authors{'Dune'}='Frank Herbert';
```

In this example, you assign to an element in the hash %Authors. The key for this element is the word Dune, and the data is the name Frank Herbert. This assignment creates a relationship in the hash between Dune and Frank Herbert. The value associated with the key, $Authors{'Dune'}, can be treated like any other scalar; it can be passed to functions, modified by operators, printed, or reassigned. When you're changing a hash element, always remember that you're modifying the value stored in the hash element, not the hash itself.

Why does the example use `$Authors{}` instead of `%Authors{}`? Like arrays, when hashes are represented as a whole, they have their own marker in front of the variable name (`%`). When you access an individual element of a hash, you are accessing a scalar value, so you precede the variable name with a dollar sign (`$`) indicating a single value is being referenced, and you use the braces around the key to indicate that you mean the value in the hash associated with that key, not an element in an array or an unrelated scalar with the same name as the hash. To Perl, `$Authors{'Dune'}` represents a single scalar value—in this case, `Frank Herbert`.

A hash with just one key isn't particularly useful. To put several values into a hash, you could use a series of assignments, as shown in the following:

```
$food {'apple'} = 'fruit';
$food{'pear'} = 'fruit';
$food{'carrot'} = 'vegetable';
```

To make this operation shorter, you can initialize the hash with a list. The list should consist of pairings of keys and values, as shown here:

```
%food = ('apple', 'fruit', 'pear', 'fruit', 'carrot', 'vegetable');
```

This example looks similar to array initializations discussed in Hour 4, "Stacking Building Blocks: Lists and Arrays." In fact, as you'll learn later in this hour, hashes can be treated as a special kind of array in many contexts.

When you're initializing a hash, keeping track of which items are keys and which items are values in a large list can be confusing. Perl has a special operator called a comma-arrow operator, `=>`. Using the `=>` operator and taking advantage of the fact that Perl ignores whitespace, you can write hash initializations like the following:

```
%food = ( 'apple' => 'fruit',
    'pear'   => 'fruit',
    'carrot' => 'vegetable',
    );
```

Perl programmers, holding laziness as a virtue, have two additional shortcuts for hash initializations. The left side of the `=>` operator is expected to be a simple string and does not need to be quoted. Also, a single-word hash key inside the curly braces is automatically quoted. So the initializations shown previously become the following:

```
$Books{Dune} = 'Frank Herbert';
%food =( apple => 'fruit',  pear => 'fruit',  carrot => 'vegetable' );
```

The comma-arrow operator is called that because it acts like a comma (when it is separating list items) and it looks like an arrow.

Getting Data Out of a Hash

As you have seen, to retrieve a single value from a hash, simply use a $, the name of the hash, and (in curly braces) the key whose value you want to retrieve. Now consider this example:

```
%Movies = ( 'The Shining' => 'Kubrick', 'Ten Commandments' => 'DeMille',
        Goonies => 'Donner');
print $Movies{'The Shining'};
```

These lines print the value associated with the key The Shining in the hash %Movies. This example would print Kubrick.

Sometimes examining all the elements of a hash is useful. If all the keys of the hash are known, you can access them individually by key as shown previously. Most of the time, though, accessing each key by name isn't convenient. Some of the key names might not be known, or the keys may be too numerous to enumerate individually.

You can use the keys function to retrieve all the keys of a hash returned as a list. That list can then be examined to find all the elements of the hash. The keys of the hash aren't stored in any particular order internally, and the keys function doesn't return them in any particular order. To print all the movies in this hash, for example, you could use the following:

```
foreach $film (keys %Movies) {
    print "$film\n";
}
```

Here, $film takes on the value of each element of the list returned by keys %Movies. If you want to print all the directors' names in addition to the movie titles, you can enter the following:

```
foreach $film (keys %Movies) {
    print "$film was directed by $Movies{$film}.\n";
}
```

This snippet might print the following output:

```
Ten Commandments was directed by DeMille.
The Shining was directed by Kubrick.
Goonies was directed by Donner.
```

Because $film contains the value of a hash key, $Movies{$film} retrieves the value of the element of the hash represented by that key. You can print both of them to see the key-value relationship in the hash. (Remember that your output might appear in a different order, because the keys are returned in no particular order by the keys function.)

Perl also provides the values function to retrieve all the values stored in a hash. Retrieving the values alone usually isn't useful, because you can't tell which key is associated with which value. The values of a hash are returned in the same order as the keys function would return the keys. Now consider the following example:

```
@Directors=values %Movies;
@Films=keys %Movies;
```

Here, each subscript of @Directors and @Films contains a reference to the same key-value pair from %Movies. The name of the director contained in $Directors[0] corresponds to the name of the movie stored in $Films[0], and so on.

Sometimes you need to retrieve individual elements from the hash by value instead of by key. The best method of retrieving by value is to *invert the hash*. This means that you make a new hash in which all the keys of the original hash become values, and all their values in the original hash become keys in the new hash. The following is an example:

```
%Movies = ( 'The Shining' => 'Kubrick', 'Ten Commandments' => 'DeMille',
        Goonies => 'Donner');
%ByDirector = reverse %Movies;
```

What's this? When you use the reverse function on a hash, Perl unwinds the hash into a flat list—perhaps something like this:

```
('The Shining', 'Kubrick', 'Ten Commandments', 'DeMille', 'Goonies',
        'Donner')
```

Perl then reverses the order of the elements in the list, and you get the following output:

```
('Donner', 'Goonies', 'DeMille', 'Ten Commandments', 'Kubrick',
        'The Shining')
```

Notice that now all the key-value pairs are switched around (values are now first). When you assign this list to %ByDirector, the resulting hash is identical to the original, except that all the keys are now values and all the values are now keys. Beware, however, if your hash has duplicate values for some reason. If the values (which are to become keys) are not unique, you end up with a hash with fewer elements than you started with. As the duplicate values collide in the new hash, old keys are replaced with the new ones.

7

Lists and Hashes

When I discussed how to initialize a hash, I hinted that hashes and arrays are somehow related. Whenever a hash is used in a list context, Perl unwinds the hash back into a flat list of keys and values. This list can be assigned to arrays, like any other list:

```
%Movies = ( 'The Shining' => 'Kubrick', 'Ten Commandments' => 'DeMille',
       Goonies => 'Donner');
@Data = %Movies;
```

At this point, @Data is an array containing six elements. (The even elements—zero included—are directors' names, and the odd elements are movie titles.) You can perform any normal array operation on @Data, and then you can reassign the array to %Movies, as shown here:

```
%Movies = @Data;
```

Perl stores hash keys in a seemingly random order, useful only to Perl. Perl makes no effort to remember the order in which the keys were placed into the hash, and it doesn't put them into any particular sequence when retrieving the keys. Getting them in order for display requires that you sort them (see the "Useful Things to Do with a Hash" section, later in this hour) or somehow remember the order they were inserted in (see the "Q&A" section at the end of this hour).

Arrays and hashes are similar in other respects. To copy a hash, you can simply assign the hash to another hash, like this:

```
%New_Hash = %Old_Hash;
```

When you put %Old_Hash on the right side of a hash initialization, where Perl would normally expect a list or array, Perl unwinds the hash into a list. This list is then used to initialize %New_Hash. In the same way, you can combine and manipulate hashes in ways similar to lists, as you can see here:

```
%Both = (%First, %Second);
%Additional = (%Both, key1 => 'value1', key2 => 'value2');
```

The first line combines two hashes, %First and %Second, into a third hash, %Both. Something to remember about this example is that if %First has keys that also appear in %Second, the second occurrence of the key-value pair replaces the first in %Both. In the second example, %Both is represented as a list of key-value pairs in the parentheses. Two additional key-value pairs are also in the parentheses. The entire list is then used to initialize %Additional.

Hash Odds and Ends

Some operations on hashes aren't obvious if you're new to Perl. Because of the special nature of hashes, a couple of common operations require functions that aren't necessary for scalars and arrays.

Testing for Keys in a Hash

To test to see whether a key exists in a hash, for example, you might be tempted to try the following syntax:

```
if ( $Hash{keyval} ) {          # WRONG, in this case
    :
}
```

This example doesn't work, for a few reasons. First, this snippet doesn't test to see whether keyval is a key in a hash; it actually tests the value associated with the key keyval in the hash.

Does it work to test whether the key is defined, as in the following?

```
if ( defined $Hash{keyval} ) {    # WRONG, again in this case
    :
}
```

Again, this example doesn't quite work. This snippet still tests the data associated with the key keyval, and not whether the key exists. undef is a perfectly valid value to associate with a hash key, as in the following:

```
$Hash{keyval} = undef;
```

The preceding test of defined returns false because it doesn't test for the existence of a key in a hash; it tests the data associated with the key. So what's the right way? Perl has a special function just for this purpose; it's called exists. The exists function, shown here, tests for the presence of the hash key in the hash and returns true if it's there or false otherwise:

```
if ( exists $Hash{keyval} ) {    # RIGHT!
    :
}
```

Removing Keys from a Hash

The other operation that isn't obvious is removing a key from a hash. As you saw earlier, simply setting the hash element to undef doesn't work. To remove a single hash key, you can use the delete function, as follows:

```
delete $Hash{keyval};
```

7

To remove all the keys and values from a hash, simply reinitialize the hash to an empty
list like this:

```
%Hash = ();
```

Useful Things to Do with a Hash

Hashes are often used in Perl for more reasons than to store records by keys for later
retrieval. The advantages to using a hash are fast individual access to keys and the fact
that all keys in a hash are unique. These properties lend themselves to some useful data
manipulations. Not surprisingly, because arrays and hashes are so similar, many of the
interesting things you can do with hashes are array manipulations.

Determining Frequency Distributions

In Hour 6, "Pattern Matching," you learned how to take a line of text and split it into
words. Examine the following snippet of code:

```
while ( <> ) {
    while ( /(\w[\w-]*)/g  ) {   # Iterate over words, setting $1 to each.
        $Words{$1}++;
    }
}
```

The first line reads the standard input one line at a time, setting $_ to each line.

The next while() loop then iterates over each word in $_. Recall from Hour 6 that using
the pattern-matching operator (//) in a scalar context with the g modifier returns each
pattern match until no more are left. The pattern being looked for is a word character \w,
followed by zero or more word characters or dashes [\w-]*. In this case, you use parentheses to remember the string matched in the special variable $1.

The next line, although short, is where the snippet gets interesting. $1 is set, in turn, to
each word matched by the pattern on the second line. That word is used as the key to the
hash %Words. The first time the word is seen, the key does not already exist in the hash,
so Perl returns a value of undef for that key-value pair. By incrementing it, Perl sets the
value to 1, creating the pair. The second time a word is seen, the key (that word) already
exists in the hash %Words, and it is incremented from 1 to 2. This process continues until
no input is left.

When you're finished, the hash %Words contains a frequency distribution of the words
read in. To look at the frequency distribution, you can use the following code:

```
foreach ( keys %Words ) {
        print "$_ $Words{$_}\n";
}
```

Finding Unique Elements in Arrays

The technique shown in the preceding code is also useful for finding which elements in an array occur only once. Suppose you have already extracted all the words from the input into an array instead of a hash, and you have made no particular effort to make sure that a word wasn't already in the list before putting it in again. In this case, you would have a list with a lot of duplicated words.

If your input text were the opening lines of *One Fish, Two Fish,* the list would look something like the following:

```
@fishwords=('one', 'fish', 'two', 'fish', 'red', 'fish', 'blue', 'fish');
```

If you are given this list of words (in @fishwords), and you need only the unique elements of the list, a hash works nicely for this purpose, as shown in Listing 7.1.

LISTING 7.1   Finding Unique Elements in an Array

```
1:    %seen = ();
2:    foreach (@fishwords) {
3:        $seen{$_} = 1;
4:    }
5:    @uniquewords = keys %seen;
```

Line 1: This line initializes a temporary hash %seen, which holds all your words.

Line 2: This line iterates over the list of words, setting $_ to each word in turn.

Line 3: If the word in $_ is not already a key in the hash %seen, this line creates an entry with that key. Whether the key previously existed or not, a dummy value is assigned to the data for that key.

Line 5: This line simply extracts all the keys from the hash and stores them in @uniquewords. No matter how many times a word (fish, for example) occurs in the original list, it appears as only one key.

Computing the Intersection and Difference of Arrays

A common problem with arrays is finding the *intersection* of two arrays (the list of the elements that they both have) and the *difference* between two arrays (the list of elements that appear in only one array or the other). In the following example, you have two lists: one containing a list of movie stars and one containing a list of politicians. It is your task

7

to find all the politicians who were also movie stars. Here are your two (woefully incomplete) arrays:

```
@stars=('R. Reagan', 'C. Eastwood', 'M. Jackson', 'Cher', 'S. Bono');
@pols  = ('N. Gingrich', 'S. Thurmond', 'R. Reagan',
                        'S. Bono', 'C. Eastwood', 'M. Thatcher');
```

The code to find the intersection is shown in Listing 7.2.

LISTING 7.2   Computing the Intersection of Arrays

```
1:    %seen=();
2:    foreach (@stars) {
3:        $seen{$_}=1;
4:    }
5:    @intersection=grep($seen{$_}, @pols);
```

Line 1: This line initializes the hash %seen. This temporary hash is used to hold all the movie stars' names.

Line 2: This line iterates over the list of movie stars, setting $_ to each name in turn.

Line 3: This line fills the hash %seen using the stars' names for the keys and setting the value to 1, which could actually be any true value you want.

Line 5: This line looks more complicated than it is. The grep function iterates over the list of politicians (in @pols), setting $_ to each one in turn. Then that name is looked for in the hash %seen. If the name returns true, it's in the hash, and the expression $seen{$_} evaluates to true. If the expression evaluates to true, grep returns the value of $_, which gets put into @intersection. The process is repeated until @pols has been completely examined by grep. When the snippet is finished, @intersection contains the names of all the members of both @stars and @pols.

The code to find the difference between two arrays (those elements in one but not the other) is almost identical. You can use Listing 7.3 to look for all the politicians who are not movie stars.

LISTING 7.3   Computing the Difference Between Arrays

```
1:    %seen=();
2:    foreach (@stars) {
3:        $seen{$_} = 1;
4:    }
5:    @difference = grep(! $seen{$_}, @pols);
```

The only line that has changed between Listing 7.2 and here is line 5. It still looks for each politician's name in the hash %seen, but now it returns false if it's found. Conversely, it returns true if the name isn't there. All the names of politicians that appear in the hash %seen do *not* get returned to @difference. If you want to find all the stars who are not politicians, the code would be almost exactly the same, except that you would need to switch @stars and @pols.

Sorting Hashes

Often it's not enough to retrieve the keys from a hash in the default order (which is pretty much random). The word frequency distribution problem discussed earlier is one of those cases. You can print the frequency distribution you've created in two sensible ways: alphabetically by word or by frequency. Because the keys function returns a simple list, you can use the sort function, introduced in Hour 4, as follows to order that list:

```
foreach( sort keys %Words ) {
    print "$_ $Words{$_}\n";
}
```

Sorting the list by frequency isn't much different. Remember from Hour 4 that the sort function, by default, simply sorts the given list in ASCII order, but you can perform a more complex sort by calling the sort function with a block of code that specifies the sort order. The following code demonstrates sorting the hash by values:

```
foreach ( sort  { $Words{$a} <=> $Words{$b} } keys %Words ) {
    print "$_ $Words{$_}\n";
}
```

Recall that the block you supply to sort is called repeatedly, with $a and $b set to each pair of values that sort needs to have ordered by your code. In this case, $a and $b are set to various keys in the hash %Words. Instead of comparing $a and $b directly, the code looks up the value of those keys in the hash %Words and compares them.

Exercise: Creating a Simple Customer Database with Perl

When you call a customer service center and finally make it through the Touch-Tone menus, the first thing the human being on the other end of the phone asks you for is your telephone number. Well, almost every time. Sometimes the customer service representative wants your customer number or even your Social Security number. What this person is after is something that uniquely identifies you to the computer he or she is using. These numbers serve as keys for retrieving information about you in a database. Sounds like Perl's hashes, doesn't it?

7

For this exercise, you're going to search a customer database. This program assumes that the database already exists, and it doesn't provide any way to update that database—yet. Here, you're going to allow the user to search on one of two different fields.

To begin this exercise, you need some data. Fire up your text editor, key in the text in Listing 7.4 (or something similar), and save it as customers.txt. Don't worry about the number of spaces between the columns or aligning them, as long as you leave at least one space between each column.

LISTING 7.4   Sample Data for the Customer Program

```
Smith,John    (248)-555-9430 jsmith@aol.com
Hunter,Apryl  (810)-555-3029 april@showers.org
Stewart,Pat   (405)-555-8710 pats@starfleet.co.uk
Ching,Iris    (305)-555-0919 iching@zen.org
Doe,John      (212)-555-0912 jdoe@morgue.com
Jones,Tom     (312)-555-3321 tj2342@aol.com
Smith,John    (607)-555-0023 smith@pocahontas.com
Crosby,Dave   (405)-555-1516 cros@csny.org
Johns,Pam     (313)-555-6790 pj@sleepy.com
Jeter,Linda   (810)-555-8761 netless@earthlink.net
Garland,Judy  (305)-555-1231 ozgal@rainbow.com
```

In the same directory, key in the short program in Listing 7.5 and save it as Customer. As usual, don't type the line numbers, and, if you can, be sure to make the program executable according to the instructions you learned in Hour 1, "Introduction to the Perl Language."

When you're done, try running the program by typing the following at a command line:

```
Customer
```

or, if you cannot make the program executable on your system,

```
perl -w Customer
```

LISTING 7.5   Complete Listing of the Customer Program

```
1:   #!/usr/bin/perl -w
2:
3:   open(PH, "customers.txt") or die "Cannot open customers.txt: $!\n";
4:   while(<PH>) {
5:       chomp;
6:       ($number, $email) = ( split(/\s+/, $_) )[1,2];
7:       $Phone{$number} = $_;
8:       $Email{$email} = $_;
```

continues

LISTING 7.5 Continued

```
 9:    }
10:    close(PH);
11:
12:    print "Type 'q' to exit\n";
13:    while (1) {
14:        print "\nNumber? ";
15:        $number = <STDIN>;   chomp($number);
16:        $address = "";
17:        if (! $number ) {
18:            print "E-Mail? ";
19:            $address = <STDIN>;   chomp($address);
20:        }
21:
22:        next if (! $number and ! $address);
23:        last if ($number eq 'q' or $address eq 'q');
24:
25:        if ( $number and exists $Phone{$number} ) {
26:            print "Customer: $Phone{$number}\n";
27:            next;
28:        }
29:
30:        if ($address and exists $Email{$address} ) {
31:                print "Customer: $Email{$address}\n";
32:                next;
33:        }
34:        print "Customer record not found.\n";
35:        next;
36:    }
36:    print "\nAll done.\n";
```

Listing 7.6 shows the output of the Customer program.

LISTING 7.6 Sample Output from Customer

```
Type 'q' to exit
Number? <return>
E-Mail? cros@csny.org
Customer: Crosby, Dave      (405)-555-1516   cros@csny.org

Number? (305)-555-0919
Customer: Ching,Iris      (305)-555-0919   iching@zen.org

Number? q

All done.
```

7

Line 1: This line contains the path to the interpreter (you can change it so that it's appropriate to your system) and the -w switch. Always have warnings enabled!

Line 3: The customers.txt file is opened for reading on the filehandle PH. Of course, errors are checked for and reported.

Lines 4–5: The PH filehandle is read, each line being assigned to $_. $_ is chomped to remove the trailing newline character.

Line 6: The line (in $_) is split on whitespace (\s+). Surrounding the split statement is a set of parentheses, and brackets follow them. Because you're interested in only the phone number and email address from each line, you take a slice of the return values from the split. The two values are assigned to $number and $email.

Lines 7–8: %Email is used to store the customer record, the key being the email address. %Phone is used to store the customer record also, but keyed by phone number.

Line 10: This line closes the filehandle.

Line 13: This while loop encloses the portion of code that needs to be repeated. The statement while(1) is a Perl idiom that means "loop forever." To exit this loop, a last statement will eventually be used.

Lines 14–15: The phone number is read, and the newline character is removed.

Lines 17–20: If no phone number is available, these lines prompt for an email address.

Lines 22–23: If nothing was entered, this line repeats the loop. If either response was a q, then the loop is exited.

Lines 25–28: If a number was entered, and it is valid, line 26 prints the customer record. Control is passed back to the top of the block with a next statement.

Lines 30–33: If an address was entered, and it's valid, the customer record is printed. Control is passed back to the top of the block with next.

Lines 34–35: Either an address or a phone number was entered, and it was found not to be valid. These lines print an appropriate message and repeat the block with next.

This example demonstrates a few Perl features. Hashes are used for quick lookups of data based on a key. Because Perl implements hashes very efficiently, response time for a query should not become inefficient even if this program has thousands or tens of thousands of records in the hashes. Also, this program serves as a demonstration of program flow control using a simpleblock instead of other control structures (`while`, `do`, `until`, and so on).

Summary

Hashes provide the Perl programmer with many useful tools. Beyond simple record storage and retrieval, hashes provide mechanisms for doing useful transformations and analysis on data. The formulas for array manipulation, record storage, and retrieval will benefit you greatly. In the hours to come, hashes will provide the gateway to your learning about such topics as handling DBM (Data Base Manager) files, working with complex data structures, and interacting with your system's environment.

Q&A

Q Can I store more than one thing in a hash—for instance, if I need to store several things (a list) by one key?

A Yes. Two basic methods are involved. The first (and most cumbersome) is to format the value portion of the hash element into something recognizable, such as a comma-separated list. Whenever you store the hash element, you assemble the list into a scalar by using `join`, and whenever you retrieve a value from a hash, you split the scalar back into a list by using `split`. This method is cumbersome and error-prone.

The other method is to use a *reference*. References allow you to create hashes of arrays, hashes of hashes, and other complex data types. Using references to create complex structures is easy when you get the hang of it. This topic will be covered in Hour 13, "References and Structures."

Q How can I keep my keys in the order in which I assigned them to the hash?

A Again, you can keep them in order in a couple of ways. The first method, which isn't easy, is to keep track of the insertion order yourself. One technique is to use an array that mirrors the hash. As you put new elements into the hash, you use `push` to put the same key into an array. When you need to see the insertion order, simply use the array instead of the `keys` function. This method is complicated and likely to be buggy.

The far superior method is to use the module `Tie::IxHash`. This module causes the `keys` function to return the hash keys in insertion order, just as you wanted. You can find an explanation of how to use modules in Hour 14, "Using Modules."

7

Q Can you suggest a convenient way to write my hash into a file?

A Yes. Modules such as `Data::Dumper` or `Storable` can reformat data types such as hashes and arrays into easily storable scalar values, which can be written to text files. These modules also have functions that take those formatted scalars and re-create the original structure you stored.

In Hour 15, "Finding Permanence," you'll see that an even easier way to write a hash into a file is to use DBM files. DBM files allow you to tie your hash to a disk file. When you alter the hash, the disk file changes. The disk file causes your hash to be preserved as long as the file is intact.

Workshop

Quiz

1. Why would `name` have been an inappropriate search key for the Customer program you wrote in this hour, especially if the customer list were much, much longer?

   a. Combinations of last name and first name would have been more than Perl's hashes would allow.

   b. People's names are not unique keys.

   c. No one would ever want to search a customer database by name.

2. What's the difference between an associative array and a hash?

   a. There is no difference.

   b. Associative arrays are used on more formal data sets, such as billing records.

   c. Hashes aren't really associative arrays in Perl, so they have a different name.

3. What kinds of data are best suited for hashes?

   a. Simple lists of items

   b. Potatoes and corned beef

   c. Lists of key-value pairs

Answers

1. b. Perl's hashes are virtually unlimited in size, and users will (inevitably) ask for a search by name. But people's names are inappropriate, because they're not unique. The phone book has many, many duplicate names such as John Smith and Robert Jones.

2. a. Hashes and associative arrays are identical. The only difference is that *hash* is much easier to say and to spell.

3. c. Choice c is the correct answer, although a nice corned-beef hash can really round out breakfast.

Activities

- Modify the Customer program to allow a search by name. Because you cannot use `name` as a hash key, you need to search through the values in the hash.

- Modify the Customer program to allow searching by a partial key (for example, part of a phone number or part of an email address). You can use regular expressions to search for the patterns. Simply keep in mind that you could find multiple results and you should return each one.

7

HOUR 8

Functions

Almost all computer languages support *functions*. A function is a grouping of code statements that can be called by name to do some work and then return some value. You've been using functions throughout this book; for example, you've used print, chomp, sort, open, close, split, and so on. These functions are built into Perl.

Perl also allows you to write your own functions. In Perl, user-defined functions are called *subroutines,* or *subs*. Like Perl's built-in functions, user-defined functions can take arguments and return values to the caller.

Perl also supports the concept of *scope*. Scope determines the set of variables that a given statement in the program can access as it is executed. Because of Perl's scope features, you can write functions that can behave autonomously from the rest of your program. Well-written functions can be reused in other programs.

In this chapter you will learn

- How to define your own functions and call them
- How to pass values into functions and return values
- How to write programs with use strict to enforce structure

Creating and Calling Subroutines

You create user-defined subroutines in Perl by using the following syntax:

```
sub subroutine_name {
    statement1;
    :
    statementx;
}
```

Subroutine names in Perl follow the same naming conventions as scalars, arrays, and hashes outlined in Hour 2, "Perl's Building Blocks: Numbers and Strings." Subroutine names can have the same names as existing variables. However, you should avoid creating subroutine names that are the same as those of Perl's built-in functions and operators. Creating two subroutines with the same name in Perl causes Perl to emit a warning if warnings are enabled; otherwise, the second definition causes the first to be forgotten.

Here is an example of a subroutine:

```
sub  countdown {
    for ($i=10; $i>=0; $i--) {
        print "$i -";
    }
}
```

When the program needs to use the code in the subroutine, you can use either of the following syntax lines to *call* (or *invoke*) the subroutine:

```
&countdown();
```

or

```
countdown();
```

You can use the second syntax (without the &) if the subroutine has been declared in the code already, although the &countdown() syntax is acceptable anywhere, and some consider it more readable. In this book, I'll declare subroutines ahead of where they're first called, and I'll use the form without the &, although either is acceptable.

When the subroutine is invoked, Perl remembers where it was, executes the subroutine's code, and then returns to the remembered place in the program when the subroutine is complete, as in the following example:

```
print "T-minus: ";
countdown();
print "Blastoff!\n";
```

prints

```
T-minus: 10 -9 -8 -7 -6 -5 -4 -3 -2 -1 -0 -Blastoff!
```

Perl subroutines can be called anywhere within your program, including within other subroutines, as shown here:

```
sub world {
    print "World!";
}
sub hello {
    print "Hello, ";
    world();
}
hello();
```

Returning Values from Subroutines

A subroutine isn't just for grouping code together by a convenient name. A subroutine, like Perl's functions, operators, and expressions, also has a value, called the subroutine's *return value*. The return value of a subroutine is the value of the last expression evaluated in the subroutine or a value explicitly returned by the `return` statement.

The return value of the subroutine, computed when the subroutine is called, can then be used in whatever code called the subroutine. Consider the following example:

```
sub two_by_four {      # A silly subroutine
    2 * 4;
}
print 8*two_by_four();
```

In the preceding snippet, for Perl to evaluate the expression `8*two_by_four()`, the subroutine `two_by_four()` is run and the value `8` returned. The expression `8*8` is then evaluated, and `64` is printed.

Values can also be explicitly returned from a subroutine with the `return` statement. Use a `return` statement when your program needs to return before the end of the subroutine or when you want to be explicit about what value is being returned—instead of just "falling off" the end of the subroutine and using the last expression's value. The following snippet uses both methods:

```
sub x_greaterthan100 {
    # Relies on the value of $x being set elsewhere
    return(1) if ( $x > 100 );
    0;
}
$x = 70;
if (x_greaterthan100()) {
    print "$x is greater than 100\n";
}
```

Subroutines can return arrays and hashes as well as scalars, as shown here:

```
sub shift_to_uppercase {
    @words = qw( cia fbi un nato unicef );
    foreach (@words) {
        $_ = uc($_);
    }
    return (@words);
}
@acronyms=shift_to_uppercase();
```

Arguments

All the preceding examples of subroutines have one thing in common: They act on either data that was hard-coded (2*4) or variables that just happened to have the right data in them ($x for x_greaterthan100()). This limitation creates a problem because functions that rely on hard-coded data or expect variables to be set outside the function aren't really portable. It would be nice to call a function and say, "Take *this* data and do something with it," and then call it later and say, "Take this *other* data and do something with it." The result of calling a function, then, can change depending on what is passed to it.

These values given to functions to change their results are called *arguments*, and you've been using them throughout this book. Perl's built-in functions (grep, sort, reverse, print, and so on) take arguments, and now yours can too. To pass a subroutine arguments, you can use any of the following:

```
subname(arg1, arg2, arg3);
subname arg1, arg2, arg3;
&subname(arg1, arg2, arg3);
```

You can use the second form—without the parentheses—only if Perl has encountered the subroutine definition already.

In a subroutine, any arguments that were passed to it are accessible through the Perl special variable @_. This snippet demonstrates passing arguments—the three string literals—and printing them with a function:

```
sub printargs {
    print join(',', @_);
}
printargs('market', 'home', 'roast beef');
```

To access individual arguments that were passed in, as shown in the following example, you use an index on the array @_ as you would any other array. Just remember that $_[0]—an element of @_—has nothing to do with the scalar variable $_.

```
sub print_third_argument {
    print $_[2];
}
```

8

Working with variable names like $_[3] isn't exactly a "clear" style of programming. Functions that take multiple arguments often begin by giving names to those arguments; this practice makes it clearer what they do. To see what I mean, check out the following example:

```
sub display_box_score {
    ($num_hits, $num_at_bats)=@_;
    print "For $num_at_bats trips to the plate, ";
    print "he's hitting ", $num_hits/$num_at_bats, "\n";
}
display_box_score(50, 210);
```

In the preceding subroutine, the array @_ is copied to the list ($num_hits, $num_at_bats). The first element of @_—$_[0]—becomes $num_hits, and the second $num_at_bats. The variable names are simply used here for readability.

> The variable @_ actually contains aliases to the original arguments that were passed to the subroutine. Modifying @_ (or any element of @_) modifies the original variables in the argument list. Doing so unexpectedly is considered bad form; your function shouldn't interfere with arguments from callers to the function unless the users of the function are expecting this.

Passing Arrays and Hashes

Arguments to subroutines don't have to be scalars. You can pass arrays and hashes to subroutines, but doing so requires some thought. You pass an array—or hash—to a subroutine the same way you pass a scalar:

```
@sorted_items=sort_numerically(@items);
```

In the subroutine, the entire array @items is referenced through @_:

```
sub sort_numerically {
    print "Sorting...";
    return( sort { $a <=> $b} @_);
}
```

You do hit a small snag when passing hashes and arrays to subroutines: Passing two or more hashes (or arrays) to a subroutine doesn't usually do what you want. Examine this snippet of code:

```
sub display_arrays {
    (@a, @b) = @_;
    print "The first array: @a\n";
    print "The second array: @b\n";
}
display_arrays(@first, @second);
```

The two arrays `@first` and `@second` are put into a list together, and the elements are put into `@_` during the subroutine call. The end of the `@first`'s elements are indistinguishable from the beginning of `@second`'s elements in `@_`; it's just one large flat list. Inside the subroutine, the assignment `(@a, @b)=@_` takes all the elements in `@_` and assigns them to `@a`. The array `@b` gets no elements. (The reason for this was explained in Hour 4, "Stacking Building Blocks: Lists and Arrays.")

One or more scalars can be passed along with a *single* array or hash, as long as the scalars are passed first in the argument list and you know how many you have. That way, the hash or array encompasses all the values beyond the last scalar, as in this example:

```
sub lots_of_args {
    ($first, $second, $third, %hash) = @_;
    # rest of subroutine...
}
lots_of_args($foo, $bar, $baz, %myhash);
```

If you must pass multiple arrays and hashes into a subroutine (and be able to distinguish them later), you must use *references*. You'll learn how to pass references in Hour 13, "References and Structures."

Scope

In the introduction for this hour, you learned that subroutines are used to take pieces of code and bundle them up and give them a name. You then can use this name to execute the code whenever you need it. You can also write the code within the subroutine so that it functions autonomously. That is, you can make it run and produce its return value using nothing but its arguments, the language's built-in functions and operators, and literal expressions within it. In that case, you can reuse the subroutine in other programs, because it no longer relies on the context it's being called in; it simply takes its arguments and data defined internally and produces a return value. The subroutine becomes a black box—stuff goes in, stuff comes out—and outside it you don't care what happens on the inside. Such a subroutine is called a *pure function*.

Now examine the following two snippets:

```
# One fairly good way to write this function
sub moonweight {
    ($weight) = @_;
    return($weight / 6);
}
print moonweight(150);
```

```
# A poor way to write this function.
sub moonweight {
    return( $weight/6 );
}
$weight = 150;
print moonweight;
```

In the long run, the first implementation shown here is a better one. It doesn't rely on any external variables—those outside the function—being set. It takes its argument, which it copies to $weight, and then does its calculations. The second implementation cannot easily be reused in another program; you would have to ensure that $weight is set properly and is not being used for some other value. If it were being used for something else, you would have to edit the moonweight() subroutine to use a different variable. That's not very efficient.

So, the first example is a better subroutine, but it's still missing something. The variable $weight could conflict with a variable named $weight somewhere else in the program.

Perl permits you to reuse variable names over and over and for different purposes within a large program. Perl's variables, by default, are visible in the main body of your program and in the subroutines; these kinds of variables are called *global variables*.

What you need to do in the moonweight example is to make the variable $weight a *private variable* in the subroutine. To do so, you use the my operator:

```
sub moonweight {
    my $weight;
    ($weight)=@_;
    return($weight/6);
}
```

Inside moonweight(), $weight is now private. Neither the main body nor any other subroutines in the program can access the value of $weight. Any other variables with the name $weight are completely separate from the moonweight() subroutine's $weight, so they are not affected by the assignment to $weight inside moonweight(). This subroutine is now completely self-contained.

The portion of the program in which the variable is visible is called the variable's *scope*.

You can use the my operator to declare scalar, array, and hash variables private to a subroutine. Filehandles, subroutines, and Perl's special variables—$!, $_, and @_, for example—cannot be marked as private to a subroutine. You can declare multiple variables private if you use parentheses with my:

```
my($larry, @curly, %moe);
```

Variables that are private to subroutines are stored in a completely different manner than global variables are. Global variables and private variables can have the same names, but they have nothing to do with each other, as shown here:

```
sub myfunc {
    my $x;
    $x=20;      # This is a private $x
    print "$x\n";
}
$x=10;          # This is a global $x
print "$x\n";
myfunc();
print "$x\n";
```

The preceding snippet prints 10, 20, and then 10. The $x inside the myfunc() subroutine is a completely different $x from the one outside. (Is it possible for a subroutine to use *both* its private $x and the global $x? Yes, but the answer is somewhat complicated and beyond this introductory book on Perl.)

Most of the time, Perl subroutines start by assigning @_ to a list of variable names and then declaring the list private to the subroutine:

```
sub player_stats {
    my($num_at_bats, $num_hits, $num_walks)=@_;
    # Rest of function...
}
```

This technique makes for a programmer-friendly subroutine: The variables are all private to the subroutine, so they cannot affect or be affected by other subroutines or the main body of the program. When a subroutine ends, any private variables are destroyed.

Other Places for my

You can also declare variables to have a scope that's even smaller than a subroutine. The my operator actually declares variables to be private to the enclosing block, which might or might not be a subroutine block. For example, in this snippet, the private variable $y (the one declared with my) is visible only within the block:

```
$y=20;
{
    my $y=500;
    print "The value of \$y is $y\n";   # Will print 500
}
print "$y\n";                           # Will print 20.
```

The declaration can even take place within one of the control structures, such as `for`, `foreach`, `while`, or `if`. Essentially, anywhere you have a block, a variable can be scoped so that it's visible only within that block, as in this example:

```
while($testval) {
    my $stuff;      # Visible only within the while() loop.
    :
}
foreach(@t) {
    my %hash;       # Visible only within the foreach loop.
}
```

In the preceding snippet, the `my` variables—`$stuff` and `%hash`—are created anew each time through the loops.

Perl versions 5.004 and newer allow the iterator in `for` and `foreach` loops and the test conditions in `while` and `if` structures to be declared as private to the block:

```
foreach my $element (@array) {
# $element is only visible in the foreach()
}

while(my $line=<STDIN>) {
    # $line is visible only in the while()
}
```

Again, when an enclosing block ends, any variables private to that block—and their values—are destroyed.

Exercise: Statistics

Now that you've learned about subroutines, you should begin to see the benefits of encapsulating code in self-contained subroutines. They provide code that can be easily reused. In this exercise, three subs provide some analysis on groups of numbers.

Just to refresh your memory from school, the *mean,* also called an *arithmetic mean* or *average,* of a set of numbers is simply the sum of all the numbers in the set divided by how many numbers there are in the set. The *median* is the number that would be in the middle if you were to sort the set numerically; with an even number of elements, the median is the average of the two numbers that would be in the middle. The *standard deviation* gives an idea of how "bunched" the numbers are around the mean. A high standard deviation that means the numbers are widely distributed; a small one means they're bunched tightly around the average. In many sets of numbers commonly found in nature, the mean, plus or minus the standard deviation, represents about 68 percent of the set of the numbers; plus or minus two standard deviations, 95 percent of the set of numbers.

Here is a program that finds the mean, median, and standard deviation for a set of numbers that the user types at the keyboard.

Using your text editor, type the program from Listing 8.1 and save it as `stats`. Again, do not type line numbers, and if possible, be sure to make the program executable according to the instructions you learned in Hour 1, "Introduction to the Perl Language."

When you're all done, try running the program by typing the following at a command line:

```
stats
```

or, if your system cannot make the program executable,

```
perl Stats
```

LISTING 8.1   Complete Listing for Stats Program

```
 1:   #!/usr/bin/perl -w
 2:
 3:   use strict;
 4:   sub mean {
 5:       my(@data) = @_;
 6:       my $sum;
 7:       foreach(@data) {
 8:           $sum += $_;
 9:       }
10:       return($sum / @data);
11:   }
12:   sub median {
13:       my(@data)=sort { $a <=> $b} @_;
14:       if (scalar(@data) % 2) {
15:           return($data[@data / 2]);
16:       } else {
17:           my($upper, $lower);
18:           $lower=$data[@data / 2];
19:           $upper=$data[@data / 2 - 1];
20:           return(mean($lower, $upper));
21:       }
22:   }
23:   sub std_dev {
24:       my(@data)=@_;
25:       my($sq_dev_sum, $avg)=(0,0);
26:
27:       $avg = mean(@data);
28:       foreach my $elem (@data) {
29:           $sq_dev_sum += ($avg - $elem) **2;
30:       }
31:       return(sqrt($sq_dev_sum / ( @data - 1 )));
```

continues

8

LISTING 8.1 Continued

```
32:  }
33:  my($data, @dataset);
34:  print "Please enter data, separated by commas: ";
35:  $data = <STDIN>;  chomp $data;
36:  @dataset = split(/[\s,]+/, $data);
37:
38:  print "Median: ", median(@dataset), "\n";
39:  print "Mean: ", mean(@dataset), "\n";
40:  print "Standard Dev.: ", std_dev(@dataset), "\n";
```

Line 1: This line contains the path to the interpreter (you can change it so that it's appropriate to your system) and the -w switch. Always have warnings enabled!

Line 3: The use strict directive means that all variables must be declared with my and that bare words must be quoted.

Lines 4–11: The mean() function works by using a foreach loop to add up all the numbers in $sum and then divides by the number of numbers.

Lines 12–21: The median() function works in two ways. With an odd number of elements, it simply picks the middle element by taking the length of the array and dividing it by two and then using the integer portion. With an even number of elements, it does the same but instead takes the two middle numbers. Those numbers—in $upper and $lower—are then averaged with the mean() function and returned as the median.

Lines 23–32: The std_dev() function is simple, but mostly just math. In short, each element in @data is subtracted from the mean and squared. The result is then accumulated in $sq_dev_sum. To find the standard deviation, the sum of the squared differences is divided by the number of elements minus 1, and then the square root is taken.

Lines 33–35: The variables needed in the main body of the program are declared as lexicals (with my), and the user is prompted for $data. The variable $data is then split into the array @dataset using the pattern /[\s,]+/. This pattern splits the line on commas and spaces. Extra spaces and commas are ignored.

Lines 38–40: The output is produced. Notice that this isn't the only place the functions mean(), median(), and std_dev() are called. They also call each other: std_dev() and median() both use mean(), which is a good example of code reuse!

Listing 8.2 shows a sample of the statistics program's output.

LISTING 8.2 Sample Output from Stats

```
Please enter data, separated by commas: 14.5,6,8,9,10,34
Median: 9.5
Mean: 13.5833333333333
Standard Dev.: 10.3943093405318
```

Function Footnotes

Now that you know about scope, there are some things that can be done effectively only with scope. One is recursive subroutines, and the other is the use strict Perl statement that enables a stricter Perl, possibly preventing you from making mistakes.

Declaring Variables `local`

Perl version 4 didn't have private variables. Instead, Perl 4 had variables that were "almost private." This concept of almost-private variables is still around in Perl 5. You declare these variables by using the local operator, as in this example:

```
sub myfunc {
    local($foo)= 56;
    # rest of function...
}
```

In the preceding snippet, $foo is declared to be local to the myfunc() subroutine. A variable that has been declared with local acts almost identically to one declared with my: It can be scoped to a subroutine, block, or eval, and its value is destroyed upon leaving the subroutine or block.

The difference is that a variable declared local can be seen within its scoped block and within any subroutines called from that block. Table 8.1 shows a side-by-side comparison.

TABLE 8.1 Comparing *my* and *local*

```
sub mess_with_foo {                  sub mess_with_foo {

    $foo=0;                              $foo=0;

}                                    }

sub myfunc {                         sub myfunc {

    my $foo=20;                          local $foo=20;

    mess_with_foo();                     mess_with_foo();

    print $foo;                          print $foo;

}                                    }

myfunc();                            myfunc();
```

8

The two snippets shown in Table 8.1 are identical except for the declaration of $foo in myfunc(). On the left, it's declared with my; on the right, with local.

When the code on the left runs, $foo is created private to myfunc(). When mess_with_foo() is called, the $foo that's changed inside mess_with_foo() is the global variable $foo. When control returns to myfunc(), the value of 20 is printed, because the $foo in myfunc() was never changed.

When the code on the right runs, $foo is created and declared local to myfunc(). When mess_with_foo() is called, $foo is set to 0. That $foo is the same $foo from myfunc(); the "privateness" is passed down to the called subroutine. Upon returning to myfunc(), the value of 0 is printed.

> If you're picky about terminology, local variables are technically known as *dynamically scoped* variables, because their scope changes depending on what subroutines are called. Variables declared with my are called *lexically scoped* variables, because their scope can be determined by simply reading the code and noting what block they were declared in, and the scope does not change.

Whenever your program needs a variable that's private to a subroutine, you almost always want a variable declared with my.

Making a Stricter Perl

Perl is a permissive language. It doesn't try to get in your way; it allows you to just get your work done without complaining too much about what your code looks like. However, you can also tell Perl to be a bit more strict about your code. For example, Perl can help you avoid silly mistakes if you use the warning switch on the command line— or on the #! line. Perl warns you when you're using undefined variables, using a variable name only once, and so on.

In large software projects, and as your own programs get larger and larger, it's nice to have Perl help you keep yourself in line. In addition to using the -w switch, you can tell the Perl interpreter at compile time to turn on more warnings. You do so by using use strict:

```
use strict;
sub mysub {
    my $x;
    :
}
mysub();
```

The `use strict` statement is actually something called a *compiler directive*. It tells Perl to flag the following situations as runtime errors that point onward in the current block or file:

- Attempts to use variable names (other than special variables) that are not declared with `my`
- Attempts to use a bare word as a function name when the function definition hasn't been seen yet
- Other potential errors

The `use strict` directive, for now, helps you avoid the last two problems. Having Perl flag variables not declared with `my` prevents you from using a global variable when you actually intend to use a private variable; it's a way of helping you write more self-contained code and not rely on global variables.

The last trap that `use strict` catches is that of bare keywords. Examine this code:

```
$var=value;
```

In this case, do you mean for `value` to be interpreted as a subroutine call, as a string (but you forgot the quotes), or as a variable (but you forgot the type identifier)? Perl's `use strict` directive would note that this code is ambiguous and disallow the syntax, unless the subroutine `value` was already declared before this statement was reached.

From this point on, I will include `use strict` in all the exercises and longer program listings in this book.

Recursion

You will probably run into a special class of subroutines sooner or later. These subroutines actually call themselves in order to do their work. They are called *recursive* subroutines.

Recursive subroutines are used wherever tasks can be broken down into smaller and smaller identical tasks. One example of a recursive task is searching a directory tree for a file. After searching the topmost directory, as subdirectories are found, those directories must be searched. And within those directories, if subdirectories are found, those directories must be searched. You should begin to see a pattern here.

Another recursive task is computing factorials, which are frequently used in statistics. For example, the number of ways the six letters *ABCDEF* can be arranged is 6-factorial, written 6! in mathematics. The factorial of an integer is the product of that integer and all the smaller integers down to 1. So the factorial of 6 is $6 \times 5 \times 4 \times 3 \times 2 \times 1$, or 720, and the factorial of 5 is $5 \times 4 \times 3 \times 2 \times 1$, or 120. Notice that 6! is equal to $6 \times 5!$. So one way to compute the factorial of 6 is to compute the factorial of 5 and multiply that by 6. To compute the factorial of 5, you compute the factorial of 4 and multiply that by 5, and so on. The factorial of 1, on the other hand, is just 1 by the definition. The factorial of 0 is also defined as 1, so that 1! equals $1 \times 0!$ regularly. These facts lead us to a recursive subroutine for computing factorials, which is shown in Listing 8.3.

LISTING 8.3 Factorials

```
1:    sub factorial {
2:        my ($num)=@_;
3:        return(1) if ($num <= 1);
4:        return($num * factorial($num - 1));
5:    }
6:    print factorial(6);
```

Line 2: The argument to the `factorial()` subroutine is copied to `$num`, which is declared private to the subroutine.

Line 3: Every recursive subroutine needs to have a *termination condition*. That is, there needs to be some argument value at which the subroutine no longer calls itself for an answer. Otherwise the subroutine would try to call itself infinitely and never return an answer. For the `factorial()` subroutine, the termination condition is 1-factorial (or 0-factorial); as stated previously, those two values are both 1. The `factorial()` subroutine will execute the `return(1)` when called with 1 or 0 (`$num<=1`).

Line 4: Otherwise, if the argument is not 0 or 1, the factorial of the next smaller sequence must be computed. Observe the following:

If $num is:	Line #4 evaluates as follows:
6	return(6 * factorial(5))
5	return(5 * factorial(4))
4	return(4 * factorial(3))
3	return(3 * factorial(2))
2	return(2 * factorial(1))
1	Line #4 is not reached; `factorial(1)` returns 1.

After the next-smaller factorials are computed (all the way down to 1), the subroutine starts returning values up through the chain of calls until finally 6-factorial can be computed.

Recursive subroutines aren't very common. Large ones are complicated to construct and difficult to debug. Any task that can be done through iteration (using for, while, foreach) can be done with recursion, and any recursive task can be accomplished iteratively. Recursion is usually reserved for a small set of tasks that lend themselves to it easily.

Summary

Perl supports user-definable functions, called subroutines or subs, that behave just like the built-in functions: They can take arguments, do work, and then return values to the caller if necessary. Perl subroutines can call other subroutines and even themselves. Perl also allows you to declare variables private to a subroutine (or any block of code) and create self-contained pieces of code that can then be reused.

Q&A

Q Is there really any difference between using & and not using & when calling a subroutine?

A None that should concern you at this point. A subtle difference does exist between `&foo` and `foo` when subroutine prototypes are used or when a subroutine is called without parentheses. These are topics well beyond the scope of this book, but for the curious, they're documented in the perlsub manual page.

Q When I use `my($var)` in a program, Perl responds with a `syntax error, next 2 tokens my(` message.

A You either have mistyped something or have Perl version 4 installed. Type `perl -v` at a command prompt. If Perl responds with version 4, you should upgrade immediately.

Q How do I pass (or return) functions, filehandles, multiple arrays, or hashes to a subroutine?

A For passing functions, multiple arrays, and hashes, you need to use a reference, which is covered in Hour 13. For passing filehandles to and from a subroutine, you need to use either something called a *typeglob* or the `IO::Handle` module, both of which are beyond the scope of this book.

Q A function I'm using returns many values, but I'm interested in only one. How do I skip some return values?

A One method is to make a literal list out of the function by wrapping the entire function call in parentheses. When it's a list, you can use ordinary list slices to get pieces of the list. The following extracts just the year (current year minus 1900) from the built-in function `localtime`, which actually has nine return values:

```
print "It is now ", 1900+ (localtime)[5];
```

The other method is to assign the return value from the function into a list and simply assign the unwanted values to `undef` or a dummy variable:

```
(undef, undef, undef, undef, undef, $year_offset)=localtime;
```

Workshop

Quiz

Examine the following block of code:

```
sub bar {
    ($a,$b)=@_;
    $b=100;
    $a=$a+1;
}
sub foo {
    my($a)=67;
    local($b)=@_;
    bar($a, $b);
}
foo(5,10)
```

1. After you run `bar($a, $b)`, what is the value in `$b`?

   a. 5

   b. 100

   c. 68

2. What is the return value from `foo()`?

   a. 67

   b. 68

   c. `undef`

3. Inside `foo()`, how is `$b` scoped?

   a. Lexically

   b. Dynamically

   c. Globally

Answers

1. b. `$b` is declared with `local` in `foo()` so that every called subroutine shares the same value for `$b` (unless they later declare `$b` again with `local` or `my`). After calling `bar()`, where `$b` is modified, `$b` is set to 100.

2. b. Surprised? The last statement in `foo()` is `bar($a, $b)`. `bar()` returns 68 because the value of `$a` is passed to `bar()`, and it's incremented. `foo()` returns the value of the last expression, which is 68.

3. b. Variables declared with `local` are called dynamically scoped variables.

Activities

- Use the functions from the statistics exercise in this hour and the word-counting code from Hour 7, "Hashes," to examine the length of the words in a document. Compute their mean, median, and standard deviation.

- Write a function to print part of the Fibonacci series. This series begins 0, 1, 1, 2, 3, 5, 8 and continues forever. The Fibonacci series is a recurring pattern in mathematics and nature. Each successive number is the sum of the previous two (except 0 and 1). These numbers can be computed iteratively or recursively.

Part II
Advanced Features

Hour

HOUR 9

More Functions and Operators

The Perl culture follows the tradition of "There Is More Than One Way To Do It," and in this hour, you will look more closely at that philosophy. You will learn a potpourri of new functions and operators.

For scalar searching and manipulation, you've been using regular expressions until this point. There is more than one way to do the job, so Perl provides a variety of functions for searching and editing scalars. In this hour, some of the other ways will be presented.

Also, you've viewed arrays as linear lists of items to be iterated through with foreach or joined together with join to make scalars. In this hour, you'll learn a whole new way of looking at arrays.

Finally, the plain vanilla print function will be revisited—and spiced up a bit. With a new and improved print function, you too can write nicely formatted reports suitable for presentation to others.

In this hour you'll learn

- How to do simple string searches on scalars
- How to do character substitutions
- How to use the `print` function
- How to use arrays as stacks and queues

Searching Scalars

Regular expressions are nice for searching scalars for patterns, but sometimes they're overkill. In Perl, some overhead—but not much—is involved with assembling the pattern and then searching for the pattern within scalars. Also, you can easily make mistakes when writing regular expressions. Perl provides several functions for searching and extracting simple information from scalars.

Searching with `index`

If you merely want to find one string within another scalar, Perl provides the `index` function. The syntax for `index` is as follows:

```
index string, substring
index string, substring, start_position
```

The `index` function starts at the left of *string* and searches for *substring*. The `index` function returns the position at which *substring* is found, with 0 being the leftmost character. If the *substring* is not found, `index` returns –1. The string to be searched can be a string literal, a scalar, or any expression that returns a string value. The *substring* is not a regular expression; it's just another scalar.

The following are some examples. Remember that you can write Perl's functions and operators with or without parentheses enclosing the arguments.

```
index "Ring around the rosy", "around";     # Returns 5
index("Pocket full of posies", "ket");      # Returns 3
$a="Ashes, ashes, we all fall down";
index($a, "she");                           # Returns 1
index $a, "they";                           # Returns -1 (not found)
@a=qw(oats     peas       beans);
index join(" ", @a), "peas";                # Returns 5
```

Optionally, you can give the `index` function a start position in the string to start searching, as shown in the following example. To start searching at the left, you use the start position of –0.

```
$reindeer="dasher dancer prancer vixen";
index($reindeer, "da");          # Returns 0
index($reindeer, "da", 1);       # Returns 7
```

You also can use the `index` function with a starting position to "walk" through a string and find all the occurrences of a smaller string, as shown here:

```
$source="One fish, two fish, red fish, blue fish.";
$start=-1;
# Use an increasing beginning index, $start, to find all fish
while( ($start=index($source, "fish", $start)) != -1) {
    print "Found a fish at $start\n";
    $start++;
}
```

The preceding example slides through `$source`, as shown here:

Searching Backward with `rindex`

The function `rindex` works the same as `index`, except that the search starts on the right and works its way left. The syntax is as follows:

```
rindex string, substring
rindex string, substring, start_position
```

When the search is exhausted, the `rindex` function returns –1. The following are some examples:

```
$a="She loves you yeah, yeah, yeah.";
rindex($a, "yeah");        # Returns 26.
rindex($a, "yeah", 25);    # Returns 20
```

The walk-through loop used with `index` looks a little different searching backward with `rindex`. The `rindex` start position must start at (or after) the end of the string—`length($source)` in the following example—but still finishes when –1 is returned. After each find, `$start` must be decremented by 1, rather than incremented as it was with `index`.

```
$source="One fish, two fish, red fish, blue fish.";
$start=length($source);
while( ($start = rindex($source, "fish", $start)) != -1) {
    print "Found a fish at $start\n";
    $start--'
}
```

Picking Apart Scalars with `substr`

The `substr` function is often overlooked and easily forgotten, but it provides a general-purpose method for extracting information from scalars and editing scalars. The syntax of `substr` is as follows:

```
substr string, offset
substr string, offset, length
```

The `substr` function takes `string`, starting at position `offset`, and returns the rest of the string from `offset` to the end. If `length` is specified, then `length` characters are taken— or until the end of the string is found, whichever comes first—as shown in this example:

```
#Character positions in $a
#   0         10        20        30
$a="I do not like green eggs and ham.";
print substr($a, 25);      # prints "and ham."
print substr($a, 14, 5);   # prints "green"
```

If the `offset` specified is negative, `substr` starts counting from the right. For example, `substr($a, -5)` returns the last five characters of `$a`. If the `length` specified is negative, `substr` returns from its starting position to the end of the string, less `length` characters, as in this example:

```
print substr($a, 5, -10);    # prints "not like green egg"
```

In the preceding snippet, `substr` starts at position 5 and returns the rest of the string except the last 10 characters.

You can also use the `substr` function on the left side of an assignment expression. When used on the left, `substr` indicates what characters are to be replaced in a scalar. When `substr` is used on the left side of an assignment, the first argument must be an assignable value— such as a scalar variable—and not a string literal. The following is an example of editing a string with `substr`:

```
$a="countrymen, lend me your wallets";
# Replace first character of $a with "Romans, C"
substr($a, 0, 1)="Romans, C";

# Insert "Friends" at the beginning of $a
substr($a, 0, 0)="Friends, ";

substr($a, -7, 7)="ears.";          # Replace last 7 characters.
```

Transliteration, Not Substitution

For this next operator, the *transliteration* operator (sometimes called the *translation* operator), think back to how regular expression substitutions work: The substitution operator, which looks like `s/pattern/replacement/` and was discussed in Hour 6, works against the `$_` variable unless another scalar is specified with a binding operator `=~`. The transliteration operator works something like that, except that it doesn't use regular expressions and works completely differently. Still follow? The syntax for the transliteration operator is as follows:

`tr/searchlist/replacementlist/`

The transliteration operator—`tr///`—searches a string for the elements in `searchlist` and replaces them with the corresponding elements in `replacementlist`. By default, the transliteration operator searches and modifies the variable `$_`. To search and modify other variables, you use a binding operator as you would for regular expression matches, as shown here:

```
tr/ABC/XYZ/;          # In $_, replaces all A's with X's, B's with Y's, etc..
$r=~tr/ABC/XYZ/;      # Does the same, but with $r
```

Logical groups of characters are accepted with dashes between them. For example, `A-Z` represents the capital letters `A` through `Z`, so that you don't have to write them all out, as in this example:

```
tr/A-Z/a-z/;              # Change all uppercase to lowercase
tr/A-Za-z/a-zA-Z/;        # Invert upper and lowercase
```

If `replacementlist` is empty or identical to `searchlist`, the characters matched are counted by `tr///` and returned. The target string is not modified, as in the following example:

```
$eyes=$potato=~tr/i//;    # Count the i's in $potato, return to $eyes
$nums=tr/0-9//;           # Count digits in $_, return to $nums
```

Finally, for historical reasons, `tr///` can also be written as `y///` with the same results, because `y` is a synonym for `tr`. The `tr///` operator (and hence, `y///`) also allows you to specify an alternate set of delimiters for `searchlist` and `replacementlist`. They can be any naturally paired set such as parentheses or any other character, as you can see here:

```
tr(a-z)(n-za-m);          # Rotate all characters 13 to the left in $_
y[,._-][;:=|];            # Switch around some punctuation
```

 The `tr///` operator actually has additional functionality, but it isn't used often. To read about all the other tasks `tr///` can perform, look at the online documentation in the perlop section.

A Better Way to `print`

The `print` function is a very simple output function; it provides almost no formatting capability. To have fine-grained control over the appearance of expression values, such as left and right alignment, number of digits of decimal precision, and fixed-width output, you must use the Perl `printf` function instead.

Formatted Printing with `printf`

The `printf` function was borrowed (almost verbatim) from the C programming language, but other languages have a similar function, such as BASIC's `print using` function. The syntax for `printf` is as follows:

```
printf formatstring, list
printf filehandle formatstring, list
```

The *formatstring* is a string that describes the format of the output, which is described shortly. The *list* is a list of values that you want `printf` to display—somewhat similar to the arguments to the `print` function. Normally, `printf` displays its output to the STDOUT filehandle, but, as with `print`, if you specify a filehandle, `printf` uses that filehandle instead. Note that no comma is used between the *filehandle* name and the *formatstring*.

Specifying the Field Formats

The *formatstring* is a string literal (usually) or a scalar that describes what the output should look like. Every character in the *formatstring* is printed literally, except those character sequences beginning with a %. The % indicates the start of a *field specifier*. The format of a field specifier is shown here:

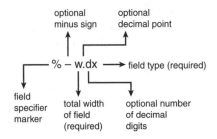

As seen in the figure, field specifiers have the form %-*w.dx*, where *w* is the total desired width of the field. *d* is the number of positions to the right of the decimal point (for numbers) and the total allowable width of the field (for strings). *x* indicates what kind of data is to be printed. A minus sign (a hyphen) before the *w* specifier indicates that the field is to be left-justified within *w* characters; otherwise, it's right-justified. Only the % and *x* are mandatory. Table 9.1 lists some of the different types of field specifiers (that is, values for the x position).

TABLE 9.1 Partial List of *printf* Field Specifier Types

Field Type	Meaning
c	Character
s	String
d	Decimal integer; fraction is truncated
f	Floating-point number

A full list of field specifier types is included in the online manual. You can view it by typing **perldoc -f printf** at a command prompt.

The following are some examples of using printf:

```
printf("%20s", "Jack");       # Right-justify "Jack" in 20-characters
printf("%-20s", "Jill");      # Left-justify "Jill" in 20 characters
$amt=7.12;
printf("%6.2f", $amt);        # prints "  7.12"
$amt=7.127;
printf("%6.2f", $amt);        # prints "  7.13", extra digits rounded
printf("%c", 65);             # prints ASCII character for 65, "A"
$amt=9.4;
printf("%6.2f", $amt);        # prints "  9.40"

printf("%6d", $amt);          # prints "     9"
```

Each field specifier uses one item from the list, as shown in the figure below. For each item, there should be a field specifier; for every field specifier, there should be a list element.

print f ("Totals: %6.2f %15s %7.2f %6d", $a $b $c $d);

To print leading zeros in a number, simply put a 0 in front of the width in the field specifier, as follows:

```
printf("%06.2f", $amt);   # prints "009.40"
```

What if you want a literal percent sign in your output? The sequence %% represents a percent sign:

```
$newprice = 1.449;
$oldprice = 1.229;
printf("The price went up by %3.1f%%!\n", 100*(($newprice/$oldprice) - 1));
#    prints "The price went up by 17.9%!"
```

9

Formatted Output to a String

The `sprintf` function is nearly identical to `printf`, except that instead of being printed, the formatted output is returned from `sprintf`—ready for you to assign to a scalar or use in another expression, as you can see here:

```
$weight=85;
# Format result nicely to 2-decimals
$moonweight = sprintf("%.2f", $weight / 6);
print "You weigh $moonweight on the moon.";
```

Remember that `printf` and `sprintf` with the `%f` format specifier will round your results to the specified number of decimal places for you.

Exercise: A Formatted Report

A task that comes up inevitably when you're dealing with computers is formatting raw data into a report. Computer programs exchange data in formats that are difficult for humans to read, and a common task is taking that data and formatting it into a human-friendly report.

For this exercise, you're given a set of employee records that contain information about some mythical employees, including hourly wages, number of hours worked, names, and employee numbers. The exercise takes that data and reformats it into a nice report.

You can easily modify this same kind of program to print other kinds of reports. The data for the exercise is contained within an array initialized at the beginning of the program. In a real report, the data would probably come from a file on disk. Modifying this exercise to use an external file is left as an exercise for later.

Using your text editor, type the program from Listing 9.1 and save it as `Employee`. Do not type the line numbers. Make the program executable according to the instructions you learned in Hour 1, "Introduction to the Perl Language."

When you're all done, try running the program by typing the following at a command line:

Employee

or, if you cannot make the program executable,

perl Employee

LISTING 9.1 Complete Listing of Employee Program

```
1:   #!/usr/bin/perl -w
2:
3:   use strict;
4:
5:   my @employees = (
6:       'Smith,Bob,123101,9.35,40',
7:       'Franklin,Alice,132912,10.15,35',
8:       'Wojohowicz,Ted,198131,6.50,39',
9:       'Ng,Wendy,141512,9.50,40',
10:      'Cliburn,Stan,131211,11.25,40',
11:  );
12:
13:  sub print_emp {
14:      my($last,$first,$emp,$hourly,$time)=
15:          split(',', $_[0]);
16:      my $fullname;
17:      $fullname = sprintf("%s %s", $first, $last);
18:      printf("%6d %-20s %6.2f %3d %7.2f\n",
19:          $emp, $fullname, $hourly, $time,
20:          ($hourly * $time) + .005 );
21:  }
22:
23:  @employees = sort {
24:      my ($L1, $F1)=split(',', $a);
25:      my ($L2, $F2)=split(',', $b);
26:      return( $L1 cmp $L2   # Compare last names
27:          ||    # If they're the same...
28:          $F1 cmp $F2   # Compare first
29:          );
30:  } @employees;
31:
32:  foreach (@employees) {
33:      print_emp($_);
34:  }
```

Line 1: This line contains the path to the interpreter (you can change it so that it's appropriate to your system) and the -w switch. Always have warnings enabled!

Line 3: The use strict directive means that all variables must be declared with my and that bare words must be quoted.

Lines 5–11: The list of employees is assigned to @employees. Each element in the array consists of a last name, first name, employee number, hourly wage, and number of hours worked.

Lines 23–30: The @employees array is sorted by last name and first name.

Line 24: The first element to be sorted ($a) is split apart into fields. The last name is assigned to $L1 and the first name to $F1. Both of these are declared private to the sort block with my.

Line 25: The same is done with another element, $b. The names are assigned to $L2 and $F2.

Line 26–29: The names are compared alphabetically using something similar to the sort shown in Listing 4.1 in Hour 4, "Stacking Building Blocks: Lists and Arrays."

Lines 32–24: The sorted list in @employees is passed, one element at a time, to print_emp().

Lines 13–21: The print_emp() function prints the employee records nicely formatted.

Lines 14–15: The passed-in record—in $_[0]—is split into fields and assigned to variables—$last, $first, and so on—which are all private to this subroutine. Remember, $_[0] represents the first argument passed to a function — the first element of @_.

Line 17: The last name and first name are combined into a single field so that the two fields can be padded to a certain width and justified together.

Lines 18–20: The record is printed. $hours and $time are multiplied to give the total amount earned. The amount .005 is added to the total so that, when the product is truncated to two digits, it's properly rounded.

Listing 9.2 shows a sample of the Employee program's output.

LISTING 9.2 Output from the Employee Program

```
131211 Stan Cliburn      11.25  40  450.00
132912 Alice Franklin    10.15  35  355.25
141512 Wendy Ng           9.50  40  380.00
123101 Bob Smith          9.35  40  374.00
198131 Ted Wojohowicz     6.50  39  253.50
```

New Ways with Arrays

In the following section, we will discuss a set of array functions that make several powerful data structures possible in Perl.

A List as a Stack

Until now, lists (and arrays) have been presented as linear arrangements of data with indexes that make it possible to access each element, as shown here:

0	1	2	3	4	5
Apple	Peach	Pear	Plum	Mango	Guava

Use your imagination for a moment and imagine the array elements piled up vertically with the element having the highest index at the top, as shown here:

Guava
Mango
Plum
Pear
Peach
Apple

Notice that there are no index numbers in this figure. The reason is that the functions we will discuss here are concerned with only the top and the bottom of the array, not with anything in the middle. In computer terminology, this list is called a *stack*. Stacks are useful for accumulating tasks that you want processed in order. A good example is a game of Klondike solitaire (like the Solitaire game often installed with Windows). Each of the seven piles of cards represents a stack. Initially, cards are placed onto the stack face down. As they are needed, they are turned over and removed from the top of the stack, or additional cards can be placed on top of the newly turned-over cards, but cards cannot be removed or inserted in the middle of the stack or at the bottom.

Stacks in Perl are (usually) implemented with arrays. To place items on top of a stack, you use the push function. To remove from the top of the stack, you use the pop function.

A stack implemented as a Perl array can also be modified from the bottom, like dealing from the bottom of the deck of cards. The shift function removes elements from the bottom, and unshift adds elements to the bottom of the stack. All four operations are shown here:

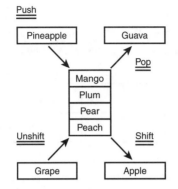

The syntax for each function is as follows:

```
pop target_array
```

```
shift target_array
```

```
unshift target_array, new_list
```

```
push target_array, new_list
```

The pop and shift functions each remove one element from the *target_array*. If the *target_array* isn't specified, an element is removed from either @_ (inside a subroutine) or @ARGV (in the main body of the program). The pop and shift functions return the element removed, or undef if the array is empty. The size of the array shrinks accordingly.

> Inside a subroutine the pop, shift, unshift and push functions will modify @_ if no other array is specified. Outside a subroutine, in the main body of your program, these functions will modify the array @ARGV if no other array is specified.

The push and unshift functions add the elements of *new_list* to the *target_array*; the size of the array grows to accommodate the new elements. An item to be pushed or unshifted onto the *target_array* can either be a list or a scalar, as in the following example:

```
@band = qw(trombone);
push @band, qw( ukulele clarinet );
# @band now contains trombone, ukulele, clarinet

$brass=shift @band;    # $brass now has "trombone",
$wind=pop @band;       # $wind now has "clarinet"
```

```
# @band now contains only "ukulele"
unshift @band, "harmonica";
# @band now contains harmonica, ukulele
```

 When you're adding elements to an array, pushing (or shifting) elements into the array is much more efficient than adding to the end of the array manually. For example, push(@list, @newitems) is more efficient than @list=(@list, @newitems). Perl's push, shift, unshift, and pop functions are all optimized for these kinds of manipulations.

The array elements in a "stack" are still just normal array elements and can be addressed with indexes. The "bottom" of the stack is element 0, and the "top" of the stack is the last element in the array.

If you use push to add elements to the array and pop to remove them, or if you use unshift to add elements and shift to remove them, you get the elements out in reverse order from the way they went in. This is what computer textbooks usually mean by the word *stack*. You can get elements out in the same order they went in if you use unshift to add elements and pop to remove them, or if you use push to add elements and shift to remove them. Such a list is called a *queue* in computer textbooks.

Splicing Arrays

So far, you've learned that arrays can by addressed by element, sliced, shifted, popped, unshifted, and pushed. The last tool for array manipulation is splice. The syntax for splice is as follows:

```
splice array, offset
splice array, offset, length
splice array, offset, length, list
```

The splice function removes elements from *array* starting at *offset*, and a list of the removed array elements is returned. Negative values of *offset* cause the element counting to begin at the end of the array. If *length* is specified, only *length* elements are removed. If *list* is specified, then *length* elements are removed and replaced with the elements of *list*. Through this process, the array grows or shrinks as necessary, as you can see here:

```
@veg=qw( carrots corn );
splice(@veg, 0, 1);                     # @veg is corn
splice(@veg, 0, 0, qw(peas));           # @veg is peas, corn
splice(@veg, -1, 1, qw(barley, turnip)); # @veg is peas, barley, turnip
splice(@veg, 1, 1);                     # @veg is peas, turnip
```

Summary

In this hour, you learned that searching for strings within other strings doesn't have to involve regular expressions; you can perform simple searches by using `index` and `rindex`. You also can make simple substitutions by using the `tr///` operator. The `substr` function can be used for both extracting data from strings and editing them. You can create nicely formatted output in Perl by using the `printf` and `sprintf` statements. Additionally, you saw arrays used as stacks of items instead of flat lists, and you learned how to manipulate those stacks.

Q&A

Q   Are `substr`, `index`, and `rindex` really necessary? Why do they exist when regular expressions can be used for most of those operations?

A   First, regular expressions for simple string searches are generally slower than `index` and `rindex`. Second, writing substitution expressions for fixed character positions with regular expressions can be messy; `substr` is a much more elegant solution sometimes. Third, Perl is a rich language. Use what you like; you have plenty of choices.

Q   What happens with `substr` (or `index` or `rindex`) if I specify an index that's beyond the end of the scalar?

A   One nice thing about computers is that they're consistent and have limitless amounts of patience. With questions like "What happens if I...?" sometimes just trying it is easiest! What's the worst that can happen?

In this case, accessing a portion of a scalar that doesn't exist might cause a `use of undefined value` error if you have warnings enabled, as you should. For example, if you use `$a="Foo"; substr($a, 5);`, the `substr` function returns `undef`.

Workshop

Quiz

1. Given the following code, what's left in `@A` afterward:

```
@A=qw(oats peas beans);
shift @A;
push @A, "barley";
pop;
```

   a. `oats peas beans`

   b. `beans barley`

   c. `peas beans barley`

2. What does `printf("%18.3f", $a)` do?

   a. It prints a floating-point number that is 18 characters wide: 15 to the left and 3 to the right of the decimal point.

   b. It prints a floating-point number 18 characters to the left of the decimal, a decimal point, and then 3 more digits.

   c. It prints a floating-point number that is 18 characters wide, 14 to the left and 3 to the right of the decimal point.

3. If `tr/a-z/A-Z/` is run against a string, will `tr/A-Z/a-z/` restore the string to its original form?

   a. Yes, of course

   b. Probably not

9

Answers

1. c. The `shift` removed `oats`, and the `push` added `barley` to the end. The final `pop` was a ruse: No array was specified, so it popped something from the array `@_` or from `@ARGV`, which causes nothing to happen to `@A`.

2. c. If you guessed a, you didn't count the decimal point, which occupies a position in the total (18=14+1+3).

3. b. The string `"Rosebud"` transformed by `tr/a-z/A-Z/` becomes `"ROSEBUD"`. Trying to transform it back with `tr/A-Z/a-z/` yields `"rosebud"`—not the original string.

Activities

- Rewrite the Hangman game from Hour 4 to use scalars instead of arrays. You can use `substr` to manipulate individual characters in the scalars.

- Modify Listing 9.2 to read from a file instead of getting data from an array. Open the file, read the data into an array, and continue as normal. You will have to create the file on disk, of course.

HOUR **10**

Files and Directories

Files in your operating system provide a convenient set of storage concepts for data. The OS enables a name to be given to the data (a filename) and provides an organizational structure, called a *file system,* so that you can find the data later. Your computer's file system then organizes files into groups called *directories*—sometimes called *folders*. These directories can store files or other directories.

This nesting of directories inside directories provides a treelike structure to the file system on your computer. Each file is part of a directory, and each directory is part of a parent directory. In addition to providing an organizational structure for your files, the operating system also stores data about the file: when the file was last read, when it was last modified, who created it, the current size of the file, and so on—called metadata (see Hour 5, "Working with Files"). This organization is true of almost all modern computer operating systems.

In the case of the Macintosh, this structure still holds true, except that the top-level directory is called a volume, and the subdirectories area is called Folders.

Perl allows you to access this structure, modify the organization, and examine the information about the files. The functions that Perl uses for these tasks are all derived from the Unix operating system, but they work just fine under whatever operating system Perl happens to be running on. Perl's file system manipulation functions are portable, meaning that if you use Perl's functions to manipulate your files and query them, you should have no problems running your code under any operating system Perl supports, providing that the directories are structured similarly.

In this hour you'll learn

- How to get a directory listing
- How to create and remove files
- How to create and remove directories
- How to get information about files

Getting a Directory Listing

The first step in obtaining directory information from your system is to create a *directory handle*. A directory handle is something like a filehandle, except that instead of a file's contents, you read the contents of a directory through the directory handle. To open a directory handle, you use the `opendir` function:

```
opendir dirhandle, directory
```

In this syntax, `dirhandle` is the directory handle you want to open and `directory` is the name of the directory you want to read. If the directory handle cannot be opened—because you don't have permission to read the directory, the directory doesn't exist, or some other reason—the `opendir` function returns false. Directory handle variable names should be constructed similarly to filehandles—using the rules for variable names outlined in Hour 2, "Perl's Building Blocks: Numbers and Strings"—and, like filehandles, they should be all uppercase to avoid conflicts with Perl's keywords. The following is an example:

```
opendir(TEMPDIR, '/tmp') || die "Cannot open /tmp: $!";
```

All the examples in this hour use forward slashes (/) in the Unix style because it is less confusing than the backslashes (\) used by Windows and MSDOS and works just as well with those operating systems as with Unix.

Now that the directory handle is open, you use the `readdir` function to read it:

```
readdir dirhandle;
```

In a scalar context, `readdir` returns the next entry in the directory, or `undef` if none are left. In a list context, `readdir` returns all the (remaining) directory entries. The names returned by `readdir` include files, directories, and (for Unix) special files; they are returned in no particular order. The directory entries . and .. (representing the current directory and its parent directory) are also returned by `readdir`. The directory entries returned by `readdir` do not include the pathname as part of the name returned.

When you're done with the directory handle, you should close it by using `closedir`:

```
closedir dirhandle;
```

The following example shows how to read a directory:

```
opendir(TEMP, '/tmp') || die "Cannot open /tmp: $!";
@FILES=readdir TEMP;
closedir(TEMP);
```

In this preceding snippet, the entire directory is read into @FILES. Most of the time, however, you're not interested in the . and .. files. To read the filehandle and eliminate those files, you can enter the following:

```
@FILES=grep(!/^\.\.?}$/, readdir TEMP);
```

The regular expression (`/^\.\.?$/`) matches a leading literal dot (or two) that's also at the end of the line, and `grep` eliminates them. To get all the files with a particular extension, you use the following:

```
@FILES=grep(/\.txt$/i, readdir TEMP);
```

The filenames returned by `readdir` do not contain the pathname used by `opendir`. Thus, the following example will probably not work:

```
opendir(TD, "/tmp") || die "Cannot open /tmp: $!";
while($file = readdir TD) {
    # The following is WRONG
    open(FILEH, $file) || die "Cannot open $file: $!\n";
    :
}
closedir(TD);
```

Unless you happen to be working in the /tmp directory when you run this code, the `open(FILEH, $file)` statement will fail. For example, if the file myfile.txt exists in /tmp, `readdir` returns myfile.txt. When you open myfile.txt, you actually need to open /tmp/myfile.txt using the full pathname. The corrected code is as follows:

```
opendir(TD, "/tmp") || die "Cannot open /tmp: $!";
while($file=readdir TD) {
    # Right!
    open(FILEH, "/tmp/$file") || die "Cannot open $file: $!\n";
    :
}
closedir(TD);
```

10

Globbing

The other method of reading the names of files in a directory is called *globbing*. If you're familiar with the command prompt in MS-DOS, you know that the command `dir *.txt` prints a directory listing of all the files that end in .txt. In Unix, the globbing (sometimes called wildcard matching) is done by the shell, but `ls *.txt` has nearly the same result: The files whose names end in `.txt` are listed.

Perl has an operator for doing just this job; it's called `glob`. The syntax for `glob` is

glob *pattern*

where *pattern* is the filename pattern you want to match. The *pattern* can contain directory names and portions of filenames. In addition, the *pattern* can contain any of the special characters listed in Table 10.1. In a list context, `glob` returns all the files (and directories) that match the pattern. In a scalar context, the files are returned one at a time each time `glob` is queried.

> Glob patterns are not the same as regular expressions.

TABLE 10.1   Globbing Patterns

Character	Matches	Example
?	Single character	f?d matches *fud, fid, fdd,* and so on
*	Any number of characters	f*d matches *fd, fdd, food, filled,* and so on
[chars]	Matches any of chars; this feature supported in MacPerl	f[ou]d matches *fod* and *fud* but not *fad*
{a,b,...}	Matches either of the strings *a* or *b*; this feature not supported in MacPerl	f*.{txt,doc} matches files that begin with *f* and that end in either .txt or .doc

> Unix fans, please note: Perl's `glob` operator uses C shell-style file globbing, as opposed to Bourne (or Korn) shell file globbing. This is true on any Unix system in which Perl is installed, regardless of whatever shell you personally use. The Bourne shell globbing and Korn shell globbing are different from the C shell's. They are very similar in some respects—* and ? behave the same—but quite different in others. Beware.

Now check out these examples of globbing:

```
# All of the .h files in /usr/include
my @hfiles=glob('/usr/include/*.h');
# Text or document files that contain 1999
my @curfiles=glob('*1999*.{txt,doc}')
# Printing a numbered list of filenames
$count=1;
while( $name=glob('*') ) {
    print "$count. $name\n";
    $count++;
}
```

An important difference betwen `glob` and `opendir`/`readdir`/`closedir` is that `glob` returns the pathname used in the pattern, whereas the `opendir`/`readdir`/`closedir` functions do not. For example, `glob('/usr/include/*.h')` returns `'/usr/include'` as part of any matches; `readdir` does not.

So which should you use? It's completely up to you. However, using the `opendir`/`readdir`/`closedir` functions tends to be a much more flexible solution and will be used in most of the examples throughout this book.

Perl offers an alternative way to write pattern globs. Simply placing the pattern inside the angle operator (`<>`) makes the angle operator behave like `glob`:

```
@cfiles = <*.c>;  # All files ending in .c
```

The syntax that uses the angle operator for globbing is older and can be confusing. In this book, I will continue to use the `glob` operator instead for clarity.

Exercise: The Unix `grep`

As you get further along in this book, the exercises will present you with more and more useful tools. This exercise presents a stripped-down version of the Unix `grep` utility. The Unix `grep`—not to be confused with Perl's `grep` function, introduced in Hour 6, "Pattern Matching"—searches files for patterns. This exercise presents a utility that will prompt for a directory name and a pattern. Every file in that directory will be searched for that pattern, and lines matching that pattern will be printed.

In future exercises, this utility will be modified to search subdirectories (Hour 15, "Finding Permanence") and to take command-line arguments (Hour 12, "Using Perl's Command-Line Tools"). Stay tuned for details.

Using your text editor, type the program from Listing 10.1 and save it as `mygrep`. If possible, be sure to make the program executable according to the instructions you learned in Hour 1, "Introduction to the Perl Language." Also, make sure that you don't rename this file to grep on a Unix system, because it could be mistaken for the real grep utility.

When you're all done, try running the program by typing the following at a command line:

perl -w mygrep

or, if your system enables you to make the file executable,

mygrep

LISTING 10.1   Complete Listing for *mygrep*

```
1:    #!/usr/bin/perl -w
2:
3:    use strict;
4:
5:    print "Directory to search: ";
6:    my $dir=<STDIN>; chomp $dir;
7:    print "Pattern to look for: ";
8:    my $pat=<STDIN>; chomp $pat;
9:
10:   my($file);
11:
12:   opendir(DH, $dir) || die "Cannot open $dir: $!";
13:   while ($file=readdir DH) {
14:       next if (-d "$dir/$file");
15:       if (! open(F, "$dir/$file") ) {
16:           warn "Cannot search $file: $!";
17:           next;
18:       }
19:       while(<F>) {
20:           if (/$pat/) {
21:               print "$file: $_";
22:           }
23:       }
24:       close(F);
25:   }
26:   closedir(DH);
```

Line 1: This line contains the path to the interpreter (you can change it so that it's appropriate to your system) and the -w switch. Always have warnings enabled!

Line 3: The use strict directive means that all variables must be declared with my and that bare words must be quoted.

Lines 5–8: $dir, the directory to be searched, and $pat, the pattern to search for, are retrieved from STDIN. The newlines at the end of each are removed.

Line 10: $file is declared as private to satisfy use strict. $file is used later in this program.

Line 12: The directory $dir is opened; an error message is printed if this operation fails.

Line 13: The entries are retrieved from the directory one at a time and stored in $file.

Line 14: Any directory entry that's really a directory itself (-d)is rejected. Notice that the pathname checked is $dir/$file. This path must be checked because $file doesn't necessarily exist in the current directory; it exists in $dir. So the full path-name to the file is $dir/$file.

Lines 15–18: The file is opened, again using the full pathname $dir/$file, and rejected if it does not open.

Lines 19–23: The file is searched, line by line, for a line that contains $pat. A match-ing line is printed.

Listing 10.2 shows a sample of the mygrep program's output.

LISTING 10.2 Output from *mygrep*

```
Directory to search: /home/clintp
Pattern to look for: printer
mailbox: lot of luck re-inking Epson printer ribbons with
config.pl: # the following allows the user to pick a printer for
```

Directories

Thus far in this hour, I've been sort of handwaving over the topic of directory structure. Full pathnames are sometimes needed to open files, and the readdir function can read directories. But actually navigating directories, adding or removing them, and cleaning them out takes a little bit more Perl.

Navigating Directories

When you run software, your operating system keeps track of what directory you're in when you run the software. When you log in to a Unix machine and run a software package, you are usually placed in your home directory. If you type the operating system command pwd, the shell shows you what directory you are in. If you use MS-DOS or Windows and open a *command prompt,* the prompt reflects what directory you are in at the time—for example, C:\WINDOWS. Alternatively, you can type the operating system command cd at the MS-DOS prompt, and MS-DOS tells you what directory you are in. The directory that you're cur-rently using is called your *current directory* or your *current working directory.*

If you're using a program editor or an integrated editor/debugger and running your Perl programs directly from there, your "current directory" might not be what you think. It might be the directory that the Perl program is in, the directory your editor is in, or any other directory—it depends on your editor. Use the cwd function below from inside your Perl program to determine exactly where your current directory is.

If you do not specify a full pathname when you try to open a file—for example, open(FH, "file") || die —Perl will attempt to open the file in your current working directory. To change your current directory, you can use the Perl chdir function, as follows:

```
chdir newdir;
```

The chdir function changes the current working directory to *newdir*. If the *newdir* directory does not exist, or you don't have permission to access *newdir*, chdir returns false. The directory change from chdir is temporary; as soon as your Perl program ends, you return to the directory that you were working in before you ran the Perl program.

Running the chdir function without a directory as an argument causes chdir to change to your home directory. On a Unix system, the home directory is usually the directory that you were placed in when you logged in. On a Windows 95, Windows NT, or MS-DOS machine, chdir takes you to the directory indicated in the HOME environment variable. If HOME isn't set, chdir doesn't change your current directory at all.

Perl doesn't have a built-in function for figuring out what your current directory is—because of the way some operating systems are written, it's not easy to tell. To find the current directory, you must use two statements together. Somewhere in your program—preferably near the beginning—you must use the statement use Cwd and then, when you want to retrieve the current directory, use the cwd function:

```
use Cwd;

print "Your current directory is: ", cwd, "\n";
chdir '/tmp' or warn "Directory /tmp not accessible: $!";
print "You are now in: ", cwd, "\n";
```

You have to execute the use Cwd statement only once; afterward, you can use the cwd function as often as necessary.

The statement use Cwd actually instructs Perl to load a module called Cwd that extends the Perl language with new functions, such as cwd. If the preceding snippet returns an error saying Can't locate Cwd.pm in @INC, or you don't understand modules completely, don't worry about it right now. Modules will be fully discussed in Hour 14, "Using Modules."

Creating and Removing Directories

To create a new directory, you can use the Perl mkdir function. The mkdir function's syntax is as follows:

```
mkdir newdir, permissions;
```

The mkdir function returns true if the directory newdir can be created. Otherwise, it returns false and sets $! to the reason that mkdir failed. The permissions are really important only on Unix implementations of Perl, but they must be present on all versions. For the following example, use the value 0755; this value will be explained in the section "Unix Stuff" later in this hour. For MS-DOS and Windows users, just use the value 0755; it's good enough and will spare you a long explanation.

```
print "Directory to create?";
my $newdir=<STDIN>;
chomp $newdir;
mkdir( $newdir, 0755 ) || die "Failed to create $newdir: $!";
```

To remove a directory, you use the rmdir function. The syntax for rmdir is as follows:

```
rmdir pathname;
```

The rmdir function returns true if the directory pathname can be removed. If pathname cannot be removed, rmdir returns false and sets $! to the reason that rmdir failed, as shown here:

```
print "Directory to be removed?";
my $baddir=<STDIN>;
chomp $baddir;
rmdir($baddir) || die "Failed to remove $baddir: $!";
```

The rmdir function removes only directories that are completely empty. This means that before a directory can be removed, all the files and subdirectories must be removed first.

Removing Files

To remove files from a directory, you use the unlink function:

```
unlink list_of_files;
```

The `unlink` function removes all the files in the *list_of_files* and returns the number of files removed. If *list_of_files* is omitted, the filename named in $_ is removed. Consider this example:

```
"glob("*.bat")";
$erased=unlink 'old.exe', 'a.out', 'personal.txt';
unlink @badfiles;
unlink;      # Removes the filename in $_
```

To check whether the list of files was removed, you must compare the number of files you tried to remove with the number of files removed, as in this example:

```
"glob("*.txt")";
my $erased=unlink @files;

# Compare actual erased number, to original number
if ($erased != @files) {
    print "Files failed to erase: ",
        join(',', <*.txt>), "\n";
}
```

In the preceding snippet, the number of files actually erased by `unlink` is stored in $erased. After the `unlink`, $erased is compared to the number of elements in @files: They should be the same. If they're not, an error message is printed showing the "leftover" files.

> Files erased with `unlink` are irrevocably erased. There is no recovery, and they are not moved to a "trash" or "recycle bin." Be careful with `unlink`!

Renaming Files

Renaming files or directories in Perl is simple; you use the `rename` function, as follows:

```
rename oldname, newname;
```

The `rename` function takes the file named *oldname*, tries to change its name to *newname*, and returns true if the rename is successful. If the *oldname* and *newname* are directories, those directories are renamed. If the rename is unsuccessful, `rename` returns false and sets $! to the reason why, as shown here:

```
if (! rename "myfile.txt", "archive.txt") {
    warn "Could not rename myfile.txt: $!";
}
```

The `rename` function also moves the file from one directory to another if you specify full pathnames instead of just filenames, as in this example:

```
rename "myfile.txt", "/tmp/myfile.txt";   # Effectively it moves the file.
```

If the file *newname* already exists, it is destroyed.

The `rename` function will not move files from one directory to another if they're on different file systems.

Unix Stuff

This portion of the hour is primarily for the users of Perl who are working under the Unix operating system. If you don't use Perl on a Unix system, you can safely skip this section and not miss anything important; you can read it if you're curious about Unix, however.

Unix users should know that Perl has a deep Unix heritage, and some Perl functions come right from Unix commands and operating system functions. Most of these functions you will not use. Some functions—like `unlink`—come from Unix but have meanings that are not really tied to Unix at all. Every operating system deletes files, and Perl ensures that `unlink` does the right thing on every operating system. Perl makes a great effort to ensure that concepts—such as file I/O—that should be portable between operating systems actually are portable, and it hides all the compatibility issues from you if it can.

The fact that many Unix functions and commands are embedded in the Perl language—which has been ported to many non-Unix operating systems—is a tribute to the desire of Unix developers and administrators to take a little bit of the Unix toolkit with them wherever they go.

As the next section header suggests, this description is not to be taken as a full explanation of Unix file system permissions and how to manipulate them. For a full explanation, consult your operating system's documentation or any good book on Unix, such as *Sams Teach Yourself UNIX in 24 Hours*.

A Crash Course in File Permissions

In Hour 1, to make a Perl program run as though it were a regular command, you were given the command `chmod 755 scriptname` without any real explanation of what it meant. First of all, `chmod` is a command in Unix that sets the permissions on files. Next, the `755` is a description of the permissions being given to the file `scriptname`. Each of the three digits represents one set of permissions, given to the owner of the file, the group that the file belongs to, and any nonowner and nongroup—called other—user. In this case, the owner has permission `7`, whereas the group and others have permission `5`, as shown next.

```
      7   5   5
     /    |    \
  owner group other
```

Table 10.2 lists the possible values of the digit for each possible combination of permissions.

TABLE 10.2 File Permissions

Permission	Allows that permision group
7	Reading, writing, and executing the file
6	Reading and Writing the file
5	Reading and executing the file
4	Reading the file only
3	Writing and executing the file
2	Writing the file only
1	Executing the file only

To set permissions on a file in Perl, you use the built-in function called chmod:

```
chmod mode, list_of_files;
```

The chmod function changes the permission on all the files in `list_of_files` and returns the number of files whose permissions were changed. The *mode* must be a four-digit number beginning with 0 (because it's a literal octal number, as mentioned in Hour 2 and later in this hour) followed by the digits that you want to indicate permission. The following are some examples of chmod. Note that R stands for read permission, W for write permission, and X for execute permission:

```
chmod 0755, 'file.pl';      # Grants RWX to owner, RX to group and non-owners
chmod 0644, 'mydata.txt';   # Grants RW to owner, and R to group and non-owners
chmod 0777, 'script.pl';    # Grants RWX to everyone (usually, not very smart)
chmod 0000, 'cia.dat';      # Nobody can do anything with this file
```

Earlier this hour, you learned about the mkdir function. The first argument of mkdir is a file permission—the same kind that chmod uses:

```
mkdir "/usr/tmp", 0777;   # Publicly readable/writable/executable
mkdir "myfiles", 0700;    # A very private directory
```

The permissions on a Unix file are often called its *mode*. So chmod is simply short for "change mode."

Everything You Ever Wanted to Know About THAT File

To find out, in excruciating detail, everything you might want to know about a file, you can use Perl's `stat` function. The `stat` function originated in Unix, and the return values differ slightly between Unix and non-Unix systems. The syntax for `stat` is as follows:

```
stat filehandle;
stat filename;
```

The `stat` function can retrieve information either about an open filehandle or about a particular file. Under any operating system, `stat` returns a 13-element list describing the attributes of the file. The actual values in the list differ slightly depending on which operating system you're running, because some operating systems include features that others do not implement. Table 10.3 shows what each element in `stat`'s return value stands for.

TABLE 10.3   Return Values from `stat`

Index	Name	Unix	Windows
0	dev	Device number	Drive number (C: is usually 2, D: is usually 3, and so on)
1	ino	Inode number	Zero, always
2	mode	File's mode (permissions)	Not relevant
3	nlink	Number of links	Usually 0; Windows NT; file system might allow links
4	uid	User ID (UID) of the owner	Zero, always
5	gid	Group ID (GID) of the owner	Zero, always
6	rdev	Special file info	Drive number (again)
7	size	Size of file in bytes	Size of file in bytes bytes
8	atime	Time of last access	Time of last access
9	mtime	Time of last modification	Time of last modification
10	ctime	Inode change time	File creation time
11	blksz	Disk block size	Zero, always
12	blocks	Number of blocks in file	Zero, always

10

Many of the values in Table 10.3 you will probably never use, but they are presented for completeness. For the more obscure values—especially in the Unix return values—you might want to consult your operating system's reference manual.

The following is an example of using `stat` on a file:

```
@stuff=stat "myfile";
```

Normally, the returned values from `stat` are copied into an assignable list of scalars for clarity:

```
($dev, $ino, $mode, $nlink, $uid, $gid, $rdev, $size,
$atime, $mtime, $ctime, $blksize, $blocks)=stat("myfile");
```

To print the permissions for a file in the three-digit form described in the section "A Crash Course in File Permissions," you use this bit of code, where `@stuff` contains the permissions:

```
printf "%04o\n", $mode&0777;
```

The preceding snippet contains elements you might not understand. That's okay; some of it has not been presented to you yet. The permissions as they're retrieved by `stat`—in `$mode` in this case—contain lots of "extra" information. The `&0777` strips out just the portion of the information you're interested in here. Finally, `%o` is a `printf` format that prints numbers in octal—the 0–7 form in which Unix expects permissions to be formatted.

> *Octal* is a base-8 representation of numbers. It's used in Unix for largely historical reasons, but it came along with Perl anyway. If you're still lost, don't panic. Just use the `printf` shown previously if you ever need to display a file's permissions. It doesn't happen that often; don't worry if you don't quite get that part.

The three time stamps mentioned in Table 10.3—access, modification, and change (or create) time—are stored in a peculiar format. The time stamps are stored as the number of seconds from midnight, January 1, 1970, Greenwich mean time. To print them in a usable format, you use the `localtime` function, as follows:

```
print scalar localtime($mtime);
```

This function prints the modification time of the file in a format similar to `Sat Jul 3 23:35:11 EDT 1999`. The access time is the time that the file was last read (or opened for reading). The modification time is the time when the file was last written to. Under Unix, the "change" time is the time when the information about the file—the ownership, number of links, permissions, and so on—was changed; it is not the creation time of the file but often happens to be by coincidence. Under Microsoft Windows, the `ctime` field actually stores the time the file was created.

Sometimes you might be interested in retrieving just one value from the list returned by `stat`. To do so, you can wrap the entire `stat` function in parentheses and use subscripts to slice out the values you want from it:

```
print "The file has", (stat("file"))[7], " bytes of data";
```

Exercise: Renaming Files En Masse

This exercise will provide another (small) tool for your toolkit. This utility allows you to rename files given a directory name, a pattern to look for, and a pattern to change it to. For example, if a directory contains the filenames Chapter_01.rtf, Chapter_02.rtf, Chapter_04.rtf, and so on, you could rename all the files to Hour_01.rtf, Hour_02.rtf, Hour_04.rtf, and so on. This task normally isn't easy at a command prompt and just silly when you're using a GUI-based file browser.

Using your text editor, type the program from Listing 10.3 and save it as `Renamer`. If you can, be sure to make the program executable according to the instructions you learned in Hour 1.

When you're done, try running the program by typing the following at a command line:

perl -w Renamer

or, if you could make the program executable,

Renamer

Listing 10.4 shows some sample output from this program.

LISTING 10.3 Complete Listing for *Renamer*

```
1:    #!/usr/bin/perl -w
2:
3:    use strict;
4:
5:    my($dir, $oldpat, $newpat);
6:    print "Directory: ";
7:    chomp($dir=<STDIN>);
8:    print "Old pattern: ";
9:    chomp($oldpat=<STDIN>);
10:   print "New pattern: ";
11:   chomp($newpat=<STDIN>);
12:
```

continues

LISTING 10.3   Continued

```
13:   opendir(DH, $dir) || die "Cannot open $dir: $!";
14:   my @files=readdir DH;
15:   close(DH);
16:   my $oldname;
17:   foreach(@files) {
18:       $oldname=$_;
19:       s/$oldpat/$newpat/;
20:       next if (-e "$dir/$_");
21:       if (! rename "$dir/$oldname", "$dir/$_") {
22:           warn "Could not rename $oldname to $_: $!"
23:       } else {
24:           print "File $oldname renamed to $_\n";
25:       }
26:   }
```

Lines 13–15: The entries in the directory indicated by `$dir` are read into `@files`.

Lines 17–19: Each file from `@files` is assigned to `$_` and that name is saved in `$oldname`. The original filename in `$_` is then changed to the new name on line 19.

Line 20: Before renaming the file, this line makes sure the target filename doesn't already exist. Otherwise, the program could rename a file into an existing name—destroying the original data.

Lines 21–25: The file is renamed, and warnings are printed if the rename fails. Notice that the original directory name needs to be appended onto the filenames—for example, `$dir/$oldname`—because `@files` doesn't contain full pathnames, which you need for the rename.

LISTING 10.4   Sample Output from *Renamer*

```
Directory: /tmp
Old Pattern: Chapter
New Pattern: Hour
File Chapter_02.rtf renamed to Hour_02.rtf
File Chapter_10.rtf renamed to Hour_10.rtf
```

Summary

This hour you learned how to create, remove, and rename directory entries by using the `mkdir`, `rm`, and `rename` functions in Perl. Also, you learned how to query the file system with `stat` to find out information about files, not just what's in them. During the course of this hour, the two exercises provided small but useful tools that you can use to make yourself more productive.

Q&A

Q I'm having problems with the following program. No files are read in, even though they're in the directory!

```
opendir(DIRHANDLE, "/mydir") || die;
@files=<DIRHANDLE> ;
closedir(DIRHANDLE);
```

A Whoops! The problem is in the second line. DIRHANDLE is a directory handle, not a filehandle. You cannot read directory handles with the angle operators (<>). The correct way to read the directory is @files=readdir DIRHANDLE.

Q Why doesn't glob("*.*") match all the files in a directory?

A Because "*.*" matches only filenames with a dot in them. To match all the files in a directory, use glob("*"). The glob function's patterns are designed to be portable across many operating systems and thus do not behave the same as the *.* pattern in DOS.

Q I modified the mygrep exercise to search subdirectories by using opendir and some more loops, but it seems to have bugs.

A In short: Don't Do That. Descending a directory tree is an old problem, it's not particularly easy, it's been solved many times before, and you don't need to do it for yourself. (Doing all that work on a problem that's already been solved is called "reinventing the wheel.") If you're doing it only for fun, that's wonderful, but don't spend too much time on it. Hold on until Hour 15, where you'll learn to use the File::Find module instead. It's a lot simpler to use—and, more importantly, it's debugged.

Q The program in Listing 10.3 gives an error if I try to change *.bat to *.tmp. Why?

A The program wasn't expecting you to type *.bat as a pattern to look for. *.bat isn't valid to have in a regular expression—* must follow some other character. If you had entered *\.bat, the program would have accepted the input just fine— although it might not have worked as expected, because filenames hardly ever have a literal * in them.

To fix this error, either give the program the input it expects (simple strings) or change line 19 to read s/\Q$oldpat/$newpat/ so that "special characters" are disabled in the regular expression patterns.

10

Workshop

Quiz

1. To print the last modification time of the file `foofile`, use

    a. `print glob("foofile");`

    b. `print (stat("foofile"))[9];`

    c. `print scalar localtime (stat("foofile"))[9];`

2. The `unlink` function returns

    a. The number of files actually deleted

    b. True or false, depending on success

    c. The number of file deletions that were attempted

Answers

1. b. or c. Choice b prints the time expressed as the number of seconds since 1970—not very useful. Choice c prints the time as a nicely formatted string.

2. a. However, choice b is also somewhat true. If no files can be deleted, `unlink` returns 0, which is false.

Activities

- As a programming exercise *only,* try to write a program that lists all the files in a directory, in its subdirectories, and so on.

Hour 11

System Interaction

All the Perl you've learned up until now has been fairly self-contained: If you wanted something done, you had to do it yourself—sorting data, creating directory listings, divining configuration information, and so on. The problem is that it's a lot of work, and you're repeating work that might have been done elsewhere.

One of the current buzzwords being touted about Perl is that it's an excellent *glue* language. What this means is that Perl can use other programs that are installed with your operating system as components, connecting them together to create larger programs. It can start your OS utilities and use them to gather information, interact with you, and then shut them down.

Perl can glue together these smaller utilities to produce a much larger and more useful utility. This capability has the added benefit of allowing you to quickly write code that might otherwise have taken a long time to write and debug. You should use any leverage at your advantage to write code quickly and accurately. Gluing system utilities together can offer a large advantage.

In this hour you'll learn about

- The `system()` function
- Capturing output
- Portability

> The examples in this hour—for the most part—have two versions, one for Windows and MS-DOS systems and the other for Unix systems. Where only one example is provided, you'll find a note in the text about what to change for the other kind of system—and usually that change is minor.

The `system()` Function

The simplest way to run a command outside Perl is to use the `system` function. The `system` function pauses the Perl program, runs the external command, and then continues running your Perl program. The syntax for `system` is

```
system command;
```

where `command` is the command that you want run. The return value from `system` is 0 if everything goes okay or nonzero if a problem occurs. Notice that this result is *backward* from the normal Perl values of true and false.

The following is an example of `system` under Unix:

```
system("ls -lF");          # Print a file listing
# print system's documentation
if ( system("perldoc -f system") ) {
    print "Your documentation isn't installed correctly!\n";
}
```

This next example shows `system` under MS-DOS/Windows:

```
system("dir /w");          # Print a file listing
# print system's documentation
if ( system("perldoc -f system") ) {
    print "Your documentation isn't installed correctly!\n";
}
```

For the most part, `system` works the same under both architectures. The point to remember is that the commands are fundamentally different from one OS to another. To get a file listing in MS-DOS, you use the `dir` command; to get a file listing under Unix, you use the `ls` command. In very rare instances—`perldoc`, for example—the commands are similar under Unix and MS-DOS.

When the `system` function is running the external command, the output of that command is displayed on your screen as though your Perl program were printing it. If that external command needs input, the input comes from your terminal the same way your Perl programs read input from the terminal. The command run by `system` inherits the STDIN and STDOUT file descriptors, so the external command does I/O from the exact same place as your Perl program. Invoking fully interactive programs from `system` is possible.

Consider the following example under Unix:

```
$file="myfile.txt";
system("vi $file");
```

Now consider this example under Windows/MS-DOS:

```
$file="myfile.txt";
system("edit $file");
```

Each of the preceding examples runs an editor on myfile.txt—`vi` for Unix and `edit` for DOS. The editor runs full screen, of course, and all the normal editor commands work. When the editor exits, control returns to Perl.

You can use the `system` function to run any program, not just console-mode programs (text). Under Unix, this example runs a graphical clock:

```
system("xclock -update 1");
```

Under MS-DOS/Windows, the following example invokes a graphical file editor:

```
system("notepad.exe myfile.txt");
```

The Underlying Command Interpreter

The `system` function (and actually most of the functions in this hour) allows you to use any of your command interpreter's features that would be available to you at the command prompt. You can do so because the Perl `system` command invokes a copy of a shell (/bin/sh on Unix, command.com in MS-DOS/Windows) and then gives your `system` command to that shell. As a result, you can perform redirection (>), piping (|), and background tasks under Unix (&), as well as use other features your command interpreter may offer.

For example, to run an external command and capture its output in a file, you use the following command:

```
system("perldoc perlfaq5 > faqfile.txt");
```

The preceding command runs `perldoc perlfaq5` and captures its output in a file called faqfile.txt. This particular syntax works on both DOS and Unix.

Some features, such as pipes and background tasks, work as you would expect under the
Unix operating system, as you can see here:

```
# Sort the file whose name is in $f and print it
system("sort $f | lp");  # Some systems use "lpr"

# Run "xterm" and immediately return
system("xterm &");
```

In the last example, the xterm program is started, but the & causes the Unix shell to start
the process in the *background*. This means that, although the process continues to run,
the system function finishes and returns control to Perl. Perl does not wait for xterm to
finish.

 Under Unix, Perl always uses /bin/sh—or a reasonable facsimile—for the
system function, pipes, and backticks (discussed later in this hour). It does
so regardless of what your personal shell is configured to be. This use provides some measure of portability across Unix systems.

Capturing Output

The system function does have a small shortcoming: It doesn't offer any particularly
good way to capture the command's output and bring it into Perl for analysis. To do so in
a roundabout way, you could use this workaround:

```
# 'ls' and 'dir' used for example only. opendir/readdir
# would be more efficient in most cases.
system("dir > outfile");     # Use "ls" instead of "dir" for Unix
open(OF, "outfile") || die "Cannot open output: $!";
@data=<OF>;
close(OF);-
```

In the preceding snippet, the command run by system has its output redirected to a file
called outfile. The file is then opened and read into an array. The array @data now contains the output of the dir command.

This method is messy and not too clever. Not surprisingly, Perl has another way of
dealing with this situation: *backticks,* also called *backquotes.* Any command that is surrounded by backticks (` `) is run by Perl as an external command—as though through
system—and the output is captured and returned as the return value from the backticks.
Consider this example using backticks:

```
$directory=`dir`;    # Unix users, use ls instead of dir
```

In the preceding snippet, the dir command is run, and the output is captured in $directory.

Inside the backticks, all normal shell processing is observed: > does redirection, | does piping, and under Unix, & starts tasks in the background. Keep in mind, though, that commands that have been run in the background or that have had their output redirected with > have no output to capture.

In a scalar context, backticks return the output of the command as a single string. If the command output contains many lines of text, those lines all appear in the string, separated by record separator characters ("\n"). In a list context, the output is assigned to the list, with record separators at the end of each line.

Now consider this example:

```
@dir=`dir`;  # Use 'ls' for Unix users
foreach(@dir) {
    # Process each line individually.
}
```

In the preceding snippet, the output in @dir is processed in the foreach loop, one line at a time.

Perl has another way of representing backticks—that is, to use the notation qx{}. The command you want to execute goes between the braces ({}), as in this example:

```
$perldoc=qx{perldoc perl};
```

By using the qx operator, you can avoid the trouble of having to put backslashes in front of backticks when they appear as part of the command, as shown here:

```
$complex=`sort \`grep -l 'conf' *\``;   # Somewhat messy
```

You can rewrite the preceding snippet as follows:

```
$complex=qx{ sort `grep -l 'conf' *` }; # Little easier.
```

Any characters can be used instead of {}, and balanced pairs or characters such as <>, (), and [] can be used as well.

Avoiding Your Shell

Sometimes the boundary between Perl and your command interpreter can get a little blurry. Consider the following two examples:

For Unix:

```
$myhome=`ls $HOME`;
```

Or, for MS-DOS and Windows:

```
$windows=`dir %windir%`;
```

In the first example, is $HOME the Perl variable $HOME or the shell's environment variable $HOME? In the MS-DOS example, is %windir% the command.com variable windir, or is it the Perl hash %windir followed by a % sign?

The bad news is that $HOME is interpolated by Perl—meaning that $HOME is Perl's scalar variable $HOME, which is probably not what you wanted. Inside backticks, variables expand into their respective values, just as they do with double quotes (""). The potential variable name %windir, though, doesn't expand inside double quotes—only scalars and array names are interpolated.

To avoid this confusion, you can just precede the variables (array and scalars) that you don't want Perl to interpolate with a backslash, as in these examples:

```
$myhome=`ls \$HOME`;  # The \ hides $HOME
```

or

```
$windows=`dir %windir%`  # Remember, hashes don't interpolate
```

Now $HOME is the Unix shell's HOME variable, and %windir% is command.com's windir variable.

The alternative method is to use the qx{} notation for backticks and to use a single quotation mark to delimit the qx, as in these examples:

```
$myhome=qx' ls $HOME ';
```

or

```
$windows=qx' dir %windir% ';
```

Perl recognizes the qx'' sequence as special and does not expand Perl variables inside it; therefore, you can use backticks and not have to backslash-escape other backticks that might occur in your command.

Pipes

Pipes in Unix and MS-DOS/Windows are used for connecting different processes together so that the output of one process becomes the input of the next process. Consider the following set of commands, which would almost work in Unix (if you change the dir to ls) or MS-DOS:

```
dir > outfile
sort outfile > newfile
more newfile
```

The output of dir is collected in outfile. Then sort is used to sort outfile, and the output from sort is stored in newfile. Then more shows the contents of newfile a screenful at a time.

Pipes allow you to perform that same sequence, but without outfile and newfile, like this:

```
dir | sort | more
```

The output of dir is given to sort, which then sorts the data. The output from sort is then given to more for page-at-a-time display. No redirection (>) or temporary files are needed.

This kind of command line is called a *pipeline*, and the vertical line between the commands is called a *pipe*. Unix relies heavily on pipes to connect its small utilities. MS-DOS and Windows support pipes but have far fewer command-line utilities that work with them.

Perl programs can participate in a pipeline in different ways. First of all, if you have a Perl program that accepts standard input, transforms it, and sends it to standard output, then you can write a command line to insert that Perl program into a pipeline, as in the following example:

```
dir /B | sort | perl Totaler | more
```

In the preceding pipeline, Totaler could be a Perl program you write to print the sum of the directory listing and maybe some statistics, along with the directory listing itself. If you're using Unix, change the dir /B to ls -1, and the pipeline works as expected. Listing 11.1 contains the Totaler program.

LISTING 11.1 Complete Listing for Totaler

```
 1:    #!/usr/bin/perl
 2:
 3:    use strict;
 4:    my($dirs,$sizes,$total);
 5:
 6:    while(<STDIN>) {
 7:        chomp;
 8:        $total++;
 9:        if (-d $_) {
10:            $dirs++;
11:            print "$_\n";
12:            next;
13:        }
14:        $sizes+=(stat($_))[7];
15:        print "$_\n";
16:    }
17:    print "$total files, $dirs directories\n";
18:    print "Average file size: ", $sizes/($total-$dirs), "\n";
```

11

Line 6: Each line of input is read from STDIN and assigned to $_. On a pipeline, a program's STDIN is connected to the previous program's STDOUT. So, in the example given, STDIN is being fed by dir /B through sort.

Lines 9–13: If a directory is encountered, its number is totaled separately in $dirs, the directory name is printed, and the loop is started again.

Lines 14–15: Otherwise, the sizes of the files are accumulated in $sizes, and the filenames are printed.

Lines 17–18: The average size of the file is printed, along with the total number of files and directories.

The other way Perl can participate in a pipeline is to treat a pipeline like a file that can either be read from or written to. This is done with the open function in Perl, as shown here:

```
# Replace "dir /B" with "ls -1" for Unix
open(RHANDLE, "dir /B| sort |") || die "Cannot open pipe for reading: $!";
```

In the preceding snippet of code, the open function opens a pipeline for reading from dir/B | sort. The fact that Perl is reading from this pipeline is indicated by having the final pipe (|) on the right. When the open function is run, Perl starts the dir /B | sort commands. When the filehandle RHANDLE is read, the output from sort is read into the Perl program.

Now consider this example:

```
open(WHANDLE, "| more") || die "Cannot open pipe for writing: $!";
```

This open function opens a pipeline for writing to the more command. The pipe symbol on the left means that Perl is going to write to the pipe. All printing to the WHANDLE filehandle is buffered by more and displayed a page at a time. Writing the function like this might be a good way to get your program's output displayed a page at a time.

When you are done with a filehandle that has been opened to a program—like RHANDLE and WHANDLE—it is very important that you close the filehandle properly. The reason is that the programs started by open must be properly shut down, and using close on the filehandle ensures that. Failing to close the filehandle when you're done with it could result in the programs continuing to run even after your Perl program has ended.

When closing a filehandle that's been opened on a pipe, the close function indicates whether the pipeline was successful. Therefore, you should be careful to check the return value of close like this:

```
close(WHANDLE) || warn "pipe to more failed: $!";
```

The reason that the `open` function might not tell you whether the pipeline was successfully started has to do with Unix's design. When Perl constructs the pipeline and starts it, it's not sure that the pipeline will actually work; if the pipeline is assembled properly and starts, it's assumed that it will finish properly. When the last program in the pipe completes, it should return a successful exit status. The `close` function can read that status to tell whether everything went all right; otherwise, an error results.

First Lesson in Portability

Portability: It's one of the things that Perl is good at. Whether your Perl code is run on a VMS machine, Unix, a Macintosh, or under MS-DOS, there's a very high probability that the Perl code you write will work seamlessly under any architecture that Perl supports. When you need to interact with the underlying operating system, such as when you're doing file I/O, Perl tries to hide all the nitty-gritty details for you so that your code will just work.

Some of the reasons that Perl is so portable are discussed at great length in Hour 16, "The Perl Community."

Sometimes, though, there's a limit to what Perl can hide from you.

Throughout this hour, the examples have read "do this for Windows and MS-DOS, do this for Unix," and either one has worked, depending on the architecture you're using. Trying to accommodate both Windows and Unix with your own programs means that you'll have to create two versions of each program—one for Windows and one for Unix. Developing two versions creates further problems when your program is successful and moved to an even more alien architecture like Mac OS 9.

It's not at all uncommon for a program to be written for one architecture—such as Windows NT—to find itself being run under a different architecture—such as Unix. Because Perl runs on so many different architectures, many people assume that running a Perl program under Windows NT is the same as running it under Unix. Web servers and other applications move frequently between architectures; it's just good business sense to keep your software portable.

Creating a different version of your program for each architecture that would work under every possible situation is time consuming, wasteful, and unproductive. By following a few rules, you can create programs that will work everywhere, or at least try to work everywhere, and that are easy to fix if they do not.

11

The following are some general rules for writing "go anywhere" code:

1. Always have warnings turned on, and use the `use strict` directive. This way, you can make sure that your code will probably run with various versions of Perl and that there aren't any obvious bugs.

2. Always check the return value from system requests—for example, use `open || die`, never just `open`. Checking the value will help you find errors when moving your application from one server to another—not just between architectures.

3. Print good, descriptive error messages.

4. Use Perl's built-in functions to perform tasks you might otherwise do by using `system` or backticks (` `` `).

5. Wrap system-dependent operations (file I/O, terminal I/O, process control, and so on) in subroutines, and check to make sure those operations are supported on the current operating system.

The first two points you should already be familiar with. All throughout this book, the examples have checked the exit status of critical functions, and since Hour 8, "Functions," all larger examples have demonstrated `use strict` and warnings.

Point 3, having good error messages, cannot be overlooked. Of the following messages, which is the most helpful?

```
(no message, or wrong output)
Died at line 15.
Cannot open Foofile.txt: No such file or directory
Cannot open Foofile.txt: No such file or directory at myscript.pl line 24
```

Obviously, the last one is the most helpful. After you've installed the program, and a problem arises months (or years) later, the last message indicates what program failed ("myscript.pl"), what it wanted ("Foofile.txt"), why it failed ("No such file..."), and where it failed ("line 24"). This information will help you fix the problems quickly. A little bit of time spent writing a good, descriptive error message always pays off.

Point 4 simply means that you should use Perl whenever possible. To retrieve a directory listing, it's tempting just to use `$dir=`dir`;` but this will fail if the program is ever moved to a non-Windows system. A good solution would be to use `<*>`. A better solution would be to use the `opendir`/`readdir`/`closedir` functions whenever possible. These solutions will work no matter where your program is moved.

Telling the Difference: An Example

The last two points for writing "go anywhere" code—wrapping system-dependent things in subroutines and checking the architecture of the machine that the program is running on—bear a little more explanation and a demonstration.

As you sit typing your Perl programs, you should remember that one day your Perl program might be used on a machine other than the one you're currently using. You may develop the next Amazon.com Web site, and it may move from your PC to a large Windows NT server to a cluster of Sun Enterprise 10000 Unix servers. Or you may simply have personal CGI programs and change Web providers only to find that your new provider has a different kind of server. These situations happen all of the time and need consideration.

So how does your program know the difference between Windows NT and Unix? Simple. The Perl special variable $^O—that's a dollar sign, a caret, and the capital letter *O*—contains the architecture name that the program is running under. For example, under Windows and MS-DOS, it contains the string MSWin32. Under Unix, it contains the type of Unix you're running—linux, aix, solaris, and so on.

The following are some tasks that depend on what operating system you are running:

- Finding out anything about the system's configuration
- Working with the disk and directory structure
- Using system services (such as email)

For this example, you're going to examine a piece of code to find the amount of available disk space on a system. This exercise might be useful if someone wants to upload a file to a server and you need to find out whether the file would fit first. A code snippet to find the free disk space in the current drive of a Windows system might look like the following:

```
# The last line of 'dir' reports something like:
#      10 dir(s)    67,502,080 bytes free
# Or on Win98, "MB" instead of "bytes"
my(@dir,$free);
@dir=`dir`;
$free=$dir[$#dir];
$free=~s/.*([\d,]+) \w+ free/$1/;
$free=~s/,//g;
```

The preceding snippet takes the last line of the directory listing—in @dir—and uses regular expressions to remove everything but the size—the digits and commas preceding bytes free. Finally, the commas are removed so that $free contains just the raw free disk space. This approach works well for Windows systems. For Unix—Linux, in particular—the following snippet works:

```
# Last lines of df -k . reports something like this:
# Filesystem          1024-blocks  Used     Available Capacity Mounted on
# /dev/hda1               938485      709863 180139        80%      /
# And the 4th field is the number of free 1024K disk blocks
```

```
# This format may be particular to Linux.
my(@dir, $free);
@dir=`df -k .`;
$free=(split(/\s+/, $dir[$#dir]))[3];
$free=$free*1024;
```

Notice the differences between this snippet and the previous one. The utility under Windows to find the disk space is `dir`; under Unix, it is `df -k .`. The last line of output of `df -k .` is split apart, and the fourth field is placed in `$field`. Output of `df` varies slightly between Unix systems; usually, the number of fields reported is different, or they're in a different order. Your Perl code can easily compensate by simply picking a different field.

So now you have two completely different routines to find free disk space. You can combine them and have the appropriate one run on each architecture, as follows:

```
if ( $^O eq 'MSWin32') {
    # The last line of 'dir' reports something like:
    #       10 dir(s)    67,502,080 bytes free
    my(@dir,$free);
    @dir=`dir`;
    $free=$dir[$#dir];
    $free=~s/.*([\d,]+) \w+ free/$1/;
    $free=~s/,//g;
} elsif ($^O eq 'linux' ) {
    # Last line of df -k . reports something like this:
    # /dev/hda1     938485 709863 180139    80%   /
    # And the 4th field is the number of free 1024K disk blocks
    my(@dir, $free);
    @dir=`df -k .`;
    $free=(split(/\s+/, $dir[$#dir]))[3];
    $free=$free*1024;
} else {
    warn "Cannot determine free space on this machine\n";
}
```

The sample program has now been expanded to include both the MS-DOS/Windows version and the Linux version. If it's run under any other kind of machine, a warning is printed.

The routine is almost finished. What you need to do now is isolate this routine in a subroutine so that the variables needed can be declared private and the final product can be cut and pasted into any program and used whenever needed.

```
# Computes free space in current directory
sub freespace {
    my(@dir, $free);
    if ( $^O eq 'MSWin32') {
        # The last line of 'dir' reports something like:
        #       10 dir(s)    67,502,080 bytes free
        @dir=`dir`;
        $free=$dir[$#dir];
```

```
        $free=~s/.*([\d,]+) bytes free/$1/;
        $free=~s/,//g;
    } elsif ($^O eq 'linux' ) {
        # Last line of df -k . reports something like this:
        # /dev/hda1      938485 709863 180139    80%  /
        # And the 4th field is the number of free 1024K disk blocks
        @dir=`df -k .`;
        $free=(split(/\s+/, $dir[$#dir]))[3];
        $free=$free*1024;
    } else {
        $free=0; # A default value
        warn "Cannot determine free space on this machine\n";
    }
    return $free;
}
```

Now whenever your programs need to find the amount of free disk space, you can simply call the `freespace()` subroutine, and the answer is returned. If you try running this subroutine on another architecture that's not listed, an error message is printed. However, adding another Unix-like OS to the function wouldn't be difficult; you can just add another `elsif` clause.

Summary

This hour you learned about how to leverage your system's utilities to do work for you. The `system` function allows you to run a system utility (or a pipeline). The backticks (`` ` ``) run a system utility and then capture the output. The captured output can then be stored in a variable for use by Perl. The `open` function can open not only files but programs as well. The programs can be written to with `print` or read from with the angle operator (`<>`). Finally, you were shown some techniques for using these utilities on many different kinds of systems without having to write different programs for each.

Q&A

Q How do I open a pipe both to and from a command? For example, `open(P, "| cmd |")` doesn't seem to work.

A This task can actually be quite complicated because reading and writing from the same process can cause *deadlock*. At this point, your program is expecting `cmd` to print something and is waiting for data with `<P>`. Meanwhile, because of some snafu, `cmd` is actually waiting for your program to print something with `print P "..."`. In fact, if you have warnings enabled, Perl will inform you with this message: `Can't do bidirectional pipe`.

If you're prepared for this kind of problem, the `IPC::Open2` module will allow you to open a bidirectional pipe. Modules will be discussed in Hour 14, "Using Modules."

Q The code `$a=system("cmd")` didn't capture the output of `cmd` in `$a` as I expected. Why not?

A You're confusing `system` with backticks (``` `` ```). The `system` function doesn't capture `cmd`'s output. What you probably wanted was `$a=`cmd`.`

Q When I run external programs under Unix with backticks (``` `` ```), the error messages are not captured. Why not?

A Because all Unix programs—including Perl—have two output file descriptors: `STDOUT` and `STDERR`. The `STDOUT` file descriptor is for normal program output. The `STDERR` file descriptor is reserved for error messages. Backticks—and `open` with pipes—capture only `STDOUT`. The short answer is to use the shell to redirect `STDOUT` into `STDERR` and then run your command as follows:

```
$a=`cmd 2>&1`;    # run "cmd", capturing output and errors
```

The Perl FAQ has a lengthy explanation of this and many other techniques for capturing a command's errors. Type `perldoc perlfaq8` for the appropriate section of the FAQ.

Workshop

Quiz

1. To have data generated by your program display a page at a time, use

   a. `perl myprog.pl | more`

   b. `open(M, "| more") || die; print M "data...data...data....\n";`

   c. `open(M, ">more") || die; print M "data..data...data...\n";`

2. Which value of `$foo` is used in this statement: `$r=`dir $foo`?`

   a. The shell's value for `$foo`.

   b. Perl's value of `$foo` is substituted, and then the `dir` is run.

3. Which of the following tasks changes depending on what system you have?

   a. Finding the amount of free disk space

   b. Getting a directory listing

   c. Deleting a directory

Answers

1. Either a or b. In the case of a, all output of myprog.pl is fed to `more`. In the case of b, any data written to the `M` file descriptor is fed to `more` for paging.

2. b. To protect `$foo` from Perl's expansion, you use `qx`dir $foo``.

3. a only. Choice b can be done with `glob`, `<*>` or `opendir` and `readdir`, and c is done with `rmdir`.

Activities

- Use the statistics functions in Hour 8, "Functions," to display even more statistics about the sizes of files in Listing 11.1.

- If you have a Unix system, add your particular flavor of Unix to the `freespace()` function. Use the Linux example as a starting point.

11

Hour **12**

Using Perl's Command-Line Tools

Until now, the Perl interpreter has been a fairly simple program to use. You type a program into a file and then invoke the Perl interpreter to run your program. The Perl interpreter is much more flexible than this, however.

Built into the interpreter is a debugger. The debugger allows you to play your Perl program like a videotape. You can rewind your program to the beginning, play it slow, play it fast, and freeze-frame it to examine the innards closely. The debugger is an often underutilized tool for finding problems in Perl programs.

Perl can also run programs that are not typed into files. For example, you can run small programs directly from your system's command prompt.

In this chapter you'll learn

- How to use Perl's debugger
- How to use command-line switches to write small Perl programs

What Is the Debugger?

The Perl debugger is a built-in feature of the Perl interpreter. It allows you to take any Perl program and step through that program statement by statement. Along the way, you can examine variables, change them, let the program run for a while longer, interrupt the program, or start it over again.

From your program's perspective, nothing is different. Input still comes from the keyboard, and output still goes to the screen. The program doesn't know when it's stopped or when it's running. In fact, you can examine your program's workings without disturbing them at all.

Starting the Debugger

If you are a Macintosh user running Perl, to use the debugger you need only select Debugger from the Script menu, and a Debugger window opens with a prompt for you.

Under any other operating system, to start the Perl debugger you must be at your operating system's command prompt. For DOS and Windows users, this means the standard MS-DOS c:\ prompt. For Unix users, this means the prompt that you were presented with when you logged in (usually % or $).

All the examples in this section use the Employee program from Listing 9.1 in Hour 9, "More Functions and Operators." You might find it handy to put a bookmark on that page and flip back and forth for reference.

To start the debugger at the prompt—an MS-DOS prompt is used for the example—type this line:

```
C:\> perl -d Employee
```

The -d switch to perl causes Perl to start up in debugging mode; the program to be debugged is also indicated on the command line. Some messages giving version information are then displayed, as shown here:

```
Loading DB routines from perl5db.pl version 1.0401

Emacs support available.

Enter h or 'h h' for help.

main::(Employee:5):        my @employees=(
main::(Employee:6):            'Smith,Bob,123101,9.35,40',
main::(Employee:7):            'Franklin,Alice,132912,10.15,35',
main::(Employee:8):            'Wojohowicz,Ted,198131,6.50,39',
main::(Employee:9):            'Ng,Wendy,141512,9.50,40',
main::(Employee:10):           'Cliburn,Stan,131211,11.25,40',
main::(Employee:11):       );
  DB<1>__
```

The debugger first displays the version number (1.0401—yours will vary) and the help prompt. Next, the first executable line of the program is displayed. Because the first statement is actually seven lines long—starting with `my @employees=(` and ending with `);`—all seven lines of the statement are shown along with a description that shows what file they came from (Employee) and what line or lines of the file they were found on (5 through 11).

Last, you see the debugger prompt DB<1>. The 1 signifies that the debugger is waiting for its first command. The cursor waits at the debugger prompt for your command.

At this point, your Perl program is not running. The program is actually paused just before the first instruction -my @employees=(, and so on. Whenever the debugger shows you a statement from your program, it is the statement *about to be executed,* not the last statement run.

The debugger is now ready for your commands.

Basic Debugger Commands

The first—and most important—command you can give the debugger is the help command. If you type h at the debugger prompt, all the available debugger commands are printed. You also can use some variations: h h prints a summary of commands and syntax, and h *cmd* prints help for a specific command.

The list of help commands is probably longer than your screen will allow, and the first few commands will probably scroll right off. To make any debugger command's output display a screen at a time, put a | in front of the command. So, to see the help a screen at a time, the command is |h.

The most-used feature of the debugger is the capability to run Perl code an instruction at a time. So, continuing with the previous example, to go to the next statement in your Perl program, you use the debugger's n command:

```
main::(Employee:5):      my @employees=(
main::(Employee:6):           'Smith,Bob,123101,9,35,40',
main::(Employee:7):           'Franklin,Alice,132912,10,15,35',
main::(Employee:8):           'Wojohowicz,Ted,198131,6,50,39',
main::(Employee:9):           'Ng,Wendy,141512,9,50,40',
main::(Employee:10):          'Cliburn,Stan,131211,11,25,40',
main::(Employee:11):     );
  DB<1> n                ←Command for "next" instruction
main::(Employee:24):                my ($L1, $F1)=split(',', $a):
  DB<1>
```

12

After you type the n command, Perl executes the statement from lines 5 to 11 of the Employee program. The debugger then prints, but does not yet run, the next statement to be executed—my($L1, $F1)=split(',', $a);—and displays another prompt.

At this point in the execution, @employees is initialized to the five names, salaries, and so on. To view them, you can simply print them:

```
DB<1> print @employees
Smith,Bob,123101,9.35,40Franklin,Alice,132912,10.15,35Wojohowicz,Ted,198131,6.50
  ,39Ng,Wendy,141512,9.50,40Cliburn,Stan,131211,11.25,40
DB<2> __
```

In fact, any Perl statement can be run at a debugger prompt. Notice that the array elements from @employees are all run together. You can enter the following to print them nicely:

```
DB<2> print join("\n", @employees)
Smith,Bob,123101,9.35,40
Franklin,Alice,132912,10.15,35
Wojohowicz,Ted,198131,6.50,39
Ng,Wendy,141512,9.50,40
Cliburn,Stan,131211,11.25,40
DB<3> __
```

To continue stepping through the program, just keep typing n, as shown here:

```
DB<3> n
main::(Employee:23):        @employees=sort {
  DB<3> n
main::(Employee:25):                my ($L2, $F2)=split(',', $b);
  DB<3> n
main::(Employee:26):             return( $L1 cmp $L2
main::(Employee:27):                         ||
main::(Employee:28):                  $F1 cmp $F2
main::(Employee:29):              );
  DB<3> n
main::(Employee:23):        @employees=sort {
  DB<3>
```

Apparently, the debugger moves backward through the program here; line 23 is about to be executed again. The Perl sort statement is actually a kind of loop, and the debugger steps through each statement in the block of the sort. If you keep typing n, the debugger keeps looping until the sort is finished—which might take awhile.

To repeat the previous command, you can also just press the Enter key at a debugger prompt.

Breakpoints

Instead of stepping through the program an instruction at a time, you also can have the debugger continue to run your Perl program until a certain statement is reached and then stop. These places to stop are called *breakpoints*.

To set a breakpoint, you must first select a place in the program to stop. The `l` command lists the next 10 lines of the program. Typing `l` again lists the next 10 lines, and so on. To list the program starting at a particular line, type `l` *lineno*, where *lineno* is the line number of the program. You can also specify a range of lines by using the command `l start-end`.

In the listing, a `===>` marks the current line about to be executed by the debugger, as you can see here:

```
    DB<3> l  11
23:==>    @employees=sort {
24:                 my ($L1, $F1)=split(',', $a);
25:                 my ($L2, $F2)=split(',', $b);
26:                 return( $L1 cmp $L2
27:                                     ||
28:                         $F1 cmp $F2
29:                     );
30:                 } @employees;
31:
32:         foreach(@employees) {
33:                 print_emp($_);
    DB<3> __
```

In this case, line 33 is a good place for a breakpoint: It's after the `sort` statement, and it's the first statement inside the main loop of the program. You can set a breakpoint anywhere in a Perl program as long as the breakpoint is a valid Perl statement; you cannot break on a brace (line 30), punctuation (line 29), a blank line (line 31), or a line containing only a comment.

To set the breakpoint, use the `b` *breakpoint* command, where *breakpoint* can be a line number or a subroutine name. To set the breakpoint at line 33, for example, you enter the following:

```
    DB<3> b 33
    DB<4>
```

The other command you need to know with breakpoints is the continue command, `c`. The `c` command instructs the debugger to let the Perl program run until the next breakpoint is reached or the end of the program is reached—whichever comes first:

12

```
  DB<5> c
main::(Employee:33):                        print_emp($_);
  DB<6>
```

In this case, the debugger stops the Perl program at line 33 before the `print_emp` function is called, as expected. The breakpoint is still set, so typing another `c` causes the program to continue, run the `print_emp()` function, and stop again on line 33:

```
DB<8> L
Employee:
 33:                        print_emp($_);
```

To examine the breakpoints you have set in your program, you can use the `L` command like this:

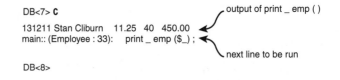

This example shows that the debugger has one breakpoint, in the file Employee at line 33.

To get rid of a breakpoint in the program, you use the `d` command in the same way you set the breakpoint—`d` *line* or `d` *subname*:

```
DB<9> d 33
DB<10>
```

Other Debugger Commands

If you want to examine the workings of the `print_emp()` function, you can do so in a few different ways. First, restart the program by using the `R` command:

```
DB<11> R
```

Warning: some settings and command-line options may be lost!

Loading DB routines from perl5db.pl version 1.0401

Emacs support available.

Enter h or `h h' for help.

```
main::(Employee:5):      my @employees=(
main::(Employee:6):              'Smith,Bob,123101,9.35,40',
main::(Employee:7):              'Franklin,Alice,132912,10.15,35',
main::(Employee:8):              'Wojohowicz,Ted,198131,6.50,39',
main::(Employee:9):              'Ng,Wendy,141512,9.50,40',
```

```
main::(Employee:10):                'Cliburn,Stan,131211,11.25,40',
main::(Employee:11):     );
  DB<12> b 33
```

The R command resets the Perl program to the beginning and prepares to execute it again. Any breakpoints you have set remain set, and any variables in the Perl program are reset. In the preceding example, a breakpoint is set at line 33. Then you can continue the program with the following:

```
  DB<13> c
main::(Employee:33):                        print_emp($_);
  DB<14> __
```

Executing the **n** command would execute the next instruction:

```
  DB<14> n
131211 Stan Cliburn                  11.25   40   450.00
main::(Employee:32):        foreach(@employees) {
  DB<15> n
main::(Employee:33):                        print_emp($_);
  DB<16> __
```

Moving through the program this way doesn't allow you to examine what's *in* print_emp(). To step into print_emp(), instead of the n command, you should use s, the step command. The s command works just like n, but instead of simply executing subroutines and moving to the next instruction, s stops at the first instruction *inside* the subroutine, as you can see here:

```
main::(Employee:33):                        print_emp($_);
  DB<16> s
main::print_emp(Employee:14):        my($last,$first,$emp,$hourly,$time)=
main::print_emp(Employee:15):                        split(',', $_[0]);
  DB<17>__
```

Here, the first statement of print_emp() is shown. (You could also have stopped in print_emp() by setting a breakpoint with b print_emp.) You can now continue using the n command to step through the function, as follows:

```
  DB<18> n
main::print_emp(Employee:16):        my $fullname;
  DB<19> n
main::print_emp(Employee:17):        $fullname=sprintf("%s %s", $first, $last);
  DB<20> n
main::print_emp(Employee:18):        printf("%6d %-20s %6.2f %3d %7.2f\n",
main::print_emp(Employee:19):                        $emp, $fullname, $hourly, $time,
main::print_emp(Employee:20):                        $hourly * $time);
  DB<21> __
```

12

You also can modify the variables in the Perl program as it's running. For example, to give the employee a temporary $2.50 per hour raise, you enter the following:

```
  DB<21> print $hourly
10.15
  DB<22> $hourly=$hourly+2.50

  DB<23> n
132912 Alice Franklin              12.65  35   442.75
main::(Employee:32):       foreach(@employees) {
  DB<24>
```

In the preceding snippet, the variable $hourly is printed (10.15), increased by 2.50, and the program is allowed to continue running. The printf statement prints the new value for $hourly.

Finally, to quit the debugger, simply type q at a debugger prompt.

Exercise: Finding the Bug

This exercise shows you how to use the debugger. The program in Listing 12.1 has a problem—actually two. It's supposed to print these messages:

```
20 glasses of Lemonade on the wall
19 glasses of Lemonade on the wall
:
1 glass of Lemonade on the wall
0 glasses of Lemonade on the wall
```

But it does not. Your task is to type the program in Listing 12.1 and try to find the bugs. Neither of the bugs is a syntax problem—Perl's warnings are not triggered, and use strict prints no messages—but the debugger should make the bugs fairly obvious to find.

After you type the program, run Perl with the debugger to try to find the errors. Remember to print relevant variables and expressions occasionally and step through the function calls one at a time.

LISTING 12.1 Buggy

```
1:  # !/usr/bin/perl -w
2:  # This program contains TWO errors
3:  use strict;
4:
5:  sub message {
6:      my($quant)=@_;
7:      my $mess;
8:      $mess="$quant glasses of Lemonade on the wall\n";
```

continues

LISTING 12.1   Continued

```
 9:     if ($quant eq 1) {
10:                     $mess=s/glasses/glass/;
11:         }
12:         print $mess;
13:  }
14:
15:  foreach(20..0) {
16:         &message($_);
17:  }
```

The solution is presented in the "Quiz" section at the end of this hour.

Other Command-Line Stuff

The debugger isn't the only feature of the Perl interpreter that can be activated by command-line switches. In fact, many useful Perl programs can be written just at the command prompt.

Macintosh users should run these command-line examples by selecting 1-liners from the Script menu and then typing the command in the dialog box.

One-Liners

The key to such programs is the -e switch given to Perl on the command line. Following the -e can be any Perl statements at all, as in this example:

```
C:\> perl -e "print 'Hello, world';"
Hello, world
```

You can use multiple -e statements to insert multiple statements or separate them with semicolons, as shown here:

```
C:\> perl -e "print 'Hello, world';" -e "print 'Howzit goin?'"
Hello, worldHowzit goin?
```

A word of caution: Most command interpreters have rules about quotation marks. The Windows/MS-DOS command interpreter—command.com or the NT command shell—allows you to use double quotes to group words—such as print and Hello, World in the preceding example—but you cannot easily put double quotes inside other double quotes. Nor can you easily put >, <, |, or ^ inside the double quotes. Consult your operating system's manual for a complete list of MS-DOS/Windows quoting rules.

12

Under Unix, generally as long as the quotes are balanced—every open quote has a close quote—and embedded quotation marks have a \ in front of them, you should be okay:

```
$ perl -e 'print "Hello, World\n";' -e 'print "Howzit goin?\n"'
```

The preceding example works under most Unix shells—csh, ksh, bash, and so on—and prints the message with the correct newlines. For a complete list of your shell's quoting rules, consult your shell's online manual page.

One frequent—and very useful—use of the -e switch is to combine it with -d and drop into Perl's debugger directly—without having a program to debug:

```
C:\> perl -d -e 1

Loading DB routines from perl5db.pl version 1
Emacs support available.

Enter h or `h h' for help.

main::(-e:1):    1
  DB<1> _ _
```

The debugger is now waiting for your commands. This particular incantation is useful for testing Perl syntax without your actually having to write a whole program, test, debug, edit, test, debug, and so on. Simply try your statements in the debugger until they work. The 1 on the command line is a minimalist Perl program; it's an expression that evaluates to—and returns—1.

Other Switches

The -c switch to the Perl interpreter causes Perl to examine your code for syntax problems—but not actually run the program:

```
C:\> perl -c Example.pl
Example.pl syntax OK
```

If a syntax error occurs, Perl may print a message like this:

```
C:\> perl -c Example.pl
syntax error at Example.pl line 5, near "print"
Example.pl had compilation errors
```

Combined with -w, the -c switch compiles your program and shows any warning messages that Perl thinks is appropriate.

When you're asking a more knowledgeable Perl user or your system administrator about debugging code, you are often requested to supply the version of the interpreter being used. The version of the Perl language that's in use primarily is Perl 5. The interpreter itself has a version that you can gather by using the -v switch on the command line, as shown here:

```
C:\> perl -v

This is perl, version 5.004_02

Copyright 1987-1997, Larry Wall

Perl may be copied only under the terms of either the Artistic License or the
GNU General Public License, which may be found in the Perl 5.0 source kit.
```

In the preceding example, the version of the Perl interpreter is 5.004_02. To get even more detailed information about how the interpreter was built, when it was built, and so on, you can run the interpreter with the -v switch, like this:

```
C:\> perl -V
Summary of my perl5 (5.0 patchlevel 4 subversion 02) configuration:
  Platform:
   osname=MSWin32, osvers=4.0, archname=MSWin32
   :
Compiler:
   cc='bcc32', optimize='-O', gccversion=
   :
Characteristics of this binary (from libperl):
  Compile-time options: DEBUGGING
  Built under MSWin32
  Compiled at Aug  9 1997 21:42:37
  @INC:   C:\PERL\lib\siteC:\PERL\lib
  c:\perl\lib    c:\perl\lib\site c:\perl\lib\site  .
```

This output might be useful if you're trying to debug a problem with the interpreter itself—perhaps a problem with the installation. At the end, note the values for @INC. This particular installation of Perl expects to find its modules in these directories. (Modules will be discussed in Hour 14, "Using Modules.") After Perl is installed, it cannot simply be moved from one directory to another. The interpreter itself has a built-in idea of where to find its modules, and moving it causes Perl to look in the wrong place for its modules.

Empty Angle Brackets and More One-Liners

The angle operator (<>) discussed so far have had a couple of functions:

1. With a filehandle, the angle operators allow you to read the filehandle—for example, <STDIN>.

2. With a pattern, the angle operators return a list of files matching that pattern, called a glob—for example, <*.bat>.

12

The angle operators have yet another function: A set of angle operators with nothing between them reads all the contents of all the files on the command line or, if no filenames are given, from the standard input. Sometimes an empty angle operator is called a *diamond operator* (the name comes from its shape). For example, examine this small Perl program:

```
#!/usr/bin/perl -w

while(<>) {
    print $_;
}
```

If you save the preceding program as `Example.pl`, then running the program with the command line

```
C:\> perl -w Example.pl file1 file2 file3
```

would cause the `<>` to read the contents of `file1` one line at a time, then `file2`, and then `file3`. If no files are specified, the angle operators read from the STDIN filehandle. This behavior mimics Unix utilities—such as sed, awk, and so on—that read input from files if given on the command line, and otherwise use standard input.

> After the Perl interpreter switches (`-w`, `-c`, `-d`, `-e`, and so on) are stripped away, the arguments to the Perl program are stored in an array called @ARGV. For example, for the previous snippet's arguments, `$ARGV[0]` would contain `file1`, `$ARGV[1]` would contain `file2`, and so on.

The `-n` switch to Perl wraps up any following statements on the command line into this small program:

```
LINE:
while(<>) {
... # Command-line Perl statements here.
}
```

So, to create a one-liner to remove leading spaces from input, you could write the following:

```
C:\> perl -n -e 's/^\s+//g; print $_;' file1
```

The preceding command actually runs a Perl program that looks like this:

```
LINE:
while(<>) {
    s/^\s+//g;
    print $_;
}
```

In the preceding snippet, the file named file1 is opened and assigned to $_ in the `while` loop, one line at a time. The line is edited with `s/^\s+//g` and then printed.

The `-p` switch is identical to `-n` except that lines are printed automatically after your statements are executed. So, rewriting the previous example would yield the following line:

```
C:\> perl -p -e 's/^\s+//g' file1
```

When you're editing a file with a Perl one-liner, you must be careful not to open the file for reading while trying to write to it at the same time, as in this example:

```
C:\>perl -p -e 's/\r//g' dosfile > dosfile
```

The preceding snippet tries to remove carriage returns from a file called dosfile. The problem is that dosfile is overwritten by `>` `dosfile` before the Perl command is even processed. The correct way to edit a file is to redirect the output to another file and rename it to the original name, like this:

```
C:\>perl -p -e 's/\r//g' dosfile > tempfile
C:\>rename tempfile dosfile
```

Writing short "one-liners" is considered a pastime for some Perl enthusiasts; the more convoluted and capable the program, the better. *The Perl Journal*, a quarterly magazine for Perl, scatters one-liners throughout each issue.

Summary

12

In this hour, you learned how to use the debugger effectively to find problems in your Perl programs. You learned that the angle operators (<>) have yet another mode that allows Perl to process all the files on the command line. Also, you learned how to use the `-n` and `-p` switches to the Perl interpreter to write small, one-line Perl programs.

Q&A

Q I'd really prefer a graphical debugger for Perl. Does such a thing exist?

A Yes, there are a few. If you're using Perl under Windows, ActiveState has a very nice graphical debugger.

Q What's the `main::` stuff that the debugger keeps printing?

A It has to do with Perl's package naming conventions. Some of this information will be covered in the next hour, so don't worry too much about it for now.

Q Does Perl have other command-line switches?

A Yes, several. You can view the full list in the online manual. To access this information, type `perldoc perlrun` at a command prompt.

Workshop

Quiz

1. What were the bugs in the Listing 12.1?

2. If no files are given on the command line, reading `<>` returns

   a. `undef`

   b. lines from standard input

   c. True

3. The Perl debugger can print Perl statements as they execute. This is called trace mode. How do you put the debugger into trace mode? (Hint: You need to look at the debugger's help message for this answer.)

   a. Use the `T` command, for trace

   b. Use the `t` command, for trace

Answers

1. First, in line 15 the range `(20..0)` is not valid. The range operator—`..`—does not count down, only up. This line should be changed to a `for($_=20; $_>-1; $_--)` loop, reverse(0..20) or something similar. Second, at line 10 the `$mess=s/glasses/glass/` looks like a substitution on `$mess`, but it's not. The substitution is actually getting performed on `$_` because the assignment (`=`) should actually be a bind (`=~`).

2. b. If no filenames are given, `<>` begins reading `STDIN`.

3. b. The `t` command prints all your program's statements as they execute. The `T` command prints a *stack trace,* which is a listing of what function is currently being executed, the function that called that function, the function that called that function, and so on.

Hour **13**

References and Structures

If Perl is your first programming language, you'll find this hour especially interesting. In most programming languages, one piece of data can be used as a reference to some other piece of data. Sometimes the piece of data used that way is called a *pointer* (Pascal or C); sometimes the technique is called *indirect referencing* (assembly language); some languages have no explicit concept of pointers at all (BASIC or Java). If you've never used references, pointers, or indirect referencing before, you may need to read parts of this chapter more than once; it can be confusing.

In Perl these pointers, called *references,* are used for many purposes. During this hour you will learn how to use references to call functions with multiple arguments of complex types and how to construct complex data types such as lists of lists.

A reference is much like a card in an old-fashioned library card catalog. Each index card in the catalog refers to a book on the library shelves. The card indicates the kind of book it is (fiction, nonfiction, reference) and its location. Card catalogs can have several references for the same book, in different categories, and even refer to other cards in the catalog ("See Also").

In Perl, references work much the same way by pointing to individual pieces of data. The references know the kind of data they point to (scalar, array, or hash) and its location. References can be copied without changing anything about the original data, and multiple references can be made to the same piece of data. References can, in fact, refer to other references.

Keeping these points in mind, settle down, and take the next few pages slowly and with a clear head while we cover the following topics:

- The basics of references
- Common structures of references
- A brief example to help all this make sense

Reference Basics

You create and assign a normal scalar variable by using an assignment operator, as follows:

```
$a="Stones";  # A normal scalar
```

After this snippet, a scalar variable called $a is created, and it contains the string "Stones". Now, somewhere within the computer's memory, there is a place labeled $a that contains that string, as illustrated here:

```
      $a
  +---------+
  | Stones  |
  +---------+
```

If you were to assign the scalar $a to $b—like $b=$a;—you would wind up with two copies of the data, with two different names, as shown here:

Having two copies might be acceptable if you want separate, independent copies of the data. However, if you want both $a and $b to refer to the *same* piece of data—not a copy—you must create a *reference*. Just as the library catalog card for a book does not contain a copy of the book's text, a reference does not contain any real data; it is simply a pointer to a piece of data. The reference is usually stored in another scalar variable.

To create a reference to any given variable, you must put a backslash in front of the variable name with its type identifier. For example, to create a reference to $a called $ref, you would assign the reference to $ref as follows:

```
$ref=\$a;   # Create a reference to $a
```

This assignment creates a situation like the following:

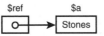

$ref doesn't contain any data for itself; it simply is a reference to $a. The variable $a isn't changed; it can still be assigned to ($a="Foo") or displayed (print $a) as normal.

The variable $ref now contains a reference to $a. You cannot simply manipulate $ref as you would $a, because it doesn't contain a normal scalar value. In fact, printing $ref would display something similar to SCALAR(0x0000). To get to the value inside $a through $ref, you must *dereference* $ref. Think of dereferencing as following the arrow in the preceding block diagram. To print the value of $a through the reference $ref, you would need to use an extra $ like this:

```
print $$ref
```

In the preceding snippet, $ref contains, of course, the reference. The extra $ tells Perl that the reference in $ref refers to a scalar value. The scalar value that $ref refers to is fetched and printed.

You can also modify the original value through the reference—something you can't do with a copy. The following code modifies the original value in $a:

```
$$ref="Sticks";    # De-references $c
```

This modification creates something like the following:

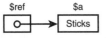

If you had used $ref instead of $$ref

```
$ref="Break";
```

then the reference stored in $ref would have been destroyed and replaced with a real value, as shown next:

13

After the preceding snippet, `$ref` no longer contains a reference; it is just another scalar. You can assign such a reference as you would any other scalar value:

```
$name="Gandalf";
$nref=\$name;            # Has a reference to $name
$oref=$nref;             # Has a copy of the reference to $name
```

You get this result:

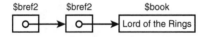

After the preceding snippet, `$$oref` and `$$nref` both can be used to get to the value `"Gandalf"`. You can also store a reference to a reference, as follows:

```
$book="Lord of the Rings";
$bref=\$book;    # A reference to $book
$bref2=\$bref;   # A reference to $bref (not to $book!)
```

In this case, the chain of references looks like the following:

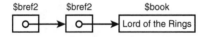

To print the book title given `$bref`, you would use `$$bref`. To print the book title given `$bref2`, you would use `$$$bref2`, with an extra dollar sign, requiring one more level of dereferencing to get to the original value.

References to Arrays

References can also be created to arrays and hashes. Such references are created in the same way a reference is created to a scalar—by using a backslash:

```
$aref=\@arr;
```

Now the scalar variable `$aref` contains a reference to the entire array `@arr`. Visually, it might resemble the following:

To access portions of @arr using the reference $aref, you would use one of the following examples:

```
$$aref[0]                       The first element of @arr
@$aref[2,3]                     A slice of @arr
@$aref                          The whole of array @arr
```

For clarity, you can use braces to separate the reference from the portions dealing with the array itself, as shown here:

```
$$aref[0]            is the same as        ${$aref}[0]
@$aref[2,3]          is the same as        @{$aref}[2,3]
@$aref               is the same as        @{$aref}
```

For example, to print all the elements of @arr using the array reference $aref, you can use this code:

```
foreach $element (@{$aref}) {
   print $element;
}
```

References to Hashes

To create a reference to a hash, you use the backslash, just as as you did with scalars and arrays:

```
$href=\%hash;
```

The preceding snippet creates a reference to the hash %hash and stores it in $href. This snippet creates a reference structure something like this:

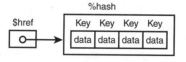

To access portions of %hash using the hash reference %href, you can use the following examples:

```
$$href{key}                    An individual key in %hash, also ${$href}{key}
%$href                         The whole hash, also %{$href}
```

13

To iterate through the hash printing all the values, you can use this code:

```
foreach $key (keys %$href) {
    print $$href{$key};  # same as $hash{$key}
}
```

References as Arguments

Because an entire array or hash can be referenced and the reference stored in a scalar, you can now call functions with multiple arrays or hashes. You may recall from Hour 8, "Functions," that the following type of snippet does not work:

```
# Buggy!
sub getarrays {
    my(@a, @b)=@_;
      :
}
@fruit=qw(apples oranges banana);
@veggies=qw(carrot cabbage turnip);
getarrays(@fruit, @veggies);
```

This code does not work because `getarrays(@fruit, @veggies)` flattens both arrays into the single array `@_`. Inside the `getarrays()` function, assigning `@a` and `@b` to `@_` causes all the elements of `@fruits` and `@vegetables`—now stored in `@_`—to be assigned to `@a`.

After all the arrays are squashed into `@_`, there's no way to tell when one array ends and the next begins; you just have one big, flat list.

This is where references come in. Instead of passing the entire array to `getarrays`, just passing the references to those arrays works splendidly:

```
# Works OK!
sub getarrays {
    my($fruit_ref, $veg_ref)=@_;
      :
}
@fruit=qw(apples oranges banana);
@veggies=qw(carrot cabbage turnip);
getarrays(\@fruit, \@veggies);
```

The function `getarrays()` always receives two values—references—no matter the length of the arrays those references point to. Now `$fruit_ref` and `$veg_ref` can be used to display or edit the data, as shown here:

```
sub getarrays {
    my($fruit_ref, $veg_ref)=@_;

    print "Fruits:", join(',', @$fruit_ref);
    print "Veggies:", join(',', @$veg_ref);

}
```

When passing references to scalars, arrays, or hashes into functions as arguments, keep in mind that the function can manipulate the original data to which the reference points. Notice these two examples:

```
# Passing Values                          # Passing references
sub changehash {                          sub changehash {
  my(%local_hash)=@_;                       my($href)=@_;
  $local_hash{mammal}='bear';               $$href{mammal}='bear';
  return;                                   return;
}                                         }
%hash=(fish => 'shark',                   %hash=(fish => 'shark',
bird=> 'robin');                          bird=> 'robin');
changehash(%hash);                        changehash(\%hash);
```

In the example on the left, when the hash is passed normally, @_ takes on the values of each key-value pair in the original hash, %hash. Inside the subroutine changehash(), the hash elements—now in @_—are copied to a new hash called %local_hash. The hash %local_hash is modified, and the subroutine returns. After the subroutine returns, %local_hash is destroyed and %hash in the main portion of the program remains unmodified.

In the example on the right, a reference to %hash is passed into the subroutine changehash() via @_. The reference is copied to the scalar $href; however, it still refers to the original hash %hash. Inside the subroutine, the hash referred to by $href is changed, and the subroutine returns. After changehash() returns, the original hash %hash contains the new key bear.

> The array @_ is an array of references when it is used to pass subroutine arguments. Modifying the @_ array's elements changes the original values passed into the function. Modifying arguments passed to subroutines is generally considered rude. If you want your subroutines to modify the arguments passed into them, pass references to the arguments into the subroutine instead. This approach is clearer; and when you pass a reference, it's expected that the original value may be modified.

13

Building Structures

Creating references to arrays and hashes is useful for passing them back and forth to subroutines and for creating complex structures that you'll learn about momentarily. However, consider that after you've created a reference to a hash or an array, you no longer need the original hash or array. As long as a reference to a hash or array exists, Perl keeps the hash and array elements around, even if the original data no longer exists.

In the following snippet, a hash, %hash, is created inside a block of code, and the hash is private to that block:

```
my $href;
{
   my %hash=(phone=> 'Bell', light=> 'Edison');
   $href=\%hash;
}
print $$href{light};  # It will print "Edison"!
```

Within the block, the scalar $href is assigned to a reference to %hash. When the block exits, the reference in $href is still valid even though %hash has disappeared (because %hash was private to the block). References to a structure can exist after the structure itself has gone out of scope. Thus the hash referred to by $href can still be modified.

If you look at the preceding block of code, you can see that its only purpose seems to be to create a reference to a hash. Perl provides a mechanism for creating such a reference without using the intermediate hash %hash. It is called *anonymous storage*. The following example creates a reference to an anonymous hash and stores it in $ahref:

```
$ahref={ phone => 'Bell', light => 'Edison' };
```

The braces ({}) enclose a hash and return a reference to it without actually creating a new variable. You can manipulate the anonymous hash using all the techniques described previously under the section titled "References to Hashes."

You can construct an anonymous array by using brackets ([]):

```
$aaref=[ qw( Crosby Stills Nash Young ) ];
```

Again, this array reference can be manipulated as described previously in "References to Arrays."

If a reference points to a private variable, the data it points to vanishes completely when the reference variable itself goes out of scope, as shown here:

```
{
   my $ref;
   {
   $ref=[ qw ( oats peas beans barley ) ];
   }
   print $$ref[0];         # Prints "oats", $ref is still in scope
}
print $$ref[0];            # $ref is no longer in scope--this is an error.
```

The preceding snippet does not even compile if use strict is in effect; in such cases, Perl recognizes the last instance to $ref as being a global variable, which is not allowed. Even without use strict, Perl's -w warnings will probably print an undefined value message.

These anonymous hashes and anonymous arrays can be combined into structures, as you'll see in the next section. Each hash and array reference represents one scalar value, and because it's a single scalar value, it can be stored in other arrays and hashes, as shown here:

```
$a=[ qw( rock pop classical ) ];
$b=[ qw( mystery action drama ) ];
$c=[ qw( biography novel periodical )];

# A hash of references to arrays
%media=( music => $a, film => $b, 'print' =>$c);
```

Recipes for Structures

The following sections present some of the more common arrangements of lists and hashes into structures.

Example: A List of Lists

Lists of lists in Perl are often used to represent a common structure called a *two-dimensional array*. That is, a normal array is a linear list of values, as illustrated here:

[0]	[1]	[2]	[3]
VAL1	VAL2	VAL3	VAL4

A two-dimensional array is like a grid of values in which each element is addressed like a point with coordinates along two axes. The first part of the index indicates a row number (starting with 0), and the second is the column, as you can see here:

[0] [0]	[0] [1]	[0] [2]
data	data	data
[1] [0]	[1] [1]	[1] [2]
data	data	data
[2] [0]	[2] [1]	[2] [2]
data	data	data

13

Perl doesn't really support a true two-dimensional array. However, Perl does allow you to emulate the two-dimensional array using an array of array references.

To create an array of arrays, use this literal representation:

```
@list_of_lists=(
    [ qw( Mustang Bronco Ranger ) ],
    [ qw( Cavalier Suburban Buick ) ],
    [ qw( LeBaron Ram ) ],
);
```

Look carefully at the preceding snippet. A regular list—@list_of_lists—is being created, but it consists of references to other lists. To access individual elements of the innermost lists—cells in the two-dimensional array—you can use the following code:

```
$list_of_lists[0][1];      # Bronco. 1st row, 2nd entry
$list_of_lists[1][2];      # Buick. 2nd row, 3rd entry
```

To find the number of elements in the outer list, do so as you would for any other array—use the $# notation or use the array name in a scalar context:

```
$#list_of_lists;           # Last element of @list_of_lists: 2
scalar(@list_of_lists);    # Number of rows in @list_of_lists: 3
```

Finding the number of elements in one of the inner lists is a little trickier. The syntax $list_of_lists[1] returns the reference in the second row of @list_of_lists. Printing it displays something like ARRAY(0x00000). To treat an element of @list_of_lists as if it were an array, put an @ sign in front of it, like this:

```
scalar(@{$list_of_lists[2]});    # Number of elements in the 3rd row
$#{$list_of_lists[1]};           # Index of last element in the 2nd row
```

To traverse every element in the list of lists, you can use this code:

```
foreach my $outer (@list_of_lists) {
    foreach my $inner (@{$outer}) {
            print "$inner ";
    }
    print "\n";
}
```

You can add to the structure like this:

```
push(@list_of_lists, [ qw( Mercedes BMW Lexus ) ]);   # A new row
push(@{$list_of_lists[0]}, qw( Taurus ) );            # A new element to one list
```

Other Structures

In the preceding section, you learned how to create a basic Perl structure, a lists of lists, by using references and arrays. Actually, an unlimited number of variations of arrays, scalars, and hashes can be combined to create more and more complex data structures, such as the following:

- Lists of hashes
- Hashes of lists
- Hashes of hashes
- Hashes that contain lists, which contain hashes, and so on

There isn't enough room in this book to describe all of these structures. However, the online documentation that comes with each Perl installation contains a document titled the *Perl Data Structures Cookbook*. It is a very detailed but understandable description of each of these structures and many others. With each structure, the *Perl Data Structures Cookbook* details

- Declaring your structure (literal representation)
- Filling your structure
- Adding elements
- Accessing elements
- Traversing the entire structure

To view the *Perl Data Structures Cookbook,* at a command prompt, type `perldoc perldsc`.

Debugging with References

When debugging programs with references, it's not uncommon for new programmers to get confused about which references point to which kinds of structures. Also, the syntax can be confusing until you get used to it. For that reason, Perl provides some facilities to help you figure out what's going on.

First, you can simply print the reference. Perl displays what the reference points to. For example, the line

```
print $mystery_reference;
```

might display

```
ARRAY(0x1231920)
```

This result means that the variable `$mystery_reference` is a reference to an array. Other possibilities include references to scalars (SCALAR), hashes (HASH), or subroutines (CODE). To print the array referred to by `$mystery_reference`, you can treat it like an array, as shown here:

```
print join(',', @{$mystery_reference});
```

13

Perl's debugger also has facilities to help you determine what a reference refers to. In the debugger, you can print the reference as normal. The following snippet shows a reference named $ref being examined:

```
DB<1> print $ref
HASH(0x20114dac)
```

Apparently, $ref refers to a hash. The debugger contains a command, the x command, that will print the reference and its internal structure:

```
 DB<2> x $ref
0 HASH(0x20114dac)
  'fruit' => 'grape'
  'vegetable' => 'bean'
```

In this case, the reference contains a hash with two elements (keys of 'fruit' and 'vegetable'). The debugger can even print complex structures such as lists of lists, as shown here:

```
 DB<1> x $a
0 ARRAY(0x20170bd4)
  0 ARRAY(0x20115484)        <---- First row in a list of lists
   0 5
   1 6                       <---- Elements in the first row
   2 7
  1 ARRAY(0x2011fbb4)        <---- Second row in the list of lists
   0 9
   1 10
   2 11
  2 ARRAY(0x2011faa0)        <---- Third row in a list of lists
   0 'a'
   1 'b'
   2 'c'
```

The preceding example shows a reference—$a—which points to an array (ARRAY(0x20170bd4)). That array, inturn, contains three other array references—ARRAY(0x20115484), ARRAY(0x2011fbb4), and ARRAY(0x2011faa0)—each with three elements.

The module Data::Dumper contains functions that display the contents of references. Data::Dumper is unique in that the output format is valid Perl, which can be stored into files and retrieved later to provide storable structures. The Data::Dumper module will be covered in Hour 14.

Exercise: Another Game, Maze

After learning so many new and strange concepts—references and structures—you deserve a little diversion. The following exercise demonstrates a structure and a few references by allowing you to play a simple game.

In the manner of classic games such as Adventure, Zork, and Hunt the Wumpus, you will be placed in a maze from which you must find your way out. The maze is featureless, consisting of only rooms with at least one doorway. The doorways lead to adjacent rooms to the north, south, east, or west. The object is to find the secret room. You'll soon learn, however, that only a couple of paths actually lead to that room; there are many dead-end paths.

To get started, type Listing 13.1 and save it as Maze. Running the program gives output similar to Listing 13.2.

LISTING 13.1 The Complete Listing for Maze

```
 1:  #!/usr/bin/perl -w
 2:  use strict;
 3:
 4:  my @maze=(
 5:        [ qw( e   swe we ws ) ],
 6:        [ qw( se new sw ns ) ],
 7:        [ qw( ns -       ns n ) ],
 8:        [ qw( ne w       ne w  ) ],
 9:  );
10:  my %direction=( n=> [ -1, 0], s=> [1, 0],
11:        e=> [ 0, 1], w=> [0, -1]);
12:
13:  my %full=( e => 'East', n => 'North', w=>'West', s=>'South');
14:  my($curr_x, $curr_y, $x, $y)=(0,0,3,3);
15:  my $move;
16:
17:  sub disp_location {
18:        my($cx, $cy)=@_;
19:        print "You may move ";
20:        while($maze[$cx][$cy]=~/([nsew])/g) {
21:                print "$full{$1} ";
22:        }
23:        print "($maze[$cx][$cy])\n";
24:  }
25:  sub move_to {
26:        my($new, $xref, $yref)=@_;
27:
28:        $new=substr(lc($new),0,1);
29:        if ($maze[$$xref][$$yref]!~/$new/) {
30:                print "Invalid direction, $new.\n";
31:                return;
32:        }
33:        $$xref += $direction{$new}[0];
34:        $$yref += $direction{$new}[1];
35:  }
36:
```

13

continues

LISTING 13.1 Continued

```
37: until ( $curr_x == $x and $curr_y == $y ) {
38:         disp_location($curr_x, $curr_y);
39:         print "Which way? ";
40:         $move=<STDIN>; chomp $move;
41:         exit if ($move=~/^q/);
42:         move_to($move, \$curr_x, \$curr_y);
43: }
44:
45: print "You made it through the maze!\n";
```

Lines 1–2: These lines are a normal beginning to a Perl program. Warnings are enabled with -w, and use strict is used to catch mistakes and bad programming practices.

Lines 4–9: The structure that describes the maze, @maze, is defined. The maze shown is a 4×4 grid, represented by a list of lists. Each element of the list describes which doors are available in any room in the maze, so if you redesign this maze, make sure you leave a path out! The current maze looks like this:

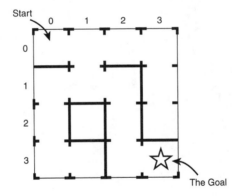

One room is inaccessible (2,1) and is designated by a - in the structure; actually, any string not matching n, s, e, or w would work as well.

Lines 10–11: As the player moves north, south, and so on, the current position in the maze needs to be changed. The hash %direction is used to calculate the player's new position, given the old position and direction. Moving "north" changes the player's *x* coordinate by −1 (going up), and the *y* coordinate remains unchanged. Moving "east" leaves the player's *x* coordinate where it is but increases the *y* coordinate by 1. You'll see how this is used in lines 33–34.

Lines 13–15: The variables used in the program are declared with `my` to make `use strict` happy. The player's current position—stored in `$curr_x` and `$curr_y`—is set to 0,0. The final destination—`$x` and `$y`—is set to 3,3.

Line 17: Given an *x,y* coordinate pair in the grid, this function displays the directions the player is allowed to move in each room.

Line 20: The letters `n`, `s`, `e`, and `w` are picked out of the room description in `$maze[$cx][$cy]` one letter at a time. The appropriate description for the `nsew` directions is displayed from the hash `%full`. This hash is used only for translating the short name (`n`) into the long name (`North`) for display.

Line 25: This function takes a direction (stored in `$new`) and references to the player's current coordinates.

Line 28: The direction is shifted to lowercase with `lc`, and `substr` takes just the first letter and assigns it to `$new`. Thus, `East` becomes `e`, `West` becomes `w`, and `s` remains `s`.

Line 29: The current room—`$maze[$$xref][$$yref]`—is searched for the direction given (`n`, `s`, `e`, or `w`). If it doesn't exist, it's not valid for this room, and a message is printed.

Lines 33–34: The player's *x* and *y* coordinates are changed. If the direction is `e`, then `$direction{e}` is a two-element array reference to (0, 1). The *x* coordinate would be increased by 0—`$direction{e}[0]`. The *y* coordinate would be increased by 1—`$direction{e}[1]`.

Line 37: The main body of the program starts here. The loop will continue until the player's *x* and *y* coordinates (`$curr_x`, `$curr_y`) match the hidden room's coordinates (`$x`, `$y`).

Line 38: The "map" of the current room is displayed.

13

Lines 39–41: The desired direction is read into `$move`, and the newline character is removed with `chomp`. If the player types anything beginning with a `q`, the game ends.

Line 42: The `move_to()` subroutine is called with the player's current desired move and references to the player's coordinates. The `move_to()` subroutine moves the player appropriately by adjusting `$curr_x` and `$curr_y`.

LISTING 13.2 Sample Output from `Maze`

```
You may move East (e)
Which way? e
You may move South West East (swe)
Which way? e
    :
Which way? e
You made it through the maze!
```

To change the maze to have a different layout, simply change the grid stored in `@maze`. The maze doesn't necessarily need to be square, nor does each room need to be mapped, nor does a valid path need to exist. Remember, though, not to provide a door that would lead off the edge of the maze; the program does not check the validity of the maze, although Perl does emit warnings if you construct an invalid maze. You can move the secret room by altering the values of `$x` and `$y`.

Summary

During this hour you learned the basics of references. First, you learned how to take references to Perl's basic data types: scalars, arrays, and hashes. Then, using those references, you learned how to manipulate the original structures. You then learned that it was possible to take a reference to a hash or array that didn't have a variable name associated with it—anonymous storage. Finally, you learned how to use references to create complex data structures and where to find a cookbook of ready-made data structures.

Q&A

Q When I print a list of lists with `print "@LOL"`, it prints `ARRAY(0x101210),ARRAY(0x101400)`, and so on. Why?

A With a normal array, `print "@array"` would print the elements of the array with a space between them. The `print "@LOL"` is doing just that, printing the array elements in `@LOL`. To print the components of each of the arrays in `@LOL`, you must use the technique described in the "Example: List of Lists" section earlier in this hour.

Q I tried to take a reference to a list by using `$ref=\( $a, $b, $c)` and ended up with `$ref` containing a reference to a scalar value instead of a list. Why?

A In Perl, `\($a, $b, $c)` is actually shorthand for `(\$a, \$b, \$c)`! What you wound up with is a reference to the last element in the parentheses, `$c`. To take a reference to an anonymous array, you should have used `$ref=[$a, $b, $c];` instead.

Workshop

Quiz

1. What does `$ref` contain after the statement `$ref=\"peanuts";`?

   a. Nothing. That syntax isn't valid.

   b. `peanuts`

   c. A reference to an anonymous scalar.

2. What does this structure create?

   ```
   $a=[
        { name=> "Rose", kids=> [ qw( Ted Bobby John ) ] },
        { name=> "Marge", kids=>[ qw( Maggie Lisa Bart ) ] },
   ];
   ```

   a. A hash of hashes, which contains a list

   b. A list of hashes, which contains a list

   c. A list of lists, which contains another list

Answers

1. c. A reference can be taken to any value, not just scalar, array, and hash variables. You can take references to a number also with `$ref=\100;`. If you answered a, it's a good idea to try new things with a short program or in the debugger to see what they do if you're unsure.

2. b. This structure wasn't covered explicitly in this hour, but you should have been able to guess the answer. A list (the outer brackets) of hashes (the braces) contains a list (the data for `kids`).

Activities

- Modify the Maze game to take diagonal direction as well. You might want to use four new keys to indicate those directions (`ne`, `nw`, `se`, and `sw` would be difficult to program). Hint: The secret is modifying `@maze` to use the new symbols and `%direction` to indicate which way they should go—`[1,1]`, `[-1,-1]`, and so on.

- Design a structure—even if just on paper—to describe a phone bill. The bill itself contains keys and data like a hash (name, phone, address), and some parts of the bill are lists (itemized calls). Each itemized call could also be considered a hash (destination, time).

13

Hour **14**

Using Modules

Perl, as you've noticed, is an extremely flexible language. Not only does it deal with files, text, math, algorithms, and other issues normally found in any computer language; much of Perl is dedicated to special-purpose functions. Regular expressions are a core part of the language and are very important to the way that Perl is used, although many languages do just fine without them. Likewise, Perl's handling of external programs (backticks, pipes, and system from Hour 11, "System Interaction") is also extensive, whereas many languages don't handle them at all.

A temptation in designing a language is to include anything and everything useful in the core of the language itself. Being so inclusive can, however, create a language that is very large and difficult to use. For example, some language designers feel that support for access to the World Wide Web should be included in the core of the language. That's a useful feature, but not necessarily one that everyone needs. If the Web (using present protocols) is less important 10 years from now than it is today, a decision will have to be made to remove that support and a lot of already-written software will be broken.

For this reason, Perl has taken a different track. Starting with Perl 5, the language itself can be extended through the use of *modules*. Modules are collections of routines that allow you to extend Perl's reach. You'll find modules that add Web browsing, graphics, Windows Object Linking and Embedding (OLE), databases, and almost anything imaginable to Perl. Remember, however, that Perl does not need modules to run. It's completely functional without them.

By using modules, you can gain access to a large library of working code to help you write your programs. The last third of this book, in fact, is dedicated to writing CGI (Common Gateway Interface) programs using Perl modules.

At the time of this writing, more than 4000 modules are available, and more than two dozen are distributed with Perl. These modules, for the most part, can be freely redistributed. You can use them in your own programs for almost any purpose. Consequently, many difficult problems that you may encounter have already been solved for you; all you need to do is install the correct module and use it appropriately.

In this hour you will

- Learn how to use modules in your Perl programs
- Take a quick tour of some built-in modules
- Review the list of the core modules distributed with Perl

A Gentle Introduction

The `use` directive allows you to use a module in your Perl program. For example, to include the `Cwd` module in your program, simply place the following somewhere in your code:

```
use Cwd;
```

It doesn't matter where in your code you place the `use Cwd`, although for clarity and maintainability, it should probably be placed near the beginning of the program.

You may recall that we used the following module in Hour 10, "Files and Directories." At that time, however, you didn't know how it worked. When you run a program with `use Cwd`, what actually happens is this:

1. The Perl interpreter opens your program and reads in all the code until the `use Cwd` statement is found.

2. When your Perl interpreter was installed, it was informed which directory it should search for modules (which is usually Perl's installation directory). That directory is searched for a module called Cwd. This module is a file containing Perl code.

3. Perl reads the module, and all the functions and variables that are required for the module to work are initialized.

4. The Perl interpreter continues reading and compiling your program where it left off.

That's all there is to it. Once Perl has read your entire program, it's ready to run, using all the functionality that the module provides.

> You might notice that use strict looks a lot like use Cwd. Without confusing the issue too much, let's just say that the use statement is a general-purpose instructionto the Perl interpreter to do something (this is called a *pragma*). In the case of use strict, it changes the behavior of the interpreter to be strict about references and bare words; there is no module called strict. In the case of use Cwd, it's to include a module in your program. Don't worry too much about the difference; it's subtle and won't affect you much.

When you include use Cwd in your program, a new function is made available to you: cwd. The cwd function returns the name of your current working directory.

Reading the Documentation

All Perl modules come with their own documentation. In fact, if the module is available to you, then the documentation should be available too, because the documentation is often embedded right in the module itself.

To view a module's documentation, use the perldoc program with the module name. For example, to view the documentation for Cwd, simply type the following at your operating system's command prompt:

```
perldoc Cwd
```

The documentation is then displayed a page at a time. A sample is shown here—shortened somewhat:

```
Cwd(3)              13/Oct/98 (perl 5.005, patch 02)              Cwd(3)

     NAME
              getcwd - get pathname of current working directory

     SYNOPSIS
                        use Cwd;
                        $dir = cwd;

                        use Cwd;
                        $dir = getcwd;

                        use Cwd;
                        $dir = fastgetcwd;

     DESCRIPTION
              The getcwd() function re-implements the getcwd(3) (or
              getwd(3)) functions in Perl.

              The abs_path() function takes a single argument and returns
              the absolute pathname for that argument. It uses the same
              algorithm as getcwd(). (actually getcwd() is abs_path("."))
              :

              :
```

In this case, the Cwd module actually allows you to use three new functions: cwd, getcwd, and fastgetcwd. If you want to use them, feel free to read the documentation for the Cwd module.

> If you're curious as to how the modules work, go look! The modules are mostly written in Perl and are stored in your system's file tree. The Cwd module is stored in a file called Cwd.pm. The location of the file varies, but it is usually stored somewhere under Perl's installation directory. The variable @INC contains the names of possible locations of Cwd.pm; you can print it by typing perl -V at a command prompt. You can also get a list of installed modules by typing **perldoc perllocal**.

Because modules are freely contributed by many different Perl programmers, the quality of documentation varies significantly. The more mainstream modules—the standard distribution, the modules mentioned in this book, and popularmodules such as Tk and LWP—have rather good documentation. Documentation on more obscure modules is usually accurate but may be sparse. If you're having trouble understanding how a module works, see Hour 16, "The Perl Community," for some resources to check or request assistance from the module's author.

What Can Go Wrong?

If your Perl installation was done correctly and has not been corrupted in any way, nothing should go wrong. However, the world is not a perfect place and sometimes things do go wrong.

If you receive the error

```
syntax error in file XXXX at line YYY, next two tokens "use Cwd"
```

you should check your Perl installation's version. Then, at your system's command prompt, try the following command:

```
perl -v
```

If Perl reports a version number less than 5—4.036, for example—you have a very old version of Perl, and you must upgrade to take advantage of features that were added in Perl 5 and to avoid security hazards. In fact, as you may already have experienced, none of the examples in Hour 13, "References and Structures," will work in Perl 4. Upgrade immediately.

Another potential error might read as follows:

```
Can't locate Cwd.pm in @INC (@INC contains: path...path...path...)
BEGIN failed--compilation aborted
```

This error usually means one of three things:

- You've misspelled the name of the module.

  The names of modules are case sensitive; use Cwd is different from use cwd. Some module names have colons (::) within the names—File::Find, for example; you must type them correctly as well.

- The module you're trying to use is not part of the standard distribution and has not been installed on this system in the correct location.

  Every Perl installation comes with approximately 150 modules—the "standard distribution." Some of them are listed later in this hour. All of them should work without any problems. If you need a module that is not in the standard distribution, you or your system administrator must install it.

  Appendix A, "Installing Modules," has instructions on how to install these extra modules.

- The Perl installation is incomplete, corrupted, or has been improperly built and installed.

  Sadly, this happens on occasion.

14

The Perl interpreter goes looking for the installed modules in the pathnames in @INC printed by the error message. If they have been moved, deleted, or otherwise made unavailable, the easiest solution is to reinstall Perl. Before you go through this trouble, however, make sure that the broken module is indeed a standard module. Any additional modules you may have installed can wind up in other places—and that's normal. See Appendix A for details on how to install—and use—modules in nonstandard locations.

A Quick Tour

What follows is a quick tour of some of the modules already installed on your system as part of the core Perl distribution.

Exploring Files and Directories

In Hour 10, you learned how to open directories and read lists of filenames contained within those directories. At that time, when the subject of reading subdirectories came up, you were told not to be concerned. Now you'll learn how to traverse directories and subdirectories recursively.

You might write a common program to find a particular file without knowing exactly what directory it's in. For example, suppose you want to find a file named important.doc somewhere beneath the directory documents, as shown here:

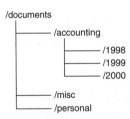

This illustration shows a directory structure under a parent directory named documents. Finding a file somewhere under documents, using only opendir/readdir/closedir, is not easy. First, documents must be searched for the file. Then each of the directories under documents must be searched—accounting, misc, and personal—and then each directory under those directories, and so on.

This is an old problem, solved again and again by programmers over the last 30 years. Writing your own solution to it would be a waste of time. Naturally, the designers of Perl have included an easy solution: the File::Find module. To use the File::Find module in your program, simply enter the following in your program—preferably somewhere near the top:

```
use File::Find;
```

A new function called `find` then becomes available to you. The `find` function's syntax is as follows:

```
find subref, dirlist
```

The second argument to find is a list of directories to search. The first argument is new to you; it's a *subroutine reference*. A subroutine reference is created just like a scalar or array reference: It's simply the subroutine name with a backslash in front of it. You *must* use the `&` in front of the subroutine name to take a reference to it. The subroutine named will be called for each file and directory found in `dirlist`.

The program to find the missing important.doc is shown in Listing 14.1.

LISTING 14.1   Finding a File

```
1:   #!/usr/bin/perl -w
2:   use strict;
3:   use File::Find;
4:
5:   sub wanted {
6:    if ($_ eq "important.doc") {
7:            print $File::Find::name;
8:    }
9:   }
10:  find \&wanted, '/documents';
```

Lines 1–2: These lines provide the usual start to your Perl programs. Warnings are enabled with `-w`, and `use strict` is used to catch errors.

Line 3: The `File::Find` module is brought into your program. It makes the `find` function available to you.

Line 5: This function is called for each file and directory under `'/documents'`. If you have 100 files and 12 directories, this routine will be called 112 times.

Line 6: When the `wanted()` function is called, `$File::Find::name` will contain the pathname to the current file being examined and `$_` will contain just the name. This line determines whether the filename is important.doc; if so, it prints the full pathname.

14

Line 10: The `find` function is called with a subroutine reference—`\&wanted`—and a directory. The `wanted()` function is called for each file and directory under `'/documents'`.

The function called by `find` will have the following variables available to it:

- `$File::Find::name`—The current pathname, directory, and filename.
- `$File::Find::dir`—The current directory name.
- `$_`—The current filename (without the directory). It's important that you don't change the value of `$_` in your function, or if you do, change it back when you're done.

Listing 14.2 contains another `File::Find` example. This example removes all the files on the C: and D: drives with the extension .tmp; these temporary files accumulate and tend to clutter your hard disk. You can easily adapt this program to remove files from a Unix system or perform any kind of file maintenance.

LISTING 14.2   Removing Temporary Files

```
 1:   #!/usr/bin/perl -w
 2:   use strict;
 3:   use File::Find;
 4:
 5:   sub wanted {
 6:   # Check to see if the filename is not a directory
 7:   if ( -f $File::Find::name ) {
 8:           # Verify the filename eds in .tmp
 9:           if ( $File::Find::name=~/\.tmp$/i) {
10:                   print "Removing $File::Find::name";
11:                   unlink $File::Find::name;
12:               }
13:           }
14:   }
15:   find(\&wanted, 'c:/', 'd:/');
```

Most of the program in Listing 14.2 is similar to the one shown in Listing 14.1, with the following differences.

Line 7: The filename passed in is tested to ensure it is a regular file. Remember, this subroutine gets called for both files and directories.

Lines 9–11: The filename is checked to see whether it contains .tmp at the end of the name. If so, the file is deleted with `unlink`.

Copying Files

Another common task—copying files—can be done the hard way in Perl:

1. Open the source file for reading.

2. Open the destination file for writing.

3. Read the source file and write to the destination.

4. Close both files.

And, of course, after each step, you must make sure that no errors occurred and that each write was successful. That's the hard way. An easier way is to take advantage of Perl's `File::Copy` module, which does the file copying for you. The following is an example of this module:

```
use File::Copy;
copy("sourcefile", "destination") || warn "Could not copy files: $!";
```

The preceding snippet copies the contents of `sourcefile` to `destination`. The `copy` function returns 1 on success or 0 if a problem occurred, and it sets the variable `$!` to the proper error.

The `File::Copy` module also provides a `move` function, which moves a file from one directory to another. If the file can be moved by simply renaming it, it's renamed; this is usually the case when the source file and the destination file are on the same file system or disk. If simply renaming the file isn't possible, first the file is copied to the destination filename, and then the original file is removed. Consider this example:

```
use File::Copy;
if (not move("important.doc", "d:/archives/documents/important.doc")) {
   warn "important.doc could not be moved: $!";
   unlink "d:/archives/documents/important.doc";
}
```

In the preceding snippet, the file important.doc is moved from its current directory to the target directory d:/archives/documents. If the `move` function fails, it's possible that a partial target file exists. The `unlink` function removes the partially copied target file if the `move` fails.

Is Anybody Out There?

Perl's modules aren't limited to just manipulating your files and directories. For example, you can use the `Net::Ping` module to determine whether your system can communicate properly on a network.

`Net::Ping` gets its name from a Unix utility called `ping`, which got its name from the "ping" sound that submarines use in echo location. The `ping` utility sends a packet to another system on the network. If that system is up and running, it sends a reply, and the `ping` command reports success. `Net::Ping`, shown here, works the same way:

```
use Net::Ping;

if ( pingecho("www.yahoo.com", 15) ) {
   print "Yahoo is on the network.";
} else {
   print "Yahoo is unreachable.";
}
```

In the preceding snippet, the `Net::Ping` module provides a function called `pingecho`. The `pingecho` function takes two arguments, the first is a host to find—www.yahoo.com in this case. The second argument indicates how long `pingecho` should wait for a response in seconds.

Due to the nature of Perl on Microsoft Windows platforms, the `Net::Ping` module does not currently work. `Net::Ping` relies on the `alarm` function, which does not work under Windows. ActiveState, a major developer of Perl for Windows, has announced plans to implement many missing functions for Windows and may incorporate those changes into Perl eventually.

Once Again, in English?

The `English` module allows some of Perl's obscure special variables to be addressed by more verbose names, as in this example:

```
use English;

while(<>) {
   print $ARG;
}
```

In the preceding snippet, `while(<>)` normally reads a line of input from STDIN and assigns it to $_. It still does. With use `English`, however, the variable $_ is also known as $ARG. A partial list of special variables and their English equivalents is shown here:

Special Variable	English Name
$_	$ARG
@_	@ARG
$!	$OS_ERROR
$^O	$OSNAME
$0	$PROGRAM_NAME

You can find a full list of special variables and the English equivalents in the `English` module's online documentation.

More Diagnostics

The Perl module `diagnostics` can help you find bugs in your program. As you were typing in the examples from this book, the Perl interpreter may have emitted an error message that you didn't quite understand. For example, the short program

```
#!/usr/bin/perl -w

use strict;
print "For help, send mail to help@support.org\n";
```

causes Perl to emit this warning message:

```
In string, @support now must be written as \@support at line 4
Global symbol "@support" requires explicit package name at line 4
```

The `diagnostics` module causes Perl to emit a wordy explanation of its errors and warnings. You can change the sample program to include the `diagnostics` module like this:

```
#!/usr/bin/perl -w
use strict;
use diagnostics;

print "For help, send mail to help@support.com\n";
```

The revised program causes a wordier diagnostic message to print:

```
In string, @support now must be written as \@support at line 4
Global symbol "@support" requires explicit package name at ./diag.pl line 5 (#1)

    (F) You've said "use strict vars", which indicates that all variables
    must either be lexically scoped (using "my"), or explicitly qualified to
    say which package the global variable is in (using "::").
```

If you think for a moment about the two messages, it's apparent that they're related. The first message is obvious. Perl wants your email message to be written as `help\@support.com`. The second message, now that it's been explained, is a bit more obvious: Because `use strict` was in effect, the `@support` variable should have been declared with `my`. Of course, `@support` isn't a variable; it was supposed to be part of an e-mail address, but Perl was misled by the special character `@`.

The letter in front of the message indicates what kind of error you have. `(W)` indicates a warning, `(D)` indicates you've used a deprecated syntax, `(S)` is a severe warning, and `(F)` is a fatal error. For all message types except `(F)`, your Perl program will continue to run.

14

Perl has 60 pages of descriptions to its error messages. If you're having problems figuring out Perl's terse error messages, use diagnostics can sometimes help.

> The full list of error messages and diagnostic information is available for you to browse in the perldiag manual page.

Full List of Standard Modules

A lengthy description of the full list of modules included with Perl is well beyond the scope of this book. The following is a listing of the modules in the standard Perl distribution with a brief description. If you're curious about what the module does and how it works, use perldoc to view the documentation for a specific module.

Module Name	Description
AutoLoader	Allows Perl to compile functions only when needed.
AutoSplit	Splits modules for autoloading.
Benchmark	Allows repetitive timing of Perl functions for speed benchmarking.
CGI	Allows easy access to the Common Gateway Interface for Web programming, covered in Hours 17 to 24.
CPAN	Provides access to the archive of Perl's modules, for installing new modules.
Carp	Generates error messages.
DirHandle	Provides an object interface to directory handles.
Env	Maps the operating system's environment into variables.
Exporter	Allows you to write your own modules.
ExtUtils::*	Allow you to write your own modules or install modules.

continues

Module Name	Description
`File::*`	Offer more file-manipulation operations, such as `File::Copy`.
`File::Spec::*`	Allows OS-independent operations on filenames.
`FileCache`	Opens more files than the OS normally allows.
`FindBin`	Finds the name of the current executing program.
`Getopt::*`	Allow you to process command-line options in your programs.
`I18N::Collate`	Allows locale-specific sorting.
`IPC::*`	Provide Interprocess Communications; two- and three-ended pipes, for example.
`Math::*`	Allow you to use extended math libraries with arbitrary-precision floating-point, integer, and complex numbers.
`Net::*`	Allow you to get information on network hosts. For example, `Net::hostent` translates IP addresses—such as `204.71.200.68`—into host names—such as `www.yahoo.com`.
`Pod::*`	Provide access to Perl's Plain Old Documentation formatting routines.
`Symbol`	Allows you to view or manipulate Perl's own symbol table.
`Sys::Hostname`	Obtains your system's IP hostname.
`Sys::Syslog`	Allows writing to a Unix system's error log.
`Term::*`	Provide terminal-controlling functions interface for cursor positioning, screen cleaning, and so on.

continues

14

Module Name	Description
Text::Abbrev	Builds abbreviation tables.
Text::ParseWords	Allows you to parse text to search for words.
Text::Soundex	Categorizes words based on pronunciation, using the Soundex method.
Tie::*	Connects Perl's variables to functions so that you can implement your own arrays and hashes.
Time::*	Allows you to parse and manipulate time. For example, you can convert times such as "Sat Jul 24 16:21:38 EDT 1999" back into the number of seconds since January 1, 1970.
constant	Allows you to define constant values.
integer	Causes Perl to do its math in integers instead of floating-point numbers (sometimes).
locale	Causes locale-based string comparison (international character string comparison).

Where Do You Go from Here?

If you want to get a feel for the kinds of modules available to you—for free—use a Web browser and head to http://www.cpan.org. The modules are organized (roughly) by category.

Some modules require a C compiler and a minimal development environment for installation. They may not be available on a Windows machine. ActiveState's Perl installation contains a utility called PPM, which can be used to browse and install prebuilt modules.

The Appendix contains step-by-step instructions for installing modules on Unix and Windows machines. These instructions will explain how to use the CPAN module (for Unix) and ActiveState's PPM utility to install new modules.

Summary

In this hour, you learned how modules are used to extend the Perl language to perform many other tasks. This general-purpose method of adding new functionality to Perl will be used throughout the rest of the book. Also, a few common modules were presented, and the full listing of modules included with the standard distribution was reviewed.

Q&A

Q In the `File::Find` module, what are the colons (`::`) in the variable names? Like `$File::Find::dir`?

A Perl modules can create alternate areas for variable names, called *namespaces*, so that the module's global variable names and your global variable names don't get mixed up. So a global variable in the `Cwd` module would be known as `$Cwd::x`. Most of your global variables actually have the full name of `$main::x` for `$x`. But for now, that's not important.

Q I have a Windows 95/98/NT machine, and the module I want to use is not available through ActiveState's `PPM`. How can I install it?

A Unfortunately, most of CPAN's modules assume that you have a full Unix-like development environment to compile and install modules; this kind of environment is not easy to put together on a Windows machine. If you're very handy with a C compiler, you can download a development environment and build your own module, but doing so is not easy. Some modules are written entirely in Perl, and it may just be a matter of opening the distribution and putting the files in the correct places.

Q I have an older Perl program with `require` instead of `use`. What's `require`?

A The `require` statement is similar to `use`, and because Perl 4 did not have the `use` keyword, it used `require`. (Follow that?) The `require` statement causes the interpreter to find a library file and include it in your program—similar to `use`. However, the key difference is that a `require` happens whenever the `require` statement is run (at runtime), whereas the `use` directive happens when your program is first loaded (at compile time).

Workshop

Quiz

1. If you want to use the `cwd` function twice in a program, how many times do you have to `use Cwd;`?

    a. Once.

    b. Once for each instance of `cwd`, so two times.

    c. None. `cwd` is a built-in function.

2. What module provides an alias for the `$_` variable?

    a. `LongVars`

    b. `English`

    c. `$_` does not have an alias.

14

Answers

1. a. After a module has been pulled into your program with `use`, all its functions are available to use throughout the rest of your program.

2. b. `use English` causes `$_` to be known by the name `$ARG`.

Activities

1. Flip to Appendix A and try using the instructions there for installing the module `Bundle::LWP` from CPAN. You'll need a module in that bundle for the examples in Hour 24, "Making an Interactive Site."

HOUR 15

Finding Permanence

Writing Perl programs that find data in files or interact with the user is all well and good. But what happens when the program ends? The results are gone, you've got nothing to show for your effort, and you're left with this empty feeling—as though nothing had happened at all.

You may already be thinking of ways in which you could solve this problem in Perl based on what you have learned in previous hours, such as files, lists, and hashes. That would, of course, be the Hard Way.

Storing information for later retrieval the Easy Way is what databases are all about. A database is a set of one or more files in a particular format that specialized software can access for storing data and retrieving it later. A properly designed database can be used by many kinds of programs for queries, reports, and data entry. To design a database, you need to think carefully about what kind of data you want to store and how you want to store it. You also need to consider how the data will be accessed: by one person at a time or by many users simultaneously.

In this hour you'll learn how to

- Create a DBM file and store data in it
- Treat regular text files as a database
- Read and write to random positions in files
- Lock files for concurrent access

DBM Files

One of the simplest ways for your Perl program to remember data in an organized way is through the use of DBM files. A DBM file is a file that's been connected to a Perl hash. To read and write a DBM file, you simply manipulate a hash, just as you've been doing since Hour 7, "Hashes."

To tie your hash to a DBM file, use the Perl function dbmopen, as shown here:

```
dbmopen(hash, filename, mode)
```

The dbmopen function connects the *hash* to a DBM file. The *filename* you supply actually creates one or two different files on your hard disk with names that are a variation on *filename*: *filename*.pag, *filename*.dir, or filename.db. Perl uses these files to store the hash. These files are not text files, and you should *not* attempt to use an editor on them. Also, if one of the files is empty, or seems very large relative to the amount of data in it, don't worry about it; that's normal.

The *mode* is the permissions on the two DBM files that Perl creates. Recall that permissions were discussed in the section "A Crash Course in File Permissions" in Hour 10, "Files and Directories." For Unix, use a sensible set of permissions; they control who can access your DBM file. For example, 0666 allows everyone read and write access to your DBM files. Mode 0644 allows you to read and write the files, but others to read them only. For Windows, you can simply use 0666, because you don't have any file system permissions to worry about.

The dbmopen function returns true if the hash has been successfully tied to the DBM file; it returns false otherwise. Now consider this example:

```
dbmopen(%hash, "dbmfile", 0644) || die "Cannot open DBM dbmfile: $!";
```

After the preceding statement is executed, the hash %hash is connected to a DBM file called dbmfile. Perl creates a pair of files on your disk, called dbmfile.pag and dbmfile.dir, to keep the hash in. If you assign a value to the hash, as shown here, Perl updates the DBM files with that information:

```
$hash{feline}="cat";
$hash{canine}="dog";
```

Fetching information causes Perl to retrieve the key and data from the DBM file, as follows:

```
print $hash{canine};
```

To disconnect the hash from the DBM file, use `dbmclose` with the hash name like this:

```
dbmclose(%hash);
```

After you've disconnected from the DBM file, the items that were stored in it—the keys `feline` and `canine` with the values associated with them—are still in the DBM file, which is the whole point of a DBM file. The key-value pairs stored in a hash tied to a DBM file are retained between invocations of a Perl program.

Functions you would normally perform with a hash can be performed with a hash that's tied to a DBM file. The hash functions `keys`, `values`, and `delete` work normally (`exists` does not work). You can empty the hash—and the DBM file—by assigning the hash to an empty list like this: `%hash=()`. You can even initialize the hash by assigning it to a list after it's tied to the DBM file with `dbmopen`.

Important Points to Know

The following are just a few small points you need to know about tying hashes to DBM files:

- The length of your keys and data is now limited. Normal hashes have (virtually) unlimited key length and value length. Hashes that are tied to a DBM file have a limited key and value length, typically around 1,024 characters for both the key and the value combined—this is a limitation of DBM files. The total number of keys and values that can be stored has not changed; it is limited only by your file system.

- The values in the hash before `dbmopen` are lost, so it's best just to use a fresh hash. Now consider this example:
  ```
  %h=();
  $h{dromedary}="camel";
  dbmopen(%h, "database", 0644) || die "Cannot open: $!";
  print $h{dromedary};  # Likely will print nothing at all
  dbmclose(%h);
  ```

  In the preceding snippet, the value in the hash %h—the key of `dromedary`—is lost when `dbmopen` is executed.

- The values in the hash while it's tied to the DBM filedisappear after `dbmclose` is performed:
  ```
  dbmopen(%h, "database", 0644) || die "Cannot open: $!";
  $h{bovine}="cow";
  dbmclose(%h);
  print $h{bovine};    # Likely will print nothing
  ```

  The values in the hash *while* it is connected to the DBM file are retained in the DBM file. Afterward, the hash itself is empty.

Walking Through DBM-Tied Hashes

Consider for a moment a hash that's been tied to a DBM file. For example, if you write a Perl program to keep appointments, phone numbers, and other information in that hash, after a while the hash can become large. Because the hash's values are retained between runs of your Perl program, they never quite go away—unless you delete them on purpose.

If your DBM file (called `records`) has collected a lot of information, this snippet might have some problems:

```
dbmopen(%recs, "records", 0644) || die "Cannot open records: $!";
foreach my $key (keys %recs) {
    print " $key  = $recs{$key}\n";
}
dbmclose(%recs);
```

There's no problem with the code. The hash `%recs` is first tied to a DBM file, and then the keys from the hash are extracted with `keys %recs`. The list of keys is iterated over with `foreach my $key`, and each key and its value are printed.

If the list of keys in `%recs` is large, however, the statement `keys %recs` could take some time to execute. Perl has another function that allows you to iterate over a hash one key at a time; it's called `each`. The syntax for `each` is as follows:

```
 ($key, $val)=each(%hash);
```

The `each` function returns a two-element list: a key and a value from the hash. Each successive call to `each` returns the next key-value pair from the hash. When the keys are exhausted, `each` returns an empty list. A better way to iterate over a potentially large hash would be to use the following example:

```
dbmopen(%recs, "records", 0644) || die "Cannot open records: $!";
while( ($key, $value)=each %recs) {
    print " $key  = $value\n";
}
dbmclose(%recs);
```

> You don't necessarily have to use `each` with a hash tied to a DBM file; you can use it with any hash at all.

Exercise: A Free-Form Memo Pad

Now that you have an easy way to keep data on the disk, it's time to put it to good use. This exercise presents a free-form memo pad that keeps information based on keys and allows you to search and retrieve that information with simple queries.

A sample session with the program (called memopad) is shown in Listing 15.1.

To query the memopad program, simply type the name of a topic, followed by a question mark. To program in a new fact, type a phrase in the form "*X* is *Y*", where *X* is the topic and *Y* is the information to associate with that topic. You can search the database for similarities by typing "**like** *pattern?*" where *pattern* is a regular expression to search for in the topics. All topics matching that expression will be printed. To exit the program, type **quit** at the prompt.

LISTING 15.1 Sample Session with *memopad*

```
Your question: perl?
I don't know about "perl"
Your question: perl is a programming language
Ok, I'll remember "perl" as "a programming language"
Your question: perl's homepage is at http://www.perl.org
Ok, I'll remember "perl's homepage" as "at http://www.perl.org"
Your question: perl?
perl is a programming language
Your question: like perl?
perl is like perl
perl's homepage is like perl
Your question: quit
```

All the information given to the memopad program will be remembered each time the program is run, because the data is stored in a hash tied to a DBM file. The code for memopad is shown in Listing 15.2.

LISTING 15.2 Full Listing of *memopad*

```
 1:  #!/usr/bin/perl -w
 2:  use strict;
 3:
 4:  my(%answers, $subject, $info, $pattern);
 5:
 6:  dbmopen(%answers, "answers", 0666) || die "Cannot open answer DBM: $!";
 7:  while(1) {
 8:      print "Your question ('quit' to quit): ";
 9:      chomp($_=lc(<STDIN>));
10:      last if (/^quit$/);
11:      if (/like\s+(.*)\?/) {
12:          $pattern=$1;
13:          while( ($subject,$info)=each(%answers) ) {
14:              if ($subject=~/$pattern/) {
15:                  print "$subject is like $pattern\n";
16:              }
```

continues

LISTING 15.2   Continued

```
17:            }
18:       } elsif (/(.*)\?/) {
19:           $subject=$1;
20:           if ($answers{$subject}) {
21:               print "$subject is $answers{$subject}\n";
22:           } else {
23:               print qq{I don't know about "$subject"\n};
24:           }
25:       } elsif (/(.*)\sis\s(.*)/) {
26:           $subject=$1;
27:           $info=$2;
28:           $answers{$subject}=$info;
29:           print qq{Ok, I'll remember "$subject" as "$info"\n};
30:       } else {
31:           print "I'm sorry, I don't understand.\n";
32:       }
33:   }
34:   dbmclose(%answers);
```

Lines 1–2: These lines provide the usual start to Perl programs: a #! line with -w, which means that warnings are enabled. Also, a use strict directive keeps you from making silly mistakes.

Line 6: The hash %answers is tied to the DBM file answers with dbmopen. Two files will be created on disk—answers.pag and answers.dir.

Line 7: while(1) executes the loop forever. Somewhere in the loop is a last or exit to get out of the loop.

Line 9: This line looks confusing because several things are happening at once. lc shifts its scalar argument to lowercase. Because <STDIN> is being used in a scalar context, one line of input from STDIN is read in and subsequently shifted to lowercase, and the result is assigned to $_. chomp is used to remove the trailing newline character.

Line 10: If the input line consists of only the word quit, the while loop is exited.

Line 11: If the input line (now in $_) matches the word like and then some text and then a ?, the text is saved in $1 by the parentheses in the pattern match . . .

Line 12: and the string in the pattern match from line 11 is saved into $pattern.

Lines 13–17: The hash %answers is searched key by key for a key that matches the string in $pattern. As each key is found, it is printed.

Line 18: (This line is a continuation of the `if` started on line 11.) Otherwise, if the input line ends in a question mark, everything up to—but not including—the question mark is remembered in `$1` with parentheses.

Line 19: The pattern in `$1` is saved into `$subject`.

Lines 20–24: If the key `$subject` is in the hash `%answers`, then the key and the associated data are printed. Otherwise, the program responds with `I don't know`.

Lines 25–27: (This line is a continuation of the `if` started on line 11.) Otherwise, if the input line is in the form `X is Y`, the first part (*X*) is remembered in `$subject` and the last part in `$info`.

Line 28: The information in `$info` is stored in the hash `%answers` as `$subject`.

Line 34: The DBM files are disconnected from `%answers`.

Text Files as Databases

Often, databases are small, simple arrangements: a list of users on a small system, local hosts on a small network, a list of favorite Web sites, or a personal address file. These are all simple forms of databases, and for simple databases, normal text files will often do. But before using text files as databases, you need to consider some pros and cons.

The good news: Using a text file as a database has a few distinct advantages over using more complicated alternatives such as DBM files or large databases such as Oracle or Sybase. Some of these advantages are:

- Text file databases are portable. They can be moved between vastly different kinds of systems without too much trouble.

- Text file databases can be edited with a text editor and printed to paper without any special tools.

- Text file databases are simple to construct initially.

- Text file databases can be imported into other programs—spreadsheets, word processors, or other databases—without hassles. Almost any program that allows you to import data allows you to import text.

Now, as you would expect, there is some bad news. To understand the bad news fully, consider how text files are usually constructed. Text file databases are traditionally arranged so that each line in the text file is a record and columns within each line are fields.

To your system, however, a text file is simply a stream of characters. So a text file database that looks like

    Bob 555-1212

    Maury 555-0912

    Paul 555-0012

    Ann-Marie 555-1190

is actually stored as a continuous stream of characters like

    Bob[space]555-1212[newline]Maury[space]555-0912[newline]Paul[space] . . .

where [space] represents a space character and [newline] represents a record separator (newline character, "\n") for your operating system, as discussed in Hour 5. The characters for each record and each field are all packed together in one long stream of characters; the nice column-row display is simply the human-readable way that editors, printers, and Perl represent the data.

Keeping that structure in mind, consider the disadvantages of a text file database:

- Text files cannot be inserted into; they can only be overwritten—partially or completely. Inserting new data anywhere, except at the end of the file, involves copying all the data following the newly inserted data further down in the file.

  New data: Susan 555-6613 to be inserted after "Bob"

  Bob[space]555-1212[newline]Maury[space]555-0912[newline]Paul[space] . . .

  All this data must be copied →

  Bob[space]555-1212[newline]Susan[space]555-6613[newline]Maury[space] . . .

  Copying data within a file is error-prone and slow.

- The reverse is also true: Removing data from the middle of a text file is difficult. All the data following the removed portion must be copied into the gap. For example, you would remove Maury from the original text database like this:

  By removing this

  Bob[space]555-1212[newline]Maury[space]555-0912[newline]Paul[space] . . .

  ← All this data must be copied

  Bob[space]555-1212[newline]Paul[space]555-0012[newline]Ann-Marie[space] . . .

- To find a particular record in a text file database, you must search the file sequentially—normally from the top down. Unlike a DBM file, in which finding a record is as easy as looking for it in a hash, each line of a text file must be examined to see whether it's the correct record. This process is slow, and it gets progressively slower the larger the database gets.

Inserting into or Removing from a Text File

Text file databases aren't completely hopeless. With a small text file database, you can easily insert or delete from the database if you treat the text file like an array. For example, if the database

Bob 555-1212

Maury 555-0912

Paul 555-0012

Ann-Marie 555-1190

were saved into a file called phone.txt, a short Perl program could read the database into an array like this:

```perl
#!/usr/bin/perl -w
use strict;

sub readdata {
    open(PH, "phone.txt") || die "Cannot open phone.txt: $!";
    my(@DATA)=<PH>;
    chomp @DATA;
    close(PH);
    return(@DATA);
}
```

Here, the `readdata()` function reads phone.txt and puts the data into @DATA—without the newline characters—and returns the array. If you add another function, `writedata()`, as follows, the database can be read and written:

```perl
sub writedata {
    my(@DATA)=@_;    # Accept new contents
    open(PH, ">phone.txt") || die "Cannot open phone.txt: $!";
    foreach(@DATA) {
        print PH "$_\n";
    }
    close(PH);
}
```

Now, to insert records into the database, simply read the data with `readdata()` into an array; use `push`, `unshift`, or `splice` to insert a record into the array; and then write the array out again with `writedata()` like this:

```perl
@PHONELIST=readdata();    # Put all of the records in @PHONELIST
push(@PHONELIST, "April 555-1314");
writedata(@PHONELIST);  # Write them out again.
```

To remove text from the text file database, use `splice`, `pop`, or `shift` on the array @PHONELIST before writing it back out. You can also manually edit the array with a loop, such as with `grep`:

```
@PHONELIST=readdata();     # Read all records into @PHONELIST
# Remove everyone named "Ann" (or Annie, Annette, etc..)
@PHONELIST=grep(! /Ann/, @PHONELIST);
writedata(@PHONELIST);
```

In the preceding snippet, the records are copied into @PHONELIST from `readdata()`. The `grep` iterates over @PHONELIST, testing each element to see whether it does not match Ann; those that do not match are assigned to @PHONELIST again. The @PHONELIST array is then given back to `writedata()` for writing.

Random File Access

If you're adventurous, you can do random reads and writes within a file, as previously mentioned. The following sections briefly cover some tools you'll need to do random reads and writes; they are not covered more extensively because you shouldn't need them often.

Opening Files for Read and Write

Until now, you've looked at three methods for opening files. Files could be opened for reading, they could be opened for writing, or they could be opened for appending. Files can also be opened for both reading and writing at the same time. Table 15.1 lists the various modes available for opening files.

TABLE 15.1 Summary of Open Modes

open *Command*	Reading?	Writing?	Append?	Creates if Does Not Exist?	Truncates Any Existing Data?
open(F, "<file") or open(F, "file")	Yes	No	No	No	No
open(F, ">file")	No	Yes	No	Yes	Yes
open(F, ">>file")	No	Yes	Yes	Yes	No
open(F, "+<file")	Yes	Yes	No	No	No
open(F, "+>file")	Yes	Yes	No	Yes	Yes
open(F, "+>>file")	Yes	Yes	Yes	Yes	No

Notice the following:

- Modes that specify "Append" can be tricky. On some systems such as Unix, data written to the file is always written at the end of the file, regardless of where the read pointer is. (You'll read more about that in a moment.)

- You should almost never use +>. The contents of the file are erased as soon as it's opened.

Moving Around in a Read/Write File

When a file is opened, the operating system keeps track of where in the file you happen to be. This pointer is called the *read pointer*. For example, when a file is first opened for reading, the read pointer is at the beginning of the file, as shown here:

After you've read through the whole file, the read pointer is at the end of the file, as shown here:

To reposition the pointer to any spot within the file, you must use the seek function. The seek function takes two arguments: The first is an open filehandle, and the second is the offset in the file that you want to seek. The last argument is what the offset is relative to: 0, the beginning of the file; 1, the current position in the file; or 2, the end of the file. The following are some examples of seeking within a file:

```
# open existing file for reading and writing
open(F, "+<file.txt") || die "file.txt error: $!";
seek(F, 0, 2);                # Seek to the end of the file
print F "On the end";         # Appended to the end of the file
seek(F, 0, 0);                # Seek back to the beginning of the file
print F "This is at the beginning";
```

The tell function returns the position of the current read pointer in a file. For example, after running the preceding snippet, tell(F) would return 24—the length of "This is at the beginning"—because the read pointer is sitting immediately after that text.

This section barely touched upon the seek, tell, and open commands. For more information on these commands, consult your online documentation. The seek, tell, and open functions are documented in the perlfunc manual, which you can access by typing perldoc perlfunc at the command prompt. Additionally, a longer explanation of open is in a manual section called perlopentut; for that documentation, type perldoc perlopentut at a command prompt.

Locking

Imagine that you've written a wonderful Perl program and that the whole world wants to use it. If you're on a Unix or Windows NT machine, or even on a Windows 95 or 98 machine, more than one person might be running your program *at the same time*. Or, your program may be put onto a Web server, and it's run so frequently that instances of your program overlap.

Now suppose that your program uses a database for its work, such as the text file database just described—but this discussion applies to any kind of database. Look at the following code, which uses functions described in the preceding section:

```
chomp($newrecord=<STDIN>);       # Get a new record from the user
@PHONEL=readdata();              # Read data into @PHONEL
push(@PHONEL, $newrecord);       # Put the record into the array
writedata(@PHONEL);              # Write out the array
```

Looks harmless, doesn't it? But if two people run your program at nearly the same time and try adding different records, it's not harmless at all; it's quite buggy. In the following diagram, this particular set of Perl statements is run at nearly the same time, on the same system, by two different people (Person 2 is working slightly behind Person 1). Watch carefully.

Time	Sequence	Person 1	Person 2
	1	$newrecord = "David 555-1212";	
	2	@PHONEL = readdata ();	$newrecord = "Joy 555-6611";
	3	push (@PHONEL, $newrecord);	@PHONEL = readdata ();
	4	writedata (@PHONEL);	push (@PHONEL, $newrecord);
	5		writedata (@PHONEL);

From Person 1's perspective, the data is read in at step 2, and the new record ("David") is added to @PHONEL in step 3 and written at step 4.

15

From Person 2's perspective, the data is read in at step 3, the new record (`"Joy"`) is added to @PHONEL in step 4, and @PHONEL is written out in step 5.

Here's the bug: The data read in by Person 2 in step 3 does not contain the record `"David."` That record hasn't been written yet by Person 1. So Person 2 adds `"Joy"` to the array @PHONEL, which does not contain `"David."` At the same time, Person 1 writes a copy of @PHONEL to the database—which does contain `"David."`

When Person 2's instance of the program finally makes it to step 5, it overwrites the data written by Person 1. The database winds up with `"Joy"`, but not `"David"`—clearly a bug.

> The problem is actually *worse* than you just learned; the preceding explanation is vastly oversimplified. The additional headaches come from the fact that the `writedata()` functions seemingly open and write the data all in one burst—but they don't. Multiprocessing operating systems can actually stop a program in the middle of writing data, go run another program for a moment, and resume it later—milliseconds later, but later nonetheless. Both programs can be writing to the same file, with different data, at the same time. This can cause your data file to become corrupted or even erased.

The kind of problem we have just seen has a formal name; it's called a *race condition*. That is, what gets stored in the file depends on which user "wins" or "loses" the race. Race conditions are difficult to debug in programs, because they come and go depending on how many instances of the program are running at the same time, and because the bugs associated with race conditions aren't always obvious.

Allowing multiple programs to update the same data at the same time is a tricky proposition, but it can be handled using a mechanism called *locks*. File locks are used to prevent multiple instances of a program from altering a file at the same time.

Locking files poses several problems, but the foremost among them is that different operating systems and different kinds of file systems require different types of locking mechanisms. The next sections describe how to lock files to prevent this kind of disaster.

Locking with Unix and Windows NT

To lock files under Unix and Windows NT, you can use Perl's `flock` function. The `flock` function provides an *advisory* locking mechanism. This means that any programs you write that need to access the file must also use `flock` to make sure that no one else is writing to the file at the same time. However, other programs can still modify the file; this is why the mechanism is called *advisory locking*, not *mandatory locking*.

You're familiar with one kind of advisory lock already: a traffic stop light. The signal is there to prevent multiple vehicles from entering the same part of the intersection at the same time. But the signal works only if everyone obeys it. The same holds true for file locks. Every program that can potentially access a file at the same time must use `flock` to prevent an accident. An advisory lock doesn't keep other processes from accessing the data; it prevents other processes only from obtaining a lock.

The `flock` function takes two arguments—a filehandle and a lock type—as you can see in the following syntax:

```
use Fcntl qw(:flock);

flock(FILEHANDLE, lock_type);
```

The `flock` function returns true if the lock is successful; it returns false otherwise. Sometimes calling `flock` causes your program to pause and wait for other locks to clear (more about this in a moment). The `use Fcntl qw(:flock)` allows you to use symbolic names for the `lock_type` instead of harder-to-remember numbers.

There are two kinds of locks: shared and exclusive. Normally, you get a shared lock when you want to read a file and an exclusive lock when you want to write to it. If a process has an exclusive lock on a file, then that's the only lock there is—no other process can have locks at all. But many processes can have shared locks at the same time as long as there are no exclusive locks. In such cases, it's safe to have many processes reading the file at the same time as long as nobody is writing.

Some possible values for `lock_type` are as follows:

- `LOCK_SH`—This value requests a shared lock on the file. If another process has an exclusive lock on the file, then `flock` pauses until the exclusive lock is cleared before taking out the shared lock on the file.
- `LOCK_EX`—This value requests an exclusive lock on a file opened for writing. If other processes have a lock (either shared or exclusive), then `flock` pauses until those locks are cleared.
- `LOCK_UN`—This value releases a lock, but it is rarely needed; simply closing the file writes out any unwritten data and releases the lock. Releasing the lock on a file that is still open can cause data corruption.

Locks taken with `flock` are released when you close the file or when your program exits—even if it exits with an error.

Taking out a lock on a file that you're also trying to read or write can be tricky. Problems arise because opening a filehandle and locking the file is at least a two-step process: You have to have the file open before you can lock it. If you open a file with `open(FH, ">filename")` and then get a lock with `flock`, you've modified the file (truncated with >) before you obtain the lock. This could potentially modify the file (by truncating it) while some other process has a lock on it.

Solving this problem involves something called a *semaphore file*. A semaphore file is just a sacrificial file whose contents aren't important; whoever holds a lock on that file can proceed.

To use a semaphore file, all you need is a filename that can be used as a semaphore and a couple of functions to lock and unlock the semaphore file, as shown in Listing 15.3. This is not a complete program; it is meant to be included as a part of other programs.

LISTING 15.3   General-Purpose Locking Functions

```
1:   use Fcntl qw(:flock);
2:   # Any file name will do for semaphore.
3:   my $semaphore_file="/tmp/sample.sem";
4:
5:   # Function to lock (waits indefinitely)
6:   sub get_lock {
7:       open(SEM, ">$semaphore_file")
8:           || die "Cannot create semaphore: $!";
9:       flock(SEM, LOCK_EX) || die "Lock failed: $!";
10:  }
11:
12:  # Function to unlock
13:  sub release_lock {
14:      close(SEM);
15:  }
```

These locking functions can surround any code that you do not want to be run concurrently, even if that code has nothing to do with reading or writing files. For example, this snippet—even if run by several processes at the same time—allows only one process at a time to print a message:

```
get_lock();       # waits for a lock.
print "Hello, World!\n";
release_lock();   # Let someone else print now...
```

The `get_lock()` and `release_lock()` functions we have just seen will be used throughout the rest of this book for locking files when locks are needed.

Waiting for user input (or any other potentially slow events) while holding a lock is not a good idea. All other programs that need that lock will stop and wait for the lock to be released. You therefore should obtain your lock, do your locking-sensitive code, and then release your lock.

Reading and Writing with a Lock

Now is a good time to show the text file database `readdata()` and `writedata()` functions being used with file locking. To do this, all you'll need is a semaphore file and the `get_lock()` and `release_lock()` subroutines from the previous section.

The first part of Listing 15.4 is the locking code from the previous section.

LISTING 15.4   Demonstration of Text File I/O with Locking

```perl
 1:  #!/usr/bin/perl -w
 2:  use strict;
 3:  use Fcntl qw(:flock);
 4:
 5:  my $semaphore_file="/tmp/list154.sem";
 6:
 7:  # Function to lock (waits indefinitely)
 8:  sub get_lock {
 9:      open(SEM, ">$semaphore_file")
10:          || die "Cannot create semaphore: $!";
11:      flock(SEM, LOCK_EX) || die "Lock failed: $!";
12:  }
13:
14:  # Function to unlock
15:  sub release_lock {
16:      close(SEM);
17:  }
18:
19:  sub readdata {
20:      open(PH, "phone.txt") || die "Cannot open phone.txt $!";
21:      my(@DATA)=<PH>;
22:      chomp(@DATA);
23:      close(PH);
24:      return(@DATA);
25:  }
26:  sub writedata {
27:      my(@DATA)=@_;
28:      open(PH, ">phone.txt") || die "Cannot open phone.txt $!";
29:      foreach(@DATA) {
30:          print PH "$_\n";
31:      }
```

continues

LISTING 15.4 Continued

```
32:     close(PH);    # Releases the lock, too
33:  }
34:  my @PHONEL;
35:
36:  get_lock();
37:  @PHONEL=readdata();
38:  push(@PHONEL, "Calvin 555-1012");
39:  writedata(@PHONEL);
40:  release_lock()
```

Most of Listing 15.4 is code you've already seen. The functions get_lock(), release_lock(), readdata(), and writedata() were all outlined earlier in this hour.

The meat of this program starts at line 34. There, a lock is taken out with get_lock(). The file is then read into @PHONEL with readdata(), the data is manipulated, and then written back out to the same file with writedata(). When all of this is done, release_lock() releases the lock in case other programs are waiting for it.

Locking with Windows 95 and Windows 98

Windows 95 , 98, and ME do not support file locking. Why not? Because under these operating systems, only one program is allowed to have the file open at a time anyway, so file locking is unimplemented. If you use flock on a Windows 95, 98, or ME system, you get the following error message:

```
flock() unimplemented on this platform at line...
```

Fortunately, however, these operating systems tend to support only one user at a time.

> The listings throughout this book that involve file locking use the functions get_lock() and release_lock() demonstrated earlier. These functions will cause errors when used, because flock is not implemented under Windows 95, 98, or ME. You can omit them from these listings for those operating systems. Notes will be in the listings to remind you.

Locking Elsewhere

In some situations, you may have multiple programs reading and writing a file at the same time, and for some reason, flock isn't available to you. Even on platforms where flock is available, it might not be applicable in all situations. For example, under Unix flock is not reliable on files over a Network File System (NFS). Or you might be in a mixed environment with Unix servers and Windows NT clients where Unix would normally support flock, but the underlying file system may not.

In the Perl Frequently Asked Questions (FAQ) list, section 5, "Files and Formats," you'll find suggestions for locking files without flock. To read about them, look in the perlfaq5 section of the documentation.

Summary

In this hour, you learned a few ways to store data between invocations of your Perl programs. First you learned about DBM files and how they can be used to tie a hash to your hard disk. Next you learned about text files and how they can be used for simple database purposes. Finally, to prevent problems with concurrent access to files, you learned about how to lock files and keep data safe.

Q&A

Q Can I store the structures from Hour 13, "References and Structures," in a DBM file or a text file?

A The short answer is no, not easily. The longer answer is yes, but first you need to convert the "structure" over to a string that represents the data and the structure that contains it, and you then need to use that as a value in the DBM-tied hash. The module to do so is Data::Dumper.

Q How do I lock DBM files?

A DBM files can be locked using the semaphore locking system shown previously. Simply use the get_lock() and release_lock() functions from Listing 15.3 and put these around the DBM open and close functions:

```
get_lock();
dbmopen(%hash, "foo", 0644) || die "dmbopen: $!";
$hash{newkey}="Value";
dbmclose(%hash);
release_lock();
```

Q Can I somehow just check to see whether flock is going to pause without actually having it stop?

A Yes you can. A value that can be passed to flock causes it not to pause. (It is called a nonblocking flock.) To find out whether a flock would pause, put a |LOCK_NB after the lock type like this:

```
use Fcntl qw(:flock);
# Attempt to get an exclusive lock, but don't wait for it.
if (not flock( LF, LOCK_EX|LOCK_NB )) {
    print "Could not get the lock: $!";
}
```

You can even wait for a lock for a while, and then print a message if you don't get it eventually:

```
use Fcntl qw(:flock);
$lock_attempts = 3;
while (not flock( LF, LOCK_EX|LOCK_NB )) {
    sleep 5;  # Wait 5 seconds
    $lock_attempts--;  # Count down chances...
    die "Could not get lock!" if (not $attempts);
}
```

Workshop

Quiz

1. Keys in hashes tied to DBM files can store keys with unlimited length.

   a. True

   b. False

2. Why is it difficult to insert data into normal files?

   a. The surrounding data has to be moved to accommodate it.

   b. Normal files cannot be opened for reading and writing at the same time.

   c. The file must be locked while the file is being edited.

3. Locking files is covered in which section of the FAQ?

Answers

1. b. The total combined length of a key and value in a DBM file is 1,024 characters, by default.

2. a. Data cannot easily be moved "up" and "down" within a file, so moving the surrounding data can be exceedingly difficult. Choice c is also true, but only when the file may be used by more than one program at a time.

3. Section 5, "Files and Formats."

Activities

- Write a small program to update a counter in a file so that each time the program is run, the counter increases by 1. Remember to use locking in case multiple instances of your program are run at the same time.

HOUR 16

The Perl Community

This hour, you get to take a break. So, sit down in a comfortable spot with something to nibble on, and learn a bit about Perl's history and culture.

You may have expected this hour to be an appendix or an introduction, but those sections of any book are often overlooked. To use Perl to its fullest potential, you must understand at least a little about the Perl Community.

Knowing what makes the Perl Community tick will help you understand what resources are available to you, why they're there, how they work, and why Perl is what it is. Many resources are out there to help you, and this hour will help you find them.

In this hour you'll learn

- A bit about Perl's history
- What the CPAN is, and how you can use it
- Where to go for help from here

What's Perl All About, Anyway?

To get a sense of the culture of Perl, how it works, and what resources are available to you, it's necessary to learn what makes Perl tick.

A Brief History of Perl

In 1988, the Internet was a different place. First, it was a lot smaller and looked much different than it does today. The Internet, at the time, had roughly 60,000 machines on it. Today that number is hundreds of millions.

At the time, the World Wide Web didn't exist. It wouldn't be conceived until 1991 at CERN in Europe, and the first graphical browser, Mosaic, wouldn't be invented until 1993.

Most of the traffic on the Internet was textual. Usenet news provided a messaging system so that interest groups could keep in touch. E-mail strongly resembled what it is today—that is, mostly textual. File transfers and remote logins rounded out the traffic on the Internet.

In January 1988, Larry Wall announced that he had just written a replacement for the awk and sed tools under Unix; he called it "Perl." The original manual for Perl described it as follows:

> Perl is a interpreted language optimized for scanning arbitrary text files, extracting information from those text files, and printing reports based on that information. It's also a good language for many system management tasks. The language is intended to be practical (easy to use, efficient, complete) rather than beautiful (tiny, elegant, minimal). It combines (in the author's opinion, anyway) some of the best features of C, sed, awk, and sh, so people familiar with those languages should have little difficulty with it. (Language historians will also note some vestiges of csh, Pascal, and even BASIC-PLUS.) Expression syntax corresponds quite closely to C expression syntax. If you have a problem that would ordinarily use sed or awk or sh, but it exceeds their capabilities or must run a little faster, and you don't want to write the silly thing in C, then perl may be for you. There are also translators to turn your sed and awk scripts into perl scripts.

Perl version 2 was released in June 1988, and it looked very much like modern-day Perl: You would recognize and be able to use most of the features of Perl 2. It was, and is, a rich, fully functional programming language. As the description said, Perl's features at the time were geared toward text processing and system programming tasks.

For Perl, 1991 was a banner year. In January, the first edition of *Programming Perl* by Larry Wall and Randal Schwartz was published. This book was (and remains, in its later editions) the definitive reference book for the Perl language. On the pink cover was featured a camel, the official mascot of the Perl language. (It's not a handsome animal, but it's reliable, trustworthy, and very utilitarian.)

The first edition of *Programming Perl* coincided with the release of Perl version 4. This version of Perl was the first widely distributed version of Perl, and remnants of it can still be found today in far-flung corners of the Net, despite the fact that it was last patched in 1992. You probably shouldn't use it if you run across it.

16

In October 1994, Perl version 5 was released. Features such as private variables, references, modules, and objects—which you haven't seen yet—were introduced. In October 1996, the second edition of *Programming Perl* ("The Blue Camel") was released, documenting these new features.

Open Source

One of the reasons for Perl's success has to do with how the Perl language is developed and distributed. The Perl interpreter is a piece of Open Source software. *Open Source* is the new term given to an old concept among software programmers: freely redistributable software. This software can be given away for free, and the source code for the software can be viewed, fixed, and adapted by anyone who wishes to change it. Other software packages that follow this model are the Linux and FreeBSD operating systems, the Apache Web server, and Mozilla, Netscape/AOL's Open Source browser.

Using the Open Source model is a very effective way to develop software. Because the code is written by volunteers, unnecessary code tends not to be included in the package. Features that are deemed necessary are proposed and included. The software's quality is very good because everyone with an interest in the software has the right, and duty, to watch the development carefully to look for bugs. The more people who look at the code, the fewer bugs tend to survive.

> Eric S. Raymond has written an excellent series of essays on the Open Source model of development that include why it works so well, why it's economically beneficial, and how it developed. The first essay, "The Cathedral and the Bazaar," is a good introduction to how the Open Source development model works. The URL for these essays is listed in the "Other Resources" section of this hour.

The Perl interpreter is copyrighted by Larry Wall; he owns it, and it's his to do with as he pleases. However, like most software, Perl can be licensed for use. A software license describes how the software can be used and distributed; it's the fine print you find when opening store-bought software. Larry Wall offers two different licenses for you to choose from: the GNU General Public License and the Perl Artistic License. After reading both, you can choose to follow the terms of either agreement when redistributing Perl.

The text of both licenses is quite lengthy, but let me summarize briefly:

- You may redistribute the source code for the Perl interpreter, but you must duplicate the copyright notices.
- You may modify the original source code if your changes are clearly marked as your own and you either give away the changes or clearly indicate that it is not the standard version of Perl. You must provide the standard version as well.
- You can charge a reasonable fee for distributing Perl. You can charge a fee for support, but you cannot sell Perl itself. You can include Perl in other products you do sell.
- Programs that are written using Perl are not subject to this license.
- No warranties are made about Perl.

You shouldn't rely on a brief summary like this for legal purposes; I provided it only to give you a feel for the licenses themselves.

Before you attempt to include Perl within another package, it is important that you read the licenses yourself and determine whether what you're doing follows either of the licenses. The Perl Artistic License is included with every Perl distribution as a file named Artistic. You can view the GNU General Public License at http://www.gnu.org.

The licenses allow Perl to be developed and enhanced in an open forum. In this way, all the source code for Perl is visible to whoever wants to read it and suggest changes. This approach encourages good programming and prevents getting locked into proprietary, hidden, and obscured software solutions.

The Development of Perl

The development of the Perl interpreter, the language, and the modules that go along with it in the standard distribution takes place on a mailing list where the developers of Perl propose changes, examine bug reports, and debate what changes should be made to the Perl source code.

Anyone is welcome to participate in this process; that's what Open Source is all about. However, to prevent chaos, the changes are filtered through a group of core developers, who approve or reject the changes and maintain the core of Perl's development. Changes are evaluated on the basis of what's good for Perl, how useful the changes are, and whether anyone has attempted the changes successfully. Larry Wall, who oversees this process, acts in the role of a benevolent dictator, allowing the beneficial changes to occur and vetoing changes he considers harmful.

16

Released Perl versions are numbered in two different ways. Until August 1999, they were numbered in a *major.minor_patchlevel* format. So, 4.036_18 was Perl version 4, release 36 with patches up to level 18. Sometimes the versions are referred to without the patch level such as 5.005.

The current release of Perl is 5.6.1. This reflects a new numbering scheme for releases of: *major.minor.patchlevel*. The *major* number is the version of the language (5), the *minor* number is the version of the interpreter (6) and the *patchlevel* (1) indicates the patch level of this interpreter's code.

The even-numbered *minor* releases are production quality, the odd ones (5.7, 5.9) are unstable development releases. The next production release of Perl will be called 5.8. The next production version of Perl after that will be 5.10 and so on.

The Comprehensive Perl Archive Network (CPAN)

Perl offers additional modules to expand your development environment even further. These modules are contained in the *Comprehensive Perl Archive Network* (*CPAN*).

What Is It?

CPAN is a large collection of Perl modules, programs, and documentation, contributed to the Perl Community by the volunteers who wrote them..

The list of modules available in CPAN is extensive. At the time of this writing, CPAN is approximately four years old, and more than 3,500 modules are available for installation. The modules cover a wide range of programming problems. Table 16.1 provides a short list to give you a taste of what's in CPAN.

The most important point to remember is that a module is already available for solving most problems at least partially. The solutions in CPAN have been coded, tested, and reviewed by many programmers for completeness and correctness.

TABLE 16.1   Modules in CPAN

Tk	Graphical interface for Perl programs; specific toolkit modules are available for accessing specialty graphic libraries such as the Win32 API, Gtk, Gnome, Qt, or the X11 toolkit
Net::*	Networking modules: interfaces for Mail, Telnet, IRC, LDAP, and 40+ others
Math::*	More than 30 modules for such constructs as complex numbers, fast Fourier transforms, matrix manipulation, and so on
Date::*,Time::*	Modules for converting dates/times into and out of various formats and doing manipulations on them
Data::*,Tree::*	Modules for manipulating data structures such as linked-lists and B-trees
DBI::*	Generic interface to databases
DBD::*	Interface to commercial and free databases such as Oracle, Informix, Ingres, ODBC, Msql, MySQL, Sybase, and many others
Term::*	Fine control over text-mode screens such as DOS Command window or Unix xterms
String::*, Text::*	Dozens of modules for parsing text and formatting text
CGI::*, URI::*, HTML::*, LWP::*	Modules for producing, serving, fetching, and parsing Web pages
GD, Graphics::*,Image::*	Modules for manipulating graphics and images
Win32::*,Win32API::*	Modules for manipulating Microsoft Windows

All the modules in CPAN are copyrighted by their respective authors, so you should read the README file that comes with each module to see the terms under which the module can be used. Most often, the modules are distributed under the same terms as Perl itself: by the Artistic License or by the GNU General Public License.

CPAN is also the name of a standard module used to help add additional modules into your Perl installation. The CPAN module is documented in the Appendix, "Installing Modules."

Why Do People Contribute?

Over the last half century of computer programming, programmers have solved the same problems over and over again. Searching, sorting, communicating, reading, writing—these problems have actually changed very little since the 1950s. Some books on computer programming theory and management are still applicable after 20 or 30 years.

Programmers are driven, ultimately, by solving interesting problems. Solving the same problems over and over again ("reinventing the wheel") is not always an interesting exercise and often results in inferior solutions. A typical frustrating situation for a programmer is to have spent a long time and a great deal of effort to solve a complex problem, only to discover afterward that a simple and elegant solution was possible. This frustration leads to programmers seeking ways to share code with each other. Sharing has the interesting side effect of creating better code, because other programmers may notice problems in your code that you do not.

CPAN is an effort by the Perl Community to save itself from unnecessary work. The modules are there to keep you from having the frustrating experience of reinventing someone else's wheel.

The quality in most of the CPAN modules is also very good because the modules, as well as Perl, are developed under the Open Source model of production. When you install a module on your system, you automatically have the source code for the module. You can examine the source yourself and—based on the license—use portions of the source for your own programs, modify the source, and even contact the author with suggested changes.

On the surface, the idea of CPAN seems very communal, but the actual reasons that authors contribute to CPAN are widely varied. Sometimes they contribute to help others with similar problems. Sometimes they contribute for the sake of giving to a good cause. Sometimes they do so to help gain the respect and admiration of their peers—a powerful motivator. Whatever the reason, the end result is a very large body of work that you can use in your own programs.

Your Next Steps

After reading though the first two-thirds of this book, you should have an understanding of the basics of Perl. You have by no means learned the whole language. On my bookshelf are at least half a dozen books on the Perl language with—discounting overlapping subjects—2,300 pages, and still some topics in Perl are not included.

A single resource can't cover *all* of Perl; however, the following sections provide recommendations for your next few steps.

The resources outlined here are presented roughly in the order in which you should seek them out. There are exceptions, but for the most part, following this order will solve your problems in the quickest manner possible.

Your First Step

When you have a Perl problem, trying to figure out what to do first is tough. You're frustrated, and if you've been working on the problem for a little while, you're probably upset. Take a deep breath, don't panic, and convince yourself that everything will be all right. Believe it or not, this is an important first step. Most people will become blocked on a problem after a while, and all the frustration from being blocked will prevent clear thinking, so you might wind up making things worse.

Walk away, get something to drink, calm down, and relax. You will solve this problem.

Your Most Useful Tool

The most useful tool in your Perl toolbox is Perl itself. First, you need to determine what kind of problem you have. Usually, problems fall into two categories: faulty syntax or bad and incomplete logic.

If you have a problem with syntax, you can usually break it down into two smaller problems: Either you're using some bit of Perl incorrectly, or you've made a typo. Run your program and examine the error message; it usually indicates Perl's best guess as to which line is wrong. Look at the line for any of the following:

- Does Perl's error message indicate specifically where you should look? Look there! The Perl interpreter can be your best ally in finding bugs.
- Do all the open parentheses, brackets, and braces have matches somewhere?
- Did you check your spelling carefully? Check it again. You'd be surprised at how many bugs turn out to be spelling errors.
- Did you leave something out? A comma? A period?
- Do the lines immediately before the indicated line look okay?
- If you go back to the section in this book where that particular type of syntax was addressed, can you find examples that look similar to yours?
- If you copied the code from another source, did you check someplace else for a similar piece of code? Mistakes happen.

If your Perl program runs but simply doesn't produce the right results, then you probably have a problem in your logic. Before you go tearing things apart, follow these steps:

1. Make sure that the #! line in your program contains a -w.

2. Make sure you have use strict somewhere near the top of your program.

Many apparent logic problems turn out to be simple mistakes that -w and use strict will catch. Use them, and if you still have problems, read on.

Debug Your Program

If you're certain that the syntax of your program is right, but it's just not doing the right thing, then it's time for some elementary debugging.

The first, and probably most used, technique in debugging a program is to use the lowly print statement. Used carefully in your programs, it can provide some runtime diagnostics as to what's going on. Look how print operates in this example:

```
sub foo {
    my($a1, $a2)=@_;
    # Diagnostic added to see if everything's OK.
    print STDERR "DEBUG: Made it to foo with $a1 $a2\n"
}
```

Just remember that when your program is complete, you need to take out all the debugging print statements. I recommend putting some kind of string in them ("DEBUG") so that you can find them all later. Also, by printing to the STDERR filehandle, you can separate your normal output from the diagnostics. If you include the literal symbols _ _LINE_ _ and _ _FILE_ _ in your diagnostic message, Perl will print the name of the current line and file.

The other approach you should try is to use the Perl debugger. You can use the debugger on almost any Perl program. Watching your program run step by step can be very enlightening. Instructions for using the Perl debugger are in Hour 12, "Using Perl's Command-Line Tools."

First, Help Yourself

If your syntax is all right and your logic seems to be okay, but you're just not getting the results you want, then it might be time to seek outside help. The first place you should look for answers is in the Perl documentation.

As indicated in Hour 1, "Introduction to the Perl Language," every Perl installation comes with a full set of documentation. For the 5.6 release, more than 1,850 pages of documentation are included with the distribution. Every module, every function, and most aspects of the Perl language are covered in this documentation, as well as a large Frequently Asked Questions list and tutorials.

To get a list of the available documentation, type `perldoc perl` at a command prompt. Each of the manual sections is listed, as well as a general description of Perl.

The Frequently Asked Questions list contains a list of the most commonly asked questions that beginners—and experts—have about the Perl language. It's worth browsing at least once, to get an idea of what kinds of questions are there, even if you don't completely understand the answers yet.

If, for some reason, you do not have the Perl documentation installed on your system or perldoc does not present the documentation, you should first talk to your system's administrator to find the documentation. Having the documentation correctly installed is important, because the online documentation matches the version of Perl you're running. Any other documentation may have differences.

If you cannot get access to the online documentation, you also can find the documentation at `http://www.perl.com`.

Learn from the Mistakes of Others

Usenet is a distributed messaging system that was developed in the early 1980s and spread to the fledgling Internet. Usenet is divided into tens of thousands of discussion groups, with topics ranging from meditation, gardening, computing, and science fiction to hockey and inline skating, along with regional groups for every region of the world. A few newsgroups are specific to Perl:

`comp.lang.perl.announce`	News about new Perl releases, modules, and information
`comp.lang.perl.moderated`	Low-traffic group with moderated discussions about Perl
`comp.lang.perl.misc`	High-traffic discussion group about anything related to Perl

To read Usenet news, you need a newsreader, and newsreaders are not hard to find. You can go to any software download site and grab a newsreader. You can also go to Web Archives such as `groups.google.com` that mirror the Usenet newsgroups in a Web format and require only that you have a Web browser to read news.

In these newsgroups, people post questions about problems that they're having with Perl, and other people answer the questions—all on a voluntary basis. Also, discussions about general-interest topics related to Perl take place here.

An observation that has held true through my entire programming career is as follows: *There are no original problems in computing.* Any problem that you are having, someone else has had before. The trick is finding who asked the question and what answer that person found. It's very likely that at least one person has asked a remarkably similar question to yours in one of these newsgroups.

`Google` maintains an online history for much of Usenet. Using its search engine, with a few well-chosen keywords, you'll likely find the answers to your question.

For example, say that you want to know how to write a Perl program to fetch a Web page. Go to `groups.google.com`'s Advanced Search screen, and fill in the screen with the following:

```
Keywords:  fetch web page
Group:     comp.lang.perl.misc
```

For this example, leave all the other fields blank. When the search returns—with thousands of matches—most of the matches will have to do with the topic you asked about. You should remember a few points about the articles that you read in Usenet:

- Not all the answers are correct. Anyone can ask a question, and anyone can answer it. Read a few responses, and decide for yourself which ones seem authoritative. Your mileage will vary.

- If you're unsure about whether an answer is correct, use the answer as a starting place to check the information yourself. Go read manual pages on the topic now that you know where to look.

- `Google` archives news for five or six years. Answers that may have been true five years ago may not be true now.

When All Else Fails, Ask

If you've checked the online documentation, your books, and Usenet history, and you still don't have an answer to your question, you might need to ask someone.

Asking for help should be your last resort, certainly not your first. Experts are a unique medium for answering questions. They can take your badly phrased question and sometimes come up with a genuinely good solution to your problem. However, unlike the other resources previously mentioned, people do not have an unlimited capacity for answering questions. They will get tired, they will have bad days, and they will especially get tired of answering the same questions over and over.

Although it's very likely that the person you're asking may know the answer, remember that you're borrowing that person's time and experience to get the answer to your question. It's your responsibility to do a reasonable amount of searching before asking someone else.

To ask a question in Usenet, you need to use a newsreader or one of the previously mentioned Web interfaces to news. As you're assembling your question, follow these guidelines:

1. Before you do anything else, see whether the group has a Frequently Asked Questions (FAQ) list. The Perl groups do; it was shipped with your Perl interpreter. For any other group, search `Google` for the group's FAQ before posting a message.

2. Post the question to the correct newsgroup. A general Perl language question should be posted to the group `comp.lang.perl.misc`. A CGI-specific programming question should probably be posted to `comp.infosystems.www.authoring.cgi`. By reading the FAQ for the group, you'll know whether you're posting to the right place.

3. Pick a good subject line for your post. It should describe your problem, avoid useless text ("help me" or "newbie question" are useless in a subject), and be descriptive but concise.

4. Make sure that the body includes the following:

   a. A description of what you're trying to do (maybe even an explanation why)

   b. A description of what you've tried so far

   c. A description of the errors you've encountered

   For example, if you post error messages or references to your code, you should also include enough of your code so that the responders can tell what's going on. If you're trying to process data, include a few lines for an example.

   The body should not include the following:

   a. Large code segments

   b. Postings of binaries such as .EXEs or uuencoded files

   c. MIME attachments (instead, include your examples and code in the body of the text)

5. Make sure you post with a valid e-mail address, in case someone wants to reply but not publicly.

6. Above all, be polite. You are asking for the kindness of strangers. No one is obligated to help you. Say "please" and "thank you," and avoid inflammatory remarks. Don't use gimmicks to try to get help—for example, "Help a poor little girl with her CGI program . . . " or "I'll give you a free Web page if you . . . " These gimmicks are rude and demeaning.

After you post your article to the newsgroup, wait. Usenet news can take a few days to propagate to the entire world, and people don't always keep up and read every article. Be patient, and go on to the next problem while you wait. Whatever you do, do *not* post to

Usenet again with your question too soon. Wait *at least* a couple of weeks before asking again. Rephrase your question, make sure your subject line is clear, and then try again.

The responses to your article can start immediately (within a few minutes) or could show up a month or more after you posted. As I said before, the quality of the responses will vary greatly. Some will be informative, and others will be wrong. Some respondents will be gracious and polite, and others will be exceedingly rude. It's considered good Netiquette to thank the responders and ignore any flames you've received.

In addition to Usenet, there are communities built around web sites and mailing lists that serve similar purposes. The web site `http://learn.perl.org` was formed to cater to beginners who are looking for a newbie-friendly (and flame-free) environment to ask questions. It has "a goal of providing a central place to assist those beginning to learn Perl find information and help." It currently hosts two mailing lists, `beginners` and `beginners-cgi`, to ask questions.

Other Resources

If you want to learn more about Perl, Perl programming, and the Perl Community, you might want to check out some additional resources:

- The *Perl Developer's Dictionary* by Clinton Pierce—This book serves as a reference, once you've got the basics of the language down. It contains hundreds of code examples covering every topic in Perl.

- *The Perl Cookbook* by Tom Christiansen and Nathan Torkington—This comprehensive collection of various problems, examples, solutions, and commentary on hundreds of problems is written in a cookbook format. Each problem is posed, a solution is presented, and then examples and explanations about the solution are included.

- *The Perl Journal*—This quarterly journal bills itself as "The Voice of the Perl Community." It is a true technical journal, with articles contributed by members of the Perl Community—programmers who use Perl every day—and not by pundits and professional writers. From Issue #1: "We're aiming [. . .] for an intellectually stimulating publication that explores the craft of Perl, the craft of programming and a few other crafts as well. . . . "

For further reading about these topics, check out the following:

Internet History: Hobbe's Internet Timeline
`http://www.isoc.org/zakon/Internet/History/HIT.html`

History of Perl: CPAST

`http://history.perl.org`

The *Perl Journal*

`http://www.tpj.com`

CPAN:

`http://www.perl.com/CPAN`

Online Documentation:

On your system, also `http://www.perl.com`

Eric S. Raymond's Open Source essays:

`http://www.netaxs.com/~esr/writings`

Summary

This hour you learned a bit about the history of Perl and how the Open Source development model is used with Perl. You also learned about CPAN, why it exists, and who
maintains it. Finally, you learned about what kinds of resources are available when
you're having problems with your Perl programs.

Q&A

Q If the Web was invented after Perl, why is Perl a CGI language?

A Perl is a CGI language for the same reason that computers are used to play
games—it's not what they were invented for—they're just good at it. The next hour
presents a more detailed explanation of why Perl is a good CGI language.

Q I posted to Usenet and got a rude, flaming response. What should I do?

A First, does that flame contain some good advice? If so, take that and throw the
rudeness away. Otherwise, just ignore it and go on. Life's too short to be wasted in
a flame war.

Q Is there an easy way to search CPAN?

A Yes! The Web page at `http://search.cpan.org` contains a general search function
and allows you to browse recent changes to CPAN and look through the modules
by category.

Workshop

Quiz

1. Questions about CGI programming in Perl should be sent to which Usenet group first?

   a. `comp.infosystems.www.authoring.cgi`

   b. `comp.lang.perl.misc`

2. If your system doesn't seem to have the documentation, what should you do?

   a. Bug the administrator to install it

   b. Post a message to `comp.lang.perl.misc`

   c. Try a secondary source for documentation, such as `http://www.perl.com`

Answers

1. a. `comp.lang.perl.misc` might be the second place you should consider posting CGI questions, but not the first.

2. a and c, and probably in that order. The documentation might already be installed, and the administrator can help you find it. If not, `www.perl.com` has a copy of a recent set of documentation.

PART III
Using Perl for CGI

Hour

HOUR 17

Introduction to CGI

There's no question in anyone's mind that the explosion in popularity of the Internet is mostly due to the World Wide Web. Since the introduction of the first graphical Web browser in 1993, the Internet has expanded at a phenomenal rate—going from the number of hosts doubling every 20 months around 1993 to doubling every 12 months currently. The growth of private networks—intranets—has increased even more rapidly.

The content of the Web has become more sophisticated since 1993, and the users of the Web expect each Web page to do more than simply show *static* (unchanging) Web pages. A successful Web site requires dynamic Web pages—Web pages that provide up-to-date information. Complex pages with rapidly changing content would be almost impossible to keep current if not for *Common Gateway Interface (CGI)*.

The next seven hours require you to have some knowledge of Hypertext Markup Language (HTML). If you're unfamiliar with HTML, don't despair. It's really not hard to learn, and you won't need much to complete this book.

HTML is a markup language commonly used for constructing Web pages. HTML consists of plain text, with formatting codes embedded in the text to indicate how a Web browser should display the text. For example, the text `HTML is <i>not</i> hard to learn.` is normal text except for the `<i>>/I>` markers. They are called *tags* and describe the formatting used to display the text. In this case, the word *not* should be displayed in italic by a Web browser, if it can. (Remember, not all browsers are graphical.)

A full lesson in HTML is well beyond the scope of this book. It's not difficult; there's just a lot of material to cover. The specification for HTML is maintained by the World Wide Web Consortium (W3C) at `http://www.w3c.org`, and you can find some nice tutorials there as well. One good book on HTML is *Sams Teach Yourself HTML in 24 Hours*.

In this hour you will learn

- The basics of how the Web works
- What you need to know *before* writing CGI
- How to write your first CGI program

Browsing the Web

The Web, as you know it, is simply the interaction between two different systems trying to exchange data. The system that is trying to fetch a Web page is known as the *client*. The client system usually runs a program called a *Web browser,* such as Netscape, Internet Explorer, Opera, and so on. This is the extent of the Web that you're used to using every day. The Web browser provides navigation buttons and bookmarks and is responsible for drawing Web pages on your screen.

On the other end of the Web is a system known as the *Web server*. This system takes the client's request for a page, retrieves the page from a local disk, and sends it to the client—your Web browser. This interaction is shown in Figure 17.1.

FIGURE 17.1

Web browser fetching a page.

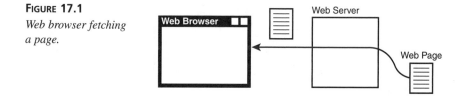

Fetching a Static Web Page

A client requests a Web page by examining a Uniform Resource Locator (URL) to determine the protocol, server, and request to make on that server. A typical URL might look like the following:

```
http://www.google.com:80/more.html
```

The parts of the URL can be broken down like this:

- `http`—This part is the protocol. HTTP, or Hypertext Transfer Protocol, is a protocol used for transferring Web pages. You may also have seen File Transfer Protocol (`ftp`) or secure HTTP (`https`).

- `www.google.com`—This part is the name of the server—also called a *host name*—that contains the document you want. Sometimes, instead of a host name, you might see an IP address, usually written as four numbers separated by dots: 209.185.108.147. These addresses tend to be less reliable than the names, though.

- `:80`—This part is a port number that determines on which port your client and the server will connect with each other. This portion is usually optional; the protocol used determines what port will be used. `http` usually means "use port 80."

- `more.html`—This is the request being made on the server. Usually it's a document you want to retrieve. Sometimes it's written as a pathname, such as `/archives/foo.html`, or it has other characters trailing at the end, such as `(?&)`, but essentially it is what the client needs the server to retrieve.

The client then follows these steps for http (see Figure 17.2):

1. The hostname (`www.google.com`) is converted to an IP address.

2. A connection is established with the server at `www.google.com` using the IP address and the port number.

3. The server is asked for the page more.html. The client waits for a response.

4. The server sends the response—in this case, the contents of more.html—and drops the connection to the server.

5. The client renders the response on the screen.

17

FIGURE 17.2
Requesting a page.

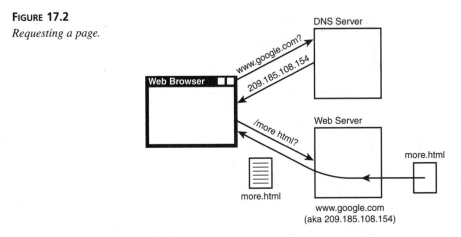

The nitty-gritty of the "conversation" between the client and the server is covered in depth in Hour 20, "Manipulating the HTTP and CGI Protocols."

Dynamic Web Content—The CGI

During a normal Web page fetch, the server simply locates the document requested, retrieves it from its disk storage, and sends it to the client, as illustrated in Figure 17.3.

FIGURE 17.3
Static Web page fetch.

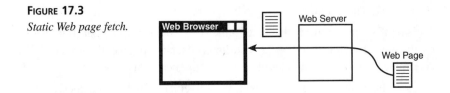

The server in Figure 17.3 doesn't process the data at all; it simply examines the request and passes the requested data back to the client.

One method to create dynamic content on the Web is through the use of CGI programs. CGI is an agreed-upon method that Web servers use to run programs on the server to generate Web content. When a URL indicates to a server that a CGI program should be run to generate the content, the server starts the program, the program generates the content, and the server passes the content back to the client, as illustrated in Figure 17.4.

FIGURE 17.4

CGI script-generated
Web page.

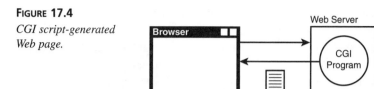

Each time the client requests a page that's really a CGI program, the following occurs:

1. The server starts a new instance of the CGI program.
2. The CGI program generates a page, or another response, using whatever information it needs.
3. The page is sent back to the client.
4. The CGI program exits.

The CGI program can be any kind of program. It can be a Perl script, which is what you'll learn about here. It can also be programmed in C, the Unix shell, Pascal, LISP, TCL, or nearly any other programming language. The fact that many CGI programs are written in Perl is a happy coincidence. Perl happens to be very well suited to writing programs that deal with text, and the output of CGI programs is often text.

The output of CGI programs can be almost anything, however. It can be images, HTML-formatted text, Zip files, streaming video, or any other kinds of content you might find on the Web. For the most part, the CGI programs you'll be writing will generate HTML-formatted text.

CGI is not a language; it has nothing to do specifically with Perl, it has nothing to do with HTML, and it has very little to do with HTTP. It's simply an agreed-upon interface between Web servers and programs run on their behalf. The specification for CGI is maintained by the National Center for Supercomputing Applications at http://www.ncsa.uiuc.edu/cgi/interface.html. You'll pick up bits and pieces of these details over the next seven hours.

Don't Skip This Section

You're almost ready to write a CGI program. Almost. You need to check a few things first; otherwise, your first experience writing CGI programs will not be a happy one. It's much easier to check things before you write, rather than while you're debugging.

To use CGI, you need a Web server. A common problem that new CGI programmers have is that they try writing CGI programs without having a Web server properly installed. For obtaining a Web server, you have a couple of options: You can rent space on a commercial Web server, or you can run your own. The decision is up to you, based on what you would like to pay, your bandwidth requirements, and how technically adept you are.

To obtain a commercial Web server, surf the Web and find one. These commercial servers are commonly known as "Web hosting" companies, and the rates they charge and the features offered can vary widely. If you're planning on writing Perl CGI programs, you should be sure to check that Perl version 5 is supported as a CGI language. A very few Web hosting companies do not support Perl as a CGI programming language or don't allow CGI at all. Avoid those companies; you have plenty of others to choose from.

You should also make sure that the Web hosting company allows you to use your own scripts. Some companies claim that they allow Perl CGI but then require that you use their programs—sometimes for a fee. You should avoid those companies as well.

Still other companies will charge a fee to "review" your CGI programs before you're allowed to use them. If you choose one of these companies, you should set up your own server for testing because this "reviewing" can be expensive.

Running your own personal Web server isn't too difficult, if you have some technical skills and are willing to read through the instructions. First, you need to pick a Web server. If you're running Windows, you can choose from dozens of free or nearly free Web servers to install. Make sure they support Perl as a CGI scripting language. A few commercial Web servers are also available for Windows, notably Microsoft's Internet Information Server (IIS).

If you have a Unix machine, a few commercial Web servers are available. Contact your Unix vendor for a list.

The most popular Web server on the Internet—Apache—is completely free. The Apache Web server is easy to install—if you have a C compiler—and fairly easy to operate if you're comfortable editing configuration files. Apache is even available precompiled for the Microsoft Windows platform. For information on Apache, go to `http://www.apache.org`.

If you run your own Web server, make sure that the Web server is working properly and can serve static Web pages before you attempt to write CGI programs. If your Web server does not serve static Web pages, it's very unlikely that CGI programs will work.

You should also check the configuration for the Web server to make sure that you have CGI scripts properly enabled. Not having this feature enabled is the cause of most beginners' frustrations with CGI programming.

The Checklist

Whether you run your own Web server or rent space from a commercial Web host, take the time to complete the following checklist—really! Write down this information; it will save you numerous headaches later.

- If you've rented space from a commercial Web host, the host will provide you with all this information. It may be located in a FAQ on the host's Web site or included in documentation sent to you when your account was set up. If you did *not* receive this information, contact your Web hosting company to get it; it's very important if you want CGI to work properly.

- If you've configured and installed your own Web server, this information should have been part of the configuration process. If you're having problems, check to see whether you can find a FAQ that answers these questions or whether you can find a configuration file to check.

This information is *required* if you're going to do CGI programming:

- Location of Perl on the Web server—You need to know where the Perl interpreter is installed on the Web server. You need this information because you need to change the #! line in your program to reflect this pathname. If your Web hosting company runs a Microsoft operating system, you might not need this information. On some servers, simply having the right extension on the script file will make it executable and Perl will be called.

- Location of the Web server's log files—You cannot easily debug your CGI scripts without knowing where the Web server's error log is kept—at least not without Herculean effort. Find this location; it's important.

- Extension to be used for CGI programs—Web servers *sometimes* distinguish between normal static pages kept on the server and CGI programs to be run based on the filename. This extension is commonly .cgi or .pl. Sometimes it's not used at all.

- Location of CGI program directory—Web servers either require an extension on CGI program filenames or require that the files be placed in a special directory. (Rarely do they require both.) Usually, this directory is called /cgi-bin and is located at (or near) the top-level directory for the Web site.

- URL of your CGI directory—Often, you just use the URL of the Web server with the CGI directory tacked on to the end—for example,

  http://www.myserver.com/cgi-bin/ or http://www.myserver.com/cgi/.

17

Your First CGI Program

After all the fanfare, warnings, checklists, and runaround, you're ready to type in your first CGI program. It is shown in Listing 17.1.

Type and save this program as hello. If, in the checklist, you are required to use a certain extension for CGI programs—as noted in the "Extension to be used for CGI programs" item—use that extension. Thus, if you're required to name your CGI programs with a .cgi extension, save this script as hello.cgi. If you're required to use .pl, save this script as hello.pl.

You *did* fill out the checklist, didn't you?

Listing 17.1   Your First CGI Program

```
1:   #!/usr/bin/perl -w
2:   use CGI qw(:standard);
3:   use strict;
4:
5:   print header;
6:   print "<b>Hello, World!</b>";
```

Line 1: This line is the standard #! line. You *must* substitute the path from the checklist item "Location of Perl on the Web server" for this script to work. The -w, of course, enables warnings.

Line 2: The CGI module is included in the program. The qw(:standard) causes the standard set of functions from the CGI module to be imported into your program.

Line 3: use strict enforces good coding practices; this is no different for CGI programs.

Line 5: The header function is imported from the CGI module. It prints a standard header that the server (and the client) must see to process the output of the CGI program.

Line 6: After the header is printed, any output will appear normally to the browser. In this case, when the CGI is run, the browser will display the words Hello, World.

That's it!

Well, not quite. You still have to *install* this CGI program and test it. You've won only half the battle.

Installing the CGI Program on the Server

How you install your CGI program depends heavily on what kind of server you have, whether you have local access to it, whether it's a server that you can only FTP files to, and so on. The following sections describe how to install for the different scenarios.

Local Access to a File System on a Unix Web Server

Use these instructions if you're able to telnet, rlogin, or otherwise log in to the Unix Web server:

1. Put the CGI program hello.cgi (or hello.pl) onto the Unix server, perhaps with FTP. You may have actually written it on the server with vi. That's fine, too.

2. Move the CGI program into the correct directory by using the mv or cp command. You should have found the correct directory in the checklist under "Location of CGI program directory."

3. Under Unix, you need to make the program *executable*. Do so by issuing the following command:

   ```
   chmod 755 hello.cgi
   ```

   Use `hello.pl` instead if it is the program's name. This command makes the file writable by the owner and readable and executable by everyone else (this is correct for a CGI program).

FTP-Only Access to a Unix Web Server

Use these instructions if you have FTP-only access:

1. Use your FTP client to put the hello.cgi (or hello.pl) program into the CGI program directory. You should have found the correct directory in the checklist under "Location of CGI program directory." Be sure to transfer the file in text mode or ASCII mode; do not transfer the CGI program to the server using binary mode. With a text-mode FTP utility, the default mode is usually text.

2. You must make the CGI program executable. For a text-only FTP program, the following command should work:

   ```
   quote site chmod 755 hello.cgi
   ```

   Use hello.pl instead if it is the program's name. This command makes the file writable by the owner, and readable and executable by everyone else (this is correct for a CGI program).

3. If you have a graphical FTP program (such as Cute-FTP), you need to find the Set Permissions, Change Mode, Set File Attributes, or Set File Access Mode tab and set the permissions there.

17

Any way you set access, the owner needs read/write/execute permissions, the group needs read/execute permissions, and others need read/execute permissions. If the program requires a numeric permission, use 755.

Local Access to a File System on an NT Web Server

If you have local access to a file system on an NT Web server, put the CGI program into the correct directory—the one you specified in "Location of CGI program directory" in the checklist—by using NT's Explorer or a file copy utility.

FTP-Only Access to an NT Web Server

If you have FTP-only access to an NT Web server, use your FTP client to put the hello.cgi (or hello.pl) program into the CGI program directory. You should have found the correct directory in the checklist under "Location of CGI program directory." Be sure to transfer the file in text mode or ASCII mode; do not transfer the CGI program to the server using binary mode. With a text-mode FTP utility, the default mode is usually text.

Running Your CGI Program

To see whether your CGI program works, fire up your browser and point it to the address you specified in the checklist—the URL of the CGI directory—with the CGI program name tacked on the end. For example, you might enter the following:

```
http://www.myserver.com/cgi-bin/hello.pl
```

You should use hello.cgi or whatever name you used for the CGI program when you saved it.

One of two things should happen:

1. Your browser loads a page with the Hello, World message.
2. It doesn't.

If your CGI program doesn't work—for whatever reason—see the next section; it's all about how to debug problems like this. The procedure for installing and debugging CGI programs is hard. *Very* hard. Don't give up because it doesn't work right away. Cheer up! Once you get it right, you don't have to debug it again.

If your CGI program does what it is supposed to, congratulations! You've successfully installed your Web server and your CGI program, and you've got your program working. You should still browse through the next section anyway. The day will come when a CGI program of yours doesn't work, and you should at least be familiar with the steps to diagnose your problem.

What to Do When Your CGI Program Doesn't Work

The following sections provide a general-purpose CGI program debugging guide. Before you read through all this information to find the problem in your first CGI program, go back through the instructions to make sure you didn't skip any steps. By the time you reach the end of this hour, you should be able to find any problems your CGI program has.

The diagnostics in these sections assume you're debugging a program named `hello.cgi`. If your program has another name, use it instead.

Is It Your CGI Program?

The first potential source of problems to eliminate is the CGI program itself. There's no sense in debugging Web server configurations if the CGI program doesn't work.

CGI programs retrieving can be run interactively like all Perl programs, and running them this way is very useful for debugging. To run your program, start it from the command prompt like this:

`perl hello.cgi`

The Perl interpreter should reply with a line that looks like this:

```
(offline mode: enter name=value pairs on standard input)
```

This prompt indicates that the CGI module is attempting to get your CGI form values; they are covered in Hour 18, "Basic Forms."

To this prompt, you should—for now—respond with just an end-of-file character. Under Unix, it is Ctrl+D; you just press the Ctrl key and type D. In Windows, you press Ctrl+Z. Perl should then print the following:

```
Content-Type: text/html


<b>Hello, World!</b>
```

The `Content-Type: text/html` message indicates that what follows should be interpreted as text or HTML. The meaning of this message is covered fully in Hour 20. For now, just know that it's important that this message is the *first* thing printed by your program—with the `header` function—and that it's necessary. If anything else is emitted before the `Content-Type` message, the CGI program will fail.

17

Problem: Perl responds with a syntax error.

Solution: Fix the syntax error.

Problem: Perl responds with `Can't locate CGI.pm in @INC....`

Solution: Your Perl installation is incomplete. The CGI module ships with Perl by default. If you need to reinstall it, see the Appendix "Installing Modules." Make sure you've spelled CGI correctly.

Server Problems

After you've eliminated your script as the cause of the problems, it's time to check the script's installation and the server's configuration.

Problem: The server responds with the message `Not Found` or `404 Not Found`.

Solution: The messages usually indicate one of the following two problems:

- The URL you used is incorrect. You typed
  `http://www.server.com/cgi/hello.cgi` when you should have
  typed `http://www.server.com/cgi-bin/hello.cgi`. Go back to the checklist
  and verify that the URL of your CGI directory is correct, you've spelled the name
  of the script right, and you have the right extension.

- You placed the script in the wrong directory on the Web server. Verify from the
  checklist that the CGI directory is correct, and if not, move the script to the correct
  location.

Problem: The text of your script is displayed.

Solution: The program is displayed because the Web server thinks that the program is really a document.

- You used the wrong extension on your CGI program. Instead of `.pl`, you used
  `.cgi` or some other wrong extension. Check the checklist, and make sure you're
  using the correct extension on your CGI program.

- You put the script in the wrong directory, *and* you're using the wrong URL to
  access it. Verify that you've put the script in the correct CGI program directory and
  that you're using the right URL.

- The server is misconfigured. If you're using your own Web server, reread the documentation and verify that you've set it up correctly. Sometimes the installation
  includes a test CGI script; if so, try it. If you're using a commercial Web hosting
  server, verify that you're placing your script in the correct directory, or contact the
  Web host for help.

Problem: The server responds with the message `Forbidden` or `403 Error`.

Solution: The permissions on the CGI program are not correct. This problem is most likely to occur on a Unix Web server.

You can view the permissions on the hello.cgi program by typing **`ls -l hello.cgi`** at a command prompt in the proper directory. If you have FTP access to the server, you can view the file permissions by typing `dir`. The permissions should look something like this:

```
-rwxr-xr-x    1 user          93 Aug 03 23:06 hello.cgi
```

The permissions are the `rwxr-xr-x` characters on the left. If they don't look exactly like this, go back to the installation instructions for details on how to properly set the permissions on the CGI program.

Fixing `Internal Server` or `500` Errors

If the server replies with an `Internal Server Error` or `500 Error` message, this means that your CGI program failed somehow. This general-purpose failure message is generated by many different problems.

The most important tool you have in debugging an "Internal Server Error" is the server's log file. As the Web server receives requests for Web pages, it writes each page request into a file for later analysis. Any errors that the server encounters are also logged, including error messages generated by CGI programs.

Find the location of the server error log file, which you should have noted in the checklist. The log is typically written by appending any new items to the bottom of the log file. To see the last few entries under Unix, at a command prompt, type

```
tail error_log
```

to see just the bottom of the file. Some Web servers have a utility—often a CGI program itself—to view the log file. If you have FTP-only access to the server, you might need to download the log file and view it on your local PC to see the error entries.

If you do not have access to the server's error logs, you have a big problem. Finding an "Internal Server Error" will be a hit-and-miss affair. Following the checklist shown here, you should find the problem eventually. (The messages you'll find in the server logs are approximated; the text will vary from server to server.)

Log entry: `No such file or directory: exec of /cgi-bin/hello.cgi failed`

Possible causes:

- The `#!` line of the script may not be correct. Make sure that the location of Perl in the `#!` line matches the location of Perl on the Web server from the checklist. Verify that Perl is actually installed there by using `ls` or `dir` in FTP or locally.

- If you used FTP to transfer the CGI program to the server, you may not have used ASCII mode for the transfer. Moving a script written in Windows to a Unix server—and vice versa—in binary mode does not work.

- The permissions are not correct on the CGI program (Unix). See the description of `Forbidden` in the "Server Problems" section.

Log entry: `Can't locate CGI.pm in @INC....`

Possible causes:

- The Perl installation is incomplete, corrupt, or very old. Perl is—apparently—unable to locate the CGI module, which is a standard part of the Perl installation. You might need to reinstall the module or contact your system administrator to have him or her reinstall Perl. See Appendix A.

Log entry: `Syntax error, warning, Global symbol requires,` etc.

Possible causes:

- Your Perl program apparently has a typo or incorrect syntax. Follow the instructions in the "Is It Your CGI Program?" section to determine the problem.

Log entry: `Premature end of script headers`

Possible causes: This catchall error message describes any situation in which your script is run, and the `Content-Type` header—printed by the CGI module's `header` function—is not the first thing emitted by the script. Sometimes a secondary message appears in the log file, immediately before or after this one. The other message may be more helpful in determining what went wrong. You can try these solutions:

- Make sure you're not printing *anything*—including error messages—before calling the `header` function. Anything printed before the `header` function causes this error.

You may see Perl CGI programs printing `"Content-Type: text/html\n\n"` at the beginning of the program instead of calling `header`. Apparently, printing this and calling `header` are supposed to do the same thing, but they don't. The `header` function takes into account that `\n\n` doesn't always mean the same thing on every server and emits the proper sequence for that server.

- A problem called *output buffering* can cause output generated by the `system` function or backticks (` `` `) to appear in the output before the `header` function's output. To make sure that the output from `header` is always shown first, you might want to try rewriting the beginning of your Perl CGI program to look like this:

```
#!/usr/bin/perl -wT
use strict;
use CGI;

$|=1;        # ensures that header's output always prints first
print header;
```

Summary

In this hour, you learned the basics of how CGI programs work. The differences between static Web pages and dynamic Web content were explained, and will be explored in further hours. You also got to write your first CGI program and, I hope, make it work.

This hour also provided a guide to debugging your CGI programs that will be useful to you in upcoming hours.

Q&A

Q I don't have the CGI module loaded. Do I *have* to use it?

A Quite frankly, yes. CGI is not an easy protocol to get right. Many programs that are published try to replicate the CGI module's functionality—and do so poorly. They are riddled with security problems and incompatibilities; plus, they do not follow Internet Standards as they should. In Hour 16, "The Perl Community," you learned why "reinventing the wheel" is a bad thing. CGI is an incredibly hard wheel to reinvent, and neither you nor I would get it right the first time or the hundredth time.

The Perl CGI module included with the standard distribution has been tested by hundreds of thousands of programmers and is very robust. Use it.

As I explain in Appendix A, you can install the module for just your use, if necessary. You don't have any excuse not to use it. All the examples in this book require the CGI module, and the explanations assume you have it installed.

17

Q I have this copy of cgi-lib.pl. Can I use *it* instead?

A You really shouldn't. All the functionality of cgi-lib.pl is in the CGI module. The cgi-lib.pl library is quite old and is no longer being maintained.

Q Why does everyone use Perl for CGI? Why not C or TCL?

A Perl has features that make it particularly useful for CGI. The short list is as follows:

1. Perl has excellent text-handling capabilities.

2. Perl's tainting capabilities—you'll learn about them soon—help make it a secure language for doing CGI programs.

3. Perl is an excellent *glue* language, good for sticking together different technologies such as operating system utilities, databases, and CGI.

4. Perl is easy to use.

Q If I have questions about Perl and CGI, should I post a message to the `comp.lang.perl.misc` newsgroup?

A Probably not. A more appropriate group would be `comp.infosystems.www.authoring.cgi`. First, though, you should check the FAQ at `http://www.w3.org/CGI/`.

Workshop

Quiz

1. CGI programs can be written in

    a. Perl, the Unix shell, or C only

    b. Perl only

    c. Almost any programming language that can be run on the server

2. The Web was invented before Perl.

    a. True

    b. False

Answers

1. c. Perl is not special in this regard; it simply has some features for making CGI programming much easier and more reliable.

2. b. Perl was invented in 1987, and the Web wasn't invented at CERN until 1991.

Activities

- Spice up your "Hello, World!" program a little bit. Print the current time (by using `localtime`), and maybe add some color and a table or two with HTML tags. Be creative. Remember that printing HTML in your Perl program will make the program appear in the final Web page when the page is loaded.

17

Hour **18**

Basic Forms

While surfing the Web, you've undoubtedly filled out a few HTML forms. HTML forms, such as email Web forms, shopping carts, guestbooks, online auction forms, mailing list subscriptions, and order forms, are used to collect information, such as login information and even Web site preference settings, from the Web browser's user.

When the user clicks the submit button on those forms, what happens? Almost always, the data from that form is passed to a CGI program. In this hour, you'll learn how to take data from a form and manipulate it in your CGI programs.

In this hour you'll learn

- How to process basic forms in Perl CGI programs
- How to debug CGI forms
- How to write safer CGI programs

How Forms Work

You've undoubtedly used forms on the Web, and you might even understand how they're laid out and how they work. Regardless, a review of HTML form basics is in order.

Short Review of HTML Form Elements

Before you jump into how a form works, you should review how HTML represents a form and the roles that all the elements in that form play.

> The HTML presented in this book should not be taken as a model of great HTML. Enough HTML is presented to demonstrate the CGI features needed, but not much else. There are generally no <head> or <body> tags shown, nor a <!DOCTYPE> in any of the HTML presented in the examples. In addition, the screens are quite plain. Feel free to add your own HTML to make the screens more attractive and complete. Most browsers will display the HTML presented here correctly.

An HTML form is a portion of an HTML document that accepts user input. When the browser loads HTML containing a form, various HTML tags create user input areas on the page. The user input is put into various form elements such as check boxes, radio buttons, selection menus, and text entry elements. After the user has manipulated the input elements with the Web browser, the form is typically submitted to a CGI program for processing.

A typical HTML form is constructed something like the one shown in Listing 18.1.

Listing 18.1   A Small HTML Form

```
<form action="http://www.server.com/cgi-bin/submit.cgi" method="get">
Name <input type="text" name="name"/><br/>
Description<br/>
<textarea name="description" rows="5" cols="40">
</textarea>
<input type="radio" name="sex" value="male"/>Male
<input type="radio" name="sex" value="female"/>Female
<br/>
<input type="submit" value="Send"/><input type="reset"/>
</form>
```

Figure 18.1 shows the form from Listing 18.1 rendered with the Netscape browser.

18

FIGURE 18.1

The form from Listing 18.1 rendered in Netscape.

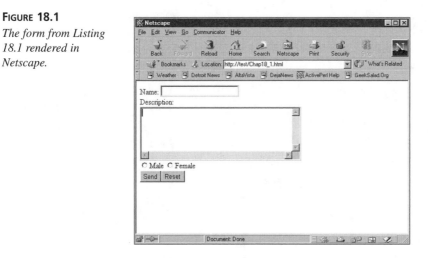

The `<form>` tag specifies the beginning of the form within the complete HTML document. The `method` attribute specifies whether this form will use the GET or POST method for form submission. If this attribute is not specified, the browser submits the form to the CGI program using the GET method. The difference between the methods is documented later. The `action` attribute specifies the URL of the CGI program that will receive the form data.

The `<input>` tag presents the user with an input field—in this case, a blank text box. The text box is assigned a name—coincidentally `"name"`.

Finally, the submit button is displayed. When the user clicks this button, the form values are passed to a CGI program for processing, as explained in the next section.

The HTML 4.0 specification contains quite a few different form element types, so I will not try to document them all fully in this book. For example, many form elements contain attributes to fix certain properties of the form element, such as `rows` and `cols` in the `textarea` in the preceding form. For the rest of this book, whenever HTML form elements are used, only the most basic attributes will be used.

You can find the full HTML 4.0 specification, including the valid form elements and their attributes, at `http://www.w3c.org`.

What Happens When You Click Submit?

After a user has filled in a form on his or her Web browser, a short chain of events takes place:

- The data on the form is collected by the Web browser into name and value pairs (see Figure 18.2). For example, in the sample form, the field named `body` takes on the value of the text entry field. The field named `sex` takes on the value of the radio buttons. The Web browser does all this work before anything else happens.

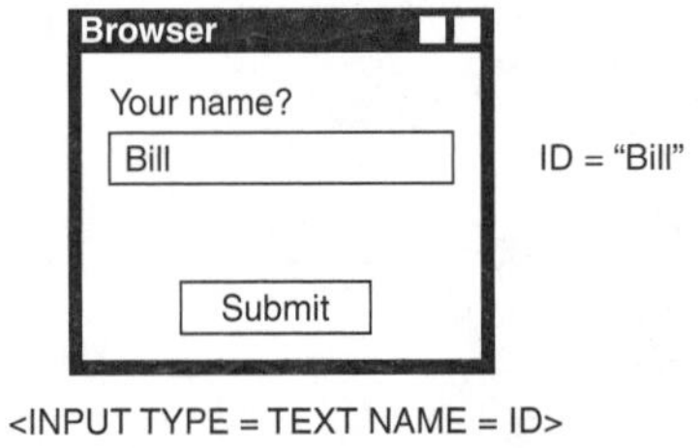

FIGURE 18.2

Browser pairing up data and field names.

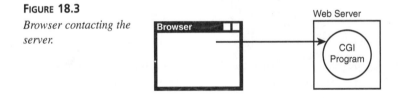

- The URL for the `action` portion of the form field is contacted. Presumably, this is the URL for a CGI program (see Figure 18.3).

FIGURE 18.3

Browser contacting the server.

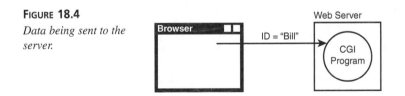

- The field names and values on the form are transmitted to the CGI program using one of the CGI methods GET or POST (see Figure 18.4). You don't have to worry too much about the mechanics of this transfer yet.

FIGURE 18.4

Data being sent to the server.

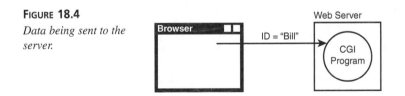

- The CGI program receives those values, generates a response, and sends the response back to the browser (see Figure 18.5). The response can be an HTML page, a page containing another form, a redirection to another URL, or anything else a CGI program can generate.

FIGURE 18.5

Web server's CGI program responding.

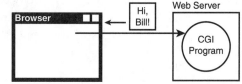

Passing Information to Your CGI Program

When a CGI program is run as the result of a form submission, the field names and values passed in from the form—called *parameters*—need to be processed by the CGI program. This is done with the `param` function.

Without any arguments, the `param` function returns the names of the fields being passed into the CGI program. If the CGI program was accepting the form in Listing 18.1, the `param` function would return `body`, `sex`, `name`, and `submit`.

With an argument, `param` returns the value of that parameter. For example, `param('sex')` would return the value of the radio buttons—either `male` or `female`—depending on which was selected.

Listing 18.2 contains a short CGI program to print these parameters.

Listing 18.2 CGI Program for Printing Parameters

```
1: #!/usr/bin/perl -w
2: use strict;
3: use CGI qw(:standard);
4:
5: print header;
6: print "<p>The name was", param('name'), "<br />";
7: print "The sex selected: ", param('sex'), "<br />";
8: print "The description was:<br />", param('description'),
9:        "</p>";
```

If the parameter specified by `param` is not used in the form, `param` returns `undef`.

GET and POST Methods

In the form in Listing 18.1, the <FORM> tag has an attribute called method. The method attribute specifies how the Web browser should transmit the data to the Web server. Currently, two methods are available.

The first method—also the default method if you don't specify one in the <FORM> tag—is called GET. With the GET method, the form values are passed to the CGI program by having their values encoded in the URL. You may have seen URLs like this while surfing the Web:

```
http://www.server.com/cgi-bin/sample.pl?name=foo&desc=Basic%20Forms
```

The CGI program, when it is run, can decode the end part of the URL (after the question mark) into fields and values. The param function essentially does the same when it's called. You should *not* try decoding these values yourself. The param function does a thorough job of it, and you don't have any reason to use anything else to extract the values.

The other method—POST—produces exactly the same result but through a different means. Instead of encoding all the form values into the URL, the Web server is contacted and the HTML form values are sent as input to the CGI program. Again, you don't need to know at this time exactly how this process works; the CGI module takes care of that for you. Simply calling the param function takes care of reading the values, decoding them, and passing them to your program.

> You may have downloaded CGI programs from the Internet or seen examples in other books that try to decode an environment variable called QUERY_STRING or use a variable called REQUEST_METHOD to figure out whether the form uses a GET or POST method. Those programs attempt to reproduce the work already done in the standard CGI module—and probably not as well. You should avoid doing this yourself.

So, which method should you choose? Each method has advantages and disadvantages. The GET method allows the Web browser to bookmark the particular URL that generated the page. For example, the URL

```
http://www.server.com/cgi-bin/sample.pl?name=foo&desc=Basic%20Forms
```

could be bookmarked and always returned to by the browser. From the perspective of the CGI program—sample.pl—it doesn't know whether or not you've just come from actually viewing the form. It receives the normal CGI parameters as it always has. The ability to call a CGI program repeatedly using the GET method's URL-encoded values is called *idempotence*.

However, you might not particularly want browsers to be able to bookmark in your site to run your CGI programs directly, and the URLs for invoking a CGI program with the GET method are, frankly, ugly.

The POST method doesn't encode the form data in the URL at all; it relies on the browser to send the data as it's negotiating for the page. However, because the data isn't encoded into the URL, you can't bookmark a page that was generated by a CGI program using the POST method.

Web Security 101

Before you put CGI programs on the World Wide Web, you need to know a few things. By putting a CGI program on a Web page, you are giving remote users (using Web browsers) limited access to your system. Using normal HTML documents, they can retrieve only static documents from your Web site. Using CGI programs, however, they're actually able to run programs on your Web server.

Knowing how to write safe and secure CGI programs will make you and the administrator of your Web server much happier. Writing such programs is not hard; you just need to follow a few simple precautions.

A Clear Link

When a Web browser retrieves a page from your Web server, the HTML is sent over a cleartext channel (see Figure 18.6). This means that as the data winds its way through the Internet, it's not encrypted, encoded, or otherwise obscured.

FIGURE 18.6

Plain text being transmitted to server.

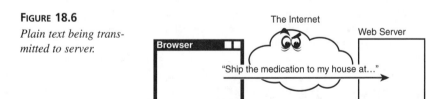

The data that a user puts into a form and submits to your CGI program is transmitted with the same protocol as the initial Web page. All the fields of the form are free for anyone to see as they go by (see Figure 18.7).

FIGURE **18.7**

Server responding in plain text.

The problem of data being transmitted in the clear is a real one that you should be concerned with. The Internet is not a secure place, and anyone along the wire between the Web browser and the Web server can eavesdrop on the information being sent out or in.

Keeping this point in mind, you should never transmit some kinds of data with normal CGI forms:

- Passwords of any kind
- Personal information (Social Security numbers, phone numbers)
- Financial information (account numbers, PINs, credit card numbers)

Keep this rule of thumb in mind: Never send anything on the Internet that you wouldn't put on a postcard. If you need to transmit data that needs to be kept secure, then you need to use extraordinary methods to do so: use a secure HTTP (https) connection (see the following note) instead of HTTP, make sure that the servers you're sending the data to are secure, and make sure that you trust the recipient with your information.

> "But wait!" you say. "I've seen forms on the Internet asking for all those pieces of information and claiming to be secure." Reasonably secure transactions can be performed over the Web with some additional tools. Secure Web transactions are actually performed by encrypting the *entire* browser/server conversation. This is done by using a secure version of the Hypertext Transfer Protocol (HTTP), called *HTTPS*.

Watching for Insecure Data

Another point to consider in writing secure CGI programs is that you're writing programs that will execute Perl commands based on the input given to you by a Web page. The Internet—and possibly your intranet—is full of people who are not nice and would take great glee and pride in harming your Web server. Also, benign users could accidentally send invalid data to your CGI program.

Consider the HTML form in Listing 18.3 and the CGI program in Listing 18.4.

Listing 18.3   Directory Listing Web Form

```
<form action="/cgi-bin/directory.cgi">
<p>What directory to list?
<input type="text" name="dirname"/>
<input type="submit" name="submit" value="Run This"/>
</p>
</form>
```

Listing 18.4   An Insecure CGI Program Named directory.cgi

```
1: #!/usr/bin/perl -w
2: # Do NOT use this CGI program, it's very insecure
3: use strict;
4: use CGI qw(:all);
5:
6: print header('text/plain');
7: my $directory=param('dirname');
8: print `ls -l $directory`;  # Do a directory listing
```

Listing 18.3 presents the user with a short form to collect a directory name and then passes the name to a CGI program called directory.cgi. In Listing 18.3, the directory.cgi program takes the directory and performs an `ls -l` on it—for DOS/Windows users, this is the equivalent of `dir`—giving the user a directory listing.

A program of this sort allows a remote Web surfer to explore your entire directory structure. The CGI program does no validation of what the directory name is, and if the browser wants to explore your sensitive data, it may be able to.

The more important point is that `$directory` might not contain a directory at all! If the Web browser had sent back the value `/home; cat /etc/passwd` for `dirname`, then the command run by the CGI program would have been as follows:

```
ls -l /home; cat /etc/passwd
```

This command would effectively transmit a copy of the system's password file back to the Web browser. In fact, any Unix shell command or MS-DOS command could be run this way. If your Web server has not been set up properly, this could allow any user on the Internet to view the information you are sending.

Perl has a mechanism to help prevent you from doing silly things like this. The `-T` switch on the `#!` line enables *data tainting*. As data is received from external sources—filehandles, network sockets, the command line, and so on—it's marked as *tainted*. Tainted data cannot be used in backticks, system calls (such as `open`), the `system` command, or other places that might compromise your security.

18

You also cannot use the `open` function, `system` function, or backticks in your Perl program when taint checking is in effect unless you explicitly set your `PATH` environment variable first.

Listing 18.5 shows a more secure version of this program.

Listing 18.5   A Somewhat More Secure Version of directory.cgi

```
1: #!/usr/bin/perl -wT
2: # tainting is enabled!
3: use strict;
4: use CGI qw(:all);
5:
6: print header('text/plain');
7: # Explicitly set the path to something reasonable
8: $ENV{PATH}='/bin:/usr/bin';
9: my $dir=param('dirname');
10: # Only allow directory listings under /home/projects
11: if ($dir=~m,^(/home/projects/[\w/]+)$, ) {
12:     $dir=$1;   # This "untaints" the data, see "perldoc perlsec"
13:     print 'ls -l $dir';
14: }
```

For more information on tainted data, how to untaint data, and Perl programs, see the perlsec manual included with the Perl distribution.

Doing the Impossible

HTML/CGI forms can also be undermined in another way. Consider the HTML in Listing 18.6.

Listing 18.6   A Simple Form

```
<form action="/cgi-bin/doit.cgi">
<p>Please type in your favorite color:
<input type="text" length="15" name="color"/>
<input type="submit" value="Submit color"/></p>
</form>
```

In this form, the maximum allowable width of the `color` field is 15, right? Almost. The HTML specification says that `length` in a text field will allow at most that many characters. However, the browser could be broken, or a malicious person could put more than 15 characters in that field by simply bypassing your form or creating a new one.

If you expect a field to have a particular value, do not rely on HTML, Java, or JavaScript to ensure that the value is okay. For example, if the absolute limit to the color field should be 15, then the Perl program could process it like this:

```
my $color=param('color');      # Get the original field value
$color=substr($color, 0, 15);  # Get just the first 15 characters...
```

Denial of Service

A Web server—any Web server—can be crippled through denial-of-service attacks. Because the Web server is processing requests on behalf of a remote user, the remote user can overwhelm a Web server by making too many requests. Sometimes this act is through malice; often it's not. Many times companies put services on the Web and are so overwhelmed with the response that they have to shut down and rethink their approach.

A denial-of-service situation can occur with static HTML pages or CGI programs.

You can't do much to prevent a denial-of-service problem except to have adequate services on hand to handle the load of browsers. If your CGI programs take a long time to execute or use a significant portion of system resources—frequency of file access, intensity of CPU usage—to operate, the server may become more vulnerable to a denial-of-service attack. Try to keep the tasks you perform in a CGI program small and quick.

18

A Guestbook

This example allows you to write a customizable *guestbook* for a Web site. A guestbook is an HTML form in which the user indicates his or her name and some comments. The guestbook can be used for collecting feedback on a topic, as a simple message board, or for submitting problems to a help desk. The data is kept in a file and can be displayed after the form is filled out; it also can be displayed on a page of its own.

Listing 18.7 provides a short bit of HTML to present a guestbook form for a fictional help desk. You can modify the form to suit your own needs.

Listing 18.7 Help Desk Form

```
<form action="/cgi-bin/helpdesk.cgi" name="helpdesk">
<p>
Problem type:
<input type="radio" name="probtype" value="hardware"/>Hardware
<input type="radio" name="probtype" value="software"/>Software
<br/>
<textarea name="problem" rows="10" cols="40">
Describe your problem.
```

continues

Listing 18.7   Continued

```
</textarea>
<br/>
Your name:
<input type="text" width="40" name="name"/><br/>
<input type="submit" name="submit" value="Submit Problem"/>
</p></form>
```

The help desk form expects a CGI program named /cgi-bin/helpdesk.cgi. This program is presented in Listing 18.8. If you need to put the CGI program somewhere else or call it by another name, be sure to put the correct URL in the help desk form in Listing 18.7.

Listing 18.8   Help Desk CGI Program

```
#!/usr/bin/perl -wT
use strict;
use CGI qw(:all);
use Fcntl qw(:flock);

# Location of the guestbook log file.  Change this to suit your needs
my $gbdata="c:/temp/guestbook";
# Any file name will do for semaphore.
my $semaphore_file="/tmp/helpdesk.sem";

# Function to lock (waits indefinitely)
sub get_lock {
   open(SEM, ">$semaphore_file")
      || die "Cannot create semaphore: $!";
   flock SEM, LOCK_EX;
}
# Function to unlock
sub release_lock {
   close(SEM);
}

# This function saves a passed-in help desk HTML form to a file
sub save {
   get_lock();
   open(GB, ">>$gbdata") || die "Cannot open $gbdata: $!";
   print GB "name: ", param('name'), "\n";
   print GB "type: ", param('probtype'), "\n";
   print GB "problem: ", param('problem'), "\n";
   close(GB);
   release_lock();
}
# This function displays the contents of the help desk log file as HTML,
```

continues

Listing 18.8 Continued

```perl
# with minimal formatting.
sub display {
    open(GB, $gbdata) || die "Cannot open $gbdata: $!";
    while(<GB>){
        print "<b>$_</b><br />";  # The name
        my($type,$prob);
        $type=<GB>;
        $prob=<GB>;
        print "$type<br />";
        print "$prob<br /><br />";
    }
    close(GB);
}

print header;
# The parameter 'submit' is only passed if this CGI program was
# executed by pressing the 'submit' button in the form in listing 18.7
if (defined param('submit')) {
    save;
    display;
} else {
    display;
}
```

18

Most of the code in Listing 18.8 is Perl that you should already be familiar with, but notice these points in particular:

- The get_lock() and release_lock() functions are absolutely necessary for this form. You must always assume with any CGI program that more than one instance of the CGI may be running at any one time. Multiple instances of helpdesk.cgi writing to the help desk log file would be bad, so the file is locked before writing to it. It's not locked before reading, because reading the log file while it's being written isn't tragic.

- This CGI program has two purposes. When called as the target action of the form in Listing 18.7, it writes new entries to the log file. When called without using the form, it simply displays the contents of the log file.

A form similar to this is presented in Hour 23, "Web Pages with Templates," but with a completely different approach.

Summary

In this hour, you learned how HTML forms and CGI programs interact and how to have your CGI programs interpret the contents of forms with the CGI module's `param` function. Also, you learned what to do to make your CGI programs more secure and how to handle tainted data. You also looked at a simple CGI guestbook application, ready to customize and modify for your own uses.

Q&A

Q I can't get the form submission to work; I keep getting an error.

A Try using the CGI debugging guide from Hour 17, "Introduction to CGI," to find your problem. Just because it's a form doesn't mean that debugging it is any different from debugging normal CGI.

Q I just found this great program on the Internet, but I don't understand why it's trying to use $ENV{QUERY_STRING} to get the form parameters.

A Because the author of that program decided to forgo the CGI module's form-processing capabilities. This fact indicates that it is either a very old Perl program that predates the CGI module or that the author decided to use his or her own form-processing code. Either way, this is a good indication that the program should be looked at skeptically and used cautiously.

Q When I run programs with the -T option in the #! line, from the command prompt, I get the error Too late for -T option and then the program stops. Why?

A The -T option must be given to Perl as soon as possible so that it knows to look for tainted data. By the time the #! line in your program was processed, it was too late—Perl had already processed your command line options without tainting. To run Perl from a command prompt—for example, in the debugger—you need to specify the –T on the command prompt as well:

```
perl -T -d foo.cgi
```

Q Will Perl's data-tainting capabilities keep me from making stupid mistakes in my CGI programs? Are they guaranteed to be secure now?

A No CGI program is completely secure. The data-tainting capabilities of Perl go a long way toward keeping you from making silly mistakes, but they do not guarantee secure programs.

Workshop

Quiz

1. The `param` function in an array context with no arguments returns

   a. `undef`

   b. The number of form elements

   c. A list of the form element names

2. The differences between the POST and GET methods are transparent if you use the CGI module.

   a. True

   b. False

3. The password field input type on an HTML form is secure because it obscures the password before sending it.

   a. False

   b. True

Answers

1. c. `param`, without arguments, returns a list of the element names from the submitted form.

2. a. True.

3. a. False. With normal HTTP and CGI, all form fields are transmitted in cleartext and are not secure. The password field input type just hides the field as you type it.

Activities

- Spice up the help desk form a bit. Add timestamps to each entry and maybe some color on the output.

- Challenge: The `display()` function prints the entries in the help desk form starting with the oldest. Change the `display()` function to print the newest entries first.

18

Complex Forms

The forms on the Web aren't limited to simple one-page forms. Sometimes forms are spread out over several pages. These complex forms appear as surveys, questionnaires, and shopping cart applications.

These more complex forms require some different programming techniques, which you'll learn about this hour.

In this hour you'll learn

- How to create multipage forms

The Stateless Web

Writing complex multipage forms using CGI programs offers a unique programming challenge. The connection between a Web browser and a Web server is not a long-term connection. The Web browser connects to the server, retrieves the page, and then disconnects from the Web server. No sustained connection is kept between the server and your browser.

To make matters more complicated, each time the browser connects to the Web server, the Web server doesn't recognize the browser as having been to the site beforehand. The server has no easy way of recognizing the browser each time.

An analogy that works well is that of a conversation between a library patron and a librarian with no memory. The patron is allowed to ask only one question at a time. The patron can ask the librarian for a book—say, on Arizona—and the librarian can retrieve it. The librarian can retrieve the book because he or she can fulfill simple requests easily. However, the patron cannot request another book on the same subject. The librarian would have no memory of the prior request and would be helpless. If the request were rephrased as "give me another book on Arizona," the librarian would still be unable to help because he or she might retrieve the same book on Arizona as he or she did for the first request.

The only way to retrieve a second book on the subject would be to say, "I need another book on Arizona; I already have *Settling of the Southwest*." That request has enough information to state the problem and let the librarian know what's not an appropriate response.

Writing multipage forms for the Web uses the same solution: Each question/answer session needs to contain enough information so that the Web server can figure out what needs to be done and what has already been done. You can create such sessions in a few different ways; one of them—using hidden HTML fields—is presented in this hour.

Hidden Fields

The easiest way to have Web forms "remember" information is to embed previous information in them by using hidden fields. Hidden fields are part of the HTML forms specification that allow fields and values to be part of an HTML form but not appear in the form when it's rendered visually. In HTML, they're written as follows:

```
<input type="hidden" name="fullname" value="Pink Floyd" />
```

If the preceding HTML were put into a form, a new name (`"fullname"`) and value (`"Pink Floyd"`) would be part of the form. If the form were submitted to a Perl CGI program, the `param` function would return a key and a value for the hidden field.

The Online Store

For an example of how to use hidden fields, consider an online store that uses a series of Web pages to allow people to shop for items from an online catalog. For now, I'll just walk you through the workings of a complex form. Later in this hour, I'll present another complex form complete with code to create an online survey.

> Do *not* use this example of an online store without implementing some kind of secure Web transaction, such as https. Consult your web server's documentation to set this up. Notice that this example doesn't contain any real personal information such as phone numbers or credit card numbers, because hidden fields are just like regular HTML forms. No security is involved at all.

The first page of the online store, illustrated in Figure 19.1, presents a list of featured items from the store.

FIGURE 19.1

The first page of an online store.

Featured Items
☐ Pickled Herring
☒ Chocolate Bananas

Go to store

19

When the user clicks the Go to Store button, the CGI program accepts the values from the form and then presents the full catalog, as shown in Figure 19.2.

FIGURE 19.2

Catalog of online store shown.

Online Store, full catalog
☒ Fish heads
☐ Chitterlings
☐ Head Cheese
☐ Elephant Ears
Hidden:
    Chocolate Bananas

Ship Items

The second page presents the full catalog. When the first page—with the featured items—was submitted, the CGI program accepted the values, and then as it was printing the HTML for the full catalog, it placed the selected quantities for the featured items on the new form as hidden fields.

Each time the CGI program receives the values from the HTML form, the new page contains the old values in hidden fields, as well as the new values in the regular form elements.

In this way, you avoid the "forgetful librarian" problem. When the form for the full cata-log is submitted, the hidden fields in the form remind the CGI program which items were selected from the first form, as well as from the current form.

If a third page is needed, the values from the first two pages can be squirreled away on the third page as hidden fields, as shown in Figure 19.3.

FIGURE 19.3

Shipping info for online store.

You should be aware of some problems with hidden fields on an HTML page. First, the val-ues in the hidden fields can be seen by anyone. To see the values, users can simply view the HTML source for the page; most Web browsers have an option for viewing the source.

Second, the values in hidden fields can be changed by remote users. Remote users can use a doctored Web browser or can submit the form manually using HTTP. For example, the online store should not store the *prices* in hidden fields—only the quantities. The CGI program should look up the prices as they are needed for display.

When you're designing forms, a look at how other people design theirs is often helpful. This way, you also get an idea whether they're using hidden fields to preserve information. Most Web browsers have a View Page Source selection. You should use it on any form you find particularly interesting to see how it was put together. Do *not* copy the form, however. Most of the time, copying violates the original author's copyright.

A Multipage Survey

Surveys are common places to find forms that span several different Web pages. They're sometimes too long to fit on a single page, and they can usually be broken up into categories.

What follows is a simple multipage Web survey to find out aspects about your personality. This survey presents four different pages but could easily be changed to support as many pages as you would like. The four pages are as follows:

- A series of general questions that are used to find out what kind of personality you have

- Some specific questions about your habits and a question based on an answer from the first survey page

- A page that allows you to enter your name and comments about the survey

- A "thank you" message that prints after the survey is complete

The same CGI program is used to perform all four functions. It decides which page to open next, depending on which page it has just displayed. The core of the survey program is shown in Listing 19.1.

19

By including the line

```
use CGI::Carp qw(fatalsToBrowser);
```

your CGI program's die() messages, which might normally go to the Web server's log file, are printed as part of the Web page. When you write longer CGI programs, this might help in debugging.

The results of the survey are saved in a text file but are not displayed by this program at all. This program simply collects the survey answers and stores them. You will have to write another CGI program to display the results.

Listing 19.1 First Part of the Survey Program

```
 1:   #!/usr/bin/perl -w
 2:   use Fcntl qw(:flock);
 3:   use CGI qw(:all);
 4:   use CGI::Carp qw(fatalsToBrowser);
 5:   use strict;
 6:   my $surveyfile="/tmp/survey.txt";
 7:   my @survey_answers=qw(pettype daytype clothes
 8:           castaway travel risky ownpet
 9:           realname comments);
10:    my $semaphore_file="/tmp/survey.sem";
11:   print header;
12:   if (! param ) {
13:       page_one();        # Survey just started
14:   } elsif (defined param('pageone')) {
15:       page_two();        # Answered one page, print the second
16:   } elsif (defined param('pagetwo')) {
17:       page_three();      # Print the last page.
18:   } else {
19:       survey_done();     # Print a thank-you note, and save
20:   }
```

Lines 7–9: During the survey, each HTML form contains input fields. The names of each of the fields appear in this array. The `save()` function and the `repeat_hidden()` functions will use this array of names later.

Lines 12–13: If this CGI program is passed no parameters—that is, it's not loaded as the result of a form posting—the function `page_one()` is called to print the first page of the survey.

Lines 14–17: If an HTML form parameter called `pageone` is passed to this CGI program, the function `page_two()` is called. If `pagetwo` is passed, then `page_three()` is called.

Line 19: If HTML form parameters are passed to this CGI program, but not `pageone` or `pagetwo`, then the survey is complete, the results are saved, and the "thank you" message is printed in the `survey_done()` function.

The submit buttons on each of the pages provide the clues as to which page should be loaded next, as you can see in Figure 19.4. Because the submit button name is passed into the CGI program as a parameter, it can be used to show which version of the page was just submitted to the program.

Listing 19.2 continues the survey program.

FIGURE 19.4

Diagram of which button causes which action.

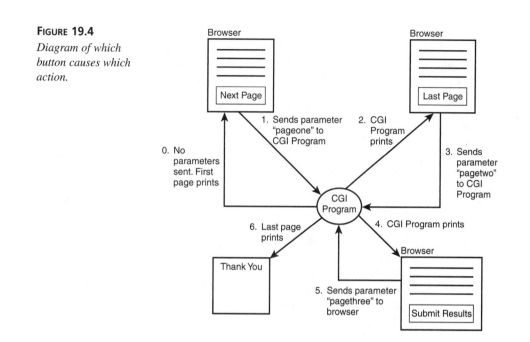

Listing 19.2 Second Part of the Survey Program

```
21:  sub page_one {
22:      print<<END_PAGE_ONE;
23:  <form>
24:  <p>Are you a "cat person" or a "dog person"?<br/>
25:  <input type="radio" name="pettype" value="dog"/>Dog<br/>
26:  <input type="radio" name="pettype" value="cat"/>Cat<br/>
27:  </p><p>
28:  Are you more of an early-riser or a night owl?<br/>
29:  <input type="radio" name="daytype" value="early"/>Early riser<br/>
30:  <input type="radio" name="daytype" value="late"/>Night Owl<br/>
31:  </p><p>
32:  At work, if you had a choice on how to dress....<br/>
33:  <input type="radio" name="clothes" value="casual"/>Casual<br/>
34:  <input type="radio" name="clothes" value="business"/>Business<br/>
35:  </p><p>
36:  If stranded on a desert island,
37:  who would you rather be stuck with?<br/>
38:  <input type="radio" name="castaway" value="ginger"/>Ginger<br/>
39:  <input type="radio" name="castaway" value="marya"/>Mary-Anne<br/>
40:  <input type="radio" name="castaway" value="prof"/>Professor<br/>
41:  <input type="radio" name="castaway" value="skipper"/>Skipper<br/>
42:  <input type="submit" name="pageone" value="Next page"/></p>
43:  </form>
44:  END_PAGE_ONE
45:  }
```

19

Lines 22 through 44 are a new Perl construct that you haven't seen yet; it's called a *here document*. A here document allows you to specify a string that spans several lines, includes other quotation marks, and acts like a normal double-quoted string. To start a here document, you use << followed by a word. The quotation continues until the next occurrence of the word at the beginning of the line, as in this example:

```
$a=<<END_OF_QUOTE;
This is included as part of the string.
END_OF_QUOTE
```

The word that identifies the beginning of the here document—END_OF_QUOTE in the previous snippet or END_PAGE_ONE in Listing 19.2—must be followed by a semicolon. At the end of the here document, the word must appear starting in the first column and must not have any trailing characters such as spaces or semicolons. Inside the here document, variables expand as they do in normal double-quoted strings (" "), so be careful using $ and @ inside a here document.

Using here documents allows you to embed a large amount of HTML in your Perl program without having to fuss with quotation marks, multiple print statements, and so on.

The function in Listing 19.2 simply prints an HTML form. The <form> tag does not contain an action or a method. When a <form> action attribute is not specified, the current CGI program (the one that produced the form) is reloaded when the form is submitted. When the method attribute is not specified, the default method, GET, is used.

Notice that the submit button on the form is named pageone. When this form is submitted, a parameter called pageone will be sent to the CGI program; the value isn't important here. When this parameter is submitted, it is the cue to the CGI program to load the second page.

Listing 19.3 continues the survey CGI program.

Listing 19.3 Third Part of the Survey Program

```
46:   # Print out any of the responses so far as hidden fields
47:   sub repeat_hidden {
48:       foreach my $answer ( @survey_answers ) {
49:           if (defined param($answer)) {
50:               print "<input type=hidden";
51:               print " name=\"$answer\" ";
52:               print " value=\"", param($answer),"\"/>\n";
53:           }
54:       }
55:   }
56:   sub page_two {
57:       my $pet=param('pettype');
```

continues

Listing 19.3   Continued

```
58:        if (! defined $pet) {
59:                $pet="goldfish";
60:        }
61:        print<<END_PAGE_TWO;
62:  <form>
63:  <p>Would you rather...<br/>
64:  <input type="radio" name="travel" value="travel"/>Travel<br/>
65:  <input type="radio" name="travel" value="home"/>Stay at home<br/>
66:  </p><p>
67:  Do you consider yourself...<br/>
68:  <input type="radio" name="risky" value="yes"/>A daredevil<br/>
69:  <input type="radio" name="risky" value="no"/>Cautious<br/>
70:  </p><p>
71:  Do you own a $pet?<br/>
72:  <input type="radio" name="ownpet" value="$pet"/>Yes<br/>
73:  <input type="radio" name="ownpet" value="no"/>No<br/>
74:  </p>
75:  <input type="submit" name="pagetwo" value="Last Page"/>
76:  END_PAGE_TWO
77:        repeat_hidden();
78:        print "</form>";
79:  }
```

Line 47: As the comment in line 46 indicates, the function in this line prints the values of all the form fields so far as hidden fields. The array `@survey_answers` contains all the possible `"name="` values on the HTML forms. When run the first time, most of the fields will not exist because those portions of the survey haven't been filled out yet.

Lines 48–49: Each of the possible parameters in `@survey_answers` is checked, and each parameter is defined. An `<input type="hidden">` HTML tag is printed to hold the value on the current form.

Line 56: This function prints the second page of the survey.

Lines 57–60: This function is called as the second page of the survey. If the first page of the survey was properly filled out, then `param('pettype')` will hold either `dog` or `cat`, and this value will be stored in `$pet`. If the responder skipped that question, and `param('pettype')` is not defined, then `goldfish` is used instead.

Lines 61–76: The rest of the second page of the form is printed, and `$pet` is substituted as a question; thus, this questionnaire is customized based on the response on the first page.

Line 77: Any HTML form parameters from the first page are carried over onto this form as hidden fields.

19

If you view the survey form at this point—the second page—all the answers from the first page are stored as hidden fields at the end of the second page. The code for the third page is shown in Listing 19.4

Listing 19.4   Fourth Part of the Survey Program

```
80:  sub page_three {
81:      print<<END_PAGE_THREE;
82:  <form><p>
83:  Last page!  This information is optional!<br/>
84:  Your name:</p><p>
85:  <input type="text" name="realname"/><br/>
86:  Any comments about this survey:<br/>
87:  <textarea name="comments" cols="40" rows="10">
88:  </textarea>
89:  </p>
90:  <input type="submit" name="pagethree"
91:      value="Submit survey results"/>
92:  END_PAGE_THREE
93:      repeat_hidden();
94:      print "</form>";
95:  }
```

The function `page_three()` is fairly straightforward, simply printing a text box and a text area in a form. At the end, it again calls `repeat_hidden()` to put all the hidden fields into the third page of the survey. The conclusion to the survey CGI program is shown in Listing 19.5.

Listing 19.5   Last Part of the Survey Program

```
96:   sub survey_done {
97:       save();
98:       print "Thank You!";
99:   }
100:  #
101:  # Save all of the survey results to $surveyfile
102:  #
103:  sub save {
104:      get_lock();
105:      open(SF, ">>$surveyfile") || die "Cannot open $surveyfile: $!";
106:      foreach my $answer (@survey_answers) {
107:          if (defined param ($answer) ) {
108:              print SF $answer, "=", param($answer), "\n";
109:          }
110:      }
111:      close(SF);
```

continues

Listing 19.5 Continued

```
112:     release_lock();
113: }
114: #
115: # Locks and Unlocks the survey file so that multiple survey-takers
116: # Don't clash and write at the same time.
117: #
118:
119: # Function to lock (waits indefinitely)
120: sub get_lock {
121:    open(SEM, ">$semaphore_file")
122:       || die "Cannot create semaphore: $!";
123:    flock SEM, LOCK_EX;
124: }
125:
126:# Function to unlock
127: sub release_lock {
128:    close(SEM);
129: }
```

Line 96: This function is called simply to print a "thank you" message—always a nice thing to do after having someone go through three pages of survey—and call the save() function.

Line 103: The save() function here is almost a clone of the save function from Hour 18, "Basic Forms." It locks the survey file with get_lock(), writes the answers to it using a mechanism similar to that in repeat_hidden(), and then unlocks the file with release_lock().

Feel free to modify this survey to suit your own needs. The design is fairly flexible and could be adapted for many purposes.

Summary

In this hour, you learned how multipage Web forms are assembled. While doing so, you learned about a few problems that need to be addressed in writing programs—most seriously, making programs remember from page to page what happened. You also learned how hidden fields are used to remember information on Web pages that can't be remembered by the server, and then you constructed a bare-bones survey form using hidden fields.

Q&A

Q Do HTML forms have to be this ugly?

A The forms in this book are simple, plain, bare-bones, and—some would say—ugly. The purpose of *Sams Teach Yourself Perl in 24 Hours* is to teach you Perl and CGI programming, not HTML. In fact, most of the HTML in this book is not up to standards and is not complete; it lacks `<head>` tags, `<html>` tags, DTD headers, and so on. By providing basic HTML, I hope you'll correct this for your own needs.

As I mentioned earlier, a good method for spicing up your forms is to explore the Web and find a form you like. By viewing the source, you can get an idea of how the pages are put together.

Q I'm getting the `Can't find string terminator "XXXX" anywhere before EOF at...` error. What is it?

A This error is caused by having an open quote somewhere in your program without a matching close quote. When you use here documents, this means that the word you've used to mark the end of the here document can't be found. The format is as follows:

```
print <<MARK;
text
text
text
MARK
```

The here document beginning and ending words—in this case, the word MARK—must be exactly the same. The terminating word must appear with nothing in front of it, on a line by itself, and with nothing after it. MS-DOS and Windows text editors sometimes do not put an end-of-line character after the last line of the program. If your here program ends at the end of the file, try putting a blank line after it.

Workshop

Quiz

1. So that your program remembers long, multipage Web transactions, you need to use

    a. Databases and cookies

    b. Hidden HTML form fields

    c. Some combination of hidden HTML form fields, cookies, and databases

2. Using an HTML `<form>` tag without an `action` attribute will

    a. Not work

    b. Cause the submit button to use the CGI program that originally generated the page

    c. Cause the submit button to reload the current page

3. The survey program, as listed, has a small bug. What is it?

    a. `print<<EOP;` is not valid syntax in Listing 19.2.

    b. The HTML is not complete because it lacks `<head>` tags and such.

    c. The survey doesn't print its results.

Answers

1. Either b or c. You can use just hidden HTML fields or just cookies. Using just a database won't quite work.

2. b. Reloading the current page would just erase all the current form answers. Without an `action` attribute, the `<form>` tag uses the URL of the current page for the submission URL.

3. b. `print<<EOP;` is certainly valid syntax, called a here document. Choice c is not correct because the program wasn't designed that way (see the "Activities" section).

Activities

- Write a short CGI program to display the results of the survey program. Possibly build a table to display them like this:

Cat/Dog	Own One?	Nocturnal	Clothes	Castaway	Traveler	Risky?
cat	no	yes	casual	Professor	yes	yes
neither	goldfish	no	business	Skipper	no	no
dog	yes	no	casual	Mary-Anne	yes	yes

- For an additional challenge, write a CGI program to summarize the survey results like this:

Cat/Dog Personality:	Cat 40%	Dog 45%	Neither 15%	
Own that pet:	Cat 20%	Dog 15%	Goldfish 30%	None 35%
Night Person?	Yes 35%	No 40%		

19

Hour **20**

Manipulating HTTP and CGI

In this hour, you'll learn a host of interesting things you can do with the Web by using CGI programs to help you make your Web site a little more flexible and easy to manage.

In this hour you'll learn

- How HTML gets from the server to your browser
- How to have CGI programs send things other than HTML
- How to pass values directly to CGI programs
- How server-side includes work
- How to query the browser and the server for information

The HTTP Conversation

In Hour 17, "Introduction to CGI," you learned about the basic conversation between the Web browser (Netscape, Internet Explorer, and so on) and the

Web server (Apache, IIS, and so on). The conversation in that hour was somewhat over-simplified. Now that you're more comfortable with CGI, it's probably a good time to take a closer look at this subject. Later in this hour, you'll learn some techniques for manipulating this "conversation" to perform some interesting tasks.

The conversation is described by a protocol known as the *Hypertext Transfer Protocol (HTTP)*. The two current versions of this standard are HTTP 1.0 and HTTP 1.1. For purposes of this discussion, either one is applicable.

The Internet standards documents that describe the protocols used on the Internet are called Request For Comments—or, more commonly, RFCs. The RFCs are maintained by the Internet Engineering Task Force (IETF) and can be viewed on the Web at `http://www.ietf.org`. The specific documents that describe HTTP are RFC 1945 and RFC 2616. Be forewarned: These documents are highly technical in nature.

When your Web browser makes a connection to the Web server, the browser sends an initial message to the server that looks something like this:

```
GET http://testserver/ HTTP/1.0
Connection: Keep-Alive
Accept: image/gif, image/x-xbitmap, image/jpeg, image/pjpeg, image/png, */*
Accept-Charset: iso-8859-1,*,utf-8
Accept-Encoding: gzip
Accept-Language: en, en-GB, de, fr, ja, ko, zh
Host: testserver:80
User-Agent: Mozilla/4.51 [en]C-c32f404p  (WinNT; U)
```

The GET line indicates what URL you're trying to receive and what version of the protocol you're accepting. In this case, you're accepting version 1.0 of the HTTP protocol.

The Connection line indicates that you would like this connection kept open for multiple page fetches. By default, a browser makes a separate connection for each frame, page, and image on a Web page. The directive Keep-Alive asks the server to keep the connection open so that multiple items can be fetched using the same connection.

The Accept lines indicate what sorts of data you're willing to accept on the connection. The */* at the end of the first Accept line indicates that you're willing to accept any kind of data. The next line (iso-8859-1 and so on) indicates what character encoding can be used for the document. The Accept-Encoding line, in this case, says that gzip (GNU Zip) can be used to compress the data from the server for a faster transfer. Finally,

`Accept-Language` indicates what languages are acceptable to this browser—English, English–Great Britain, German, French, and so on.

`Host` is the name of the system you think is hosting the Web site. Because of virtual hosting, explained later, it may be different from the host name in the URL.

Finally, the browser identifies itself to the Web server as `Mozilla/4.51 [en]C-c32f404p (WinNT; U)`. In Web terminology, the browser is called a *user agent*.

The server then sends a reply that will look something like this:

```
GET http://testserver/ --> 200 OK
Date: Thu, 02 Sep 1999 19:54:39 GMT
Server: Netscape-Enterprise/3.5.1G
Content-Length: 2222
Content-Type: text/html
Last-Modified: Wed, 01 Sep 1999 17:12:03 GMT
```

The reply is followed by the contents of the page you requested.

The `GET` line in this case indicates whether the server is going to give you the page. The status `200` indicates that everything went fine. The server also identifies itself on the `Server` line; in this case, the server is a Netscape-Enterprise/3.5.1G Web server.

The `Content-Length` line indicates that 2,222 bytes of content will be sent back to the browser. Using this information, your browser knows that a page is 50 percent complete, 60 percent complete, and so on. The `Content-Type` is the kind of page that's being sent back. For HTML pages, this line is set to `text/html`. For an image, it might be set to `image/jpeg`.

The `Last-Modified` date indicates to the browser whether the page has changed since it was last fetched. Most Web browsers *cache* pages so that if you look at a Web page twice, the date can be compared at this point to a saved copy the browser already has. If the page on the server hasn't changed, downloading the entire page again might not be necessary.

Example: Fetching a Page Manually

You can fetch a Web page manually if you'd like to. This capability is often useful when you're just testing and want to make sure that the correct replies are being sent by a Web server.

To follow this example, you need a special program called a *Telnet client*. The Telnet client is a remote-terminal access program used to remotely log in to Unix workstations; however, it's often useful for tasks such as debugging HTTP.

20

If you have a Unix machine, it's very likely that you have Telnet installed already. If you have a Microsoft Windows machine, Telnet may already be installed as part of your networking utilities. Simply use the Run option from the Start menu to run the Telnet client. If you don't have this program installed, or you're working on a Macintosh, you can find free Telnet clients at any good download site.

To start communicating with the Web server, use Telnet like this at a prompt:

```
$ telnet www.webserver.com 80
```

Here, `www.webserver.com` is the name of the Web server, and `80` is the port number you want to connect to (port 80 is typically where Web servers are listening). If your Telnet client is a graphical one, you might need to set these values in a dialog box.

When Telnet connects, you may not receive a prompt or a connection message. Don't worry; that's normal. HTTP expects the client to talk first; the server isn't expected to prompt. Under Unix, you get a message that says something like this:

```
Trying www.webserver.com
Connected to www.webserver.com
Escape character is '^]'
```

Other kinds of systems—for example, Windows and Macintosh—do not see this message.

You now need to type the following, carefully and somewhat quickly:

```
GET http://www.webserver.com/ HTTP/1.0
```

Press the Enter key *twice* after typing this line. The Web server should then respond with a normal HTTP header and the top-level page for the Web site and then disconnect.

Example: Returning Something Other Than Text

Your CGI program doesn't have to return HTML to the browser. In fact, anything your browser can fetch, your CGI program can send.

The `header` function in the CGI module informs the browser what kind of data it's about to receive using a MIME Content-Type header. The Content-Type header describes the contents of the data that follows, so that the browser knows what to do with the data.

By default, the `header` function sends a Content-Type description of `text/HTML` to the browser. The browser recognizes that the contents that follow are text with possible HTML.

By telling the browser to expect different kinds of data, you can manipulate how the browser treats the data. The data can be displayed as images, passed to a browser plug-in, or even run by an external program launched by the browser.

To have the `header` function send something other than a regular `text/html` header, use the `-type` option, like this:

```
print header(-type => MIME_type);
```

Some common MIME Content-Types that can be sent to a browser are `text/plain` for text that is not to be interpreted, `image/gif` and `image/jpeg` for GIF and JPEG images, and `application/`*appname* for data specific to an application *appname*. A special MIME Content-Type called `application/octet-stream` indicates raw binary data that the browser should just save to a file.

This could be used if you want to create something like an "image of the day" Web site or a Web page banner advertisement. Changing a Web page daily to reflect the new image would be a pain. If you were out of town, who would update the "image of the day" for you? Instead, you can have a static HTML page and have a Perl CGI program cough up a different image automatically every day.

Inside your Web page, use HTML like this:

```
<body><p>
Today's image of the day is:
<img src="/cgi-bin/daily_image.cgi"/></p>
</body>
```

In the preceding HTML, notice that the target of the `<img>` tag is a CGI program—not a .gif or .jpg. Next, you need a directory that's full of images, at least as many as the number of days in a month. You can call the images whatever you like, as long as the filenames end in .jpg; note that the program could be adapted to use GIF images easily.

The daily_image.cgi CGI program can look something like Listing 20.1.

Listing 20.1 Code for Picture of the Day

```
1:  #!/usr/bin/perl -w
2:
3:    use strict;
4:    use CGI qw(:all);
5:    my($imagedir, $day, @jpegs, $error);
6:
7:    $imagedir="/web/htdocs/pic_of_day";
8:    $error="/web/htdocs/images/error.jpg";
9:
10:  sub display_image {
11:      my($image)=@_;
12:      open(IMAGE, "$image") || exit;
13:      binmode STDOUT; binmode IMAGE;
14:      print <IMAGE>;
```

20

continues

Listing 20.1 Continued

```
15:      close(IMAGE);
16:      exit;
17:  }
18:
19:  print header(-type => 'image/jpeg');
20:
21:  # Day of the month, 1-28, 29, 30, or 31
22:  $day=(localtime)[3];
23:  $day=$day-1;    # We want day 0-27, etc..
24:
25:  opendir(IMGDIR, $imagedir) || display_image($error);
26:  @jpegs=sort grep(/\.jpg$/, readdir IMGDIR);
27:  closedir(IMGDIR);
28:
29:  my $image="$imagedir/$jpegs[$day]";
30:  $image=$error if (not defined $jpegs[$day]);
31:  display_image($image);
```

Line 7: This line specifies the directory where the images are located. You can change it to indicate where you put the pictures.

Line 8: Oddly enough, because this CGI program doesn't emit text, and because the HTML page it's embedded in doesn't display the output as text, you can't simply print error messages. The variable $error contains the name of a .jpg that will be displayed if the $imagedir directory can't be opened.

Lines 10–16: This subroutine displays images to the standard output—which will go to the browser. On Windows platforms, STDOUT is considered a text file, and printing a .jpg to STDOUT will corrupt the image. So binmode is used to make STDOUT and IMAGE binary filehandles. Under Unix, you don't need binmode, but it doesn't hurt. Notice line 12: If the image can't be opened, there's no point in printing an error message, so the program simply exits.

Line 19: This line prints a standard HTTP header, except that the Content-Type will be image/jpeg instead of the usual text/html.

Line 25: The image directory is opened to be read. If the image directory does not open, then display_image() is called with the error image $error.

Line 26: This line is complicated, so follow along. First, the directory is read with readdir. Then the filenames that end in .jpg are extracted from that list. Finally, the resulting list is sorted and assigned to @jpegs.

The Internet Explorer browser ignores the HTTP `Content-Type` header entirely (and violates several Internet standards in the process). It uses the extension on the last component of the URL that you're retrieving to determine the file type (and, thus, behavior). It's sometimes necessary then to trick the browser into accepting data and treating it as the appropriate type—because frankly, it would be silly to name your CGI scripts with a .gif and .jpg extension.

You can do this by adding an extra component onto the URL so that it appears that it's another file type, like this:

```
http://server.com/cgi-bin/daily_image.cgi/nonsense.gif
```

The extra path information will be passed to the CGI script as the environment variable PATH_INFO in Apache. For this to work in IIS, you have to tweak the server's configuration; see MS Knowledge Base article Q184320 for instructions.

More Details on Calling CGI Programs

So far, you've learned two different techniques for starting a CGI program. The first and most obvious is simply to call the CGI program's URL from a link or have the user type it in the browser. A line like this will start and run a CGI program called time.cgi:

```
<A HREF="http://server/cgi-bin/time.cgi">Click here for the time</A>
```

When this link is followed, the CGI program time.cgi is run by the Web server, and its output is displayed as a new Web page. This example is simple, easy, and straightforward—just like the "Hello, World!" CGI program in Hour 17.

The other way to start a CGI program is to make it the target of an HTML form. For example, the following form calls the CGI program process.cgi when the submit button is clicked:

```
<form method="get" action="/cgi-bin/process.cgi">
<input type="text" name="STUFF"/><br/>
<input type="submit"/>
<form>
```

This method of calling a CGI program has an added benefit: You can pass parameters to the CGI program for processing. Well, that's the whole point of an HTML form.

Passing Parameters to CGI Programs

Wouldn't it be nice to pass information into a Perl program from a link? For example, wouldn't it be nice to have a clickable link in a document that would "run cgi program foo.cgi, with value X=this and value Y=that"? It's possible with a little bit of work.

20

First, you have to use a special kind of URL in your `<A HREF>` tag. The format of this URL is illustrated in Figure 20.1.

FIGURE 20.1

URL containing parameters.

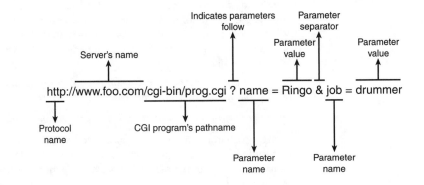

Each parameter is the name of a value that you want to pass into your CGI program—such as a named HTML form element. The value is the value for that name. For example, to create a link that, when clicked, will run a CGI program with the parameter `sign` set to `Aries` and `year` set to `1969`, you would enter the following:

```
<a href="http://www.server.com/cgi-bin/astrology.cgi?sign=Aries&year=1969">
Aries, year of the Rooster</a>
```

Inside the CGI program, the parameters are processed with the CGI module's `param` function as normal:

```
#!/usr/bin/perl -w

use CGI qw(:all);
use strict;

print header;
print "The year ", param('year'), " and being born under ",
    param('sign'), "indicates you are brilliant.\n";
```

You can pass as many parameters as you want. If you want to pass an empty parameter—one with no value—simply leave it off, as in `author` in the following example:

```
<a href="http://www.server.com/cgi-bin/book.cgi?author=&title=Beowulf">Beowulf</a>
```

Special Parameter Considerations

You need to be aware of some special considerations when calling CGI programs with parameters. Some characters are special and cannot be made part of a URL. For example, the `?` (question mark) is special: It marks the separation between the main portion of the URL and the parameters. Other characters that are special are `&`, space, and quotation marks.

The full list of special characters is enumerated in an Internet standards document called RFC 2396.

To insert one of these special characters into a URL requires that you *escape* the character. In this case, escaping the character means to translate its ASCII value into a two-digit hexadecimal number and then precede it with a percent sign. The encoding for "Hello, World!" is as follows:

```
Hello%2C%20World
```

Obviously, creating a URL-escaped string can be messy. The CGI module provides a function to create such strings automatically for you. The following snippet demonstrates how to print a URL with the proper encoding:

```perl
#!/usr/bin/perl -w

use strict;
# The 'escape' function must be pulled in manually
use CGI qw(:all escape);

print header;
my $string="Hello, World!";
print '<a href="http://www.server.com/cgi-bin/parrot.cgi?message=',
    escape($string) , '">Click Me</a>';
```

The preceding code produces a correctly URL-escaped HTML link. Notice how the CGI module is used in the code—use CGI qw(:all escape);. The escape function is not normally made available to your program if you use the CGI module; you have to ask for it explicitly.

The following program creates a much longer URL with escaped values:

```perl
#!/usr/bin/perl -w

use strict;
use CGI qw(:all escape);

my %books=( Insomnia => 'S. King',  Nutshell => 'O\'Reilly');
# Start with a base URL
my $url="http://www.server.com/cgi-bin/add_books.cgi?";

# Accumulate on the end of the URL with concatenation "."
foreach my $title (keys %books) {
    $url.=escape($title);  # Escape the title, add it
    $url.="=";
    $url.=escape($books{$title}); # Same with Author
    $url.="&";
}
```

20

```
print header;
print "<a href=\"$url\">Add books to library</a>";
```

The final value for `$url` that's constructed looks something like this:

```
http://www.server.com/cgi-
bin/add_books.cgi?Insomnia=S.%20King&Nutshell=O%27Reilly&
```

The final `&` on the end of the URL is ignored by the CGI program when it extracts the parameters with the `param` function.

Server-Side Includes

When you're designing a Web page, often most of the content on the page is static. Occasionally, portions of the page are changed, but overall the page stays the same. Consider a Web page that displays a current stock price for a company. The vast majority of the page is probably static—navigation bars, pictures, logos, usage information, headers, footers, titles, and so on. The important part of the page—the stock price—is generated by reading a database somewhere and simply filling in the blank.

To help create such pages, most Web servers support a feature called *server-side includes (SSI)*—also called *server-parsed HTML*. This feature allows the author of the Web site to construct an HTML Web page that's basically static and to have some portion of the page rewritten on-the-fly by the Web server as it's being served out (as illustrated in Figure 20.2). You can think of it as a fill-in-the-blanks HTML file; CGI programs fill in the blanks for you.

FIGURE 20.2

Web server adding things to an HTML page as it's being processed.

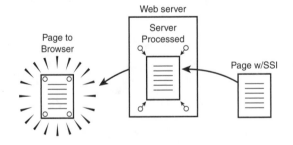

Your server administrator must enable SSI for these examples to work. For the server to read HTML with embedded SSIs properly, you sometimes need to give the HTML pages special names with `.shtml` or `.stm` extensions. Consult your server's documentation, or check with your server's administrator to find out how SSI is used on your particular Web server, since the supported directives and their syntax will vary.

The Web server—as it reads the static HTML page from the disk—looks for "tags" that cause it to substitute values. Under the Apache Web server in a server-parsed HTML page, the tag `<!--#echo var="LAST_MODIFIED"-->` causes Apache to substitute the date the page was last modified in place of the tag. The browser doesn't see this process happen; it sees only the date as it has been substituted by the server. This point is illustrated as follows:

This Web page is transformed	*Into this content by the server*
`<html>`	`<html>`
`<body>`	`<body>`
`This page was last changed:`	`This page was last changed:`
`<!--#echo var= "LAST_MODIFIED" -->`	`Wednesday, 01-Sep-1999 21:29:31 EDT`
`</body>`	`</body>`
`</html>`	`</html>`

Web servers vary in how they implement SSI. Sometimes the tags have different syntax, and some kinds of tags are supported on some servers but not others. Some Web servers do not support SSI at all; Microsoft's Personal Web Server does not, for example. The SSI HTML tags used in this hour are compatible with the Apache Web server and Microsoft's Internet Information Server, far and away the two most popular servers on the Web at the time of this writing.

20

This hour is not intended to teach you everything about SSI's features; they're too numerous, and most features are particular to specific brands of Web servers. The purpose is to introduce the SSI tag `#exec`. You use the SSI `#exec` tag like this in an HTML file:

```
<!--#exec cgi="/cgi-bin/stockprice.cgi"-->
```

When the Web server encounters this `#exec` tag, it stops and executes the stockprice.cgi CGI program. The output of that CGI program is inserted in the HTML stream as it goes to the browser. After the CGI program is complete, the rest of the HTML file following the `#exec` tag is sent to the browser.

Example: Working with SSI

For this example, you'll create a simple page that prints `"Hello, World"` and then a customized image, depending on what time of day it is. First, you need two images, one for night and one for day, as illustrated in Figure 20.3.

FIGURE 20.3

Day and Night pictures: day.jpg and night.jpg.

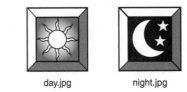

day.jpg   night.jpg

Then you need a boilerplate HTML file with the hello message, as shown next. If you're creating this example for yourself, remember that you might need to name the HTML file with a .shtml or .stm extension for the server to recognize the SSI tags.

```
<html>
<head>
<title>Welcome Page</title>
</head>
<body><p>
Welcome to this web page.  Currently, out my window I see:
<!--#exec cgi="/cgi-bin/sunmoon.cgi"--></p>
</body>
</html>
```

In the program sunmoon.cgi, you can use the code shown in Listing 20.2.

Listing 20.2   The Sun and Moon Greeting Program

```
 1:   #!/usr/bin/perl -w
 2:
 3:   use CGI qw(:all);
 4:
 5:   # The hour from localtime() is in 24-hour format
 6:   my $hour=(localtime)[2];
 7:   my $image;
 8:
 9:   # Before 6am or after 6pm, it's nighttime
10:   if ($hour<6 or $hour>18) {
11:           $image="night.jpg";
12:   } else {
13:           $image="day.jpg";
14:   }
15:   print header;
16:   print qq{<img src="$image" ALT="$image"/>\n};
```

Line 3: Because this is a CGI program, you should include the CGI module. The `qw(:all)` ensures that you can get to any functions you need.

Line 6: `localtime` in a list context returns a list of elements describing the current time; this topic was described in Hour 4, "Stacking Building Blocks: Lists and Arrays." The parentheses around `localtime` put it in a list context, and the `[2]` causes the third element of the list to be returned and assigned to `$hour`. Element #2 is the time in 24-hour format.

Line 15: A `header` must still be printed with the CGI header function, even though the output appears midway through the Web page.

Line 16: The `<img>` tag is printed with the value of either `$day` or `$night` as the image. An ALT attribute is used in case a browser is unable to display the image.

The source of the resulting Web page, when it's fetched by a browser at 8 a.m., would be as follows:

```
<html>
<head>
<title>Welcome Page</title>
</head>
<body><p>
Welcome to this web page.  Currently, out my window I see:
<img src="day.jpg"></p>
</body>
</html>
```

Remember that programs run with SSI's `#exec` feature are like CGI programs in that you're allowing the user to choose (indirectly) what's run on your web server, and you should keep security in mind when writing these programs.

20

Looking Out the Window

Most of the functions from the CGI module so far have been to control a browser—such as `redirect` or `header`—or to process parameters passed to CGI programs—such as `escape` and `param`. A whole set of functions in the CGI module has been designed to give you information about the system you're currently running on. A partial list is presented in Table 20.1, but for a full list, see the CGI module's online documentation by typing `perldoc CGI` at a command prompt.

Most of these functions rely on values that are provided by the Web server or sent by the Web browser in the HTTP protocol. Web browsers can lie about certain values—such as the `referer` value or `user_agent`—and Web servers may return inaccurate information sometimes; for example, `server_name` may not always return what you would expect.

Table 20.1 Partial List of Environment Functions

`referer`	Returns the URL of the link that sent you to this page. (Yes, it's misspelled. The original Internet Standard describing this field contained a spelling mistake, and it's now intentionally misspelled for consistency.)
`user_agent`	Returns a string that identifies the kind of Web browser that requested the page (for example, Netscape, IE, Lynx).
`remote_host`	Returns either the hostname or the IP address of the system that requested the page. Which value you get depends on how your Web server is configured and whether the hostname is available.
`script_name`	Returns the name of the program that is running this CGI program as a partial URL (for example, as `/cgi-bin/foo.cgi`).
`server_name`	Returns the name of the server hosting the CGI program.
`virtual_host`	Returns the name of the virtual host that was used to run this CGI program. This function differs from `server_name` because one server can often host many Web sites. `virtual_host` returns the name of the particular site that was requested.
`path_info`	Returns the value of the PATH_INFO environment variable. This is the portion of the URL that follows the CGI script name. IIS requires a registry patch to enable this. See the note at the end of the section "Example: Returning Something Other Than Text."

A short program to demonstrate these functions follows:

```perl
#!/usr/bin/perl -w

use strict;
use CGI qw(:all);

print header;

print "You were sent from: ", referer, "<br/>";
print "You are apparently running: ",
            user_agent, "<br/>";
print "Your system is called: ", remote_host,
            "<br/>";
print "The name of this program is: ",
            script_name, "<br/>";
```

```
print "It's running on the server: ",
              server_name, "<br/>";
print "The server's calling itself: ",
              virtual_host, "<br/>";
```

Running this program on a testing Web server produces these results:

```
You were sent from: http://testsys.net/links.html
You are apparently running: Mozilla/4.51 [en] (Win95; I)
Your system is called: 192.168.1.2
The name of this program is: /cgi/showstuff.cgi
It's running on the server: testsys
The server's calling itself: perlbook
```

Redirection

One useful trick to use in CGI programs is called *HTTP redirection*. You use redirection when you want a CGI program to load another page based on some computed value.

For example, if you have a series of pages specific to a browser—for example, they contain a plug-in that's available only to Netscape browsers under Microsoft Windows—you can send all the Web site visitors to the same URL and have a CGI program redirect them to the correct page, as illustrated in Figure 20.4.

FIGURE 20.4

One Web site redirecting to another.

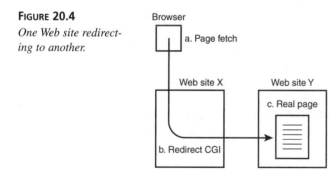

To implement a redirection, you need to use the CGI module's `redirect` function. The `redirect` function manipulates the HTTP conversation discussed earlier and causes the browser to load a new page.

Listing 20.3 contains a short program to redirect users of Netscape under Windows to one page and all other browsers to a different page.

20

The `redirect` header has to be printed before anything else is emitted from the CGI script. Don't print the output of the `header()` function or anything else before calling `redirect()`.

Listing 20.3   Redirection Based on Browser

```
1:   #!/usr/bin/perl -w
2:
3:   use CGI qw(:all);
4:   use strict;
5:   my($browser, $target);
6:
7:   # Fetch the browser's name
8:
9:   $browser=user_agent;
10:  $target="http://www.server.com/generic.html";
11:
12:  # Test for WinXX and Netscape
13:  if ($browser=~/Mozilla/ and $browser !~ /MSIE/ and $browser=~/Win/) {
14:          $target="http://www.server.com/netscape.html";
15:  }
16:  print redirect( -uri => $target );
```

Line 9: The browser type is captured in `$browser`.

Line 10: The default URL is put into `$target`. Any non-Netscape browsers will be sent here.

Line 13–14: The browser identification, stored in `$browser`, is checked to see if it contains `Mozilla` or `Win` but not MSID if so, a new target address is assigned.

Line 16: The redirection message is sent to the browser.

Redirection through CGI is seamless, whereas other techniques, such as using JavaScript and HTML extensions, have problems. JavaScript is not supported on all platforms, and using a `window.location.href` assignment in JavaScript might not produce the proper results. Using an HTML `<META HTTP-EQUIV="refresh">` tag for redirection causes a noticeable delay because the browser has to load the page completely before the redirection can take place. JavaScript shares this problem. HTTP redirection happens before any HTML is transmitted and is nearly instantaneous.

Netscape's browser identifies itself as *Mozilla* to the CGI module's `user_agent` function. This name is a play on the original graphical Web browser's name, *Mosaic*. The `user_agent` name returned by a typical Windows 95 Netscape 4.51 browser is similar to `Mozilla/4.51 -- (Win95; I)`. Microsoft Internet Explorer 5 identifies itself as `Mozilla/4.0 (compatible; MSIE 5.5; Windows 98)`. Coding a script that guesses the browser in a foolproof manner is almost impossible, though, because a browser can lie about its user agent type.

Summary

In this hour, you learned about what goes on as the Web page is being fetched from the server, and you learned a little bit about the HTTP protocol. You also learned how to call a CGI program from a link and pass parameters into the program as well, which can be used with SSI. In addition, you learned how to manipulate the HTTP conversation to perform redirection and to get information about the browser and the server.

Q&A

Q The SSI examples don't seem to be working.

A SSI might not be working for a host of reasons. First, you should verify that your Web server supports SSI; not all do. Second, make sure that SSI has been enabled on your Web server. Third, make sure you have the right extension on your HTML files to enable SSI. You may have to contact your server administrator to find out this information. Finally, make sure you're using the right syntax for your HTML SSI tags.

If you're using the `<!--#exec cgi-->` tag, be sure that the CGI program works if you run the program without SSI.

You can tell if the server is actually executing your SSI by using the "view source" option in your browser with the page loaded. If you see the SSI tags in the page source, then the server isn't recognizing them and parsing them.

Q The Telnet example doesn't work.

A If Telnet fails to connect, make sure you're using Telnet against the Web server's name and that you're using the correct port, probably 80. You might need to look at the Telnet client's documentation to set the port number properly.

Another common problem is that you can't see yourself type. Some Telnet clients echo the characters to you, and some do not. Don't worry about this; just type carefully. The characters are still being transmitted carefully. After you type the GET line, make sure that you press the Enter key *twice*.

20

Workshop

Quiz

1. The following URL will work as expected.

   ```
   <a href="/cgi/foo.pl?name=Ben Franklin&Job=printer">
   ```

   a. True.

   b. False; you can't pass two parameters to a CGI program in this way.

   c. False; the space in the name `Ben Franklin` is not allowed.

2. Server-side includes are processed and expanded by what?

   a. The browser

   b. The Web server

   c. The operating system

Answers

1. c. You should use escape to properly hide spaces and other special characters.

2. b. The Web server converts the SSI HTML tags to their final values before sending them to the browser.

Activities

- Use a Telnet client to connect to one of your favorite Web sites, and try fetching a Web page manually.

HOUR 21

Cookies

In Hour 19, "Complex Forms," you learned how to make your Web browser remember information between Web pages by using hidden fields in HTML. You must understand this process because you may need to pass information from one instance of a CGI program to another. The only way to do this is to store a piece of information with the browser.

Another way to store information with the browser is to use *HTTP cookies*. HTTP cookies are pieces of information passed between the browser and the CGI program during the HTTP connection. Using cookies can be a much more flexible method of storing information with a browser than using hidden HTML fields.

This chapter will tell you

- What a cookie is
- How to write and retrieve cookies
- How to handle or avoid common problems with cookies

Later, in Hour 23, "Web Pages with Templates," cookies will be used to establish and keep track of user *sessions*.

What's a Cookie?

You can think of a cookie as a movie theater ticket. You can go to the theater ticket booth and obtain a ticket for a subsequent showing. You can then leave the theater, come back, buy some popcorn, and do anything else you'd like. When you're ready to see the movie, you present your ticket to the ticket-taker. The ticket-taker doesn't know how, when, or why you purchased the ticket, but as long as you have it, the ticket-taker will let you into the theater. The ticket entitles the bearer to admission to a subsequent show.

An HTTP cookie is simply an information packet that the CGI program asks the browser to hold. The packet can be reclaimed at any time by another CGI program or by the same program. Cookies are even passed back to the server when regular HTML pages are requested. The cookie can contain any kind of information: information about multipage Web forms, visitation information, user preferences, and so on.

The cookie is transferred from the server to the browser whenever a CGI program requests that a cookie be created (see Figure 21.1); this process is called *setting a cookie*.

FIGURE 21.1

Cookie going to the browser from a CGI program.

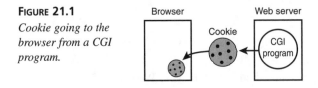

The cookie can be later reclaimed by a CGI program to retrieve the information stored in the cookie, as illustrated in Figure 21.2.

FIGURE 21.2

Cookie being returned to the server by the browser.

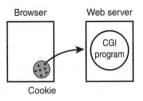

Why Is a Cookie Called a Cookie?

In computing circles, *cookie* is a very old term. It refers to any piece of information passed between routines or programs that enables the holder of the cookie to perform some operation. Some kinds of cookies are called *magic cookies* because they contain data that's obscure and meaningful only to the sender and the receiver of the cookie. CGI cookies are not magic.

How to Make Cookies

To create a cookie, you can use a CGI function called `cookie`. The syntax of the `cookie` function is as follows:

```
$cookie_object=cookie( -name => cookie_name,          # Optional
                       -value => cookie_value,
                       -expires => expiration_date,   # Optional
                       -path  => path_info,           # Optional
                       -domain => domain_info,        # Optional
                       -secure => true/false          # Optional
);
```

The `cookie` function takes arguments in an unusual way. Each argument in the call to `cookie` is named. Actually, passing arguments to a function this way in Perl is convenient because you don't have to remember the order in which the arguments occur; they simply get named in whatever order you decide to use them.

When called with the first syntax, the `cookie` function returns a cookie, which should be stored in a scalar variable and can then be given to the CGI module's `header` function to be sent to the browser. The only required argument to create a cookie is the `-value` argument. The `-name` argument allows several cookies to be sent to the browser at one time, to be retrieved individually or as a group. The other arguments—`-expires`, `-path`, `-domain`, and `-secure`— are discussed in the next section.

The `header` function in the CGI module takes care of actually transmitting the cookie to the browser. This means you must create the cookie, by using the `cookie` function, and then call the `header` function soon afterward. You shouldn't send any other kind of data to the browser until after the cookie and the header have been sent.

To create a cookie and send it to a browser in a CGI program, you can use a CGI program similar to this:

```
#!/usr/bin/perl -w
use CGI qw(:all);
use strict;

my $cookie=cookie(-name => 'Sample',
   -value => 'This cookie contains no MSG');

# Transmit the cookie to the browser
print header(-cookie => $cookie);
```

After the preceding snippet has run, a cookie called `Sample` is set on the browser. The cookie contains the information `'This cookie contains no MSG'`.

21

> Actually, the cookie may not be set. Browsers can refuse to accept a cookie for many reasons. See "Problems with Cookies" later this hour.

To retrieve cookies from the browser in your CGI program, you use the same function—cookie. When called without any arguments, as shown in the following examples, cookie returns a list of cookies that the browser has for your server:

```
@cookie_list=cookie();    # Returns names of all cookies set
```

or

```
# Returns the value for a particular cookie
$cookie_value=cookie($cookie_name);
```

By default, after the cookie is set on the browser, it is returned to any CGI program that resides on the same server. That is, only the server that set the cookies can fetch those cookies. To view the Sample cookie created previously, you can use another CGI program:

```
#!/usr/bin/perl -wT
use CGI qw(:all);
use strict;

print header();  # Print out the standard header

print "<p>Sample's value: ", cookie('Sample'), "</p>";
```

The preceding snippet uses cookie with one argument—the name of the cookie whose value you want to see. That value is retrieved and printed.

The cookie should be retained by the browser until the browser is terminated. When the browser is restarted, the cookie Sample will be gone. If you want to make a more permanent cookie, see "Remembering Cookies" later in this hour.

> Most browsers have an option to view the cookies as they're being set. In Netscape, you can find the cookie viewing options under the Preferences selection on the Advanced tab. In Internet Explorer, the selection appears on the Advanced tab of the Internet Options dialog, and a radio button controls whether you can view cookies as they're set.

Example: Using Cookies

For this example, you'll create a small program to allow the user using the Web browser to set the color of the Web page he or she is viewing. The program actually does several things at once:

1. Checks for a change in the default background color by checking for program parameters
2. Sets a cookie on the browser with the correct background color
3. Sets the background color of the page to the correct color
4. Displays a CGI form, allowing you to change the color

Listing 21.1 contains the color-changing program.

LISTING 21.1 Complete Listing for `ColorChanger`

```
 1:  #!/usr/bin/perl -w
 2:  use strict;
 3:  use CGI qw(:all);
 4:  use CGI::Carp qw(fatalsToBrowser);
 5:  my($requested_color, $old_color, $color_cookie)=("","");
 6:  $old_color="blue";  # Default value
 7:  # Is there a new color requested?
 8:  if (defined param('color')) {
 9:   $requested_color=param('color');
10:  }
11:  # What was the old color, if any?
12:  if (defined cookie('bgcolor')) {
13:        $old_color=cookie('bgcolor');
14:  }
15:  if ($requested_color and ($old_color ne $requested_color)) {
16:        # Set the cookie in the browser
17:        $color_cookie=cookie(-name => 'bgcolor',
18:                             -value => $requested_color);
19:        print header(-cookie => $color_cookie);
20:  } else {
21:        # Nothing's changed, no need to set the cookie
22:        $requested_color=$old_color;
23:        print header;
24:  }
25:  print<<END_OF_HTML;
26:  <html>
27:  <head>
28:  <title>Set your background color</title>
29:  </head>
```

continues

21

Listing 21.1 Continued

```
30:  <body bgcolor="$requested_color">
31:  <form>
32:  <select name="color">
33:                 <option value='red'/>Red
34:                 <option value='blue'/>Blue
35:                 <option value='yellow'/>Yellow
36:                 <option value='white'/>White
37:  </select>
38:  <input type="submit" value="Set the color"/>
39:  </form>
40:  </body>
41:  </html>
42:  END_OF_HTML
```

Lines 7–10: If this program is called as the target of a CGI program, the param('color') function returns a defined value—a new color. Otherwise, it returns nothing, and $requested_color remains unset.

Lines 12–14: These lines check for a cookie named bgcolor; that cookie may or may not exist. If it does exist, it is stored in $old_color, which is the last screen color value that was saved to a cookie.

Lines 15–19: If the color has changed (the cookie value doesn't match the new value), then a new cookie needs to be set with the new value.

Lines 20–24: Otherwise, a plain header is printed without a cookie. Remember: The browser will retain the previous cookie indefinitely.

Lines 25–42: These lines create a standard HTML form. Note line 30, however; on this line, the color gets substituted into the HTML output.

Another Example: The Cookie Viewer

A surprisingly short program, the cookie viewer in Listing 21.2, is an aid that helps you debug your CGI programs that use cookies. It lists any cookies stored on your Web browser that happen to come from the same Web server.

Listing 21.2 Cookie Viewer

```
1:  #!/usr/bin/perl -w
2:
3:  use strict;
4:  use CGI qw(:all);
```

continues

LISTING 21.2   Continued

```
 5:
 6:    print header();
 7:
 8:    print "Cookies set that can be seen:<P>";
 9:
10:    foreach my $cookie (cookie()) {
11:            print "<p>Cookie name: $cookie <br/>";
12:            print qq{Cookie value: "}, cookie($cookie), qq{"</p><hr/>};
13:    }
```

Line 10: The names of all of the cookies are retrieved using `cookie`, and are assigned to `$cookie`, one at a time.

Lines 11–12: The name and value of each cookie is printed.

The viewer works by getting a list of all the cookies available with `cookie()` and then iterating over each of those names, printing the name and value for each cookie.

Advanced Cookie Stuff

The basics of cookies are straightforward: you give a cookie to the browser, and the browser gives it back later. There's more to cookies than that, though. You can set cookies to last for a long time. These cookies are called *persistent cookies*. They can be told to return only to a particular URL, and they can indicate something about the security your connection.

Remembering Cookies

So far, the cookies you've set on the browser have been temporary: as soon as the browser is closed, the cookie disappears. When you're using cookies to save values among multiple pages on a form—instead of hidden HTML values—using temporary cookies is entirely appropriate. When a new browser is started, you don't want the cookie returned to the server because the user wouldn't be filling out the form starting in the middle; he or she would be starting at the beginning.

In some cases, you might like the cookie to hang around much longer. Perhaps you want the cookie to persist for days, weeks, or months after the browser is closed and restarted. Creating these cookies is easy with Perl's CGI module.

To set an expiration date for a cookie, you can use the `-expires` option when you create the cookie. The `-expires` option must be followed by a date that you want the cookie to expire. You can specify this date in several formats, as shown in Table 21.1.

21

TABLE 21.1 Formats for Cookie Expiration Dates

Format	Sample	Meaning
Number of seconds	+30s	30 seconds from now
Number of minutes	+15m	15 minutes from now
Number of hours	+12h	12 hours from now
Number of months	+6M	6 months from now
Number of years	+1y	1 year from now
	now	Cookie expires immediately
Any negative time	-10m	Cookie expires immediately
A specific time	Saturday, 28-Aug-1999 22:51:05 GMT	

When specifying an expiration time, you must follow the format listed in Table 21.1 exactly. All the other possible values are offsets from the current time, and the fully qualified time will be computed for you and sent to the browser.

This small program sets a cookie on the browser that expires in eight days:

```
#!/usr/bin/perl -w
use CGI qw(:all);
use strict;

my $cookie=cookie(-name => 'Favorite',
    -value => 'soft oatmeal raisin cookies',
    -expires => '+8d' );

# Transmit the cookie to the browser
print header(-cookie => $cookie);
```

Now for the Bad News

Persistent cookies do not last indefinitely. That is, if you send a cookie to the browser and expect that the cookie will be around weeks, months, or years from now, you may be disappointed.

As you'll learn later in "Problems with Cookies," browsers don't have to store cookies. In fact, they don't have to accept your cookies at all—and you're not informed that the cookies aren't kept.

Browsers can flush out their cookies at any time to make room for new cookies received from other sites—or for no reason at all. Some browsers can allow users to edit cookies or to add new ones.

Users can erase the cookies, either accidentally or on purpose. If the users install a new version of a browser or an operating system, the cookies can be wiped out—or misplaced. Simply using a different browser can make the cookies seem to "disappear." The cookies are usually stored in a file when the browser isn't active, and that file can be edited by users, erased, or corrupted.

> If you're curious, most browsers store the cookies in files when they're not active, and usually they're just text files that you can view with an editor. Netscape stores the cookies in a file called `cookies.txt` under the user's home directory (which varies from system to system). Internet Explorer stores cookies under `\Windows\Cookies`.

Storing critical information in an HTTP cookie, therefore, is really not a good idea. Any information that you want to store persistently in a cookie should be easily replaced—user preferences, a replaceable entry key for a restricted Web page, last-visited information, and so on.

Sending Cookies Elsewhere

By default, cookies are sent back only to the server that sent them. Sometimes sending the cookies back there is what you want, but sometimes maybe not. For example, consider the mythical Web site Congo.com, which sells books and has two Web servers—`www.congo.com` and `shopping.congo.com`—as illustrated in Figure 21.3. The main Web site (`www.congo.com`) contains all the company information, links to other sites, and—most importantly—links to the online bookstore.

FIGURE 21.3

Two Web sites, linked together.

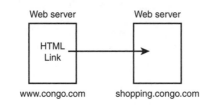

The `www.congo.com` Web server contains a registration HTML form/CGI program so that the user can add his or her name to email lists, and set preferences about the kinds of books he or she is interested in reading. Later, when cruising `www.congo.com`, the user can read about newly published books that may be of interest. The cookie on the user's browser indicates to `www.congo.com` which books he or she should be told about (see Figure 21.4).

21

FIGURE 21.4

Cookie being returned to only one Web site.

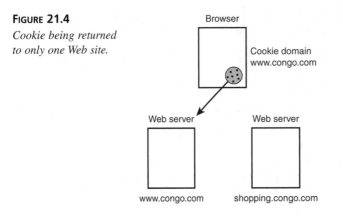

The problem is that when the user goes from www.congo.com to the online bookstore at shopping.congo.com, the cookie is not sent to the shopping.congo.com server. HTTP cookies are returned only to the server that originally sent the cookie. If www.congo.com sent the cookie, it is not returned to shopping.congo.com.

So what do you do? It would be impractical to have the user fill out another preference form and send him or her a new cookie from shopping.congo.com. A better solution is to restrict the cookie to a particular domain name. For example, when the original cookie is sent from www.congo.com, you can allow the cookie to be sent back to any congo.com Web site, as illustrated in Figure 21.5.

FIGURE 21.5

Cookie being returned to both Web sites.

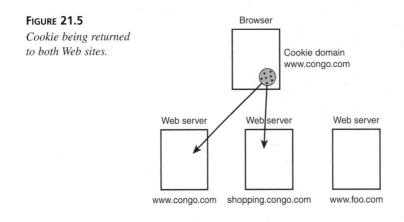

You do so by using the `-domain` argument to `cookie` when creating the cookie:

```
$cookie=cookie( -name => 'preferences',
          -value => 'mysteries, horror',
          -domain => 'congo.com');
print header(-cookie => $cookie);
```

In the preceding snippet, the cookie `$cookie` is created and is restricted to the `congo.com` domain. Any Web server with a hostname ending in `congo.com` will have this cookie returned to it by the browser.

> The domain argument must have at least two parts and cannot be a bare top-level domain—that is, `.com` or `.net`. This way, you can prevent the browser from implanting cookies from one `.com` domain to another `.com` domain.

Keeping Cookies to Yourself

It's also possible to restrict a cookie's allowed return destinations. By default, when you create a cookie, that cookie is returned to any URL on that Web site—including non-CGI URLs. For example, consider an automotive Web site organized like the diagram in Figure 21.6.

FIGURE 21.6

Directory tree of a multi-use Web site.

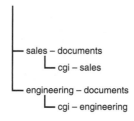

Having the sales CGI programs and the engineering CGI programs reside in different directories might make sense. If a sales CGI program were to set a cookie, the engineering CGI programs would pick it up, and vice versa. This result might not be desirable, and the people writing CGI programs for both sites need to coordinate to make sure they didn't reuse each other's cookie names.

To get around this problem, you can use the `cookie` function's `-path` option. It indicates the pathname—relativeto the top of the URL— to which the cookie should be returned. For example, to send a cookie that will be returned only to the sales CGI programs, you could use this snippet:

21

```
# Cookie only visible to sales CGI programs
$cookie=cookie( -name => 'profile',
          -value => 'sedan,luxury,2-door',
          -path => '/cgi-sales');
print header(-cookie => $cookie);
```

By default, cookies are returned to every site on the server as though you had used the option -path=>'/'. To restrict the cookie to return to only one CGI program, you can use the CGI program's URL in the -path option:

```
# Return the cookie only to this program
$cookie=cookie( -name => 'profile',
          -value => 'sedan,luxury,2-door',
          -path => script_name() );
print header(-cookie => $cookie);
```

Remember from last hour, "Manipulating HTTP and CGI," that the script_name function in the CGI module returns the partial URL of the current CGI program. This effectively creates a cookie that will be returned only to the program that set the cookie on the browser.

Cookies with Security

Some cookies you may want transmitted only over a secure connection. By using the -secure argument to cookie, you can have cookies sent from the browser only if the connection is secure. The following code sends a cookie containing an account number to the browser. A cookie containing sensitive information like this should be sent *only* over a secure connection.

```
# Caution!  Send this only over an https connection
$cookie=cookie( -name => 'account',
          -value => '00-12-3-122-1313',
          -secure => 1);
print header(-cookie => $cookie);
```

Later, to retrieve the cookie, you can simply use the cookie function as you normally would. If the connection is secure, and the cookie is on the browser, the browser sends the cookie back to the server when needed:

```
# Fetch the account number from the browser.
$account_number=cookie('account');
```

You shouldn't rely on this trick to detect whether the connection is secure. Nor should you assume that the account number is accurate. Remember, the user controls the Web browser and its cookie files. The cookie can be sent back over an insecure connection, and the account number could be invalid.

Problems with Cookies

Before using cookies in an application, you should be aware of the problems associated with cookies. For these reasons—and others that may crop up in the future—you should be careful to design your Web pages and CGI programs so that cookies are entirely *optional*.

For example, if you're using cookies to store user preferences, you should use a default set of preferences if cookies are not available. You must code defensively.

Cookies Are Ephemeral

As I've mentioned throughout this hour, cookies are ephemeral. Cookies can be deleted from the user's system, edited by the user, or simply thrown away by the browser for no apparent reason. A browser can accept the cookie, use it for a a short time, and then simply forget it for no apparent reason. If you've set up persistent cookies using -expire, the browser can still throw away the cookie without telling the user.

Cookies Aren't Always Supported

Not all browsers support HTTP cookies. The Internet standards that apply to HTTP and Web traffic don't guarantee that browsers must support cookies.

I'm not suggesting that *most* browsers don't support cookies, because they do. Netscape (since version 1.1), Internet Explorer (all versions), Lynx, Opera, and most popular Web browsers do support cookies. In most of them, though, the user has the option to turn off cookie support.

Even if you've used the CGI module's user_agent function and determined that the intended browser should support cookies, don't count on it.

Some People Don't Like Cookies

The title of this section might be hard to fathom: Why on earth would someone not like cookies?

Surfing the Web is essentially an anonymous activity. As you've seen in previous lessons, when a Web page is requested by a browser, the request happens in a vacuum. The server doesn't necessarily know where the browser's been or the last time a page on this site was requested by this particular browser.

21

Remember: One browser does not necessarily represent one user. A browser can be shared by many people in a household, kiosk, Internet café, or public access site, such as a library. Setting (or changing) a cookie for one person might actually set it for several people.

Cookies can be used to track where people have been on a particular site and what items they've clicked. If you're concerned about privacy, this might be alarming. For example, the hypothetical bookstore previously mentioned in "Sending Cookies Elsewhere"—Congo.com—might track which books the Web surfer clicked on for more information. That information can be used to tailor-make lists of books to present to the surfer.

On the surface, this feature seems convenient. For people concerned about privacy, it presents two problems. First, now an entity keeps track of the kinds of books in which the Web surfer is interested. If that information is ever correlated with the Web surfer's name and address—possibly obtained from a fill-out form from another site that is sharing information with Congo.com—the surfer might start receiving junk mail related to his or her book selections. The more information that's shared by cookie-gathering sites, the more detailed a "profile" that can be assembled about the Web surfer.

Beyond the privacy issue, if the first two books examined were categorized as "Computer" books, the Web site might stop offering books to the Web surfer in the "Romance" and "Cooking" categories. The Web site "channels" the surfer into categories that might be difficult to escape.

You might be surprised at how often cookies are used to collect and store information on your browser. Just turn on cookie confirmation in your browser, and visit any popular Web site.

People have been known to go to great lengths to avoid cookies. Web browsers that support cookies all offer features to turn off cookies, and some allow you to examine cookies as they're set on the browser. Add-on software packages are available to filter cookies that are sent to and from your browser, and allow you to edit them. Web sites are designed to allow you to surf other Web sites anonymously without having cookies gathering information about you.

In short, some people consider HTTP cookies as an invasion of privacy, so you should be careful how you you use them.

Summary

In this hour, you learned how HTTP cookies can be used to store information on the browser for later use by another CGI program. The options for having cookies expire at a predetermined time, being active for a particular Web server, or for particular directories were discussed. Finally, you reviewed the reasons for not using cookies, and the problems associated with using cookies.

Q&A

Q How do I put more than one piece of information in an HTTP cookie?

A The easiest way is to combine multiple items in a single cookie separated by a field separator, as in this example:

```
$cookie=cookie(-name => 'preferences',
    -value => 'bgcolor=blue,fgcolor=red,banners=no,java=no');
```

Later, when you retrieve the cookie, you can use `split` to separate the items:

```
      $cookie=cookie('preferences');
      @options=split(/,/,  $cookie);
# Now, make a hash with the option as the key,
# and the option's value as the hash value
foreach $option (@options) {
    ($key,$value)=split(/=/, $option)
    $Options{$key}=$value;
}
```

Q How do I use cookies to track which links a user clicks on a Web page?

A Before I give you the answer, you must realize that some people consider tracking an invasion of privacy. Having said that, let me show you the general method:

1. Write your `<a href>` links so that they go to a CGI program, passing the *real* target URL as a parameter:

   ```
   <a
   href="http://server/cgi/redirect.pl?target=http://www.congo.com">Congo</a>
   ```

2. The redirect.pl program in the example should use the CGI module's `param` function to get the real URL (`http://www.congo.com`) from the parameter `target`:

   ```
   $target_url=param('target');
   ```

3. A cookie is then created with the target URL in the value, with a name you can search for later, such as:

   ```
   $tracking_cookie=cookie(-name => 'tracker',
           -value => $target_url,
           -expires => '+1w');
   ```

21

4. The redirect is then sent to the browser along with the cookie:

```
print redirect(-uri => $target_url,
      -cookie => $tracking_cookie);
```

Later, when the browser returns to your Web site, you can look for the cookie named `tracker`, which will contain the URL that the user visited when he or she left your site.

There are other methods of tracking users; this is just one.

Q Can I transmit a cookie while redirecting the browser to another page?

A Yes. The CGI module's `redirect` function can also take a `-cookie` argument such as the `header`:

```
my $cookie=cookie(-name => 'target',
          -value => 'redirected to foo.html');
print redirect(-uri => "http://www.server.com/foo.html",
          -cookie => $cookie);
```

One complication: If you're using IIS as a web server, to send a cookie and a redirect at the same time you will need to enable Non-Parsed-Header scripts (usually done by having `nph-` at the beginning of the script name).

Workshop

Quiz

1. Why does using cookies for long-term storage sometimes fail?

   a. Browsers can "throw away" cookie information.

   b. Cookies can be lost during software updates.

   c. Users may turn off cookie support in their browsers.

2. To make a cookie expire one week from now, use the `-expire` option to the `cookie` function with what?

   a. `+7d`

   b. `+1w`

   c. `+10080m`

3. Why do some people consider cookies a privacy problem?

   a. Cookies can be used to track which links a user follows.

   b. Tracked cookie information can be shared to build a dossier on the user.

   c. Cookie information can be used to "channel" certain kinds of information to the user.

Answers

1. All the above.

2. Either choice a or c. The `+1w` argument is invalid.

3. All the above.

Activities

- Extend the background color changer to set foreground colors and fonts. Randomly select an image to display on the page by editing the target of an `<img>` tag.

21

Hour **22**

E-mail from CGI

Undoubtedly, while surfing the Web, you've filled out a form that would later be used to send e-mail. These forms are commonly used for mailing lists, trouble reports, customer support, fan mail, and every other use imaginable.

In this hour, you'll learn how to send mail from Perl, and you'll look at a short sample Web page that you can use to generate e-mail. The creative uses of this page I'll leave to you.

In this hour you'll learn

- A little bit about how Internet mail works
- How to send mail under Unix and non-Unix systems
- How to set up a Web form to send mail

A Primer in Internet Mail

Before you can unleash your programming skills by sending e-mail with Perl, you need to know something about how mail works on the Internet.

Before Perl was born, when the Web wasn't even a twinkle in NCSA's eyes and modems were slow, people worldwide communicated using e-mail over a system called *Unix-to-Unix copy (UUCP)*. When you sent e-mail using this old system, the local system bundled up your e-mail and forwarded it to the next system in a chain, which bundled up the e-mail and forwarded it on. Each system in the line added a little bit to the message, indicating that it handled the message and then passed it on, as illustrated in Figure 22.1.

FIGURE 22.1

Handing off mail from system to system.

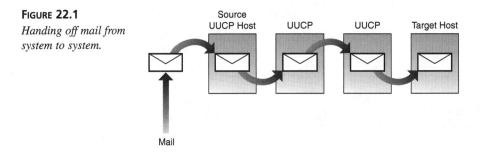

This method of mail propagation is called *store and forward,* for obvious reasons. UUCP has since been replaced, but the basic method of store and forward still persists. When you send mail from your PC, another system picks up the mail and relays it to another system; that system then relays the mail again until the target system finally receives the mail.

The protocols have all changed, though. Most commonly, *Simple Mail Transport Protocol (SMTP)* is used to send mail out onto the chain (see Figure 22.2). To receive it, the target end of the connection usually uses either *Post Office Protocol (POP)* or *Internet Message Access Protocol (IMAP)*. The part you're going to be concerned with when sending mail is SMTP.

FIGURE 22.2

Different protocols used in sending mail.

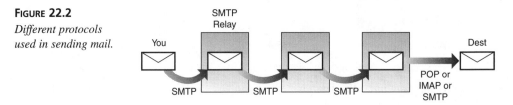

Sending a Mail Message

To send an e-mail message, you need one of two things: a *Mail Transport Agent (MTA)* or an *SMTP relay host*.

Whoa. Sorry. Those were pretty heavy terms to drop, but I'll explain.

A *Mail Transport Agent* is a program that resides on your computer—it usually comes with your operating system—and is in charge of taking e-mail messages and forwarding them correctly. An MTA is usually already configured correctly when your operating system is installed. One common MTA on Unix systems is called sendmail. The `sendmail` program takes a mail message and figures out how to deliver it to the destination. To send a mail message using Unix, at the command line you could use this syntax:

```
$ /bin/echo "Subject:Test\n\nHello, World!" | sendmail foo@bar.com
```

The preceding snippet would send a short message to `foo@bar.com`. The `sendmail` program takes care of all the difficult parts for you: deciding which mail relay to use, handling bounced (refused) mail, and so on.

If you're using a Microsoft Windows or a Macintosh operating system, you don't have a built-in MTA. Fortunately, a Perl module enables you to send mail directly. The `Net::SMTP` module can send mail without an intervening MTA, but you have to know the name of your SMTP relay host. This name is the "Mail Host" hostname for sending mail that you were given when you signed up for your account. Get the name of the relay host, and write it down somewhere; you'll need it later.

> You may have different "Mail Hosts" for sending and receiving mail. For this hour you'll need the "sending" hostname.

Remember, programs that rely on an SMTP relay need to have the correct relay host built into the software, or the process will not work.

> The correct "SMTP relay hostname" depends on where you're sending mail from. If you're sending mail from home, your home Internet service provider (ISP) account will have given you an SMTP relay hostname. If you're sending mail from an account on a rented Web server, you need the name of the relay host for that server. Mail relays usually refuse mail when it's sent from a system they don't recognize.

But First, Some Advice to Save Your Reputation

In the next section, you'll learn about a new function called `send_mail`, which you can use to send mail with a Perl program. This tool is very useful and very dangerous at the same time. Sending e-mail to someone is a small invasion of his or her privacy. You're asking the recipient of the mail to give you some of his or her time and disk space. You're also asking for every system between yours and the recipient's to relay this mail for you. This is a lot to ask from a complete stranger.

The following are some tips on Netiquette for sending mail with Perl—or any other tool:

- Test your code with well-known addresses—such as your own—and small messages first. Disasters happen all the time; avoid creating one.

- Do not send *unsolicited* commercial e-mail. Unsolicited commercial e-mail—commonly known as *spam*—has become a major problem on the Internet. A small number of people like receiving this kind of mail. The rest of the recipients have reactions ranging from annoyance to outrage. A corporate entity sending such mail will find itself the target of many angry people. When you collect an e-mail address, always ask whether it's okay to send mail back to that address at a later time. Always respect people's wishes to be removed from mailing lists.

- Do not send out large volumes of mail, whether requested or not, at one time; pace yourself. First, your local mail relay host can get overwhelmed in a hurry, and your local ISP will terminate your account to control the damage. Second, if a target ISP begins to be overwhelmed by your mail, the provider may simply block all e-mail from your domain. Losing the ability to send any mail at all to large domains—`aol.com`, `hotmail.com`, and so on—can ruin your day, will likely get your account with your ISP terminated, and may result in your being sued.

- Provide good return e-mail addresses, especially in the header. Make sure the From: (or Reply To:) address of your e-mail is correct, especially when it was sent from a machine. It *is* possible to use Perl to forge e-mail, but the forgery does contain a trail back to you. Forging mail can get you into serious trouble.

- Always use your own mail relay host. Abusing other systems' e-mail relays will get your account terminated quickly, and it may get you sued or worse.

- Do not send huge e-mail messages, or lots of smaller messages, to unsuspecting people; this is called *mailbombing*. It will likely get your ISP account terminated, and it may cause legal trouble.

Not all these tips are simply good Netiquette. Breaking some of these rules can get you removed from your Internet service provider and/or sued for damages by your ISP and recipients. When you signed up for your ISP account, you were most likely told that any

22

of the above reasons are grounds for termination, and you may possibly be liable for damages.

Be conservative in what you produce and liberal in what you accept.

> The Internet has a *very* long collective memory. People who have truly abused e-mail are long remembered and loathed. Once a reputation is soiled by spamming, it's very hard to fix.

A Mailing Function

The objective of the following sections is for you to write a short Perl function that you can use in your CGI programs to send mail. There is a problem, though. The way the function works is fairly dependent on whether you have a local MTA (such as sendmail) or whether you have to send the mail yourself to an SMTP relay host. So scan ahead, and decide which of the following sections you're going to need for your particular program.

A Mail Function for Unix Systems

If you have a Unix system, and sendmail is properly configured (it probably will be), you're reading the right section. If you don't have Unix or sendmail, and you're reading this section out of curiosity—good for you. However, the function presented in Listing 22.1 probably won't do you much good.

> Even if you have a Unix system, the next section, "A Mail Function for Non-Unix Systems," might be worth reading. A new technique for using a module—an object-oriented module—is discussed there.

LISTING 22.1   Function `send_mail`

```
1:   # Function for sending mail with an MTA like sendmail
2:   sub send_mail {
3:    my($to, $from, $subject, @body)=@_;
4:
5:    # Change this as necessary for your system
6:    my $sendmail="/usr/lib/sendmail -t -oi -odq";
7:
8:    open(MAIL, "|$sendmail") || die "Can't start sendmail: $!";
9:    print MAIL<<END_OF_HEADER;
10:  From: $from
```

continues

LISTING 22.1   Continued

```
11:   To: $to
12:   Subject: $subject
13:
14:   END_OF_HEADER
15:          foreach (@body) {
16:                         print MAIL "$_\n";
17:          }
18:          close(MAIL);
19:   }
```

Line 6: The location of sendmail and the arguments that it needs are put into a variable here. The sendmail program may be in a different location on your system, or it may take different arguments.

Line 8: The sendmail program specified in $sendmail is started and opened for writing on the filehandle MAIL.

Lines 9–14: The header of the mail message is written to MAIL.

Lines 15–17: The body of the message is written to the MAIL filehandle. Each line has a \n appended to it.

To use this function, simply call it with four arguments like this:

```
@body=("Lower mine, please.", "Thanks!");
send_mail('president@whitehouse.gov', 'owner@geeksalad.org',
   'Taxes', @body);
```

This function relies on sendmail being properly installed and configured on your system. If it's not, see the next section, "A Mail Function for Non-Unix Systems"; the solution presented there should work under Unix as well.

You need to change the variable $sendmail to the correct location of the sendmail program on your system. It's most commonly in /usr/lib, although it can be in /usr/sbin, /lib, or any other directory on your system. You might need to hunt around for it.

> If things don't work as you expect, make *sure* that mail is configured properly on your system. Use a mail utility such as mail or pine to try sending a test mail message. If these utilities don't work properly, it's very unlikely that sendmail is set up properly. You need to fix that problem first, or use the approach listed in the next section.

In Listing 22.1, the sendmail program is started with the following options; you can change them as you see fit.

-t	Takesheader fields (From, To, Subject, and so on) from the input instead of the command line.
-oi	Ignores . (a period) on a single line by itself. Not using this option could prematurely terminate your e-mail message.
-odq	Queues messages instead of trying to send them immediately. You can leave off this option if you like. If too many messages are sent immediately, however, your mail system could be swamped with requests. Using -odq is being polite.

The rest of the function send_mail() should be self-explanatory.

A Mail Function for Non-Unix Systems

Under Windows and other operating systems that do not have a built-in MTA such as sendmail, you can run into complications. MTAs are not simple beasts; trying to duplicate what they do with a few lines of Perl isn't easy, but it can be done.

First, the good news: The Perl module Net::SMTP allows you to send mail from any kind of operating system that Perl runs on. Using this module, you can easily send the mail without much hassle.

Now for the bad news: This module isn't installed with the standard Perl distribution. To get it, you need to load it onto your system where the Web server is located—or wherever you're trying to send mail from. The Net::SMTP module is part of the libnet bundle, which contains all kinds of useful networking modules.

Appendix A, "Installing Modules," has a fairly detailed how-to guide on installing Perl modules. It explains how to install modules under Unix, Windows, and Macintosh operating systems. In addition, you'll find instructions on how to install your own private copies of modules if your system administrator will not install a public copy.

The `send_mail` function for systems without an MTA is shown in Listing 22.2. It contains some rather strange, new syntax that may be unfamiliar. Be sure to read the explanation afterward.

LISTING 22.2   Function `send_mail` for Non-MTA Systems

```
 1: # Function for sending mail for systems without an MTA
 2: sub send_mail {
 3:     my($to, $from, $subject, @body)=@_;
 4:
 5:     use Net::SMTP;
 6:
 7:     # You will need to change the following line
 8:     # to your mail relay host
 9:     my $relay="relayhost.yourisp.com";
10:     my $smtp = Net::SMTP->new($relay);
11:     die "Could not open connection: $!" if (! defined $smtp);
12:
13:     $smtp->mail($from);
14:     $smtp->to($to);
15:
16:     $smtp->data();
17:     $smtp->datasend("To: $to\n");
18:     $smtp->datasend("From: $from\n");
19:     $smtp->datasend("Subject: $subject\n");
20:     $smtp->datasend("\n");
21:     foreach(@body) {
22:             $smtp->datasend("$_\n");
23:     }
24:     $smtp->dataend(); # Note the spelling: no "s"
25:     $smtp->quit;
26: }
```

Line 5: The `Net::SMTP` module is brought in to make sending mail a little easier.

Line 10: A `Net::SMTP` object is created, connected to the correct relay host, which you set on line 9.

Lines 13–23: The headers and body for the e-mail are sent to the relay host. See the explanation of the `Net::SMTP` functions that follow for more details.

To use this function, simply call it with four arguments representing the pieces of the e-mail message:

```
@body=("Lower mine, please.", "Thanks!");
send_mail('president@whitehouse.gov', 'owner@geeksalad.org',
   'Taxes', @body);
```

The first thing that should strike you as odd about this function is the line `$smtp = Net::SMTP->new($relay);`. This line creates something called an *object*. An object isn't really a scalar, a hash, or an array; it's something a little different. The value in `$smtp` now represents a connection to a mail program, which you can manipulate. Think of it as a special kind of value that allows you to call functions that are related to it.

The next thing that should strike you as odd is the line `$smtp->mail($from);`. The `->` connects an object to a function called against it. So `mail` is a function call using the `$smtp` object that was created on the previous line.

You don't really need to understand everything about object syntax to use the `Net::SMTP` module—just enough to get by. The functions that you can use against a `Net::SMTP` object are as follows:

- `$smtp->mail(addr)`—The `mail` function indicates the name you're using to send mail. Yes, you can lie about who you are sometimes.

- `$smtp->to(addr)`—The `to` function indicates to whom you're sending mail. If you call `to` with a list of names, each person receives a copy of the mail. The names of these people don't necessarily appear in the body of the message, unless you explicitly put them there yourself—for example, to send BCC (Blind Carbon Copy).

- `$smtp->data();`—The `data` function indicates that you're ready to send the message itself.

- `$smtp->datasend(data)`—This function sends the actual text of the message. You must print your own header fields (To:, From:, and so on). Header fields such as Date: and Received: are generated automatically. Between the header and the body, you must also print a blank line—`$smtp->datasend("\n")`. The body of your message follows the blank line and is also sent with `$smtp->datasend()`.

- `$smtp->dataend()`—The `dataend` function indicates that you're done with the message body; the message isn't sent until this happens.

- `$smtp->quit()`—This function disconnects from the SMTP server.

Sending Mail from a Web Page

Now that you have a mail function—`send_mail()`—the rest of sending mail from a Web page is a snap! You just have to design a page and write the CGI to go along with it. A sample e-mail HTML form is shown in Listing 22.3. The form isn't very pretty, but feel free to use your own style to spice it up.

LISTING 22.3   HTML Form for Sending E-mail

```
1.  <!--assumes a program called /cgi-bin/mailer.cgi exists-->
2.  <form method="post" action="/cgi-bin/mailer.cgi">
3.  Your address: <input type="text" name="return_addr"/><br/>
4.  Subject: <input type="text" name="subject"/><br/>
5.  <br/>
6.  Message:<br/>
7.  <textarea name="body" rows="20" cols="60" wrap="hard">
8.  Type your message here
9.  </textarea>
10. <br/>
11. <input type="submit" VALUE="Send Message"/>
12. </form>
```

The CGI program for sending the mail isn't much larger. It's shown next.

```
#!/usr/bin/perl -w
use strict;
use CGI qw(:all);
use CGI::Carp qw(fatalsToBrowser);

#
# Insert the send_mail function
# from listing 22.1 or 22.2 here!
#

print header;
my $return=param("return_addr");
if (! defined $return or ! $return) {
        print "You must supply an e-mail address<P>";
        exit;
}
my $subject=param("subject");
if (! define $subject or ! $subject) {
        print "You must supply a subject<P>";
        exit;
}

# Change this address to wherever you want your
# mail sent
send_mail('webmaster@myhost.com',
 $return,
 $subject,
            param("body"));

print "Mail sent.";
```

You should note a few points about this small program in the previous code. First, you must insert the `send_mail` function from either Listing 22.1 or Listing 22.2 for this program to work. Use whichever listing works best and is appropriate for you.

Second, notice that the To: address is hard-wired into the program—as `webmaster@myhost.com`. You need to change this address as well to the address to which you want the mail sent. The reason that the address is not taken from the users is simple: You don't want users sending mail to arbitrary addresses using a Web form. If people abuse your form and send, say, hate mail to someone, then you and your system will be targeted as the originator of the message. This is not a good idea.

If you need to be able to send to multiple targets with one form, use a drop-down list (or radio buttons) to provide a choice of addresses:

```
<INPUT TYPE=radio NAME=target Value=1 CHECKED>Support Department
<INPUT TYPE=radio NAME=target Value=2>Sales Department
<INPUT TYPE=radio NAME=target Value=3>Legal Department
```

Then, in your program, use a piece of code like this:

```
$formtarget=param('target');
%targets=( 1=> 'support@myhost.com',
           2=> 'sales@myhost.com',
           3=> 'legal@myhost.com');
if (exists($targets{$formtarget})) {
        $target=$targets{$formtarget};
} else {
        $target='webmaster@myhost.com';
}
print $target;
```

Whatever you do, do not allow the actual To: e-mail addresses to be passed in from the form and used in your program. Pass a harmless value (`1` to `3` in the example) and interpret that value in your CGI program, allowing for incorrect values to be passed—the `else` clause in the example—even if it seems impossible.

Verifying E-mail Addresses

You may have noticed that the CGI program didn't try to determine whether the e-mail address entered by the user was valid. There's a good reason for that. It's not possible.

That answer might surprise you, since one of the Holy Grails of designing an e-mail system on the Internet is to know whether the destination address is valid.

The difficulty is apparent from Figures 22.1 and 22.2 at the beginning of this hour. From the originating system's perspective, it can't see the end of the delivery chain. It has to hand off the message fully to the second system in the chain, which passes it along to the third, and so on. The delay between these "handoffs" is significant. What's even more important is that the originating system has no control over the message after it's past the first handoff.

The standard approach is to try to weed out obviously false addresses—except there's no way to tell that an address isn't valid. The Internet standard for e-mail addressing—RFC 822—has a template for standard e-mail addresses. However, some perfectly valid RFC-822–compliant addresses are not valid, and some addresses that break the RFC-822 standards are valid, deliverable addresses.

Writing regular expressions to match e-mail addresses doesn't work. For example, the expression `/^[\w.-]+\@([\w.-]\.)+\w+$/` looks reasonable. It even matches addresses like `me@somewhere.com`. However, it rejects the following perfectly valid e-mail addresses:

```
*@qz.az
clintp!sol2!westwood@dec.net
relay%me@host.com
"barney&fred"@flintstones.net
```

One regular expression to match RFC-822–compliant e-mail addresses is 4,700 characters long—a bit too long to put in this book and expect you to type. Also, it doesn't match every deliverable address on the Internet.

So what are you to do?

The only way to determine whether an e-mail address is valid is to send a message to that address and wait for a reply. If, for some reason, you need to be guaranteed that a live human being is on the other end of the address—for example, to send future messages, assuming he or she asked for them—send an e-mail message asking him or her to reply. When the reply comes back, you'll know you have a valid e-mail address.

Summary

In this hour, you learned how to send mail from a Web page. Along the way, you examined a couple of versions of a function called `send_mail()` that can be used in any Perl program to send e-mail. The basics of Internet e-mail were demonstrated, and basic e-mail Netiquette was presented.

Q&A

22

Q **Is it possible to use information gathered from the browser to get the surfer's e-mail address?**

A Although being able to do so would be nice—it would eliminate errors in fetching the e-mail address—it's just not possible. The browser doesn't contain the user's e-mail address. The return value from the `remote_host` function in the CGI module may not actually be the address where the user receives e-mail. The `remote_user` function—if you're using secure Web transactions—is probably not the user's e-mail address "name" portion. And remember, it's possible for a browser to lie about some of this information, and some plug-ins for Netscape and Internet Explorer do just that.

Also, consider that the user may be using a Web browser at a library, at a friend's house, at work, or at a kiosk, and the browser's address isn't even remotely related to the user's e-mail address.

Q **Can I validate an e-mail address? Please?**

A You can try. For example, most modern addresses contain an @ (at symbol), and you could use it for a test. However, addresses on the local machine (for example, `postmaster`, `root`) don't need an @.

Q **Hey! I tried the e-mail CGI program, and I got a "From nobody. . ." line in the message.**

A Ah, yes. The sendmail program records the user ID of the person sending the mail. The actual "person" sending the mail is the *Web server* itself. The Web server often runs as a special user ID—nobody, Web, httpd, or (heaven forbid) root—and that address gets recorded in the mail header. No need to fear. As long as you print a proper From: line as part of the mail header, when a user responds to that message, that's the line that will be seen.

Q **How to I attach a file to an e-mail message?**

A You'll want to look at the MIME modules in CPAN.

Workshop

Quiz

1. What does `$foo=Net::SMTP->new('mailhost')` do?

   (If you didn't read the section "A Mail Function for Non-Unix Systems," you might want to do so now.)

a. It causes a syntax error.

b. It creates an object called `$foo`, which represents a connection to an SMTP mail server.

c. It includes the `Net::SMTP` module in the current program.

2. Which of the following is not a (potentially) valid e-mail address?

a. `foo!bar!baz!quux`

b. `" "@bar.com`

c. `stuff%junk!"Wowzers"!foo.com!blat`

Answers

1. b. If you answered a, then either you've mistyped, or you're running Perl version 4. Choice c is incorrect because it actually describes the statement `use Net::SMTP`.

2. Trick question. They're all potentially valid e-mail addresses.

Activities

- Make these simple changes to the simple CGI mail program:

  - Collect the user's browser information, and attach it to the message body.

  - Send the user a courtesy copy of the message (be sure to tell him or her that you're doing so if you do this on a real Web site). Be careful too, because this can be abused.

- Allow the user to "preview" the message before sending it. You need to use one of the techniques from Hour 19, "Complex Forms," to make the data from the first page (the e-mail entry screen) available to the second page (the e-mail verification screen), and finally to the mail-sending CGI program.

HOUR 23

Web Pages with Templates

Templating Systems

A templating system is a general-purpose term for a document that's served on the Web, where parts of the document are replaced by the Web server. In an earlier hour, you learned about server-side includes (SSI); these could be used to merge other files into an HTML page or to do a small amount of processing within the page.

CGI programs are just one way of creating dynamic content, where the Web server runs a program on its behalf to construct the entire page. Templating systems use a static page with embedded code to change the dynamic parts as in Figure 23.1

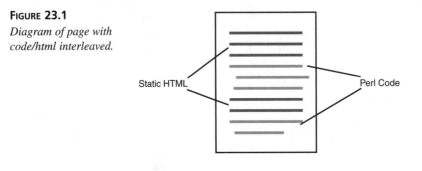

FIGURE 23.1
Diagram of page with code/html interleaved.

Static HTML

Perl Code

This technique is quite common. One popular Web development environment is Microsoft's ASP (Active Server Pages). ASP's consist of HTML pages with Visual Basic code embedded in them. Another programming language for the Web is PHP, which also uses a static document with embedded code to serve up a dynamic page.

Introduction to HTML::Mason

HTML::Mason is a module available from CPAN that allows you to construct Web pages as HTML pages with embedded Perl statements; a copy of the module is on the CD-ROM included with this book. There are other modules for Perl that accomplish the same thing (such as Text::Template), but HTML::Mason was chosen because it is common and widely used. The official Web site for HTML::Mason is http://www.masonhq.com.

Traditionally, HTML::Mason is installed as a mod_perl extension to the Apache Web server. Pages are given a special extension (such as `.mas`) and the Web server knows to treat these pages as an HTML::Mason component instead of a static HTML page or a CGI program. Instructions for doing this are at the HTML::Mason Web site.

It is also possible to run an HTML::Mason component from a CGI program; that is how the following examples will be run. This is slower than using an Apache handler directly, but this method will require less effort to install on a Web server. You can use HTML::Mason programs on a Web server to which you do not have administrator rights, and you can use it on non-Apache Web servers.

If you do have a Web server running Apache, have administrator privileges, and are comfortable with reconfiguring it, you may want to run HTML::Mason as it's distributed. See the documentation at HTML::Mason's Web site for detailed installation instructions.

The CGI HTML::Mason Handler

To install the HTML::Mason module, follow the instructions in Appendix A. After the module is installed, you'll need to create three directories. One directory will hold your HTML::Mason components. HTML::Mason uses a second directory to store temporary data, and a third directory will hold session and application data for your applications.

The components will actually contain the HTML and the Perl code to make the pages dynamic. Create the directories on the Web server, and note the full pathname (such as /home/clintp/htdocs/components) to the directories; you'll need this information to configure the CGI component loader.

Next, you'll need to install this CGI program (Listing 23.1) to handle the loading and dispatching of HTML::Mason components. Normally the Apache Web server would automatically run the components when the URL was specified, but because of previously mentioned reasons, we're not doing that here. Install this CGI program as you have the CGI programs thus far in this book.

I realize that this is the most complicated program listing in the entire book, so I'll separately summarize the overall purpose of the code, before the detailed analysis:

- A lock and unlock function is made available to the Mason components.
- Two hashes are used to store data for the components. The %session hash will store user-data for the duration of the browser's lifetime, and preferences will be stored here. The hash %application is shared by everyone for the life of the application; you should use locks around access to this hash. Locks were discussed in Hour 15, "Finding Permanence."
- The user is assigned a unique ID code in a cookie.
- The Mason component stored in the CGI parameter "comp" is loaded.

Listing 23.1 HTML::Mason Component dispatcher.

```
 1:   #!/usr/bin/perl -w
 2:
 3:   use strict;
 4:   use CGI qw(param cookie header);
 5:   use HTML::Mason;
 6:   package HTML::Mason::Commands;
 7:   use vars qw(%session %application);
 8:   use Fcntl qw(:flock);
 9:   sub get_lock {
10:       open(SEM, ">/tmp/mason.lock") ||
11:           die "Can't create lock: $!";
12:       flock(SEM, LOCK_EX) || die "Can't lock: $!";
13:   }
14:   sub release_lock {
15:       close(SEM);
16:   }
17:   package main;
18:
19:   my(%args,$id,$comp);
```

continues

Listing 23.1   Continued

```
20:    # Transform HTML form arguments into %args
21:    foreach my $key (param()) {
22:        my @values=param($key);
23:        $args{$key}=( @values == 1 ? $values[0] : \@values );
24:    }
25:
26:    # Generate a session ID for the user
27:    $id=cookie('ID');
28:    if (not defined $id) {
29:        $id=time . "$$" . rand(1000000);
30:    }
31:    print header(-cookie => cookie( -name => 'ID', -value => $id));
32:    my $session="/tmp/mason/sessions";
33:    # Launch the HTML::Mason component
34:    dbmopen(%HTML::Mason::Commands::session, "$session/dat$id", 0666) || die "$!";
35:    dbmopen(%HTML::Mason::Commands::application, "$session/app", 0666) || die "$!";
36:    my $interp = HTML::Mason::Interp->new(parser=>HTML::Mason::Parser->new(),
37:        comp_root=>'/tmp/mason/component',
38:        data_dir=>'/tmp/mason/data');
39:    if ($comp=param("comp")) {
40:        eval { $interp->exec("/$comp",%args) };
41:        print "HTML::Mason Error: $@" if $@;
42:    } else {
43:        print "No component specified.";
44:
45:    }
46:    dbmclose(%HTML::Mason::Commands::session);
47:    dbmclose(%HTML::Mason::Commands::application);
48:    while(<$session/dat*>) {           # Clean out sessions,
49:        unlink $_ if -M > .5           # older than a half-day.
50:    }
```

Make note of lines 32, 37, and 38. The variable $session must be a writeable directory where the HTML::Mason applications can store data. Later on the comp_root argument to HTML::Mason::Interp must be set to where your component files will be stored. The argument data_dir must be set to a writeable directory where HTML::Mason can create scratch files.

Remember, there's a lot of advanced magic in this script; you're not expected to understand all of it.

Lines 4–5: The HTML::Mason and CGI modules are brought into the program. We need only three functions from the CGI module, so those are named explicitly.

Line 6: This declares a namespace, where we can create variables. Normally variables exist in the namespace main::, but HTML::Mason expects its own namespace. So we temporarily switch into its namespace to do some work. You saw namespaces at work in Hour 14 with the File::Find example.

Line 7: We've got `use strict` in effect, so to have a "global" variable visible from our component we must use this directive. It effectively tells `use strict` that these variables are allowed to be used globally.

Lines 8–16: Set up locking functions for our components. These are just like the functions from Hour 15.

Line 17: We pop back into the main package.

Lines 21–24: The HTML::Mason module expects CGI arguments to be passed in by way of an array that contains references to name-value pairs or lists of name-value pairs.

Lines 27–30: The session ID is generated for the user. When the user returns, that user will have a session ID and we'll reuse that. Otherwise, we create a fairly random one and hand that over. Sessions are described later this hour.

Line 31: We print a header and send the session ID back in a cookie.

Lines 34–35: We connect the `%session` and `%application` hashes (in the HTML::Mason::Commands namespace) to DBM files in the session directory. These hashes are also explained later this hour.

Lines 36–38: An object that describes an HTML::Mason interpreter is created. (A brief explanation of objects is in Hour 22, "E-mail from CGI.")

Lines 39–45: If the CGI argument "comp" wasn't passed in, an error message is printed. Otherwise, we run the component specified in the argument using the interpreter created in line 36.

Lines 48–50: Any sessions idle for more than half a day are removed. This is necessary; otherwise the old sessions would build up and fill the disk. To use the component dispatcher, pass in the name of the component as an argument named "comp" in the URL like this:

```
http://www.myserver.com/cgi/compdisp.pl?comp=sample.mas
```

This would load the component "sample.mas" from the directory `comp_root` specified in Listing 23.1. If you load this URL without passing a "comp" parameter, it will display the message

```
No component specified
```

If you get this message (because you don't have a sample.mas yet), you know that the handler is installed correctly. The next section has sample components for you to try.

Basics of HTML::Mason Tags

HTML::Mason component files are treated as a normal HTML file, except for certain elements that HTML::Mason recognizes as special. These elements are processed, and the output of the elements is sent to the browser instead of the actual contents of the element. Normal HTML elements and HTML::Mason elements can be present in a component file.

For example, the <%perl> element contains Perl code to be run. The code can contain variable declarations, loops, subroutines, or any other legal Perl code. If the following is seen in an HTML::Mason component,

```
<h1>The time is now</h1>
<%perl>
my $time=scalar localtime;
</%perl>
```

the variable $time would be set to a string describing the current time for the duration of this component.

> Perl code run in HTML::Mason is called as though the use strict pragma is in effect. This means that variables must be declared with the my operator, as described in Hour 8, "Functions."

Once the variable is set, use the element <%> to include the variable (or any other value) in the body of an HTML document:

```
<h1>The time is now</h1>
<%perl>
my $time=scalar localtime;
</%perl>
The time is: <% $time %>
```

Save this snippet as sample.mas in your components directory, and try running it. If you've installed the CGI HTML::Mason handler correctly, then using the URL

```
http://yourserver/cgi/mason.pl?comp=sample.mas
```

should run this program to print the current time.

> If your component will not run, make sure that running the handler as
>
> `http://yourserver/cgi/mason.pl`
>
> correctly prints the "No component specified" message. If not, the handler isn't installed correctly. If it does print, but you cannot get your component to run, then double-check the directory names in the handler and make sure that your component is typed correctly.

23

Another way of running Perl code in a component is to have a line that simply begins with %. Everything up to the end of the line following % is treated as Perl code to be run.

```
% my $dir;
<h1>Where are we?</h1>
<%perl>
use Cwd;
$dir=cwd;
</%perl>
We seem to be in <% $dir %>.
```

Components can be called from other components. This powerful feature lets you compartmentalize your Web site's design into small segments that can be assembled together to form a coherent page. To include another component in the current component, use the `<&` and `&>` tags:

```
<& header.mas &>
<& navigation.mas &>
Hi, this is the body of my page!
% my $time=scalar localtime;
The time is now: <% $time %>
<& footer.mas &>
```

In this snippet, this component calls three other components to assemble the page header, navigation, and footer. Each component can have its own variables and can call other components in turn. To pass arguments to a component, call the component as you normally would, but include a keyword => value list of arguments after the component name:

```
<& header.mas, title => 'Main Screen' &>
```

The argument will be received by the component through the `<%args>` tag, explained in the next section.

HTML Forms in HTML::Mason

Forms that are submitted to CGI programs use the `param()` function to retrieve the form values. The HTML::Mason module uses a special syntax to retrieve those values. The `<%arg>` tag is used to process CGI form values. Examine this HTML form:

```
<form method='get' action="/cgi/mason.pl">
<input type="hidden" name="comp" value="process.mas"/>
<input type="text" name="partno"/>
<input type="submit"/>
</form>
```

The interesting thing to note is that the target URL for the form is the CGI HTML::Mason handler. In order for the handler to launch the correct component, we set an HTML form variable named "comp" to the component name we want processed—process.mas. The remainder of the form looks normal. To process this form we could use the HTML::Mason component `<!--process.mas` →

```
<%args>
$partno => ''
</%args>
You chose the part number: <% $partno %>
```

The `<%args>` element consists of a variable name (`$partno`), an arrow (`=>`), and a default value. If the component receives an HTML form value for an element named "partno," it will be assigned to the variable `$partno`. Otherwise, the variable will receive the default value—in this case, the empty string.

> Note that the `<%args>` syntax isn't quite legal Perl syntax; it's special to HTML::Mason. The line doesn't require a trailing semicolon, the `=>` is a pseudo-assignment operator here, and the variable doesn't have to be declared with `my`.

You can receive multiple form values in an HTML::Mason component with multiple lines in the `<%args>` tag:

```
<%args>
$partno => ''
$customer => ''
$order_date=>scalar localtime
</%args>
```

In this snippet, the variables `$partno` and `$customer` can be passed as arguments (or CGI parameters) to this component, and they will be set to null if they're not passed. The variable `$order_date` will be set to the current time if it's not passed as an argument.

Example: A Common Header File

Our first example is a simple HTML::Mason component that prints a menu of other programs to run. Not impressed? Well, this program is largely a launching pad for other programs that we'll write later in the hour, and it's an opportunity to show off using one component loading another.

Listing 23.2 should be saved in the components directory that you set up earlier this hour as `main.mas`.

23

Listing 23.2   main.mas: Application Main Menu

```
1:    <& header.mas, title=>"First Screen" &>
2:    <ul>
3:    <a href="/cgi/mason.pl?comp=preferences.mas">Change Preferences</a><br/>
4:    a href="/cgi/mason.pl?comp=grafitti.mas">Grafitti Board</a>
5:    /ul>
6:    /body>
7:    /html>
```

Line 1: The component header.mas is called with the arguments "title" and "First Screen." This will print a common header for our site.

Lines 2–7: Prints a simple Web page with a couple of links. The links are rigged to call the mason.pl CGI script with different arguments to run different components. The showy part of Listing 23.2 is the portion where we call the component header.mas to print the header. Because the header.mas file doesn't yet exist, we need to create one. This is shown in Listing 23.3.

Listing 23.3   Common Header component, header.mas

```
1:    <%args>
2:    $title => 'No Title'
3:    </%args>
4:    <%perl>
5:    my $user="Unknown user";
6:    # User name '0' is troublesome -- and ignored
7:    $user=$session{name} if $session{name};
8:    </%perl>
9:
10:    <html>
11:    <head>
12:    <title><% $title %></title>
13:    </head>
14:    <body bgcolor=<% $session{bgcolor} %> >
```

continues

Listing 23.3   Continued

```
15:    <table width="100%" border="1">
16:    <tr>
17:    <td width="25%"> <% $user %> </td>
18:    <td align="center" width="50%"><h3><% $title %></h3></td>
19:    <td align="right" width="25%"> <% scalar localtime %> </td>
20:    </tr>
21:    <tr> <td colspan="3" align="center">
22:    <a href="/cgi/mason.pl?comp=main.mas">Main Menu</a>
23:    </td> </tr>
24:    </table>
```

Lines 1–3: The `<%args>` section takes the arguments passed in and assigns them to variables. In this case, if "title" is passed in, it's assigned to `$title`. If it's not, it's assigned "No Title" by default.

Lines 5–7: The `%session` hash is checked for a "name" key. If it's there, then the user has logged in, and we'll use his name. Otherwise we use "Unknown User."

Lines 10–24: A reasonable HTML header is printed with timestamps, user ID information, and titles. A session variable ("bgcolor") is used to set a background color. The header.mas component accepts an argument named "title." The main.mas program passes the title as an additional parameter in the `<& &>` tag, and it's accepted in the header.mas component as though it were an HTML form element. If no title argument is passed, the default value of "No Title" is printed.

If everything worked correctly, you should see something resembling Figure 23.2 in your browser:

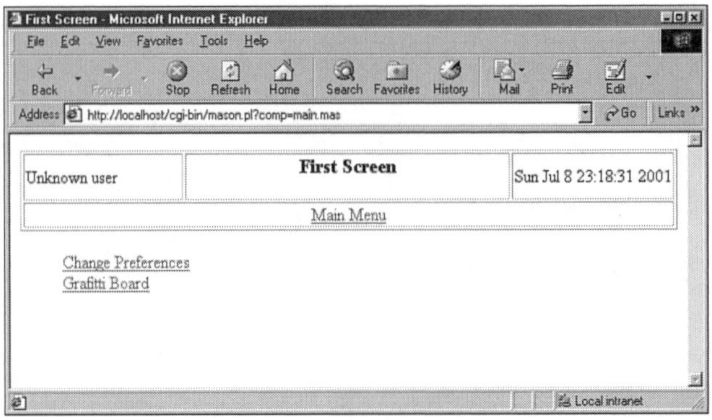

FIGURE 23.2

Main menu of application with header and default values.

Example: Managing Sessions in HTML::Mason

Obviously, the header.mas component in Listing 23.3 was looking for some additional information that wasn't provided: $session{user}. This is called *session information*. Session information is data that is identified with the current browser which the user used to connect to the Web application. Normally, HTML::Mason uses features in Apache's mod_perl to store this kind of data—but because we're running HTML::Mason as a CGI program, we're taking a slightly different approach.

When the user connects to the HTML::Mason CGI handler, a random ID string is sent back to the browser as a cookie. Each time the user reconnects to the application, the cookie is returned with the information. This way we can uniquely identify the user when the user returns.

In this application, the cookie is destroyed when the browser is closed. To change this you'll have to alter the HTML::Mason CGI handler to set an expiration time.

When a component is run, the HTML::Mason CGI handler creates a DBM file hash associated with the user—%session. So within the application, storing data in %session makes it available later when the user reconnects to the application.

Listing 23.4 contains a program that allows you to set user preferences for the current session. Currently, only two preferences can be set: the user's name and the background color of the screen. As soon as they are set, these preferences take effect for this screen and every other screen in the application that uses the component header.mas.

An interesting part of Listing 23.4 is lines 15–19. The for loop completely envelops a piece of HTML that contains HTML::Mason tags. The three lines of HTML used to create radio buttons are repeated once for each color needed in the list.

Listing 23.4 Changing Preferences, preferences.mas

```
1:    <%args>
2:    $comp=>''
3:    $name=>$session{name}
4:    $bgcolor=>$session{bgcolor}
5:    </%args>
```

continues

margin: 23

Listing 23.4 Continued

```
6:
7:      % $session{name}=$name if $name;
8:      % $session{bgcolor}=$bgcolor if $bgcolor;
9:
10:     <& header.mas, title => "Basic Preferences" &>
11:     <form method="get" action="/cgi/mason.pl" ><p>
12:     <input type=hidden name=comp value="<% $comp %>" />
13:     Username:<input type=text width=10 name="name" value="<% $name %>"/>
14:     </p><p>Background color:<blockquote>
15:     % for my $color (qw(blue red yellow white green)) {
16:         <% ucfirst($color) %> <input type="radio" name="bgcolor"
17:         value="<% $color %>"
18:         <% ($bgcolor eq $color)?"checked":"" %>/><br/>
19:     % }
20:     </blockquote><p>
21:     <input type="submit" value="Save Changes"/>
```

Lines 1–5: The arguments "comp", "name", and "bgcolor" are all accepted and assigned to variables. Sometimes they're defaulted from the user's session; sometimes they're passed in as the program calls itself during form submission.

Lines 7–8: If the CGI variables "name" and "bgcolor" are set, then they're recorded in the session.

Lines 11–22: A CGI form is displayed to the user. Note that some fields have a "default" value set from the session, if they exist in %session.

Example: Managing Applications in HTML::Mason

In the previous example, the %session hash was used to keep track of an individual user's preferences for a browser "session." These were cleaned up every half-day or so by the HTML::Mason CGI handler, and they represent temporary data used by the application.

Obviously, to create a more permanent application you're going to need a storage area that

- Is not transitory and doesn't get erased periodically
- Is shared among many users

The HTML::Mason CGI handler sets up such a database for you, and it's accessible through the %application hash. Items stored in this hash will be visible for any application using the handler, and is persistent: it will be around for future invocations as well.

Because this hash is shared between different processes, possibly running at the same time, it will be necessary to take out a lock before reading or writing this hash. The HTML::Mason CGI handler provides get_lock and release_lock functions just for this purpose. The mechanism behind the lock was described in Hour 15.

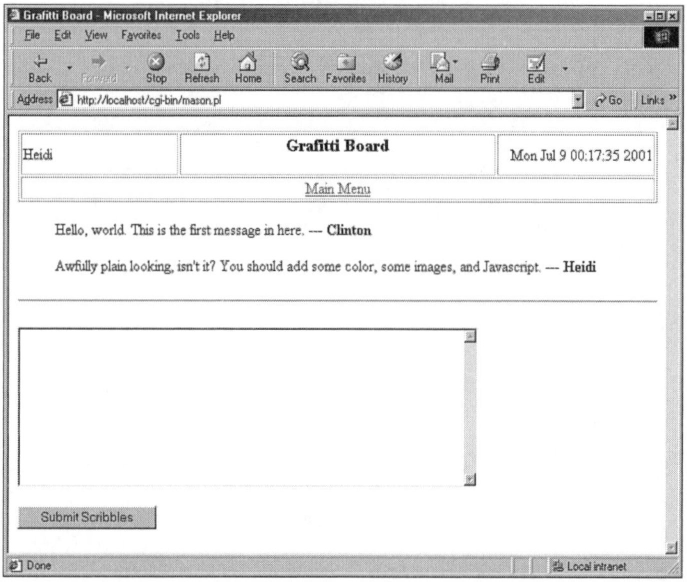

23

FIGURE 23.3

A screen shot of the "grafitti board."

To demonstrate this "shared" resource, we're going to create a stripped-down version of a Web message board system as seen in Figure 23.3. Listing 23.5 contains the code for grafitti.mas. This Web message board is very different from others (to keep it simple). In order to post a message to the board, you have to have a valid "user name" on the preferences screen. Messages are added to the bottom of the list, signed only by the given name. Otherwise, there's no "login" procedure, as in other systems.

Listing 23.5 Grafitti Board component grafitti.mas

```
1:    <%args>
2:    $comp=>''
3:    $newmessage=>''
4:    </%args>
5:
```

continues

Listing 23.5 Continued

```
6:     <%perl>
7:     if ($newmessage and $session{name}) {
8:         get_lock();
9:         my($id)=$application{lastid};
10:        $id++;
11:        $application{"msg" . $id}="$session{name}#$newmessage";
12:        $application{lastid}=$id;
13:        release_lock();
14:    }
15:    </%perl>
16:
17:    <& header.mas, title => "Grafitti Board" &>
18:    <%perl>
19:        foreach my $mesg (sort keys %application) {
20:            my($id,$person,$message);
21:            next if (not $mesg=~/msg/);
22:            $id=substr($mesg, 3); # Get the ID number
23:            ($person,$message)=split(/#/, $application{$mesg});
24:    </%perl>
25:            <blockquote>
26:            <% $message %>
27:            <b>--- <% $person %></b>
28:            </blockquote>
29:    %    }
30:    % if ($session{name}) {
31:        <hr/>
32:        <form method="post" action="/cgi/mason.pl" ><p>
33:        <input type="hidden" name="comp" value="<% $comp %>" />
34:        <textarea name="newmessage" rows="10" cols="60"></textarea></p>
35:        <p><input type="submit" value="Submit Scribbles"/></p>
36:    % } else {
37:        <i>Sorry, you have to be signed in to write to the
38:        message board!</i>
39:    % }
40:    </form>
```

Lines 1–6: Two arguments can be accepted. The argument `"newmessage"` is the message to be posted.

Lines 7–14: If a message is passed into the component via "newmessage", it's recorded in the application hash `%application`. Because this hash is shared among many components, possibly running at the same time, we need to erect a lock around access to the hash with `get_lock` and `release_lock`. The message is stored in the hash keyed by "msg" with a message number appended to the end; the value contains the message and the user ID of the person who posted it. The last message number is also stored in the hash.

Lines 19–24: The messages are retrieved from the `%application` hash. This is done by going through each key of the hash looking for ones that match `/msg/`. As they're found, `$person` and `$message` are populated by splitting apart the value.

Lines 30–35: If the user is logged in (via the preferences screen), then a message posting form is presented.

Lines 36–38: Otherwise a message telling the user to log in is shown.

23

Summary

Templating systems can be used to dramatically reduce development time in a Web application. Keeping your HTML markup and Perl code in the same file is useful for debugging and can make the application look simpler.

The HTML::Mason module provides a flexible template for creating your applications by calling components to do manageable portions of the work. HTML::Mason is most readily used with the Apache Web server, but can be called through CGI with the handler given earlier in this hour.

Q&A

Q Is HTML::Mason the only templating system available in Perl?

A No, actually it's only one of many. Another wildly popular tool is Text::Template, which is geared to be a general-purpose templating system, and is not specifically a CGI system.

Q None of the components will work! In fact, I can't even get the "No components specified" message.

A Check the following:

1. That the session, data, and components directories exist

2. That the session and data directories are writeable by the Web server.

3. Try putting:

```
use CGI::Carp qw(fatalsToBrowser);
```

in the script near the top to see if there are any errors that aren't coming through.

4. Make sure other CGI programs are working and follow the checklist in Hour 17, "Introduction to CGI."

Workshop

Quiz

1. Within a component, to get to CGI parameters, you need to use:

    a. The CGI module's `param()` function

    b. The `<%args>` section of a component

    c. The `QUERY_STRING` environment variable

2. Sessions (`%session`) are shared among users

    a. True

    b. False

Answers

1. b. The `param()` function isn't needed in HTML::Mason components.

2. False. The application hash (`%application`) is shared among users. The session is per individual user.

Exercises

- Notice that most "professionally" done Web pages not only have a common header and navigation system, but the footers are also similar. Construct a footer component and insert it into the three pages you have so far (main, grafitti, and preferences). After you've completed Hour 24, "Making an Interactive Site," revisit this chapter and consider how a hit counter could be implemented as an HTML::Mason component. Would it be simpler or more difficult than using a server-side include?

HOUR 24

Making an Interactive Site

If the reason you're using CGI programs on your Web site is to pull people in and provide them with an interesting place to visit, you're going to need to do a little bit more than put up a hit counter.

The most interesting sites on the Web are ones that provide content that is updated frequently. If your Web page has static information on it, people don't have any reason to ever come back. After a couple of visits, they'll figure out that your site doesn't change much and there's no point in returning.

In this hour you'll learn

- How to create a "hit counter"
- How to borrow content from another Web site

Hit Counters

On Web pages, you commonly see something called a *hit counter* or a *visitor number* indicator. Supposedly, it indicates how many times a Web page has been visited. An example of one is shown in Figure 24.1.

FIGURE **24.1**

Sample of a "hit counter."

Visitor counters have lots of problems. First and foremost, what does that number mean? A high number of "hits" supposedly indicates that the page is popular. If it's popular, does that mean it's a good Web page? Not necessarily. If you're visiting a Web page, either it has the information you want, or it doesn't. The quality of the page is in its value to you, not to others.

Essentially, a hit counter is a kind of beauty contest—with blind judges. The number represented is not necessarily the number of people who've visited your page. At best, it's a wildly inaccurate estimate. Why are these counters so inaccurate? I can think of several reasons.

First, no rule says that a hit counter has to start at 0. When you were issued your last checkbook, was the first check #1? More likely, when you ordered the checks, you were allowed to pick the starting sequence number. If you're smart, you'll pick a high number so that it appears as if you have a long-standing account with the bank. A low number will make store clerks look twice at your ID and maybe consider not taking your check at all. Web site operators frequently set the hit counter initially high to make their sites look more "popular" than they really are.

The second problem with hit counters is Web robots—also called *spiders, crawlers,* and so on. These automatic processes search the Web for data, sometimes simply to look for a specific piece of data and sometimes to build indexes of interesting Web sites. Have you ever wondered how AltaVista, Google, or HotBot build their indexes? They search the Web, fetch pages, and ultimately make hit counters go higher than they really should be.

The next problem is the Refresh button on Web browsers. Every time your page is "refreshed," the hit counter goes up a notch. You're not really measuring the number of "visitors" to your site if someone hits the reload button, are you?

Last—and most important—is the caching problem. In Hour 17, "Introduction to CGI," you saw a diagram of how the browser communicates with the Web server. It left out an important detail, which is shown in Figure 24.2.

FIGURE 24.2

Proxy server fetching the page for the browser.

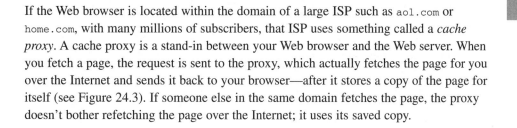

24

If the Web browser is located within the domain of a large ISP such as `aol.com` or `home.com`, with many millions of subscribers, that ISP uses something called a *cache proxy*. A cache proxy is a stand-in between your Web browser and the Web server. When you fetch a page, the request is sent to the proxy, which actually fetches the page for you over the Internet and sends it back to your browser—after it stores a copy of the page for itself (see Figure 24.3). If someone else in the same domain fetches the page, the proxy doesn't bother refetching the page over the Internet; it uses its saved copy.

FIGURE 24.3

Proxy server retrieving a page from its cache.

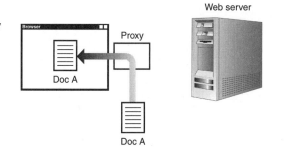

The proxy storing a copy of the page artificially deflates the number of hits that a hit counter shows. Strangely enough, it also causes the `remote_host` value to be repeated frequently, even though the page is fetched by many different people.

Web surfers at large corporations and universities are often behind firewalls that act as caching proxies. Every page fetch that happens from one of these sites has the potential for missing the hit counter because it's being intercepted by a cache proxy.

And Now, a Hit Counter

After having read the preceding section, if you're still reading you must be interested in writing a hit counter for your Web page. The two basic types of hit counters for Web pages are a simple text display and a graphical counter. The first example here is a text counter, and the next is a graphical one—along with some ideas on making rather pretty hit counters.

To use the hit counter, include it as part of a server-side include, which you learned about in Hour 20, "Manipulating HTTP and CGI." If you call the hit counter CGI program hits.cgi, you can include it in any page using SSI like this:

```
<!--#exec cgi="/cgi-bin/hits.cgi"-->
```

The source for the hit counter program is shown in Listing 24.1.

LISTING 24.1   Hit Counter Program

```
1:    #!/usr/bin/perl -w
2:
3:    use strict;
4:    use Fcntl qw(:flock);
5:    use CGI qw(:all);
6:
7:    my $semaphore_file='/tmp/webcount_lock';
8:    my $counterfile='/web/httpd/countfile';
9:    sub get_lock {
10:       open(SEM, ">$semaphore_file")
11:           || die "Cannot create semaphore: $!";
12:       flock(SEM, LOCK_EX) || die "Lock failed: $!";
13:    }
14:    # Function to unlock
15:    sub release_lock {
16:       close(SEM);
17:    }
18:    get_lock();  # Get a lock, and wait for it.
19:    my $hits=0;
20:    if ( open(CF, $counterfile) ) {
21:       $hits=<CF>;
22:       close(CF);
```

continues

LISTING 24.1 Continued

```
23:  }
24:  $hits++;  # Increase the hits by 1.
25:  print header;
26:  print "You have had $hits visitors";
27:
28:  open(CF, ">$counterfile") || die "Cannot open $counterfile: $!";
29:  print CF $hits;
30:  close(CF);
31:
32:  release_lock();  # Release the lock
```

Line 18: A lock is necessary because the hit-counter file will be read and written, possibly by many processes at the same time.

Lines 20–23: The contents of the file in $counterfile are read. This is the number of hits so far.

Lines 28–30: The hit counter is written back out to the file in $counterfile.

Line 32: Finally, the lock is released.

Most of the code in Listing 24.1 should not strike you as unusual. However, notice that file locking is used, and the example follows the file-locking formulas demonstrated in Hour 15, "Finding Permanence."

File locking is necessary in the case in which two people load the Web page at nearly the same time. If the reading and writing of the Web counter file are slightly out of sync, then the counter might increase too quickly or too slowly, or it might produce a corrupt file. These results would further diminish the accuracy of the counter.

Graphical Hit Counter

To spice up the hit counter, you could take three approaches. First, you could make up a graphic that represents each possible value of the hit counter and display it as necessary. That approach would be time consuming if you received more than a few visitors to the Web site.

Another approach is to have a Perl CGI program actually generate the necessary graphics to display the hit counter itself. The GD module, available from CPAN, is designed for creating graphics with Perl programs, so you could use it for this purpose. Unfortunately, covering the ins and outs of the GD module is well beyond the scope of this book.

By far the easiest approach is to create 10 images, representing the digits 0 to 9. Then, as the hit counter increases, your program can simply emit HTML with <IMG> tags that put the digits in the right place (see Figure 24.4). You do, of course, have to create the images to represent the digits. The Perl CGI program in Listing 24.2 expects the images to be named digit_0.jpg, digit_1.jpg, and so on, up to digit_9.jpg.

FIGURE 24.4

Graphical hit counter output.

To use the hit counter, you can include it as part of a server-side include, as described in Hour 20. If you call the hit counter CGI program graphical_hits.cgi, you can include it in any page like this:

```
<!--#exec cgi="/cgi-bin/graphical_hits.cgi"-->
```

The source for this graphical hit counter is shown in Listing 24.2.

LISTING 24.2   Graphical Hit Counter

```
1:   #!/usr/bin/perl -w
2:
3:   use strict;
4:   use Fcntl qw(:flock);
5:   use CGI qw(:all);
6:
7:   my $lockfile='/tmp/webcount_lock';
8:   my $counterfile='/web/httpd/countfile';
9:   my $image_url='http://www.server.com/images';
10:
11: sub get_lock {
12:    open(SEM, ">$lockfile")
13:        || die "Cannot create semaphore: $!";
14:    flock(SEM, LOCK_EX) || die "Lock failed: $!";
15: }
16: sub release_lock {
17:    close(SEM);
18: }
19: get_lock();  # Get a lock, and wait for it.
20: my $hits=0;
21: if ( open(CF, $counterfile) ) {
22:     $hits=<CF>;
23:     close(CF);
24: }
25: $hits++;
26:
27: open(CF, ">$counterfile") || die "Cannot open $counterfile: $!";
28: print CF $hits;
```

continues

LISTING 24.2 Continued

```
29:  close(CF);
30:  release_lock();  # Release the lock
31:
32:  # Now, create the <IMG> tags.
33:  print header;
34:  foreach my $digit (split(//, $hits)) {
35:      print "<img src=\"$image_url/digit_$digit.jpg\"/>";
36:  }
```

Listing 24.2 is essentially the same as Listing 24.1, with some small changes.

Line 9: This line now contains in `$image_url` the base URL for the images that make up the digits. Remember, it must be the URL that the browser will see to load the images, not the path to the images on the local disk.

Lines 34–35: The number in the hit counter—`$hits`—is split up on every character and assigned to `$digit` one digit at a time. The `<IMG>` tags are then printed for each digit.

24

Borrowing Content

You've probably seen Web sites that have somewhat up-to-date stock tickers, news headlines, or sports scores somewhere on the page—even if the person running the site has nothing to do with the original source of the content.

What usually happens is this: A program running on the system you're looking at occasionally goes to the original source of the information and pulls it in. The information is then reformatted and displayed on the target page. Figure 24.5 shows what this process looks like.

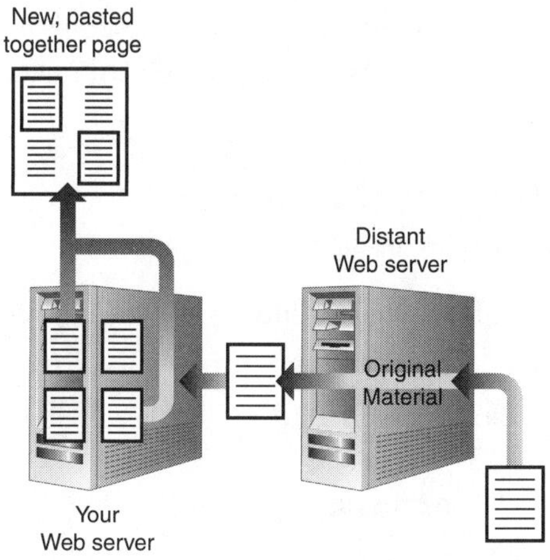

FIGURE 24.5
Fetching a Web page, altering it, and redisplaying it.

New, pasted together page

Distant Web server

Original Material

Your Web server

Here, you can see that your Web *server*—by way of its CGI programs—has become a Web *client*. When the server can fetch pages for itself, it can glue them together and present the information again.

Important: Covering Your Hide

Before you skip down and read how to borrow content, you should know a few things. First, if the information you are displaying is not your own—it comes from another Web site or database—that material is probably covered by copyright law. Borrowing material from one Web site to present on your own can get you into serious legal trouble. Violating copyright laws can get your Web site *and* your ISP shut down, and you can be fined, imprisoned, and sued.

It's also rude.

Always ask permission before using information from another source on your own Web site. Most Web site operators will let you display content from their sites. Usually, they will ask for a few considerations in return:

- You clearly indicate the source of the content—possibly with a banner, links, and text.
- You clearly specify the content's copyrights and indicate that the content is used with permission.
- You might not be allowed to "deep-link" into their Web site—that is, link to their site several pages deep. They will probably prefer that you link to a top-level page instead.
- You might be allowed to update your version only occasionally. Burying their servers under traffic to make your site look good isn't cool.

The owners of Slashdot.org, a Web site with content geared toward technical users—and with the motto "News for Nerds"—have given me permission to use their site for demonstration purposes in the examples in this book. Before you actually implement these examples on a page of your own, you should ask their permission. You can find details on contacting Slashdot.org on their Web site and in their FAQ at
http://www.slashdot.org.

Example: Fetching Headlines

The plan for displaying Slashdot's headlines on your Web site works something like this:

1. The headlines.cgi CGI program is started by way of a server-parsed HTML Web page.
2. The CGI program then checks to see whether it has a recent copy of the headlines stored on disk. If it does, it uses them. Otherwise, it fetches the headlines from Slashdot.org's Web site.
3. The CGI program then parses the headline file and displays the headlines.

To retrieve a Web page or any other content from another Web site, you need a module that's not included as part of the standard Perl distribution: LWP::Simple. The LWP modules allow you to fetch all kinds of information from the Internet: Web pages, FTP data, newsgroup articles, and so on.

> The LWP::Simple module is packaged as part of a bundle called libwww-perl. This bundle contains modules for fetching Web pages, parsing HTML, parsing URLs, traversing a Web site, and many others. The benefits of using these modules make them well worth the installation time.

The LWP::Simple module, once installed, allows you to fetch a Web page like this:

```
use LWP::Simple qw(get);
$content=get("http://www.slashdot.org");
```

And now $content contains the text of the Web page at that URL. Wasn't that easy?

The program to fetch Slashdot's headlines and display them appears in Listings 24.3 through 24.5. To use the program, you can either run it directly or inside a server-parsed HTML file.

LISTING 24.3   Part I of Slashdot's Headline Program

```
1:   #!/usr/bin/perl -w
2:
3:   use strict;
4:   use Fcntl qw(:flock);
5:   use LWP::Simple qw(get);
6:   use CGI qw(:all);
7:
8:   my $url="http://slashdot.org/slashdot.xml";
9:   my $cache="/tmp/slashcache";
10:  my $lockfile="/tmp/slashlock";
11: sub get_lock {
12:    open(SEM, ">$lockfile")
13:        || die "Cannot create lockfilee: $!";
14:    flock(SEM, LOCK_EX) || die "Lock failed: $!";
15: }
16: sub release_lock {
17:    close(SEM);
18: }
```

Lines 3–6: To write this program, you need a variety of modules. You should use the module Fcntl because you need to lock a portion of the program so that it can be run by only one user at a time. You need the LWP::Simple module—specifically, the get function—to fetch the headlines from Slashdot's Web site. And, of course, you need the CGI module because this is a CGI program.

Line 8: Contains the URL for the file, which contains just the headlines. This file's format is something like the following:

```
<story>
    <title>Ask Slashdot: Internet Voting?</title>
    <url>http://slashdot.org/askslashdot/99/09/05/1732249.shtml</url>
    <time>1999-09-05 21:34:36</time>
    <author>Cliff</author>
      :
```

Here, each story is bracketed by a <story> tag. The file is in a somewhat reduced form of a markup language called XML. This makes it very easy for a Perl program to process it, as you'll see later.

The variable $cache at line 9 contains the name of the file into which you're going to temporarily store the Slashdot headlines. You use this file so that each time the program is invoked, you don't bother Slashdot's servers for the information; you have a local copy.

And, of course, the get_lock() and release_lock() subroutines should now look familiar to you because you've seen them in three other lessons. You need them because the file in $cache should not be updated by more than one program at a time; therefore, it needs to be locked.

LISTING 24.4   Part II of Slashdot's Headline Program

```
19:
20:  print header;
21:  # If the cache is older than about an hour, rebuild it
22:  get_lock();
23:  if ( (not -e $cache ) or ( (-M $cache) > .04)) {
24:      my $doc=get($url);
25:      if (defined $doc) {
26:              open(CF, ">$cache") || die "Writing to cache: $!";
27:              print CF $doc;
28:              close(CF);
29:      }
30:  }
31:  release_lock();
32:
```

Line 23: Determines that, if the cache file doesn't exist or if the cache is more than 60 minutes old, it should be rebuilt. The -M function in Perl returns the modification time of the file since the Perl program was started, but the time is returned in *fractional days*. Thus, if the file is one day old, -M returns 1; if the file is six hours old, -M returns .25 (one-quarter day); if the file is one hour old, -M returns .0416666— approximately 1/24.

Line 24: Retrieves the URL containing the headlines, as explained previously with the LWP::Simple module's get function. The next few lines write the retrieved document in $doc into the cache file. If the get fails, it returns undef, and that's checked in line 25.

Notice that the get_lock() and release_lock() sequences are *outside* the if statement. This point is very important. If one instance of the CGI program is busy updating the cache file, you don't want another one coming along checking to see whether the cache exists or when it was last modified.

LISTING 24.5 Part III of Slashdot's Headline Program

```
33: print "<h2>Slashdot.Org's Headlines as of ",
34:     scalar(gmtime((stat $cache)[9])),
35:     "GMT </h2><p>Updated Hourly!</p>";
36:
37: open(CF, $cache) || die "Cannot open the cache: $!";
38: my($title, $link);
39: while(<CF>) {
40:     if (m,<title>(.*)</title>,) {
41:             $title=$1;
42:     }
43:     if (m,<url>(.*)</url>,) {
44:             $link=$1;
45:             print qq{<a href="$link">$title</a><br/>\n};
46:
47:     }
48: }
49: print "Copyright Slashdot.Org, used with permission.";
50: close(CF);
```

The last portion of the program is the most straightforward. Lines 33–35 print the introduction and the time the cache file was last updated. Line 34 is kind of tricky. Let me explain what's going on: First, stat gets information about the file in $cache and returns it as a list. Second, element 9 of the list (the last modification time) is extracted. Third, localtime is called with that time, which, in a scalar context, returns a nicely formatted string.

Lines 40 and 43 extract the <title> and <url> sections of the headline file from Slashdot. The matching portions of the title and URL are saved in $1 by the regular expressions and then assigned to $title and $link, respectively. Because the <url> element always occurs after the <title> element, when the <url> element is seen, both $title and $link can be printed on line 45.

These regular expressions should *not* be used to match HTML in a general case. They work here because Slashdot's headline XML file is nicely formatted with exactly one XML element per line. If the format of the file seems to change and this program can't process it, you should check Slashdot's FAQ to see what has changed.

When the program is finally run, the output looks something like that shown in Figure 24.6.

FIGURE 24.6

Output of slashdot.cgi program.

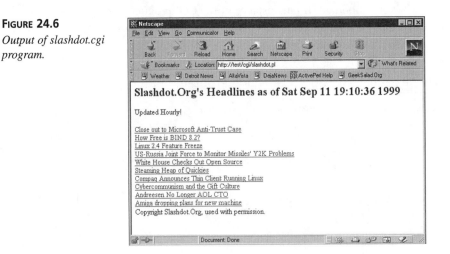

Of course, you should use your HTML skills to make this output look a little snazzier.

Summary

In this hour, you created a couple of programs to help give your Web pages some variety. First, you created a simple method to keep track of how many people have visited your web site. Next, you created a program to take content from other sites and present it on yours. You also read some advice about borrowing content from other people.

Q&A

Q Can I really be sued for borrowing just the headlines from a site?

A Yes, you can; it has happened before. In February 1999, a lawsuit was settled between Microsoft and Ticketmaster for just this kind of situation. Microsoft had allegedly used "deep links" into Ticketmaster's site, and Ticketmaster sued. In this

case, no copyright violations occurred, but there were enough grounds from "deep linking" that the case was settled. Had copyright infringement been involved, the situation would have gotten uglier.

Q I have a site I'd like to get headlines from; it's similar to Slashdot. However, it doesn't have a nice XML-ish file to parse. Instead, I have to use the normal HTML file. How should I parse that?

A If you're going to parse HTML, do *not* try to use regular expressions and parse it yourself. Parsing HTML is not as easy as it looks, and it is nearly impossible to get right. And, even if you manage to get regular expressions to parse some HTML, it won't work everywhere. The CPAN contains modules for parsing HTML. These modules are all under the HTML section of CPAN, that is, `HTML::*`.

Workshop

24

Quiz

1. To fetch an HTML file from a Web server, what should you do?

   a. Use `LWP`.

   b. Open a socket to that system and retrieve the data.

   c. Use `[ag]lynx -dump[ag]` or `[ag]netscape -print[ag]`.

2. If the `LWP::Simple` module's `get` function fails, what does it return?

   a. The error message (that is, `"No Document"`)

   b. The empty string (that is, `""`)

   c. `undef`

Answers

1. a. Although b and c would work, they're not terribly robust or easy to use.

2. c. The answer was explained in the analysis following Listing 24.2.

Activities

- Simply as a thought experiment: how could you create an independent hit counter for each page in your site? Would you use cookies? Server-side includes?

- A challenging activity, in two parts:

   1. Create a fill-in form where users can select a U.S. location for themselves.

   2. Fetch a page from http://weather.noaa.gov/weather and display (dynamically) the weather for that U.S. location. Forecasts and current conditions are both available if you dig around a bit.

The location you fetch will be a METAR code that is based on your local observation station (which is usually related to your local airport). For example, the METAR code for Detroit, Michigan, is KDTW. The page with the weather for Detroit would be

`http://tgsv22.nws.noaa.gov/weather/current/KDTW.html`

The full list of METAR codes is at the NOAA website.

- For a further challenge, store the METAR code for the user in a cookie. Have the page automatically display that user's weather when they return by fetching the last value from the cookie.

Part IV
Appendix

Installing Modules

Part IV

Appendix

APPENDIX

Installing Modules

Installing modules for Perl isn't hard, and learning how to install them is essential if you ever want to master Perl. This appendix contains information on how to install the modules you need.

 Detailed documentation on installing modules under almost any architecture is available in Perl's documentation. The document, called "perlmodinstall," even contains instructions for building under obscure operating systems such as OS/2 and VMS.

Picking the Right Module

First, you need to pick the right module. A good starting place is the CPAN itself at http://www.cpan.org. You need to decide which module you're interested in.

CPAN modules are named, roughly, based on what they do. For example, Image::Size takes an image and reports what size the image is; this module is useful for working with Web pages. Some modules have unusual names, though. LWP derives its name from a Perl library called libwww-perl.

You also can find bundles of modules on CPAN. These bundles contain several related modules—and usually prerequisite modules—all in one large package. For example, the `libnet` bundle installs like a module, but in the process, you get several modules all related to networking. `LWP` is part of the `libnet` bundle, for example.

> When you install a module, you also automatically get all the documenta-
> tion needed for that module.

Installing the Modules Under . . .

For each of the examples in the following sections, you will attempt to install the `Date::Manip` module from CPAN. To install your own module or bundle, simply substitute the name of your module in place of `Date::Manip`.

. . . Windows 95/98/NT

With Windows, the easiest solution is to use prepackaged modules available from ActiveState Tool Corp, assuming, of course, that the Perl installation you have is from ActiveState.

To install a prebuilt module under Windows, you first need to start the Perl Package Manager (PPM). This utility simplifies the module-building process for you by providing an interactive interface to module installation. To start the PPM, you need to open a DOS command prompt, as shown in Figure A.1; you should be connected to the Internet.

FIGURE A.1

You can work from the DOS command prompt.

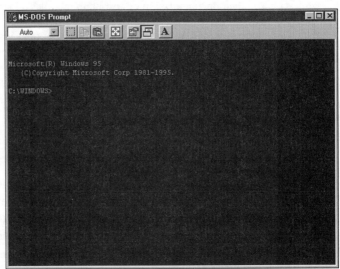

At the command prompt, simply type **ppm**, as shown here. The PPM utility should then start; if it doesn't, you need to look for the ppm.bat file that was installed with ActiveState Perl and run it with the full pathname.

```
C:\Windows>ppm
PPM interactive shell (1.0.0) - type 'help' for available commands
PPM>
```

To search for a particular module, use the search command, as shown here. You need to use this command because ActiveState doesn't have prebuilt packages for all the modules in CPAN, only the more commonly requested ones. Also, for installation, you have to be able to spell the name of the module correctly.

```
PPM> search Date
Packages available from http://www.ActiveState.com/packages:
        Date-Calc
        Date-Manip
        TimeDate
PPM>
```

After you've found the module you want—Date-Manip for this example—you can install it by using the install command, as follows:

```
PPM> install Date-Manip
Install package 'Date-Manip?' (y/N): y
Installing C:\Perl\html\lib\Date\Manip.html
Installing C:\Perl\htmlhelp\pkg-Date-Manip.chm
Installing C:\Perl\htmlhelp\pkg-Date-Manip.hhc
Installing C:\Perl\site\lib\Date\Manip.pm
Writing C:\Perl\site\lib/auto/Date-Manip/.packlist
PPM>
```

The Date::Manip module is now installed!

If you want to download the bundle and install it manually—perhaps the PC doesn't have Internet access or is behind a firewall—you can find instructions for downloading and installing modules by hand and dealing with firewalls on ActiveState's Web site (http://www.ActiveState.com). ActiveState maintains a FAQ specific to its distribution of Perl, and you can find the necessary instructions there.

> Installing modules without PPM—for example, using your own C compiler under Microsoft Windows—is well beyond the scope of this book. The source distribution of Perl contains instructions for building Perl yourself under Windows, but this job is not for beginners. If you can accomplish that, building modules for yourself shouldn't be too difficult because the processes are about the same.

. . . Unix, Using CPAN

Installing modules under Unix can be exciting and full of challenges, or it can be ridiculously easy. You need an ANSI C compiler (the one used to build Perl will be fine) and a compiler license if your vendor requires one. You also need a copy of the GNU compression program gzip/gunzip; some Unix vendors ship it as a standard utility. You can obtain a copy from `http://www.fsf.org` if you don't have it.

> Some Unix vendors—Hewlett-Packard, notably—ship their operating systems with a C compiler that is not an ANSI C compiler. It's a severely stripped-down version of a real compiler, so you have to pay for the real one, or download and install the GNU C compiler—for free.

One last thing: You'll probably need root privileges on the installation machine. Normally, Perl is installed as a systemwide utility. Installing modules into the system directories requires that you have adequate permission to do so—root permission.

The Perl installation comes with a module called CPAN that is designed to help you install other modules. To get the installation started, you start Perl using the CPAN module's shell like this:

```
$ perl -MCPAN -e shell
```

The first time you run this command, the CPAN module interrogates you to find out where you want to fetch Perl modules from and how you want them built. Most of the time, the default answers are sufficient. You are asked about the location of temporary directories, which CPAN mirror you want to use (a list is presented), and whether you're accessing the Internet through a proxy.

When CPAN is done interrogating you, you are presented with this prompt:

```
cpan shell -- CPAN exploration and modules installation (v1.3901)
ReadLine support available (try [ag][ag]install Bundle::CPAN'')

cpan>
```

At this prompt, you can use the command i */pat/* to search for information on a package, where *pat* specifies the pattern to search for. To find the Date::Manip module, for example, search like this:

```
cpan> i /Manip/
```

The CPAN module may need > to contact a CPAN server and obtain a new copy of the index. This situation happens only when necessary, and the process takes just a moment.

When the query is done, CPAN replies with something like the following information:

```
Distribution    SBECK/DateManip-5.35.tar.gz
Module          Date::Manip    (SBECK/DateManip-5.35.tar.gz)
```

To install the module, type the following:

```
cpan> install Date::Manip
```

Now, the CPAN module goes through the process of fetching, compiling, testing, and installing the module for you. The display is quite messy but looks something like this greatly abbreviated example (# comments normally do not appear; they're added for clarity here):

```
Running make for SBECK/DateManip-5.35.tar.gz
Fetching with LWP:              # Fetching the module

ftp://ftp.perl.org/pub/perl/CPAN/authors/id/SBECK/DateManip-5.35.t
ar.gz
Writing Makefile for Date::Manip
mkdir blib                      # Building the module
mkdir blib/lib
Target "makemakerdflt" is up to date.
  /usr/bin/make  -- OK
Running make test               # Testing to ensure it works
        PERL_DL_NONLAZY=1 /usr/bin/perl -Iblib/arch -Iblib/lib
-I/usr/local/lib/
perl5/5.00502/aix -I/usr/local/lib/perl5/5.00502 -e 'use
Test::Harness qw(&runte
sts $verbose); $verbose=0; runtests @ARGV;' t/*.t
t/settime..........ok
t/unixdate.........ok
All tests successful.
Files=30,  Tests=826, 178 wallclock secs (168.85 cusr +  5.23
csys = 174.08 CPU)
Target "test" is up to date.
  /usr/bin/make test -- OK
Running make install            # Installing the module
Target "install" is up to date.
  /usr/bin/make install  -- OK
```

Your output will vary considerably from the preceding. The module is now tested and installed. Enjoy!

. . . Unix, The Hard Way

Although you can install modules in Unix without using the CPAN module, most of the time you don't need to install this way. This method is presented for completeness only; you should really use the CPAN module whenever possible.

A

First, you need to download the module from CPAN. It is a gzip'ed tar bundle. If the module is `Date::Calc`, for example, you would need to obtain the latest version, which has a name something like Date-Calc-X.Y.tar.gz. After you've downloaded the bundle, go to that directory and unpack the bundle like this:

```
$ gunzip Date-Calc-4_2.tar.gz
$ tar xf Date-Calc-4_2.tar
```

Unpacking creates a subdirectory called Date-Calc-4.2. Change into that subdirectory by using `cd`, and type the following command:

```
$ perl Makefile.PL
Checking if your kit is complete...
Looks good
Writing Makefile for Date::Calc
```

Now you have a makefile, which is required for the build process. Next, build the module by using the `make` command as follows:

```
$ make
mkdir blib
mkdir blib/lib
:
Manifying blib/man3/Date::Calc.3
Target "makemakerdflt" is up to date.
```

This process might take awhile.

At the next prompt, you need to test the module to see whether it is built correctly. Just type **make test** as follows:

```
$ make test
PERL_DL_NONLAZY=1 /usr/bin/perl -Iblib/arch -Iblib/lib
-I/usr/local/lib/
perl5/5.00502/aix -I/usr/local/lib/perl5/5.00502 -e 'use
Test::Harness qw(&runte
sts $verbose); $verbose=0; runtests @ARGV;' t/*.t
t/f000..............ok
t/f001..............ok
:
t/f032..............ok
t/f033..............ok
All tests successful.
Files=34,  Tests=1823, 14 wallclock secs ( 9.81 cusr +  1.10 csys
= 10.91 CPU)
Target "test" is up to date.
```

You should *always* run the `make test` command to ensure the module was built correctly. It can save you (and others) hours of debugging later. When the test is complete, you need to install the module, as shown here. This step is usually done as the root user because the installation must write to system directories.

```
$ su
Password: *******
# make install
Installing
/usr/local/lib/perl5/site_perl/5.005/aix/auto/Date/Calc/Calc.so
:
Appending installation info to
/usr/local/lib/perl5/5.00502/aix/perllocal.pod
Target "install" is up to date.
#
```

At this point, you're done!

Installing Modules on the Macintosh

Installing modules on the Macintosh is challenging. You should consult the MacPerl FAQ for information on the droplets that can be used to install modules. The MacPerl FAQ is located at `http://www.macperl.com`.

What to Do When You're Not Allowed to Install Modules

A

If you can install programs on a system, you can install modules. Your ability to do so depends on how complex the module is and what kind of trouble you're willing to go through. Sometimes the system administrator does not allow you to install a module because he or she doesn't want it used by others. In some cases, only you, or a group of people, want specific modules, and having them installed systemwide is too much hassle.

In either case, installing private copies of Perl modules in your own directories is not difficult.

First, you need to build the module using the instructions given previously—with a small exception. You can specify to the installation program that you want the modules placed in a particular directory. With PPM under Microsoft Windows, before you install the module, you need to tell PPM that you want to install into a different directory. You do so by using the `set` command like this:

```
PPM> set root c:\myperl
PPM> set build c:\myperl
```

The module is then assembled and installed in the directory c:\myperl.

Under Unix, when you're using the CPAN module, you can specify the installation directory by using the `makepl_arg` setting like this:

```
cpan> o conf makepl_arg PREFIX="/home/clintp/perl/lib"
```

Or, if you're installing modules by hand using the make utility, you can specify the installation directory by using the PREFIX argument on the first line during the build:

```
$ perl Makefile.PL PREFIX="/home/clintp/perl/lib"
```

Using either method, the module you're trying to install is installed into /home/clintp/perl/lib. You can then move this module to another directory if you need to.

When moving the components between systems or directories, remember to keep the directory structure the same. There are often compiled object components to be moved (under an architecture-specific directory) as well as the perl module itself—be sure to move all of the components and keep them in relatively the same place.

> You should be careful not to move modules between different kinds of machines. A compiled module will only work on one kind of system, like Perl itself. Also, try not to move modules between different versions of Perl; it sometimes does not work. In that case, you have to rebuild the module.

Using Modules Installed in Strange Places

To use modules that are installed in a directory other than the standard directory, you need to use a directive called use lib. For example, if you install the module Date::Manip in the directory /home/clintp/perl/lib using the instructions in the preceding section, you would have a file tree like the one shown in Figure A.2.

FIGURE A.2

File tree after installation for Date::Manip.

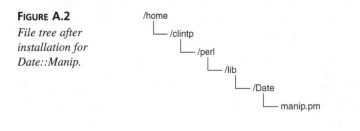

At the beginning of your program, you can simply put the following:

```
use lib '/home/clintp/perl/lib';   # Look for module here else
use Date::Manip;
```

Perl then searches that directory for the module before it searches any of its own directories. You also can use this technique to install newer versions of modules onto the system—for testing—without overwriting older versions and creating incompatibilities.

INDEX

X-Y-Z

SAMS
Teach Yourself
in 24 Hours

When you only have time for the answers™

Sams Teach Yourself in 24 Hours *gets you the results you want—fast! Work through 24 proven 1-hour lessons and learn everything you need to know to get up to speed quickly. It has the answers you need at the price you can afford.*

Sams Teach Yourself C in 24 Hours

Tony Zhang
ISBN: 0-672-31861-X
$24.99 US/$37.95 CAN

Other Sams Teach Yourself in 24 Hours Titles

TCL/TK
Venkat Sastry
ISBN: 0-672-31749-4
$24.99 US/$37.95 CAN

Java 2
Rogers Cadenhead
ISBN: 0-672-32036-3
$24.99 US/$37.95 CAN

C++
Jesse Liberty
ISBN: 0-672-31516-5
$19.99 US/$29.95 CAN

Linux
Craig & Coletta Witherspoon
ISBN: 0-672-31993-4
$24.99 US/$37.95 CAN

HTML & XHTML
Dick Oliver
ISBN: 0-672-32076-2
$24.99 US/$37.95 CAN

CGI
Rafe Colburn
ISBN: 0-672-31880-6
$24.99 US/$37.95 CAN

JavaScript
Michael Moncur
ISBN: 0-672-32025-8
$24.99 US/$37.95 CAN

All prices are subject to change.

SAMS

www.*samspublishing*.com

Hey, you've got enough worries.

Don't let IT training be one of them.

Get on the fast track to IT training at InformIT,
your total Information Technology training network.

 | **www.informit.com** | **SAMS**

■ Hundreds of timely articles on dozens of topics ■ Discounts on IT books from all our publishing partners, including Sams Publishing ■ Free, unabridged books from the InformIT Free Library ■ "Expert Q&A"—our live, online chat with IT experts ■ Faster, easier certification and training from our Web- or classroom-based training programs ■ Current IT news ■ Software downloads ■ Career-enhancing resources

InformIT is a registered trademark of Pearson. Copyright ©2001 by Pearson.
Copyright ©2001 by Sams Publishing.

Installation Instructions

Windows

1. Insert the disc into your CD-ROM drive.
2. From the Windows desktop, double-click the My Computer icon.
3. Double-click the icon representing your CD-ROM drive.
4. Double-click on `start.html`. All of the CD-ROM files can be accessed by the HTML interface.

Macintosh

1. Insert the disc into your CD-ROM drive.
2. Double-click the STYPERL242E icon when it appears on your desktop.
3. Double-click on `start.html`. All of the CD-ROM files can be accessed by the HTML interface.

Linux/Unix

These installation instructions assume that you have a passing familiarity with Unix commands and the basic setup of your machine. As Unix has many flavors, only generic commands are used. If you have any problems with the commands, please consult the appropriate manual page or your system administrator.

1. Insert the disc into your CD-ROM drive.
2. If you have a volume manager, mounting of the CD-ROM will be automatic. If you don't have a volume manager, you can mount the CD-ROM by typing

   ```
   mount -tiso9660 /dev/cdrom /mnt/cdrom
   ```

   > **NOTE:** `/mnt/cdrom` is just a mount point, but it must exist when you issue the mount command. You may also use any empty directory for a mount point if you don't want to use `/mnt/cdrom`.

3. Open the `start.html` file. All of the CD-ROM files can be accessed by the HTML interface.

By opening this package, you are agreeing to be bound by the following agreement:

You may not copy or redistribute the entire CD-ROM as a whole. Copying and redistribution of individual software programs on the CD-ROM is governed by terms set by individual copyright holders.

The installer and code from the author(s) are copyrighted by the publisher and author(s). Individual programs and other items on the CD-ROM are copyrighted by their various authors or other copyright holders. Some of the programs included with this product may be governed by an Open Source license, which allows redistribution; see the license information for each product for more information.

Other programs are included on the CD-ROM by special permission from their authors.

The book companion CD-ROM contains ActiveState's ActivePerl. ActivePerl is the latest Perl binary distribution from ActiveState and replaces what was previously distributed as Perl for Win32. The latest release of ActivePerl as well as other professional tools for Perl developers are available from the ActiveState web site at http://www.ActiveState.com. The ActiveState Repository has a large collection of modules and extensions in binary packages that are easy to install and use. To view and install these packages, use the Perl Package Manager (PPM) which is included with ActivePerl. Commercial support for ActivePerl is available through the PerlClinic at http://www.ActiveState.com. Peer support resources for ActivePerl issues can also be found at the ActiveState Web site under support at http://www.ActiveState.com/support/.

This software is provided as is without warranty of any kind, either expressed or implied, including but not limited to the implied warranties of merchantability and fitness for a particular purpose. Neither the publisher nor its dealers or distributors assume any liability for any alleged or actual damages arising from the use of this program. (Some states do not allow for the exclusion of implied warranties, so the exclusion may not apply to you.)